RUM AND REGGAE

Rum

A N D

Reggae

THE INSIDER'S GUIDE TO THE CARIBBEAN

REVISED AND EXPANDED

1994–1995 EDITION

Jonathan Runge

VILLARD BOOKS · NEW YORK · 1993

While every effort has been made to provide accurate information, prices, places, and people do change rather frequently in the Caribbean. Typographical errors also occasionally occur. Thus, please keep in mind that there may be discrepancies between what you find and what is reported here. In addition, some of the recommendations have been given by individuals interviewed by the author and may not represent the opinion of the author or of Random House, Inc. The reader assumes all responsibility when participating in the activities or excursions described in this book.

Library of Congress Cataloging-in-Publication Data
Runge, Jonathan.
Rum and reggae / Jonathan Runge.—Rev. and expanded 1994–1995 ed.
p.   cm.
Includes index.
ISBN 0-679-74716-8
1. West Indies—Guidebooks.   2. Caribbean Area—Guidebooks.
I. Title.
F1613.R86   1993   917.2904'52—dc20   93-25916

Manufactured in the United States of America on acid-free paper
9 8 7 6 5 4 3 2
Revised edition
Design by Debbie Glasserman

In memory of Warren Jacobus

ACKNOWLEDGMENTS

Contrary to what you might think, writing a book on the Caribbean is not very glamorous. The most glamorous part about doing it is answering the "So what do you do?" question at cocktail parties. It's all downhill from there. I did not spend my days on the beach or by the pool sipping a piña colada. Well, okay, *sometimes* I did. But most of the time I was running around checking out this or that and complaining about the heat. Just when I felt at home on an island, it was time to uproot myself and start all over again. Try doing that at least thirty times and you'll begin to know what I mean.

Fortunately, some wonderful people helped me out along the way. I'd like to take this opportunity to graciously thank those who did. In no particular order, they are: Barry Mattis (our Jamaican guide); Brendan Hickey and Judith Wright; Anne and Cuthbert Grey-Jean Baptiste; Irvin; Myron Clement; Leslie Cohen; Liz Elman; Lisa Herbst; Arlene Flowers; Stacy Meyrowitz; Linda Jacobsen; Beth Walsh; Laura Davidson; Deborah Bernstein; Lourdes Pena; Karen DeGoyer and Andreas Luzio; Catherine Pinder; Mari-Elena Baldwin; Alexandra P. de Fernandez; Al Block and Pedro Castillo; Grace Bruny; Walter Cappellini and Barbara Lieber; Maria Teresa Almarza; Joan and Lou Bourque; Tom Potter; Patrick-Denis Finet; Natalie Glitzenhern; Maria Elena Perez-Nevarez; Pam Barry; Brian Parmelee; Nigel Cosans; Hope Swift; Carl, Finn, Manuel and Lizi; Christophe Buey; Dennis Henry; John Caldwell, Jr.; James Brown; Sally and Mark Tramoni; Andre Nahr; David at the Old Fort; Sonja and Otmar Schaedle; Lou Keane and Marie Kingston; Carol, Cedric, and Heidi Osborne; Rose; Dan Critchett and Peter Rana; my cruising buddies: Allen Johnson, George Hobica, Rick Murray, Tom Fortier, and especially Duncan Dona-hue; Uli and Claus; Jean-Louis Papelard; Angel Cerda; Jorge Méndez-Martinez; Elvis Jiménez-Chávez; and Phil Perry.

There were also several people up north shivering through a brutal winter who provided support and assistance while I was in the land of the sun. I would like to specially thank my parents, Eunice and Albert Runge, for their tireless and enthusiastic support of me and my work. And thanks go to Nan Garland and Ed Rosner for keeping me smiling when I got *fehklempt,* and to my agent, Sallie Gouverneur.

Finally, I would like to thank my new editor, Doug Stumpf, for liking the original *Rum and Reggae* so much and having enough faith in me to bring the book to Villard (and patience when deadlines passed). Also, thanks to his assistant, Leslie Chang, for all her efforts.

To all who helped, many thanks—YES, MON!

CONTENTS

Introduction   xiii

BEFORE YOU GO   1

THE ISLANDS: 19
  Anguilla   21
  Antigua   37
  Aruba   55
  Barbados   63
  Bequia   77
  Bonaire   93
  British Virgin Islands   103
  Carriacou   121
  Culebra   131
  Dominica   139
  The Dominican Republic   155
  Grenada   183

Guadeloupe   203
Jamaica   225
Margarita Island   259
Martinique   269
Montserrat   291
Mustique   303
Puerto Rico   309
Saba   345
St. Barthélemy (St. Barts)   353
St. John   371
St. Kitts and Nevis   383
St. Lucia   405
St. Martin   429
Trinidad and Tobago   439

TOURIST BOARD ADDRESSES   463
INDEX   469

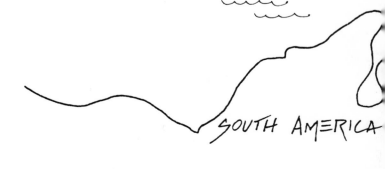

FLORIDA

BAHAMAS

CUBA

CAYMAN ISLANDS
o D

HAITI

JAMAICA

CARIBBEAN SEA

SOUTH AMERICA

RUM & REGGAE'S
CARIBBEAN

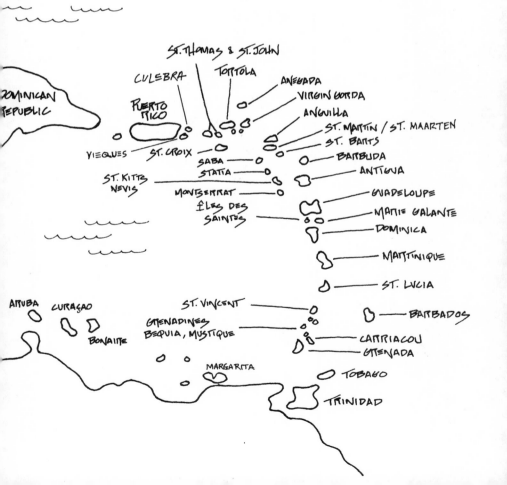

ATLANTIC OCEAN

DOMINICAN REPUBLIC

ST. THOMAS & ST. JOHN

CULEBRA

TORTOLA

ANEGADA

VIRGIN GORDA

ANGUILLA

PUERTO RICO

ST. MARTIN / ST. MAARTEN

ST. BARTS

YIEQUES

ST. CROIX

BARBUDA

SABA

STATIA

ANTIGUA

ST. KITTS
NEVIS

MONTSERRAT

GUADELOUPE

ÎLES DES
SAINTES

MARIE GALANTE

DOMINICA

MARTINIQUE

ST. LUCIA

ARUBA

CURAÇAO

ST. VINCENT

BARBADOS

GRENADINES
BEQUIA, MUSTIQUE

BONAIRE

CARRIACOU

GRENADA

MARGARITA

TOBAGO

TRINIDAD

INTRODUCTION

Ever wonder what it's like to swim in a large tank of dark rum? It feels like rubbing yourself from head to toe with Vicks VapoRub. My friend Katie used to do it all the time at a rum mill—to remain unnamed—in the islands. She would swim laps, pausing after each for a high-octane sip of liquid gold. She'd prefer swimming in rum to a swimming pool: unlike chlorine, the rum didn't cast a green tint to her naturally blond hair. After her swim, Katie would drive into town to her favorite bar to jam on some reggae music. The bartender, whose name was Pedro, would prepare a wonderfully nasty rum punch with overproof especially for her. He called her "Wassy" (pronounced waz-zy), which roughly translates from Caribbean patois to *wild fun*—for Katie knew how to have a good time.

Perhaps you may not have had the privilege of a rum dip. Don't worry, for there are many other adventures and activities awaiting you in the tropics. Just be assured that you have bought the right book, for *Rum and Reggae* will show you how to find your own wassy fun, with a twist.

This is not your typical Caribbean tourist guide. It is written with the distinct point of view of someone who grew up in suburban America in the sixties and seventies. *Rum and Reggae* is for people like you who want more out of a vacation than the standard tourist fare. You're more active—you like scuba, windsurfing, hiking, cruising, golf, or tennis. Or you're more particular, in search of secluded, hedonistic, cerebral, or hip places.

This book also differs from other guidebooks in another way. Instead of telling you that everything is "nice"—nice, that is, for the average tourist—*Rum and Reggae* offers definite opinions. I will tell you what's fantastic and what's not, from the point of view of someone who loathes the tourist label.

So mix yourself a stiff rum punch (don't forget the bitters and fresh grated nutmeg), put on some Bob Marley, and sit back and let *Rum and Reggae* take you on your own private Caribbean trip.

Before You Go

A NOTE ABOUT THIS GUIDE: I have used a number of symbols and terms to indicate prices and ambience. Here are the code breakers.

RESTAURANT PRICES

Prices represent per-person costs for the average meal from soup to nuts.

$—$0–10
$$—$11–20
$$$—$21–30
$$$$—$31–40
$$$$$—over $40

LODGING RATES

- Rates are for *high season* unless otherwise noted.
- Rates are for a single (noted as "singles" in this book) or double (noted as "doubles" in this book) room, EP unless otherwise noted.
- Expect a service and tax charge of about 15 percent or more added to your bill.
- Be sure to ask about credit cards when making your reservations if you intend to use them as payment. Many places, even expensive ones, do not accept credit cards.

DIRT CHEAP—under $30 U.S.
CHEAP—$30–50 U.S.

NOT SO CHEAP—$51–100 U.S.
PRICEY—$101–150 U.S.
VERY PRICEY—$151–200 U.S.
WICKED PRICEY—$200–300 U.S.
RIDICULOUS—$301–400 U.S.
OUTRAGEOUS—$401–500
BEYOND BELIEF—$501 and up!

MEAL CODES

EP (European Plan)—No meals included
CP (Continental Plan)—Continental breakfast (or sometimes more
extensive breakfast) included
MAP (Modified American Plan)—Full breakfast and dinner included
FAP (Full American Plan)—Full breakfast, lunch, and dinner included (sometimes with an afternoon "tea" or snack as well)

TOURISTO SCALE KEY

📷 1 What century is this?

📷 📷 2 There's no airport and there are only a few ferries a week.

📷 📷 📷 3 A nice, unspoiled yet civilized place.

📷 📷 📷 📷 4 Still unspoiled, but getting popular.

📷 📷 📷 📷 📷 5 A popular place, but still not too developed.

📷 📷 📷 📷 📷 📷 6 Busy and booming; this was not long ago
very quiet.

📷 📷 📷 📷 📷 📷 📷 7 Well-developed tourism and lots of tourists; fast-food outlets conspicuous.

📷 📷 📷 📷 📷 📷 📷 📷 8 Highly developed and tons of tourists.

📷 📷 📷 📷 📷 📷 📷 📷 📷 9 Mega-tourists, and tour groups;
fast-food outlets outnumber restaurants.

📷 📷 📷 📷 📷 📷 📷 📷 📷 📷 10 Swarms of tourists and total
development. Run for cover!

CLIMATES OF THE CARIBBEAN

The weather in the Caribbean is about as close to perfect as anywhere on earth. The temperature rarely dips below 70° or above 90° Fahrenheit (at sea level). It can get cooler at night in the mountains of some of the islands, making it ideal for sleeping. The sun shines almost every day. Rainfall comes in the form of brief, intense cloudbursts, quickly followed by sun. It's pretty hard not to get a tan.

The reasons for this ideal climate are the constant temperature of the ocean—about 80° year round—and the steady trade winds from Africa. The Caribbean is not susceptible to the harsh weather patterns of the middle latitudes. The only weather peril to a Caribbean vacation is an occasional summer tropical depression or hurricane, which can make life very exciting.

There are three basic climate categories: arid (hot and dry), lush (hot, somewhat humid, with lots of rainfall), and those islands that have a little of both (the windward side being the wetter and greener) or that fall somewhere in the middle. The larger, mountainous islands almost always fall in the latter two categories. Conversely, the flatter, smaller ones are almost exclusively arid. All are warm to hot, depending on the season and the extent of the trade winds. Summers, while only about five degrees hotter than winter, feel a lot warmer due to the increased humidity and decreased wind. The one constant is the sun. It is always *strong*, and will swiftly fry unprotected pale faces—and bodies—to a glowing shade of lobster red.

There is also another climate down here, one I measure by the "friendliness barometer." This "barometer" reveals the attitude of the local people toward tourists. Some of the island nations of the Caribbean are wonderfully warm and positive while others are fairly antagonistic. The determining factors are the amount of tourist traffic and the degree to which local governments have educated the populace as to the economic importance of tourism. For example, both St. Thomas and Barbados are flooded with tourists every season, yet the atmosphere of the former is hostile while the latter is remarkably warm—thanks to education. Other islands, because tourism is a recent phenomenon, are more open and friendly.

How do you find which "climates" are best for you? Simple, check out the chart on the next page.

CLIMATES CHART

	ARID	LUSH	BOTH
FRIENDLINESS BAROMETER			
VERY FRIENDLY	Bonaire Tobago Bequia Margarita	Montserrat Dominica Saba	Puerto Rico Trinidad
WARM	Barbados Carriacou Culebra Anegada Jost Van Dyke	Montserrat Grenada	Dominican Republic Virgin Gorda
NEUTRAL	Aruba Mustique Anguilla St. Barts	Jamaica	St. Martin St. John Tortola
COOL	Antigua	St. Vincent St. Lucia Martinique Guadeloupe	Nevis St. Kitts St. Croix
NASTY			St. Thomas

BUILDING A BASE FOR TANNING

Since the advent of electric beaches (tanning machines) and pretanning accelerators, there is absolutely no reason to get burned on your first day out in the tropical sun. With some advance attention, you can stay outside for *hours* on your first day, and let's face it, what you want to do when you step off the plane is hit the beach.

Just about every town has a tanning center with clever and cutesy names like Tanarama, Tanfastic, A Touch of Bronze, Endless Summer, Sunsational, Fake-and-Bake, and Tanfasia. Most health clubs usually have one or two tanning "coffins" lying around, beckoning pasty skins to look healthier and more attractive in a matter of *minutes.* Ultraviolet tanning is quite safe when used properly, as the UVB light doesn't have the burning rays of earlier sun lamps and, of course, the sun.

Many of these tanning centers have tanning-prep packages of ten sessions: you start with about five minutes of "sunning" and work up to twenty or thirty. Spread out over the two weeks prior to your departure, this should give you an excellent head start on a great Caribbean tan.

Recent years have also seen the development of pretan accelerators. These marvelous creams, pioneered by Estée Lauder and now available from a wide variety of manufacturers, chemically stimulate the manufacture of melanin, the pigment that darkens your skin. (Normally it takes direct exposure to the sun to start its production.) A pretan accelerator doesn't change your color (or dye your skin like QT). Rather, it prepares the skin with extra melanin so that you tan the first time rather than burn, and much faster, too.

WHAT TO WEAR AND TAKE ALONG

Less is more. That's the motto to remember when packing to go to the Caribbean. Bring only what you can carry for ten minutes at a good clip, because you'll often be schlepping your luggage for at least that time, and it's *hot.*

What you *really* need to take along are a bathing suit, shorts, T-shirts, cotton sweater, a pair of sandals, sunglasses, and a Walkman. After all, you *are* on vacation. However, these are the nineties and people tend to dress up for no reason, so you may want to bring some extra togs to look presentable at the dinner table. To help you be totally prepared (and to make your packing a lot easier), I've assembled a list of essentials for a week.

THE PACKING LIST

CLOTHES
bathing suit
T-shirts (4)—you'll end up buying at least one
polo shirts (2)
shorts (2)
nice, compatible lightweight pants (you can wear them on the plane)

sandals
cotton sweater or sweatshirt
undergarments
sneakers or topsiders

If you must have them, wear the following (with appropriate shoes) on the plane:
Men: lightweight jacket, tie
Women: lightweight dress

ESSENTIALS
toiletries
sunscreens (SPF 15+, 8, 4 [oil] and lip protector)
moisturizers (Noxema is still the old standard for sunburn; or an aloe preparation)
some good books
Cutter's or Woodsman's insect repellent (oh those nasty bugs)
sunglasses
hat/visor

HARDWARE
Walkman and tapes
camcorder or pocket camera
"credit-card" calculator (for exchange rates)

SPORTS ACCESSORIES (when applicable)
tennis racquet
golf clubs
hiking shoes
fins, mask, snorkel, regulator

PAPERWORK
passport
traveler's checks
driver's license

THE DEAL OF THE SKIES

For those of you with some time on your hands (and a sense of adventure), LIAT, the "Caribbean Airline," has a deal called the

Super Explorer Fare. It costs (at press time) $357 U.S. and allows you to fly virtually everywhere that LIAT flies for thirty days. This is roughly all the islands from Puerto Rico south to Trinidad. The major restrictions are that you can't stop at the same place twice (unless you are in transit) and that you can't change the itinerary once ticketed (a $20 U.S. surcharge every time you do) or get a refund. This is a great way to see several islands on an extended holiday. There is also another Explorer Fare, for $199 U.S. peak season and $169 off-peak, which allows for three stopovers in twenty-one days (no changes can be made).

Remember that LIAT, and other small island airlines, fly small planes, from the nineteen-seat DeHavilland Twin Otter to the forty-four-seat Dash-8. Having flown LIAT extensively, I've developed some golden rules for stress-free flying when in the friendly but sometimes tricky skies of the Caribbean.

- *Always have a reservation.*
- *Reconfirm seventy-two hours before departure.*
- *Get to the airport at least an hour before departure—overbooking can be a problem.*
- *Never fly standby, especially during peak periods—you won't get on.*
- *Go immediately to the gate once you've checked in. I was left behind when the plane arrived early and took off without me.*
- *Avoid itinerary changes when flying on Sundays. Everything, including reservation lines and ticket counters, closes down in some places.*
- *Keep luggage to a minimum. Carrying a lot in the heat is unpleasant. Also, carry all valuables with you—don't check them.*

OTHER AIRFARE TIPS

Always shop around to secure the lowest possible fare to your destination. Ask for the lowest fare, not just a discount fare. If you're adventurous, as your departure date draws nearer, call again—additional low-cost seats may have become available.

You may also want to consider buying your ticket from a consolidator (or bucket shop), such as Access International, (800) 827-3633, or a rebator, such as Travel Avenue, (800) 333-3335.

Or shop around the major carriers for a charter flight.

Island/Activities Matchup

Looking for the best island for diving, golf, restaurants, or gay nightlife? This helpful chart will give you some suggestions.

ACITIVITY/TOPIC	ISLAND	ACTIVITY/TOPIC	ISLAND
BEACHES	Anguilla	RESORTS	Aruba
	St. John		Puerto Rico
	Anegada		Barbados
	Culebra		Antigua
	Dominican Republic		Dominican Republic
PRIVACY	The Grenadines		Jamaica
	Montserrat	FOOD	Guadeloupe
	Tobago		St. Barts
	St. Kitts–Nevis		Martinique
SCUBA	Bonaire		St. Martin
	Saba		Margarita
	Cayman Islands	GOLF	Dominican Republic
HEDONISM &	Jamaica		(Casa de Campo)
NIGHTLIFE	Carnival in Trinidad		Puerto Rico
	San Juan, Puerto Rico		(Dorado/Cerromar)
	Margarita		Jamaica
	Barbados		Nevis
SAILING	British Virgin Islands	NATURE	Dominica
	Antigua		Guadeloupe
	St. Lucia		Dominican Republic
	The Grenadines		Grenada
CEREBRAL	Jamaica	QUIET	Montserrat
	Martinique		Nevis
	Dominican Republic		Anguilla
	Grenada		The Grenadines
			Bonaire
			Tobago
			Culebra
			Saba

ACITIVITY/TOPIC	ISLAND	ACTIVITY/TOPIC	ISLAND
WINDSURFING	Aruba Bonaire Barbados Puerto Rico (Rincón) Guadeloupe	GAY NIGHTLIFE	Puerto Rico (San Juan) Dominican Republic (Santo Domingo) Venezuela (Caracas)
HIP	Bequia St. Barts Margarita Bonaire Puerto Rico Mustique	NUDE BEACHES	St. Martin Guadeloupe Bonaire Jamaica
		SUN	Aruba Bonaire
LUXURY	Anguilla St. Barts Nevis		Margarita

CARIBBEAN SUPERLATIVES

BEST BEACH—**Playa Soni,** Isla de Culebra, Puerto Rico
BEST ISLAND FOR BEACHES—**Anguilla**
BEST ISLAND FOR SUN—**Aruba**
BEST LUXURY HOTEL/RESORT—**The Four Seasons Resort,** Nevis
BEST HOTEL—**Ottley's Plantation Inn,** St. Kitts
BEST GUEST HOUSE—**Julie's,** Bequia
BEST NEW AGE HOTEL—**Hostellerie des Trois Force,** St. Barts
BEST MOUNTAIN LODGING—**Papillote,** Dominica
BEST GAY ACCOMMODATION—**Hostería del Mar,** Ocean Park, San Juan, Puerto Rico
BEST ROOM WITH A VIEW—**Ladera Resort,** St. Lucia
BEST CRÉOLE RESTAURANT—**Eddie's Ghetto,** St. Barts
BEST CONTINENTAL RESTAURANT—**Château de Feuilles,** Anse Bertrand, Guadeloupe
BEST PIZZA—**Mac's Pizzeria,** Bequia
BEST ISLAND FOR FOOD—**Guadeloupe**

BEST BEER—**Carib**
BEST RUM—**Bettancourt** (Haiti)
BEST RUM PUNCH—**Betty Mascol's Plantation House**, Grenada
BEST NIGHTCLUB—**Mosquito Coast**, Margarita Island, Venezuela
BEST GAY NIGHTCLUB—**Krash**, San Juan, Puerto Rico
BEST PLACE FOR NIGHTLIFE—**San Juan**, Puerto Rico
BEST PLACE FOR GAY NIGHTLIFE—**San Juan**, Puerto Rico
BEST PLACE TO GET HIGH—**Negril**, Jamaica
BEST CARNIVAL—**Port-of-Spain**, Trinidad
BEST REGGAE MUSIC—**Reggae Sunsplash**, Kingston, Jamaica
BEST CALYPSO MUSIC—**Port-of-Spain**, Trinidad
BEST PAN MUSIC—**Port-of-Spain**, Trinidad
BEST SALSA—**San Juan**, Puerto Rico
BEST MERENGUE—**Santo Domingo**, Dominican Republic
BEST DIVING—**Bonaire**
BEST GOLF COURSE—**The Teeth of the Dog**, Casa de Campo, Dominican Republic
BEST PORT OF CALL—**Port Elizabeth**, Bequia
BEST HIKE—**Boiling Lake**, Dominica
BEST TENNIS—**Cerromar Beach**, Puerto Rico
BEST WINDSURFING—**Club Mistral**, Barbados
BEST SHOPPING—**St. Martin/St. Maarten**
BEST T-SHIRT—**Barracuda Bistro**, St. John
BEST ISLAND BARGAIN—**Margarita Island**, Venezuela
BEST HIP DESTINATION—**Bequia**
BEST-KEPT SECRET—**Isla de Culebra**, Puerto Rico

THE TEN BEST BEACHES IN THE CARIBBEAN

PLAYA SONI—Isla de Culebra, Puerto Rico
A long, deserted stretch of white sand with a view of pretty islas, rocks, and cays across the bay.

PLAYA BAVARO—Bavaro, Dominican Republic
A twenty-mile strand of coconut palms and mostly empty beaches.

ANSE GOUVERNEUR—St. Barts
Where the swells meet the swells, this is a very pretty and private beach.

SANDY CAY—Carriacou, the Grenadines
A deserted island with palm trees, white sand, and great snorkeling reefs about a mile offshore of Hillsborough.

NEGRIL BEACH—Jamaica
An experience in itself.

PLAYA BOQUERÓN—Boquerón, Puerto Rico
A gorgeous arc of sand in a tranquil and very scenic bay.

TRUNK BAY—St. John
Despite the crowds, this is still the prettiest beach in the U.S. Virgins.

PLAYA EL AGUA—Margarita
This may not be the prettiest beach, but the great restaurants, waiter service at your chaise, and all those sexy Venezuelans make it an exceptional experience.

FRENCHMAN'S BAY—Port Antonio, Jamaica
A tiny beach in a cove with a clean, sandy-bottomed freshwater river at one side makes it a great place to spend the day.

ANEGADA—British Virgin Islands
The whole island is a deserted, gorgeous beach.

NUDE BEACHES IN THE CARIBBEAN

You might expect the Caribbean to be a paradise for nudists, or "naturists" as they prefer to be called. The fact is that there are surprisingly few official buff options—the proper British heritage of most islands takes a dim view of such "uncivilized" habits. Fortunately, most of the French and Dutch islands are more lenient. It's best to use your discretion at the more deserted beaches—keep your clothes close at hand in case of disapproving visitors. Women would be well advised not to sunbathe topless or nude alone, as local men are not accustomed to naked women on their turf.

Another option is to stay at a resort with its own private beach—many have sections that are clothes-optional (don't be shy to ask when making reservations). Consult Lee Baxandall's *World Guide to Nude Beaches*.

The following are some of the better-known nude beaches. In many cases, nude beaches exist without the blessing of local laws, so please remember to check out the scene with reliable local sources (like your hotel) before shedding your clothes and cares.

- BLOODY BAY BEACH—Negril, Jamaica
  Negril is the home of Hedonism II (see pages 241–42) and is the land of anything goes. The buff area is in Bloody Bay—just east of Hedonism II.

- ANSE DE GRANDE SALINES—St. Barts
  You'll feel weird if you don't take your clothes off here. This is one of St. Barts' best.

- HAWKSBILL BEACH—Antigua
  A pretty beach and Antigua's only buff beach, it's located next to the Hawksbill Beach Hotel.

- ORIENT BAY BEACH—St. Martin
  One of the first "official" clothes-optional beaches in the Caribbean, it is also the home of Club Orient, a naturist resort.

- SALOMON BEACH—St. John, U.S. Virgin Islands
  Although there is a "No Nudity" sign posted here, most people at this beach obviously aren't paying attention. The trail to this beach is a little over a half-mile north of Cruz Bay on the left.

- ANSE TRABAUD—Martinique
  The nicest beach on Martinique, located in the southeast corner of the island, is also quite "free" during the week.

- PLAGE TARARE—Guadeloupe
  This is the primary buff beach on an island that put the "n" in nudité. There is also a smaller buff beach at the Club Med Caravelle that is open to the public.

- ANEGADA—British Virgin Islands
  Because this island is so remote to begin with (there is only one hotel—the Anegada Reef Hotel), you will have miles of beach to yourself.

- THE GRENADINES
  There are many nudie options here, particularly at the island luxury resort of Petit St. Vincent. Many of the other islands, such as Carriacou, Canouan, and Mayreau, offer discreet possibilities on deserted beaches.

This is also very true of the "out islands" reached by boat, such as the Tobago Cays (located east of Mayreau) and Sandy Cay off Carriacou.

- TOBAGO (NORTH COAST)
  There are several deserted beaches here (see pages 455–56) that could be used for discreet sunning.

- SOROBON—Lac Bay, Bonaire
  The home of the pink flamingo also has the Sorobon Resort, a naturist resort. Non-resort guests can use the beach for a fee.

- PLAGE CRAWEN—Îles des Saintes, Guadeloupe
  A pretty, private beach with lots of shade and a great lunch spot over the hill at Bois Joli.

WHAT ABOUT TENNIS?

Just about every large hotel in the Caribbean has a tennis court or access to one. However, if you're a tennis freak, be warned that the smaller islands will have fewer courts or limited access. So be sure to ask when making reservations at some remote destination.

These resorts will particularly appeal to tennis buffs:

- BUCCANEER—Gallows Bay, St. Croix
  Eight Laykold courts—two lit for night play.

- SANDY LANE—St. James, Barbados
  Eight hard-surface courts—four lit for night play.

- CURTAIN BLUFF—Old Road, Antigua
  Three hard-surface and one clay court—tournament in the spring; full-time pro.

- HALF MOON CLUB—Montego Bay, Jamaica
  Thirteen Laykold courts—seven floodlit at night. Also, videotaped lessons and four squash courts.

- CERROMAR/DORADO BEACH—Puerto Rico
  Twenty-one Laykold courts between the two resorts—two lit. (Cerromar has the most courts—fourteen.)

• CASA DE CAMPO—La Romana, Dominican Republic
Thirteen clay courts—six lit; and four lit Laykold courts.

• PALMAS DEL MAR—Puerto Rico
Fifteen hard-surface courts and five Har-Tru—four lit. Tennis packages
available.

THE TEN MOST LUXURIOUS RESORTS IN THE CARIBBEAN

MALLIOUHANA—Meads Bay, Anguilla
This is the crème de la crème of luxury and taste. Service is great and the
Haitian paintings even match the upholstery!

THE FOUR SEASONS RESORT—Pinney's Beach, Nevis
This newcomer has achieved a level of service unparalleled in the Caribbean. It has every imaginable amenity, service, and facility. Come here to
pamper yourself.

ROUND HILL HOTEL AND VILLAS—Montego Bay, Jamaica
This is where Ralph Lauren hangs his polo cap. A celeb hangout, 27
wonderful WASPY bungalows and lush vegetation maintain your privacy
on a 98-acre peninsula.

SANDY LANE—St. James, Barbados
The grande dame of the Barbados hotels, it's the ideal place to throw a
party. Double ballustrades enclose a terrace that would put the mansions
of Newport to shame.

LE TOINY—St. Barts
This very chichi small resort has fabulous villas, each with its own pool.

CAP JULUCA—Maunday's Bay, Anguilla
On the best beach in Anguilla, this Moorish-style resort is a major celeb
hangout.

PETIT ST. VINCENT RESORT (PSV)—The Grenadines
A remote, deluxe cottage-colony resort on its own island in the southern
Grenadines. Home of the flag-signal-system for room service.

CANEEL BAY RESORT—St. John
The original Rockresort, it's the pinnacle of old-money, subtle luxury with 7 beaches, an eighteenth-century sugar mill, and 3 restaurants on a 170-acre peninsula.

CARL GUSTAF—Gustavia, St. Barts
With incredible views of sunset and the Caribbean's most scenic harbor, the tony and tasteful hotel has sumptuous guest rooms.

COVE CASTLES—Shoal Bay, West End, Anguilla
The villas here are so incredibly tasteful and spacious that you will never want to leave.

HISSING

Don't be startled or offended if someone hisses at you; that's just the Caribbean way of saying "Hey, you." It's very effective—a woman once got my attention clear across the airline terminal in Guadeloupe (she wanted to tell me that the plane was boarding). It seems that the hiss can be directionally controlled, as no one but me turned around.

LAUNDRY

Doing laundry in the Caribbean can be incredibly expensive and inconvenient, especially in the French West Indies (100F, or about $20 a load). The reason is the dryer—it takes a lot of power, which is expensive down here. Laundromats as we know them don't exist except on Puerto Rico, the U.S. Virgin Islands, and few other islands with big cities. Try to bring hand-washables only.

Are you dreaming about Carnival but it's the middle of July? Don't worry, you can create your own festivity with this recipe.

Rum and Reggae Punch

Ingredients
2–3 oz. good dark rum (the stronger, the better)
2 oz. sugar syrup*
1 lime
4 oz. water
bitters
fresh grated nutmeg
ice

Directions
Squeeze the lime and add the juice to the rum and sugar syrup. Shake the bitters into the glass four times. Add the rocks, then sprinkle with fresh grated nutmeg (it must be fresh!). Yum! *Serves one.*

*To make sugar syrup, dissolve 1 lb. sugar in 2 cups of water. Keep handy for quick and easy rum punches.

The Islands

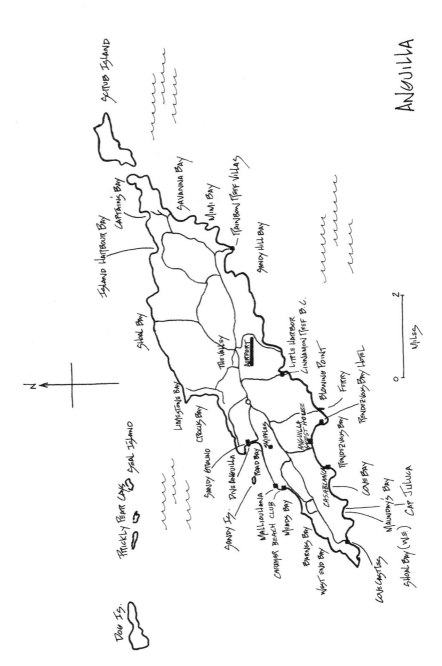

ANGUILLA

ANGUILLA

TOURISTO SCALE   📷 📷 📷 📷 📷   5

There's an old Patti Page song that goes

"If you're fond of sand dunes and salty air,
Quaint little villages, here and there,
You're sure to fall in love
With An-guil-la."

Hey, wait a minute! Isn't it "you're sure to fall in love with old Cape Cod"? Well yes, but Anguilla could easily fit into Patti's refrain. It's so reminiscent of the Cape and Nantucket twenty-five years ago that it hits you like a horsefly. Of course some adjustments have to be made—like adding palm trees, turquoise water, West Indians, that kind of thing. But the actual island itself, minus the accoutrements, has the dunes, shrubby vegetation, gentle terrain, and beautiful beaches of the aforementioned area on the forty-second parallel. Any time of the year in Anguilla feels like summer up north—minus the fog, bad weather, and cold water.

For the longest time Anguilla was really in low gear. In the shadow of St. Martin/St. Maarten, which lies only ten miles to the south, it remained the Caribbean's equivalent of a sleepy little town until about ten years ago. Then travel writers started raving about the Caribbean's "best-kept secret." Soon, the crowds on St. Martin started spilling over on ferry day-trips. And the word got out— Anguilla has some of the finest beaches in the Caribbean. So now things here are in high gear. Development is happening everywhere, but it is "controlled," so most operations are relatively small and informal. Some of the best beaches now have resorts on them. The proverbial deserted beach, here and elsewhere in the Caribbean, is definitely an endangered species and increasingly close to extinction. The almighty dollar is very persuasive in these parts.

Everything here is focused on the beach, and it's a perfect place to spend a whole week just swimming and sunning. Don't expect much else: there's the beach, a good book, and bed. But for some, that's just what the doctor ordered.

THE BRIEFEST HISTORY

The Ciboney first settled this dry, flat island well before Christ. Then the Arawaks arrived about A.D. 200 and were left undisturbed until the Carib invasion about 900 years later—the Caribs named it Malliouhana. *Anguilla*, which is Spanish for "eel" (in deference to the island's shape), was one of the only islands not "discovered" by Columbus or even mentioned in any of his expeditions. The British first colonized the island in 1650 and it had remained under the Union Jack until 1967, despite attempts by the Caribs and the French to dislodge them. That is a rarity in the Caribbean—one government for 300 years. In 1967, the island was given its independence from Britain as a part of the new Associated State of St. Kitts-Nevis-Anguilla. Well, this did not go well with the Anguillans and unrest on the island became so bad that in 1969, a British "peacekeeping force" parachuted down to the island to establish order. Then the London police took over and remained for three years until Anguilla formed its own police force. Finally, in 1980, Anguilla formally became a self-governing British possession. And it's been peaceful ever since.

ANGUILLA: KEY FACTS

LOCATION	18°N by 63°W
	10 miles north of St. Martin/St. Maarten
	1,675 miles southeast of New York
SIZE	34 square miles
	16 miles long by 3 miles wide
HIGHEST POINT	Crocus Hill (213 ft.)
POPULATION	7,500
LANGUAGE	English

TIME	Atlantic Standard Time (1 hour ahead of EST, same as EDT)
AREA CODE	809
ELECTRICITY	110 Volts AC
CURRENCY	The Eastern Caribbean dollar, EC$ (EC$2.70 = $1 U.S.); U.S. dollars are widely accepted
DRIVING	On the *left*; you'll need a temporary permit—$6 U.S. with own valid license
DOCUMENTS	Passport or proof of nationality with photo and onward or return ticket
DEPARTURE TAX	EC$16/$6 U.S. at the airport EC$5/$2 U.S. by ferry
BEER TO DRINK	Heineken
RUM TO DRINK	The "house" overproof
MUSIC TO HEAR	Dancehall

GETTING THERE

St. Maarten's Juliana Airport is the major gateway to Anguilla, with direct and nonstops from the States on AMERICAN, CONTI-NENTAL and BWIA and from Canada on BWIA. From St. Maarten, WINAIR (Windward Islands Airways) flies the ten-minute trip three times daily for $30 per person. There is limited service from other Caribbean islands as follows: Antigua—LIAT; St. Thomas—AIR BVI; St. Kitts—LIAT; San Juan—LIAT, AMERICAN EAGLE, and AIR BVI; and Tortola—LIAT and AIR BVI.

A cheaper and fun alternative to flying in from St. Maarten is to take the ferry. From Juliana, hop a cab (about $10 U.S.) and head for Marigot, where you can enjoy a delicious French repast in one of several restaurants on the waterfront. Then hop a ferry to Blowing Point, Anguilla. There are several boats that do the 20-minute trip. The fare is $9 U.S. one way. Departures are about every half-hour beginning at 7:30 A.M. with the last boat leaving St. Martin at 11 P.M. No reservations are necessary.

GETTING AROUND

A rental car is a good idea if you want to explore this island's fine beaches and leave your place of residence every once in a while. Of the international agencies, BUDGET ([809] 497-2217) and AVIS/ BENNIE & SONS ([809] 497-6221) have outposts here. If you want the car for the whole week, it's best to reserve in advance. For AVIS and BUDGET, just call their toll-free 800 numbers—(800) 331-1084 and (800) 527-0700, respectively. Two local agencies, CONNOR'S ([809] 497-6433) and ISLAND CAR RENTALS ([809] 497-2723), also have a good selection. All will offer free drop-off and pickup at your hotel, as the agencies are not conveniently located to the airport or ferry terminal—you'll have to take a cab anyway, so why not go to your hotel and have them come to you.

FOCUS ON ANGUILLA: THE BEACHES

Out of a total of more than thirty, there are ten outstanding beaches scattered throughout the island. You're never very far from a good one. All have some of the whitest sand in the Caribbean, a creamy-colored mixture of ground-up shells and coral. It's quite lovely. So starting from the west end of the island and working our way to Windward Point, here are the best beaches:

SHOAL BAY (WEST END)
(Located at the western end of the paved road)

This beach is the home of Cove Castles, the futuristic white structures that were written up in *Architectural Digest*. There is another, smaller resort next to it. The beach, however, is quite nice and empty if you walk down to the eastern end (to the left).

MAUNDAY'S BAY
(Follow the signs for Cap Juluca)

Alas, one of the top three beaches on Anguilla has been developed. Ten years ago ago there was nothing here except a half-moon arc of beach culminating in dunes and a sand wall on the western end. Now there's a very Arabesque and very white resort called Cap Juluca.

COVE BEACH
(Follow the signs for Cap Juluca, but don't turn right at the beach; go straight ahead and park)

Just to the east of Maunday's, the long sweep of beach on the western end is too rough and exposed, but the other side is calmer and deserted. A nice touch is the palm trees on the other side of the dunes, giving the illusion of tiny trees on top.

BARNES BAY
(Follow the signs for Coccoloba Plantation)

Another nice stretch of beach that has had to endure development. Most unfortunate is what was built on the eastern end, a complex called Coccoloba Plantation. You can escape much of this, however, if you walk as far away as possible in the opposite direction.

MEADS BAY
(Follow signs for Carimar Beach Club)

Malliouhana is the chichi resort that sits on a bluff on the eastern end of the beach. This is a beautiful beach, with great views at sunset. For lunch, try Caper's next to the Carimar Beach Club.

RENDEZVOUS BAY
(Directions below)

Now here's a superb and very long (almost two miles) stretch of beach. There's plenty of room despite the addition of the Anguilla Great House and Casablanca. The best way to access this beach is to enter on the dirt road on your left as you drive from The Valley (the capital and only commercial center on the island—if you can call a couple of intersections with some stores a center). Once you pass Connor's Car Rentals and Hertz, you will notice signs for Arlo's Place and Skiffle's on the right. Take the next dirt road on the left (about a quarter-mile from the signs). Stay to the left and go all the way to the end, park, and walk to the right—or west. Find a stretch of pearl-white sand to call your own and enjoy.

LIMESTONE BAY
(North of The Valley)

This small, sandy cove is a local favorite. It is reached by taking a right turn just before the Cottage Hospital and following the road a few miles to Limestone Bay.

SHOAL BAY
(Follow signs to Shoal Bay)

The great snorkeling right off the reef, the calm water, and Happy Jack's restaurant make Shoal Bay a favorite of day-trippers from St. Martin. The Shoal Bay Villa development doesn't help matters any. Your best bet here is to go all the way down to either end of the beach—my preference is the eastern end (to your right). This is a great spot to watch the sunset and fiddle about with a rum punch or Cape Codder from Uncle Ernie's, Trader Vic's, and Happy Jack's.

SAVANNA BAY
(Directions below)

This is a very pretty, long, and deserted beach on the still-undeveloped, quiet East End. It serves up some good surf and a steady onshore breeze. For calmer water, the coconut-tree–studded left side is best. The only drawback to this beach is that during heavy trade winds, the turbulent water tends to wash up debris that must have come all the way from Africa.

To get there, take the road to Island Harbour via East End. Once you've passed a semblance of a garage on your left, the road will go uphill and arc to the right. There is a small sign that says "Oil and Gas Available Here." Slow down. The road will bend to the left and you'll see a dirt road going downhill to the right—just opposite a beige-colored vacant house and a chainlink fence. Turn right and follow the road past the house on the right with a stone wall and assorted trucks in the yard. The road here is rough but a standard rental car will make it (maybe with a few scrapes and loud thuds. But don't worry, it's a rental). After you pass the house, take the right fork in the road and go straight to the beach.

CAPTAIN'S BAY
(Directions below)

The most secluded beach on Anguilla. This is a beauty—especially for basking in the buff. It's a small cove of creamy-white sand where privacy is virtually guaranteed because it's so hard to reach (the road is rough in spots).

To get here, take the same dirt road that goes to Savanna Bay, but stay to your left for the entire way (about two miles). The road is broken up in places and it's best traversed on a scooter, but a car will make it. It's worth the effort.

WHERE TO STAY

The development of the last decade and the early nineties has opened up a much greater range of accommodations than was previously available. However, don't expect Anguilla's sleepy image to be matched by sleepy prices. It is expensive to stay here, for the most part. Don't forget that an 8 percent government tax will be added to your bill, plus 10 percent for service.

All the accommodations recommended except one are on the water. Some have kitchens, which is an advantage given the cost of eating out every night.

COVE CASTLES (809) 497-6801, fax (809) 497-6051
Stateside: (800) 348-4716; in Canada: (800) 468-0023
(P.O. Box 248), Shoal Bay, West End, Anguilla, B.W.I.

When I did the first edition of *Rum and Reggae* in 1987, I drove up to the Cove Castles and just hated it. Why? Because I felt the contemporary structures overwhelmed this delicate setting. This made me mad, hence my decision to exclude it. Well, I gave it a second shot this time, and I stand corrected. The accommodations are just fabulous! I couldn't have been more wrong, and the key to this turnaround is going inside. What a great space!

The units, set in futuristic white structures on the beach amidst wild and natural landscaping, are two- and three-bedroom affairs with two baths, a fully equipped gourmet kitchen, dining room, living room, and terra-cotta–tiled veranda. They are furnished simply but beautifully in natural wicker, very comfy white cushions and décor right out of *Arch. Digest*. The tradewinds provide ample ventilation and the views are of the water and the profile of St. Martin in the distance. All are designed to ensure maximum privacy. Amenities include your own housekeeper, who does everything but cook; plus: cable TV, beach chairs and umbrellas, snorkeling gear, Sunfish sailboats, fishing gear, bikes, tennis racquets and a lighted tennis court, and a *New York Times* fax (in season). Other activities and services can be arranged by the management. An optional MAP plan offers meals served in your villa. Rates are BEYOND BELIEF (EP).

CAP JULUCA (809) 497-6666, fax (809) 497-6617
Stateside: (800) 323-0139/(212) 497-6779
(P.O. Box 240) Maunday's Bay, Anguilla, B.W.I.

Situated on the prettiest beach on Anguilla, with the whitest sand you'll ever see, this Moorish extravaganza of stucco and domed turrets is an unusual architectural statement in the West Indies. From the paisley wall coverings, tapestries, and exotically uphol- stered furniture of the main building to the curves and columned arches of the guest accommodations, the effect is striking—a little out of place but striking nonetheless.

There are 85 rooms of various degrees of size and luxury strung along this gorgeous beach. All rooms are fully-loaded, with covered lanai, air conditioning and ceiling fans, hammocks, Italian tile floors, Moroccan artifacts, Italian marble baths, and so on. You can also rent suites and villas with their own pools. On the eastern end of the beach are Pimm's and Chatterton's, the four-star French/ Caribbean restaurant and bar, respectively. There are three tennis courts, two lighted for night play; an 1,800-square-foot pool with private tanning areas separated by hedges, with attendants available at the summons of a bell provided to you; and all water sports either on the beach or through arrangement by the hotel. Rates are OUTRAGEOUS to BEYOND BELIEF (CP).

RAINBOW REEF VILLAS (809) 497-2817, fax (809) 497-3091
Stateside: (708) 325-2299
(P.O. Box 130) Anguilla, B.W.I.

If you like the steady sound of breakers rolling in on the reef, then these comfortable and well-maintained villas are for you. Rather functional in appearance, they are situated on Seafeather's Point with spectacular views of the mountains of St. Martin and the distant hills of St. Barts. There are two bedrooms, one bath, a long hall, a large living/dining/kitchen area, pantry, and covered veranda that provides optimal views and a stiff breeze. Each villa is situated to allow constant ventilation from the trades. There is daily maid service by a very friendly staff and owners Dave and Charlotte

Bergland are very helpful. There is a shallow beach good for kids but not on a par with Anguilla's better beaches.

Rates are PRICEY for singles and doubles (EP). *No credit cards accepted.*

MALLIOUHANA (809) 497-6111, fax (809) 497-6011
Stateside: (800) 835-0796
(P.O. Box 173) Meads Bay, Anguilla, B.W.I.

Like a celebrity traveling incognito, the Malliouhana doesn't disclose its whereabouts. You won't find any signs pointing the way—always a tip-off to an ultrachic resort. This is one of the Caribbean's poshest. Promising to "replenish the spirit of living," it will also most assuredly deplete your bank account. But if you have the money and want really sumptuous and tranquil surroundings, with nothing or no one else to harass you, then why not?

Everything here is carefully considered, from the tasteful color scheme of earth reds, forest greens, and sandy beiges to the small and multitiered layout of the many public loggias and alcoves. Throughout, there is a feeling of intimacy. You expect to see Jackie O. or Princess Stephanie sipping a lime squash under one of the countless oversized (and matching, of course) Haitian or West Indian paintings. The bar is particularly attractive, with very comfortable sofas, piles of pillows, muted tones, and a terrific sound system.

Outside, there are two and a half free-form pools. The half-pool is a shallow model for tots. The other two are at different levels so that one spills into the next by means of a manmade stone waterfall. But far more appealing for swimming is the little-used, spectacular deep-water access down a series of steps from the pool. Some more steps and a landing have been carved into the rock. This allows you to dive into the crystal-clear water and swim to the resort's beach (about 100 yards to the right). All water-sports activities and equipment (snorkeling, fishing, waterskiing, parasailing, out-island cruises, windsurfing, Sunfish and Hobies) are "complimentary," which is the least the resort can do considering the price you pay for a room!

And there's more: a superb and very expensive open-air restaurant overlooking the water and a pagoda-style exercise "hall" with Universal and aerobic machines, massage room, and the best view offered by any gym I've ever used. Four of the island's best tennis courts (two lit for night play), and Meads Bay beach round out the facilities. Oh yes, and the rooms—suffice it to say that they uphold the elegance of the rest of the resort. Each one has a terrace and ceiling fan, bamboo platform beds, and the same tasteful design scheme and furnishings. There's also a fabulous Japanese villa on the beach that costs buckets, but what style!

Rates are BEYOND BELIEF. *No credit cards accepted* (just Swiss bank account numbers—only kidding). Personal checks are accepted with "prior arrangement."

CINNAMON REEF BEACH CLUB (809) 497-2727, fax (809) 497-3727
Stateside: (800) 223-1108, (800) 972-4490
Little Harbour, Anguilla, B.W.I.

Many pegs down from the luxury of the Malliouhana, but certainly still high on the comfort scale, is the Cinnamon Reef. Now 10 years old, this Spanish-cast resort is situated in its own protected bay named Little Harbour. Several rather oddly designed villas spin off from the main building—a long arched loggia of terra-cotta–tiled floors, heavy Mediterranean furnishings, and painted porcelain chandeliers. The restaurant, bar, boutique, and reception are also located here. The villas themselves have walled terraces with huge circular ports, a "designer" living area, and a raised bedroom space directly behind it. The villas are spaced far enough apart to be fairly private. The landscaping, however, still needs work, six years after my last visit. A down-sized pool sits next to deco-turf tennis courts that are well maintained. The beach is okay and offers free use (for guests) of windsurfers, Sunfish, paddle boats, snorkel and fishing gear. *Note:* During the winter "high" season, no children under twelve are allowed.

Rates are WICKED PRICEY for singles and doubles (EP). Add $50 U.S. per person for MAP.

SKIFFLE'S VILLAS (809) 497-6110, no fax
Stateside: (219) 642-4855
(P.O. Box 82), Lower South Hill, Anguilla, B.W.I.

Beatles' fans will remember that the Fab Four started out as a skiffle band. Who knows whether the owner had them in mind when he named this place. Anyway, these tastefully done villas, while not on the water, are fairly out of the way and private. They also offer good panoramas of the north (with a little, palm-studded cay known as Sandy Island front and center). There are five two-bedroom, two-bath units with bamboo furnishings, lots of tile, and good light. A small pool is located in the center, though I wouldn't use it very much. Instead I'd hop on my scooter and head to one of the recommended beaches nearby.

Rates are PRICEY for singles and doubles. *No credit cards accepted.*

CARIMAR BEACH CLUB (809) 497-6881, fax (809) 497-6071
Stateside: (800) 235-8667
(P.O. Box 327), Meads Bay, Anguilla, B.W.I.

Down the hill from the Malliouhana is the Carimar Beach Club. This is a very pleasant and charming little resort that rents 23 apartments (one-, two-, and three-bedroom), each with a fully equipped kitchen, living and dining room and a spacious patio and balcony. Run by Pam Berry, who's very friendly and a great gal, this is a good alternative for families who need space and cooking facilities. But keep in mind that prices here are only slightly lower than a room (no kitchen) at Cap Juluca, so unless you are four or more you might as well go for the latter. The atmosphere here, however, is very low-key and Pam will help you with any questions or plans. There is a great beach out front, Meads Bay, and a western exposure for great sunsets. There is a tennis court and water sports are available.

Rates are RIDICULOUS to BEYOND BELIEF (EP).

CASABLANCA (809) 497-6999, fax (809) 497-6899
Stateside: (800) 231-1945/(203) 655-4200
Maunday's Bay, Anguilla, B.W.I.

This property is located just east of Cap Juluca and very oddly designed in a very Moorish/Arabesque style, particularly since Cap Juluca is next door. A mini-Arabia in Anguilla, I guess. The resort only opened in early 1993, and indeed construction was still happening when I visited the property. Owned by a Saudi family, hence the style, about the most stunning thing about this resort is the entrance—totally out of context—but stunning nonetheless.

Arches, kiosks, elaborate mosaics and colorful painting, a reflecting pool and a view of the sea and St. Martin beyond greet you as you walk into the lobby. With such an entrance, your expectations are high for what's beyond. That's where you're let down. The grounds will take several years to make what was scrub and sand into a tropical garden. The buildings that house the guest accommodations are fairly bland, although the rooms themselves are attractive, painted in bright pastels with custom-matching fabrics and great big gray marble baths. The beach, however, is not on par with its neighbor, Cap Juluca. But prices here are about $100 U.S. less per room per night, which makes a difference. You'll find all the amenities here, including water sports, tennis, and a health club. The resort borrows heavily from the movie of the same name, with such flourishes as Rick's Café Americaine. Since it's still in its infancy, this place make take a few years to grow up.

Rates are RIDICULOUS for rooms and OUTRAGEOUS to BEYOND BELIEF for suites (EP).

ANGUILLA GREAT HOUSE (809) 497-6061, fax (809) 497-6019
Stateside: (800) 241-6764
(P.O. Box 157), Rendezvous Bay, Anguilla, B.W.I.

Located midway on the long stretch of strand on Rendezvous Bay, this is a small, locally owned resort with a nice, casual ambience and very attractive rooms. While the grounds could use some water and a manicure, there is a great beach in front and you'll rarely have more than 10 people on it at one time. The style is refreshingly West Indian, with white Antillean roofs and gingerbread trim. The rooms are comfortably furnished with mahogany repros and chintz upholstery—simple but tasteful. The baths are marble and good-sized; ceiling fans keep the rooms cool. There are some comfy chaises on the long veranda outside the rooms. A pool is adjacent to the Old Caribe bar/restaurant, and there are water sports available on the beach.

Rates are VERY PRICEY for singles and WICKED PRICEY for doubles (EP).

THE INNS OF ANGUILLA (809) 497-3180, fax (809) 497-5381
Anguilla, B.W.I.

If your budget is tight, this association of twenty small hotels, guest houses, and efficiencies offer rates from $75 per day for a double

room to $150 per day for a two-bedroom villa. All the properties are locally owned and each is unique. Don't expect the Ritz: these are simple, clean accommodations—many with views and close to the beach (Patsy's Seaside Villa is on the beach).
   Rates are NOT SO CHEAP to PRICEY (EP).

WHERE TO EAT

The choices are now quite good for dining out on Anguilla. At the resorts, the restaurant at MALLIOUHANA (497-6111) and PIMM'S at CAP JULUCA (497-6666) are excellent and very expensive. But you should splurge one night and dine at one. Both feature seaside dining and French/Caribbean cuisine. Reservations are a must. Others to try are:

MANGO'S, Barnes Bay, 497-6479

This is an American/California grill with a West Indian flair. The food is fresh, simple, and good. Lunch and dinner served daily. Reservations are recommended. $$$

CAPER'S, Meads Bay, 497-6369

Now open for lunch and dinner, this restaurant is a grill with Pacific Rim flourishes, including yummy and filling dishes like Seven Stars Around the Moon (Java pork, five-spice chicken, coconut shrimp, beef tenderloin, calamari, lobster, veggies, and rice). Reservations are suggested. $$$$

KOAL KEEL, The Valley, 497-2930

The cuisine here could be best described as nouvelle West Indian. The restaurant is located in one of the oldest houses on Anguilla and is decorated with a collection of nineteenth-century island antiques. Reservations are recommended. $$$$$

BARREL STAY, Sandy Ground, 497-2831

This is a French/Créole restaurant that sits beside the beach. Fresh seafood is the specialty here—their fish soup is famous. Lunch and dinner are served daily. Reservations are recommended. $$$$$

ROY'S PLACE, Crocus Bay, 497-2470

This authentic English pub is a fave among the yachty set because of its fresh seafood and good value. Happy hour on Friday (5–7 P.M.) is a big hit here too. Reservations are recommended for dinner. $$$$

RISTORANTE LA FONTANA, Fountain Beach Hotel, Shoal Bay, 497-3492

With pastas and seafood and antipasti, this small restaurant serves Anguilla's best Italian cuisine. $$$$

THE OLD HOUSE, George Hill, 497-2228

The cuisine is West Indian and the setting is a white plantation-style house. Great for breakfast too. $$$

LEDUC'S FISH TRAP, Island Harbour Beach, 497-4488

Great French-West Indian–style seafood is served by the sea. Veronica Leduc's restaurant is chic and a local favorite. The fish and lobster come in on the fishing boats across the street. Reservations are strongly recommended at dinner. $$$

HIBERNIA, Island Harbour, 497-4290

This small restaurant has developed a reputation for its fine cuisine, an exotic mix of French and Oriental flavors. Reservations are required. $$$$

RIVIERA, Sandy Ground, 497-2833

The Riviera has the only oyster bar on the island and very good, critically acclaimed French and Créole cuisine. Reservations are suggested. $$$$$

JOHNNO'S, Sandy Ground, 497-2728

Johnno's is for good food, local-style, and great music on Saturday nights. $$$

FAT CAT GOURMET, George Hill, 497-2307

Not to be missed, particularly for those with kitchens, is the Fat Cat Gourmet. It features excellent packaged and frozen homemade dishes, such as chicken marbella, conch stew (guaranteed tender), and lobster quiche, that can be reheated whenever. Thus, you are relieved of shopping and cooking that would take up precious beach time. They make lots of desserts and will custom-bake a birthday cake or your favorite pie. Also available are pasta salads and daily specials for beach picnics as well as a catering service for any cocktail parties or dinner parties you may decide to toss. Servings for four will cost about $20 U.S., and they do deliver.

DON'T MISS

DIVE ANGUILLA WITH TAMARIAIN
WATERSPORTS, LTD. (809) 497-2020, fax (809) 497-5125
P.O. Box 247, The Valley, Anguilla, B.W.I.

This is Anguilla's only full-service PADI dive facility and the only shop with a compressor on the island. Located in Sandy Ground on Road Bay, it has much to offer, including a resort course for the scuba-curious that costs $80 U.S. for one open-water dive. Ian and Tom, the owners, also offer a PADI Open Water Certification course for enthusiasts. Most diving is done off the Prickly Pear Reef, a ten-mile-long stretch of coral providing some excellent dive sights that is only a short boat ride away.

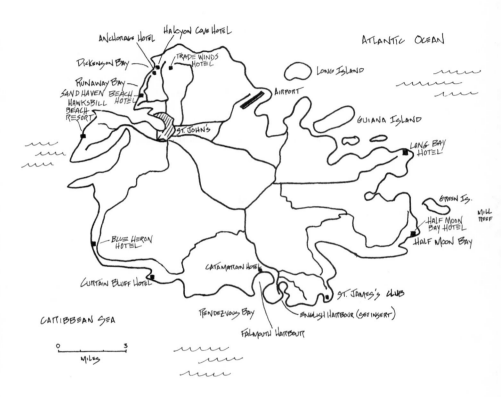

ATLANTIC OCEAN

ANCHORAGE HOTEL   HALCYON COVE HOTEL

DICKENSON BAY   TRADE WINDS HOTEL

LONG ISLAND

RUNAWAY BAY
SAND HAVEN BEACH
HAWKSBILL BEACH HOTEL   AIRPORT
BEACH
RESORT

GUIANA ISLAND

ST. JOHN'S

LONG BAY HOTEL

GREEN IS.

MILL REEF

HALF MOON BAY HOTEL

BLUE HERON HOTEL   HALF MOON BAY

CATAMARAN HOTEL

CURTAIN BLUFF HOTEL

ST. JAMES'S CLUB

RENDEZVOUS BAY   ENGLISH HARBOUR (SEE INSERT)

CARIBBEAN SEA

FALMOUTH HARBOUR

0   3
MILES

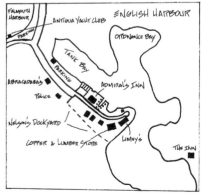

FALMOUTH HARBOUR   ENGLISH HARBOUR

ANTIGUA YACHT CLUB

PARKING

ORDNANCE BAY

TANK BAY

PARKING

ABRACADABRA'S   ADMIRAL'S INN

POLICE

NELSON'S DOCKYARD

COPPER & LUMBER STORE   LIMEY'S

THE INN

ANTIGUA

ANTIGUA

TOURISTO SCALE   🔲 🔲 🔲 🔲 🔲 🔲 🔲 🔲   8

I'm not crazy about Antigua. If it weren't for Sailing Week and V. C. Bird International Airport, where I am constantly making connections, I doubt I would ever come here. Why, you ask? It all starts at the airport at Immigration, where the very frosty officer looks at you the way you look at a cockroach, never utters a hello, and makes you feel as meaningful as a grain of sand on a beach. Shades of things to come? You hope not. But there is a definite and deliberate coolness to Antiguans. They are rather brusque and unwelcoming toward tourists. Although this is certainly not a new phenomenon (the Parisians perfected this years ago), it's a tad unsettling when you're on a small, Third-World island. There's definitely an attitude problem here.

Antigua does have its merits, however. There are many wonderful beaches (the Tourist Office claims 365—does the mud in St. John's Harbour count as a beach?), some rather nice resorts and one of the cheapest beachfront hotel options in the Caribbean, a dry climate with the trades, a happening yachting scene, great British historic sights, and an international airport where most airlines fly nonstop. Antigua is also the largest of the Leeward Islands, covering an area of about 108 square miles. It's just that with all the other choices in the Caribbean, why deal with attitude, lots of tourists, bad roads, and an island that really isn't all that pretty? Unless, of course, it's Sailing Week time (see below).

Being a major hub in the Caribbean transportation wheel, Antigua attracts all kinds of travelers. Americans, Brits, Canadians, and Germans pour in on jumbo jets. Once on the island, they head to the major resorts on the western and southern coasts. The

yachty set heads for English Harbour, one of the major boat centers in the Caribbean. And with a new cruise ship dock, the
swarms descend from the big ships into St. John's during the day
in a shopping frenzy and overwhelm the little town as well as
Nelson's Dockyard at English Harbour. With all of this commotion, there are a lot of options for the visitor and Antigua may
appeal to those who, if they are not sailors, like the activity and
variety the island offers.

THE BRIEFEST HISTORY

Antigua (pronounced An-tee-ga) has been inhabited for more than
4,000 years, starting with the Ciboney in 2400 B.C., the Arawaks
from the time of Christ until about 1100, when the Caribs took
over. Columbus sighted and named the island after Santa María de
la Antigua on his second voyage in 1493. The Caribs and the lack
of fresh spring water kept out the Europeans until 1632, when the
English landed a party from St. Kitts and eventually conquered the
Caribs. Sugar planting (mostly by imported African slaves) became
very successful and there were over 150 mills in operation at one
time. The mills also deforested the island, which is still evident
today. Antigua played an important role in the British hegemony in
the West Indies, as the "landlocked" and incognito port of English
Harbour (easily disguised from enemy French ships with palm
fronds on the ships' masts) was the key naval base for Lord Nelson
in the Caribbean. When slavery and slave labor were abolished in
1834, the economy slid downhill and conditions for the former
slaves were deplorable. This led to unrest and violence in the early
part of this century. This also may help to explain the Antiguan
demeanor. In the 1940s, V. C. Bird founded the Antigua Labour
Party to alleviate the awful plight of Antiguans; the party negotiated
with England for self-rule (granted in 1967) and full independence
with a reluctant Barbuda in 1981. V. C. Bird is still the P.M. (he's
now in his eighties). Scandal has lately rocked his government (his
son and family members were allegedly being a little overgenerous
with government funds and power), but as of press time he's still in
office.

ANTIGUA: KEY FACTS

LOCATION	17°N by 61°W
	38 miles north of Guadeloupe
	30 miles south of Barbuda
	1,800 miles southeast of New York
SIZE	108 square miles
HIGHEST POINT	Boggy Peak (1330 ft.)
POPULATION	66,000
LANGUAGE	English
TIME	Atlantic Standard Time (1 hour ahead of EST, same as EDT).
AREA CODE	809
ELECTRICITY	Most of the island's electricity is 220 volts AC, 60 cycles; however, Hodges Bay area and some hotels have 110 volts AC, 60 cycles
CURRENCY	The Eastern Caribbean dollar, EC$ (EC$2.70 = $1 U.S.)
DRIVING	On the *left*; you'll need a temporary permit— EC$30 or $12 U.S.—just present your valid U.S. or Canadian driver's license
DOCUMENTS	U.S. and Canadian citizens need proof of nationality with a photo; British citizens need a passport; all visitors must present a return or ongoing ticket
DEPARTURE TAX	EC$25 or $9 U.S.
BEER TO DRINK	Red Stripe
RUM TO DRINK	Mt. Gay
MUSIC TO HEAR	Dancehall

GETTING THERE

Antigua is centrally located and is a major gateway to the Caribbean. Its airport, V. C. Bird International, handles jumbo jets and has daily nonstop service from the States on AMERICAN and BWIA, and from Canada on AIR CANADA. AMERICAN and AMERICAN EAGLE also fly here from San Juan. BRITISH AIRWAYS and LUFTHANSA fly nonstop from London and Frankfurt, respectively. Antigua is LIAT's hub, so it is easy to fly here from other Caribbean islands.

GETTING AROUND

To really explore the island, you will need a rental car. There are plenty of agencies located at the airport to your right as you walk out of Customs. Competition is fierce, so go to each counter and ask for their best price (they will show you their rate on a piece of paper so their competitors don't shout out a lower one). I was able to get a decent economy car for $30 U.S. a day, a very good price in the Caribbean. Weekly rates will yield a better discount. You'll have to get a temporary Antiguan license from the rental agent, which costs $12 U.S.; to get one, you'll have to present a valid driver's license from home.

Check your car thoroughly to make sure everything works and to note any dents on your rental agreement. Also check the spare tire before you drive away. Among the international car-rental agencies (none have airport offices, probably a government move to help local outfits) are AVIS ([800] 331-1084), BUDGET ([800] 527-0700), DOLLAR ([800] 800-4000), and NATIONAL ([800] 227-3876). If you want to use them, make reservations and arrangements with these companies before you arrive to avoid any inconvenience when you arrive.

If you loathe driving, there are plenty of taxis available. Be sure to agree on a rate *before* you get in the cab. Rate sheets are posted in the Customs area and your hotel will also advise you.

FOCUS ON ANTIGUA: ANTIGUA SAILING WEEK

If there is one time in yachting when socializing is just as important as racing (if not more so), it is Antigua Sailing Week (also known as Race Week). Having survived 26 years of festive inebriation, it's still going strong as the premier yachting event in the Caribbean. Always held during the last week in April, this ritual puts the final wrap on the winter season. Afterward, most boats head north to the States or east to the Mediterranean for the summer.

Race Week also attracts a large crowd of nonracers. This is because of the range of activities that happen onshore. In fact, most people who participate in Race Week don't give a damn about the races and can't tell the difference between a shroud and a stay. What they want is to have a good time while rubbing elbows with the sailing set. On weekend nights, a good part of the younger Antiguan population will be there too as this is one of major events on the island (the other being Carnival in August).

People get pretty smashed during this celebration (boating people are notorious drinkers, putting Nick and Nora Charles to shame). Despite the alcohol, there is order due to what seems to be a policeman every 20 feet—a sobering effect. The presence of the police also reflects the political unease that an event as white and wealthy as yachting might create on an island that is predominantly black and poor (the average per-capita income is below $1,000). Since Sailing Week is a major tourist attraction and allows the hotels to extend their winter rates until after the event (and three weeks longer than just about every other island), the Hotel Association and government want to ensure that all goes smoothly—hence the cops. In the official programs, there is a plea to "please help us keep Antigua Sailing Week a happy, carefree, but controlled experience for the benefit of all."

Most of the activity during Sailing Week is focused on Nelson's Dockyard, a restored historic complex of old Georgian brick buildings and warehouses that sits in the middle of English Harbour. Now a national park and major tourist attraction, some of the buildings are stunning—especially the Admiral's Inn (see the "English Harbour" entry later on in the "Where to Stay" section).

In any given year, almost 200 boats from over 25 countries compete. The boats are about equally split into racing and cruising classes. So you will know for future cocktail conversation, there are five days of races and three classes of racers and cruisers, Racing Class I, II, and III, and Cruising Class I, II, and III (the first—I—being the most advanced). The Racers are semipros, traveling around the seas on the racing circuit. The Cruisers are more mellow—many of these boats are available for crewed charter any other week but this one. The Cruisers also drink a lot more during the race—beer consumption goes through the roof during Race Week. The Race Committee designs the courses, depending on conditions. The courses allow the boats to circumnavigate the island, with an Olympic Gold Cup race thrown in, in five races. Some years they go clockwise, some years they go counterclockwise, some years they go in both directions (it's sounds implausible but it works). Always check with the Race Committee—they will post the course—before heading to other parts of the island to rendezvous with the boats.

The main pre-event to Sailing Week is the Guadeloupe Race, held a few days before the start of Sailing Week. This is a 42-mile race from Deshaies, Guadeloupe, to English Harbour. There are three classes of boats in this race: Multi-hulls, Racers, and Cruisers. The cocktail party hosted by Les Amis de Voile de Point-à-Pitre is fabulous. Even more fun is the Mt. Gay open bar and barbecue held at the Galleon Beach back at English Harbour, which kicks off Sailing Week. Be sure to get one of the red Mt. Gay hats, the hottest Race Week souvenir.

Sunday is the day of the First Yacht Race. Supposing that this is a counterclockwise year, the race starts off Falmouth Harbour and runs a course around the island from east to north to west. It is 33 miles long and finishes in Dickenson Bay on the northwestern corner of Antigua.

This is where the real fun begins—many claim this is the best party of the week. The combination of almost two hundred boats in the bay, a pretty beach, a large local turnout, and several big hotels create a very festive atmosphere. A traveling band of vendors sets up on the beach, offering chicken and chips, ice-cold beer, and an endless array of mediocre T-shirts. A good reggae band provides the pulsating beat for the huge crowd on the beach. If you ever wanted to dance barefoot in the sand, this is the ideal opportunity to do so. The action actually begins around noontime, as the non-mariners arrive at the beach for sun, fun, and watching the boats come in—so plan to spend the day. You'll never be too far from the bar or a bathroom.

The Second Yacht Race is held the next day in the same area. It consists of a "Gold Cup" course similar to what the boats sail in the America's Cup. The course is about 16 miles long for the Racing Classes and 10 miles long for the Cruising Classes. After the races, it's pretty much a rerun of the night before, but not quite as much fun or as crowded.

It's back to Nelson's Dockyard for the Third Yacht Race. The boats start around 9 A.M. off Dickenson Bay and sail between 24 to 28 miles south, then east to the finish line at English Harbour. After the race, another party kicks off at 1800 hours on the waterfront in front of the Officer's Building. This is a major drinking event as the following day is Lay Day, that is, no races. A must-not-miss is Limey's Bar on the second floor overlooking the action. This is the place to rendezvous and talk about plans for the delivery north or the summer.

Lay Day is lots of fun for landlubbers, too. All the festivities are held at the Antigua Yacht Club, just down the road from Nelson's Dockyard, about a 12-minute walk, on Falmouth Harbor. The action starts in the early afternoon with a rubber-raft race, tug-of-war, boardsailing races, a beer-drinking contest, and other "why-not" games. There is also a singlehanded yacht race for boats 45 feet and under and team racing in Lasers by country/territory, which can be real fun if you're a sailor.

There are two more days of racing after Lay Day. The Fourth Yacht Race begins off Falmouth Harbour, beats east to Mill Reef, then runs west to Curtain Bluff, home of one of the most deluxe resorts—the Curtain Bluff Hotel—on the island. The course is 29 miles long for Racers and 17 miles for Cruisers. Once again, there is a party with a band in front of the hotel. For nonmariners, this is a wonderful beach on which to spend the afternoon drinking rum punches from the beach bar and greeting the arriving boats. The party starts around six and goes until your walking hangover says "enough already."

The final race, the Fifth Yacht Race, is an Ocean Triangle Course held off Falmouth Harbour and runs 24 miles for Racers and about 16 miles for the Cruising Classes. The "après" scene shifts back to Nelson's Dockyard for the last of the Race Day sailing parties. By now, you'll be feeling just a little weary and will probably want to venture over to one of the local bars outside of the Dockyard.

The most social of the local bars is undoubtedly Abracadabra's, located just across from the Dockyard parking lot. This is the place to go if you're trying to get picked up (if people still do that kind of thing in the paranoid nineties). The deck will be jammed with the sailing set—count on twenty minutes to get from end to end. Don't even think of trying to get through when the management shows video highlights of the day's races on the big screen. The crowd here is very attractive, generally bleached out and horny. In the garden, a reggae band sets up and gets to really jammin' later in the evening.

Probably the prettiest spot for having a drink or listening to music is the Admiral's Inn, located in the Dockyard. The grounds are beautiful, particularly the huge stone columns that line a narrow slipway and are the only remnants of the old boat house. The canopy created by some very old trees combined with the elegance of the inn make a quietly grand and stately sight. The bar inside is very comfortable and very nautical, with large French doors opening out onto the terrace and grounds. The live music here can be surprisingly good—one night I heard one of the best pan bands outside of Trinidad.

With the races over and the final standings posted, the atmosphere the next day becomes quite festive. Even while crews scurry around readying their boats for imminent departure, all seem to find time for a few pops here and there. Indeed, for many it's a liquid diet beginning with breakfast. So by the time things start happening, a lot of people are juiced up and ready to go. Not that there's really all that much going on, except for the greased-pole contest where local boys (the only ones daring enough) try to walk on a machine-greased wooden pole over the water. The goal is to touch a red flag before falling in. Winners get a bottle of rum and a pat on the back. It's amusing to watch for twenty minutes. Around three o'clock, the much-heralded Non-Mariner's Race takes place at the ramp in front of the Officer's Quarters. The requirements of the race are that the vessel be homemade, cost no more than $100 to build, and never have been in the water. The best part of the race is the start, when the contestants plunge into the water with their vessels. Their destination is the dock at the Admiral's Inn, where a crowd with cocktails awaits and cheers on the participants. Unfortunately, the race is over too soon and that's that. The milling around on the waterfront continues while a band kicks up to keep everyone going until the evening and Lord Nelson's Ball.

Lord Nelson's Ball is supposedly the culmination of the social events during Sailing Week, but in reality the first night at Dickenson's or the deck at Abracadabra's is much more fun. The ball is a throwback to the days when yachting was exclusively white and Anglo-Saxon. The crowd (when I attended) was almost entirely white, thanks to the jacket-tie dress code and the $30 U.S. admission fee. It just doesn't seem right in the nineties, not that it ever was. I was embarrassed for the Governor-General who spoke at the ball to an audience that was hardly his constituency (they were not invited). That said, the ball is enjoyable for the alcohol flowing freely from the open bar. Also amusing is how women manage to stow away their best taffetas in their duffel bags and then throw them on for this formal occasion. Some of the men come up with black tie, although most are dressed in natty blue blazers and button-downs with wrinkled khakis or Lilly Pulitzers. The setting of the Admiral's Inn and grounds is very stunning and very colonial. When you've had enough, head over to Abracadabra's for reggae and a much more civilized environment.

WHERE TO STAY

Antigua is loaded with hotels, most of which are on the beach. Like the other Leeward Islands, it's not cheap to stay here. However, it would certainly be worth your while to investigate package deals, as significant discounts will be offered on both airfare and accommodations. Check whether any hotels offered in a given package correspond to my recommendations below. Antigua does sport one of the best beach hotel values: the Sand Haven Beach Hotel (see below).

THE WEST COAST

There is a grand stretch of beach which begins just north of St. John's at Fort James and continues, with minor interruptions, for five miles through Runaway Bay and Dickenson Bay to Boon Point. On this strand there are no fewer than nine hotels, resorts, and condo villages. Among my recommendations:

HALCYON COVE RESORT AND CASINO (809) 462-0256, fax (809) 462-0271
in Canada: (800) 531-6767
(P.O. Box 251, St. John's), Dickenson Bay, Antigua, W.I.

While there's nothing particularly special about this large resort (over 140 rooms and suites), it does have everything, including a nice beach, and would be a good option for those looking at packages. Facilities include free water sports, three restaurants, four bars, a casino, pool, four all-weather lighted tennis courts, all rooms with phones and some with air conditioning (standard rooms do not have air conditioning). Deluxe rooms have TV and fridge.

Rates are the same for singles and doubles and are much higher for the Christmas holiday period, from WICKED PRICEY to OUTRAGEOUS. In January, rates go down almost 100 percent, to PRICEY to RIDICULOUS, and go up slightly for the rest of the high season, from VERY PRICEY to RIDICULOUS. *Hint:* Buy a package with this one!

TRADE WINDS HOTEL (809) 462-1223, fax (809) 462-5007
(P.O. Box 1390, St. John's), Dickenson Bay, Antigua, W.I.

Perched on the top of a hill overlooking Dickenson Bay, this is a great option for view and breeze fans and those who aren't keen on being on the beach. A small but attractive free-form pool centers a terrace with lots of shade and a bar. This is a very pleasant spot to hang out. There is also a good French restaurant, L'Auberge de Paris, on the grounds. Rooms are clean and simply yet handsomely furnished. Every room has a view, air conditioning, phone, and lanai. There are three types of rooms: a two-room apartment with kitchen, a studio with kitchen, and a standard room with kitchenette.

Rates are VERY PRICEY to WICKED PRICEY for singles and WICKED PRICEY to OUTRAGEOUS for doubles. All rates include MAP, taxes, and service charge.

SAND HAVEN BEACH HOTEL (809) 462-4491
(P.O. Box 405, St. John's), Antigua, W.I.

The Sand Haven is the best beachfront value on Antigua and one of the best in the Caribbean. The reasons are simple: a beautiful beach, the water 50 feet away, and the prices well under $100 a day. It's hard to find similar value anywhere in the tropics. Recently purchased by two ex-Londoners who were drawn to the "Don't Stop the Carnival" lure of a hotel in the tropics, they openly admit they are often finding their way in the dark. Operating a hotel in Antigua is not the same as working as a banker or general contractor in London. But they say they're enjoying it. With this kind of value, the accommodations are very simple, in the motel-school of décor. However, the beach at Runaway Bay is one of Antigua's best and there are few people on it to boot. So if you want value over luxury and want to be ON THE BEACH, this is the place to go. There is a relatively pricey restaurant and a beach bar on the premises.

Rates are NOT SO CHEAP for singles and doubles (EP).

HERITAGE HOTEL (809) 462-1247, fax (809) 462-2262
Heritage Quay, St. John's, Antigua, W.I.

While staying in the heart of St. John's, the major town on Antigua, wouldn't be my idea of a tropical getaway, I'm sure there are a few of you who would relish the idea (this is actually a good hotel for business travelers). While you are on the water, the major cruise-ship dock actually, there is no beach and no pool. Still interested, read on. The rooms are actually suites and are spacious, clean, and have full kitchens, lanai, air conditioning, phones, and cable TV.

Rates are NOT SO CHEAP for singles and PRICEY for doubles (EP).

THE SPANISH MAIN INN (809) 462-0660
Independence Avenue, St. John's, Antigua, W.I.

For those looking for heaps of character, this is the place. It's cheap, funky, and noisy, and it's also in town. However, it was the original American consul's residence, so it does have some history to it (though it could use a paint job). The Spanish Main is run by a nice Irish couple who relish the pub atmosphere of the place. Be sure to get a room that does not face the street and the park, as the traffic noise will not be at all restful. Wednesday night is the big pub night with live entertainment. This place attracts a lot of Brits and Irish travelers.

Rates are CHEAP for singles and doubles (EP).

HAWKSBILL BEACH RESORT (809) 462-0301, fax (809) 462-1515
Stateside: (800) 223-6510; in Canada: (800) 424-5500
(P.O. Box 108, St. John's), Five Islands, Antigua, W.I.

Set on 37 acres on a peninsula just south of St. John's, this fine resort boasts four of its own beaches, including one that is reserved for nude bathing. There are 90 pleasant rooms centered around a great house, 2 restaurants, 2 bars, a swimming pool, tennis court, and water sports. If you like beaches, especially a nude one, and a resort setting, this might be the place for you.

Rates are WICKED PRICEY for singles and RIDICULOUS for doubles (CP). Look for package deals.

THE BLUE HERON HOTEL (809) 462-8564, fax (809) 462-8005
(P.O. Box 1715, St. John's), Johnson's Point, Antigua, W.I.

A tad more deluxe and expensive than the Sand Haven (see above), this small resort on the fairly remote southwest corner of the island is another good beachfront value. Situated on its own pretty beach and facing west, this is a fine and quiet retreat for those who don't need anything fancy but still want to be on the beach. All rooms have air conditioning and phones. Superior rooms are on the water.

Rates are NOT SO CHEAP for singles and PRICEY for doubles (EP). Prices go up 80 percent during the Christmas holiday.

THE SOUTH COAST

CURTAIN BLUFF (809) 462-8400, fax (809) 462-8409
Stateside: (212) 289-8888
(P.O. Box 288, St. John's), Old Road, Antigua, W.I.

Located on a promontory jutting out into the remote south coast, Curtain Bluff is the grande dame of luxury hotels on Antigua, having been around since the early 1960s. Run on the "old school" approach to deluxe vacations (no pool aerobics here), this is a quiet, elegant if somewhat dowdy resort (men must wear a tie and jacket to dinner). Hence, the clientele tends to be more mature here. Rates are based on the Full American Plan, and the food here is reknowned as extraordinary; even wine by the glass and soft drinks are included in the price. There are 61 attractive rooms furnished in tropical décor and all have lanais, water views, and ceiling fans. Rates also include all water sports, even diving (certified divers only), laundry, and postage. Curtain Bluff has the best tennis facility on Antigua, including a resident pro, and features two private beaches. This is also one of the overnights of Sailing Week.

Rates are BEYOND BELIEF for both singles and doubles (FAP).

ENGLISH HARBOUR

If you like being at the hub of activity during Sailing Week, then I strongly suggest that you stay at Nelson's Dockyard at either the Admiral's Inn or the Copper and Lumber Store. Keep in mind that there will be a lot of noise from bands and people during this fiesta. Still close by but just a tad removed are the Inn at English Harbour and the Galleon Beach Hotel.

THE ADMIRAL'S INN (809) 460-1027, fax (809) 460-1534
Stateside: (800) 621-1270; in Canada: (800) 387-8031
(P.O. Box 713, St. John's) English Harbour, Antigua, W.I.

Set on the waterfront amid stately trees and old columns, this stunning weathered-brick and shuttered Georgian building is also the site of Lord Nelson's Ball during Sailing Week. There are 14 twin-bedded character-filled rooms of various sizes in this 200-year-old former engineer's quarters. Some rooms have air conditioning, others ceiling fans. The Admiral's Bar is festooned with tasteful nautical memorabilia, and the terrace is a grand place to sip rum punch while comparing the virtues of various winches.

Rates are NOT SO CHEAP for singles and PRICEY for doubles (EP). Add $42 U.S. per person for MAP.

THE COPPER AND LUMBER STORE HOTEL (809) 460-1058, fax (809) 460-1529
Stateside: (800) 633-7411
(P.O. Box 184, St. John's), Nelson's Dockyard, English Harbour, Antigua, W.I.

This is a wonderfully elegant hotel set in an old Georgian building in the heart of Nelson's Dockyard. It is owned by an English couple who finished restoring the hotel in 1988, giving careful attention to Georgian design and authenticity. Like the Admiral, it has a weathered-brick and shuttered/louvered exterior with 14 suites/studios and the same brick/wood décor throughout. It is the interior that makes the Copper and Lumber Store one of the classiest joints on Antigua. The restorer's detailing is evident in the Honduran mahogany woodwork, the hand-stenciled wallpaper, and the numerous and elegant antique furnishings. Even the bathrooms are special— the showers are panelled with mahogany. The best rooms are the four suites which are "très deluxe." All the rooms have kitchenettes. There is a restaurant and pub on the premises. During Sailing Week, this place is in the middle of the action, fronting the main piazza on the bay where the bands play.

Rates are VERY PRICEY to WICKED PRICEY for both singles and doubles (EP). Add $40 U.S. per person for MAP.

THE INN AT ENGLISH HARBOUR (809) 460-1014, fax (809) 460-1603
Stateside: (800) 223-6510; in Canada: (800) 424-5500
(P.O. Box 187, St. John's), English Harbour, Antigua, W.I.

This inn is located across the bay from Nelson's Dockyard on Freeman's Bay. What it lacks in charm and character, it makes up for with a great beach, water sports, and a fab view of the dockyard from the excellent Terrace Restaurant and Bar. There are 28 modernish rooms, most right on the beach. The Inn runs a frequent launch to and from the Dockyard.

Rates are WICKED PRICEY to OUTRAGEOUS for singles and doubles (MAP).

GALLEON BEACH (809) 460-1024, fax (809) 460-1450
Stateside: (800) 223-9815
(P.O. Box 1003, St. John's), Freeman's Bay, English Harbour, Antigua, W.I.

This is a spacious property situated at the entrance to English Harbour with a great beach too (and the sight of the Mt. Gay Open Bar and Barbecue during Sailing Week). There are one- and two-bedroom cottages and one-bedroom suites, all of which have living rooms, fully equipped kitchens, and lanais. Two tennis courts, water sports, and a beach eatery—Colombo's Italian Restaurant—round out the amenities.

Rates are WICKED PRICEY for singles and doubles (EP).

THE SOUTHEAST AND EAST COASTS

There are some very deluxe resorts in these parts that will cost you lots of money.

ST. JAMES'S CLUB (809) 460-5000, fax (809) 460-3015
Stateside: (800) 274-0008/(212) 486-2575; in Canada: (800) 268-9051/(416) 598-2693
(P.O. Box 63, St. John's), Mamora Bay, Antigua, W.I.

Affiliated with the St. James's Clubs in London, Paris, and L.A., this resort put the "p" in pretentious. With an "honorary committee" of Sirs and Ladies, the correct smattering of celebrities, and the appropriate amount of attitude, you'd think the Aga Khan built the place out of marble and gold. But in reality, it used to be a Holiday Inn! The main building is borderline tacky and the glass-walled pool is reminiscent of a chain hotel on Miami Beach. The villas, while interesting in design, are jammed together—hardly worth the $850-U.S.-and-up price during high season. There is an array of activities available, including the standard water sports and tennis. Some, like horseback riding, scuba, deep-sea fishing, and surf jetting, are offered for an additional charge (if you can believe it). After shelling out $850 you'd think they would throw in a masseur or masseuse. But here the motto should be "why pay less?" P.S.: Burt and Fay, the couple who run the scuba operation and Yacht Club boutique, are very nice.

Rates are OUTRAGEOUS to BEYOND BELIEF for everyone (EP).

HALF MOON BAY HOTEL (809) 460-4300, fax (809) 460-4306
Stateside: (800) 223-6510; in Canada: (800) 424-5500
(P.O. Box 144, St. John's), Half Moon Bay, Antigua, W.I.

Situated on its own lovely three-quarter-mile-long beach *and* with its own nine-hole golf course, this is a good place for those who have the bucks and want both golf and beach on Antigua at their doorstep. There are also five all-weather Laykold tennis courts for those who want more action. All 100 rooms are on the ocean and are very attractive and comfortable. A full-service resort, there are two restaurants serving fine food, two bars, and water sports in addition to all of the above. If you like country clubs, this is the place.

Rates are WICKED PRICEY to RIDICULOUS for singles and RIDICULOUS to BEYOND BELIEF for doubles (AP).

LONG BAY HOTEL (809) 463-2005, fax (809) 463-2439
(P.O. Box 442, St. John's), Long Bay, Antigua, W.I.

Owned and operated by the Lafaurie family since 1966, this small hotel has a nice, casual ambience about it and sits on a very pretty beach on the rather remote east coast. There are 20 rooms, 6 cottages, and a villa which are simply and attractively furnished. All water sports are available and a protected bay on one side of the property allows for waterskiing and sailing. There are two restaurants and two bars and the hotel shares the beach with the Pineapple Beach Club.

Rates are WICKED PRICEY for singles and RIDICULOUS for doubles (MAP). Villa and cottage rates are WICKED PRICEY to RIDICULOUS (EP).

WHERE TO EAT

With the number and size of hotels on this island in addition to just the restaurant establishments, there are hundreds of options for dining. Listed below are some of the best and/or most interesting:

LE BISTRO, Hodges Bay, 462-3881

One of the most famous restaurants on Antigua and written up in many international mags, including *Gourmet*, this is French country cuisine served in a wonderful bistro setting. Reservations are a must. Closed June and July. $$$$$

CURTAIN BLUFF, Old Road, 462-8400

If you can't stay here, at least you can eat here. True, you'll have to dress up (guys will need a jacket *and* tie), but for one night, why not? The cuisine is continental and guests continually rave about it. Curtain Bluff also has one of the most extensive wine lists in the Caribbean (over 25,000 bottles in the cellar). Reservations are a must. Closed from mid-May to mid-October. $$$$$

HEMMINGWAY'S, St. Mary's Street, St. John's, 462-2763

Serving Caribbean cuisine, this is a delightful place for lunch and especially dinner. It is situated on the second floor of an old wooden building and has a wraparound veranda with comfortable, unique booths along the rail. It's bright, airy, and attractive in a real Caribbean style. The staff is friendly and attentive. Each booth is curiously equipped with a phone jack—shades of a Polo Lounge on Antigua? It's also very romantic due to the lighting outside. Be sure to try the pumpkin soup—it's out of this world! Open for breakfast, lunch, and dinner. $$$

FRENCH QUARTER, Runaway Bay, 462-0624

This is a fun restaurant with a Cajun accent situated on the northeast side of the island. You don't need reservations here. $$$$

PIZZAS ON THE QUAY, Redcliffe Quay, St. John's, 462-2621

This is a lively and fun place where the EC$9 (about $3.50 U.S.) price for a slice of plain pizza is ridiculously expensive. The proceeds of your pizza donation probably goes to the mortgage payment on the bitchin' stereo system and reggae CD collection. Despite the high prices, it's worth a stop just to have a drink and listen to the music. Open Monday through Saturday from 8:30 A.M. to midnight. Thursday nights are really fun here. $

LA DOLCE VITA, Redcliffe Quay, St. John's, 462-2016

With very reasonably priced, simple Italian/French fare (pizzas, pastas with wine sauces, etc.), this is a casual, pleasant place for dinner on a second-floor terrace overlooking the harbor. $$.

LEMON TREE, Long and Church streets, St. John's, 462-1969

Reknowned for its rather portly woman maître d', this fun place in town has reasonable prices, a lively atmosphere, and nightly entertainment. $$$

TALK OF THE TOWN, Redcliffe Street, St. John's, 462-0535

If you want a full plate of good West Indian food for EC$10, which is really cheap, then this is the place. Given the prices, it's always packed with locals. $

GOING OUT:

Here is the Thursday through Sunday lowdown about where to find the action on Antigua:

Thursday	*Pizzas on the Quay*, Redcliffe Quay, St. John's
Friday	*Abracadabra's*, English Harbour
Saturday	*Jolly Roger*, Heritage Quay
	This is a boat cruise that costs $40 U.S., but it includes dinner and all drinks and is a nice mix of tourists and locals.
Sunday	*Shirley Heights*, above English Harbour
	3–6 P.M.—steel bands, tourists
	6–9 P.M.—reggae/dub, more locals
	Barbecue all day, great views and sunsets
	After this, people head to *Miller's* from 10 P.M. on.

Note: The island's only disco, Tropix, on Redcliffe Quay, was closed at press time, but there was talk of reopening it, so do ask around.

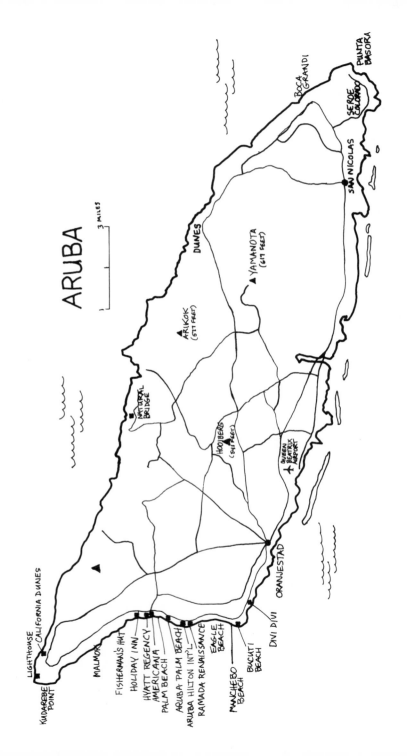

ARUBA

If all you want to do on your vacation is to esconce yourself at a deluxe resort, take in the sun, and never venture beyond the gates until you're ready to leave, then you will love Aruba. This is a desert island (not deserted, but a very arid island) where huge hotels line the nicest beaches. The climate is pretty much guaranteed to be sunny, breezy, and hot. The island is highly developed and tourism is big business, attracting more than 500,000 visitors a year. Shopping and casinos are major recreational activities here. There are more than 100 restaurants and 7,800 hotel rooms. Are you getting the picture?

Now I've seen a lot of islands in the Caribbean. I have my personal favorites, and Aruba is not one of them. Granted it does have sunny weather and constant breezes, but it's just not a pretty island. The resorts have landscaping, and inside the gates it's green and lush, but take a drive around the island and you'll find it's a dust bowl with cactus. Actually, I've never seen so much cactus in my life. When you drive over to the windward side, there are jungles of it. I like dense, lush, tropical foliage and Aruba just ain't got it.

Aruba is a major package-tour destination for Americans and Canadians. It appeals to those who like big resorts, casinos, and duty-free shopping. Actually, it's like one huge cruise ship anchored 15 miles off the coast of Venezuela—all that's missing is Kathy Lee Gifford. But as I said earlier, if what you want is just to be pampered at a deluxe resort, say, the Hyatt Regency, then you'll be quite content and you'll sport a great tan by the end of the week.

You'll notice a very strange language being spoken on Aruba that sounds a lot like Spanish but is not—it's Papiamento, a native

dialect that is a combination of Spanish, Dutch, and Portuguese
with some African and Arawak words thrown in. If you understand
Spanish, you should get the jist of it. Most locals here speak at least
four languages: Papiamento, Dutch (the official language), English,
and Spanish.

THE BRIEFEST HISTORY

The Arawak peoples first settled Aruba and were still on the island
when the Spanish claimed it in 1499. They thought the land was
useless (they didn't see high-rise hotels in their future) and left it
pretty much to the Arawaks for over a century. But the Dutch
seized the island in 1636 near the end of the eighty-year war between
Holland and Spain. They began to settle Aruba in the late 1600s at
Oranjestad. The English were in control here between 1805 and
1816 during the Napoleonic wars; when they departed, the Dutch
returned. The discovery of gold in 1824 brought new waves of
immigration from Europe and Venezuela. When the gold mines
were exhausted, aloe production kept up the economy until the
Lago oil refinery was built on the southeastern tip of the island in
1929. That brought a new wave of prosperity to Aruba and at one
time the oil industry employed 8,000 people. The refinery shut
down in 1985, causing widespread unemployment. But tourism
replaced oil as the largest employer. In 1986, Aruba became a
separate entity within the Kingdom of the Netherlands under a
political arrangement called *Status Aparte*. Before that date it was
a member of the Netherlands Antilles.

ARUBA: KEY FACTS

LOCATION	12°N by 70°W
	15 miles north of Venezuela
	2,090 miles southeast of New York
SIZE	70 square miles
HIGHEST POINT	Mount Yamanota (617 ft.)
POPULATION	66,000
LANGUAGE	Papiamento plus Dutch (the official language); English and Spanish widely spoken
TIME	Atlantic Standard Time (1 hour ahead of EST, same as EDT)

AREA CODE	Aruba *is not* part of the 809 area code that applies to most of the Caribbean; to call Aruba from the U.S. dial 011 (the international access code), then 297 (the Aruba country code), then 8 (the area code) and the five-digit local number
ELECTRICITY	110 volts AC, 60 cycles
CURRENCY	Aruban florin, AFl (1.77 AFl = $1 U.S.)
DRIVING	On the *right*; a valid U.S. or Canadian driver's license is accepted
DOCUMENTS	Passport or proof of citizenship with photo for U.S. and Canadian citizens, plus an ongoing or return ticket
DEPARTURE TAX	$10 U.S.
BEER TO DRINK	Grolsch
RUM TO DRINK	Mt. Gay
MUSIC TO HEAR	Salsa

GETTING THERE

Aruba's Queen Beatrix International Airport has nonstop flights from the States on AIR ARUBA from Newark, N.J., and Miami; on AMERICAN from New York and San Juan; on CONTINENTAL from Newark, and on BWIA from Miami. From Canada visitors can fly on AIR CANADA to Miami and make connections there for Aruba.

GETTING AROUND

If you're just going to stay at your hotel and never leave, take a cab from the airport to the hotel. If you want mobility and want to see what desert vegetation is really like, driving is easy and the roads are good and well marked. All the major rental car players are represented, including AVIS ([800] 331-1084), HERTZ ([800] 654-3131), BUDGET ([800] 527-0700), NATIONAL ([800] 227-3876/[011-297-8] 21967), THRIFTY ([800] 367-2277/[011-297-8] 35335), and DOLLAR ([800] 800-4000/[011-297-8] 22783 or 25651). Be sure to make reservations in advance to ensure availability and the best rate.

FOCUS ON ARUBA: PAMPERING YOURSELF

The sun	A chaise	A piña colada
The sea	A good book	For seven days
The beach		

WHERE TO STAY

With no shortage of hotels or hotel rooms, there are plenty of choices on Aruba. However, since the object here is to pamper yourself, only a few places will pass muster. In my opinion, by far the best resort on Aruba is the Hyatt Regency. Other resorts may be as expensive, but there's just no comparison. Opening soon is the new RAMADA RENAISSANCE HOTEL (it's a dark-glass monster on the beach) and the renovated Concorde in a new incarnation as the ARUBA HILTON (if it's like the other Hilton Internationals, it'll be great; be sure to check out package deals, which will be much less expensive than the published rack rates).

HYATT REGENCY ARUBA (011-297-8) 31234, fax (011-297-8) 21682
Stateside: (800) 233-1234
L. G. Smith Boulevard 85, Palm Beach, Aruba

The Hyatt Regency is the best and most luxurious property on Aruba. It's also the most attractive-looking of the bunch. Unlike the other behemoth hotels, it seems the Hyatt's architect actually looked at the site and the island and designed a handsome building with Spanish and Caribbean flourishes. Set on 12 acres in the middle of Palm Beach, there are 360 guest rooms, which are tastefully decorated and feature all the deluxe amenities, including 24-hour room service.

There is an 8,000-square-foot pool complex with waterfalls and a two-story waterslide. Adjacent to the pool is a lagoon with more waterfalls, black and white swans, and a restaurant built to resemble the ruins of an old plantation. The beach in front is pleasant, with all water sports available from Red Sails Sports. There are two lighted tennis courts as well. Inside there is a casino, four restaurants, two bars, and a health club.

Rates are WICKED PRICEY to RIDICULOUS for singles and doubles (EP).

ARUBA PALM BEACH RESORT & CASINO (011-297-8) 23900, fax (011-297-8) 21941
Stateside & Canada: (800) 345-2782
L. G. Smith Boulevard 79, Palm Beach, Aruba

This is your basic big hotel on the beach. It has a nice-sized pool area and beach in front. There are 173 comfortable guest rooms with wall-to-wall carpet, air conditioning, lanai, walk-in closets and cable TV. The resort has a casino, two restaurants, two bars, two pools, two lighted tennis courts, and all water sports. This is a better value than the Holiday Inn.

Rates are VERY PRICEY for singles and doubles (EP).

HOLIDAY INN ARUBA BEACH RESORT & CASINO (011-297-8) 23600, fax (011-297-8) 25165
Stateside: (800) HOLIDAY
L. G. Smith Boulevard 230, Palm Beach, Aruba

This is a very bland and sixties-ish-looking hotel with a pretty palm grove in front. It's big (there are 600 rooms), with 5 restaurants, 2 lobby bars, a pool snack bar, a beach bar, a nightclub, a casino, a shopping arcade, a pool, 6 lighted tennis courts, a health club, and all water sports. Rooms are standard Holiday Inn, wall-to-wall carpeting, with air conditioning, cable TV, lanais, and 24-hour room service. There is a laundry room on every floor—a convenience.

Rates are VERY PRICEY to WICKED PRICEY for singles and doubles (EP).

BEST WESTERN BUCUTI BEACH RESORT (011-297-8) 36141, fax (011-297-8) 25272
Stateside: (800) 528-1234
(P.O. Box 1299), L. G. Smith Boulevard 55, Eagle Beach, Aruba

This small hotel has a nice wide beach in front. There is also a beached ship, a replica of an old Dutch galleon which serves as its restaurant and backdrop for the pool. The Bucuti Beach has 63 comfortable rooms, with lanais, tile floors, fridge, microwave, air conditioning, ceiling fans, room safes, and cable TV.

Rates are VERY PRICEY to WICKED PRICEY for singles and doubles (EP).

WHERE TO EAT

All the resorts have at least one restaurant each. While these are convenient and some are quite good, they tend to be overpriced. Here are some other suggestions:

CHEZ MATHILDE, Havenstraat 23, Oranjestad, 34968

The best restaurant on the island serves French cuisine in an elegant house built in the 1800s. Reservations are a must. $$$$$

LA DOLCE VITA, Caya G. F. Croes 164, 25675

The place for Italian food (and also a great Fellini film). Reservations are recommended. $$$$

THE OLDE CUNUCU HOUSE, Palm Beach 150, 31666

Very good continental and local cuisine is served in this seventy-five-year-old Aruban country house. Reservations are suggested. $$$$

MI CUSHINA, Noord Cura Cabai 24, San Nicolas, 48335

The best local (Aruban) cuisine served on the island. The décor features antique farm tools, family photographs, and a ceiling made of coffee bags. Try the iguana soup. $$$

TALK OF THE TOWN, L. G. Smith Boulevard 12, near Palm Beach, 23380

This is a very good steak house. You'll enjoy candlelight dining here. Reservations are suggested. $$$$

STEAMBOAT BUFFET, L. G. Smith Boulevard 370, 36700

If you like buffets, the Steamboat offers one for dinner for just $12.95. $$

DON'T MISS

THE CELLAR—The happening disco/club in Oranjestad.

WINDSURFING—With its steady, strong winds, Aruba is a natural for windsurfing. It's also the site of the annual Hi-Winds Pro-Am Windsurfing Competition. Most activity occurs at Fisherman's Huts and Malmok beaches. Both ARUBA SAILBOARD VACATIONS (800) 252-1070, stateside (617) 829-8915 and ROGER'S WINDSURF PLACE (800) 225-0102 offer windsurfing/accommodations packages. Both have fully equipped shops and offer instruction.

BOCA GRANDI—This is one of the only undeveloped beaches where you can swim.

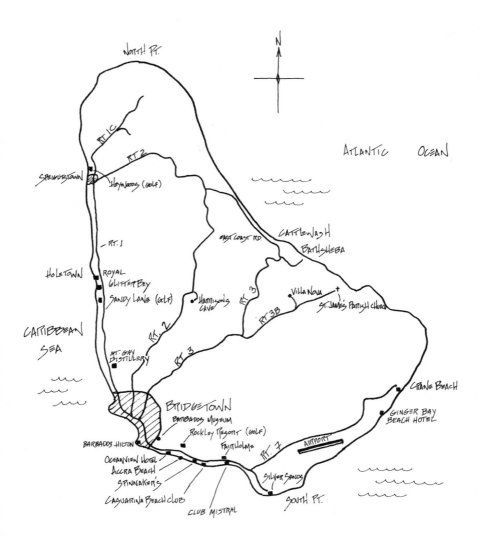

NORTH PT.

N

RT 1C

RT 2

ATLANTIC   OCEAN

SPEIGHTSTOWN

Heywoods (GOLF)

RT. 1

EAST COAST RD.

CATTLEWASH

BATHSHEBA

HOLETOWN

ROYAL
GLITTER BAY

SANDY LANE (GOLF)

HARRISON'S
CAVE

RT 3

VILLA NOVA

ST. JAMES' PARISH CHURCH

RT 3B

CARIBBEAN
SEA

RT. 2

RT 3

MT. GAY
DISTILLERY

CRANE BEACH

GINGER BAY
BEACH HOTEL

BRIDGETOWN

BARBADOS MUSEUM

ROCKLEY Tregott (GOLF)

BARBADOS HILTON

FAITHOLME

RT. 7

AIRPORT

OCEANVIEW HOTEL
ACCRA BEACH
SPINNAKER'S

CASUARINA BEACH CLUB

CLUB MISTRAL

SILVER SANDS

SOUTH PT.

0   5
MILES

BARBADOS

BARBADOS

TOURISTO SCALE   📷 📷 📷 📷 📷 📷 📷 📷   8

Barbados is the Florida of the West Indies, albeit with a distinctly Caribbean and British accent. It is highly developed, crowded (along the south coast), gets lots of tourists on packages, is flat, and not a get-away-from-it-all kind of place. It does have some fine beaches, especially on the southeast and east coasts, which are less crowded and far less developed than the south coast.

The mood here is certainly more hectic, or should I say faster paced, than other islands nearby. Actually, it's light years different from a Grenada, a Grenadine island, or a Tobago. The traveler who visits here comes for beaches, first-class resorts, diversions—such as nightlife, restaurants, shopping—basically those who want the comforts of home in the West Indies. Or they come to windsurf. They don't come for privacy—there are many more private places on other islands, especially since the beaches here are open to the general public. The ease of reaching Barbados, especially nonstop from Europe on jumbo jets, makes the package tourist the mainstay of the Barbados economy

Tourism is the business of Barbados, and the industry is more highly developed here than on any other Caribbean island. And the government makes a point of educating its citizens on the value of the tourist dollar. A banner strung across a major access road to Bridgetown, the capital, says it all: "Tourism is our business. Let's do our part." Bajans are very friendly despite the hordes of tourists who stream through Barbados (almost 400,000 a year). One gets the feeling that they view tourists as they do rain—a necessity to keep the island growing.

With all this emphasis on the tourist, there are tons of options from which to choose. Most are not worth it. The three weekly newspapers geared to the tourist—*The Visitor, The Sun Seeker,* and *What's On in Barbados*—are all crammed with activities that cater primarily to the standard tourist crowd.

There are two tourist attractions worth your while. The first is Harrison's Cave in the parish of St. Thomas (438-6640). An electric trolley runs through these fascinating caverns of stalactites, stalagmites, and running/dripping water to the accompaniment of a guide reciting a rote speech that must have been written for morons. I couldn't help but get the feeling that I was on a ride at Disney World. Yet these caves are real, and if you can get past the tourist b.s., it's very interesting. Admission is $15 BDS for adults. The other attraction is the *Atlantis II* (436-8929), a submarine that takes you down 150 feet to view marine flora and fauna from morning to night. It can hold twenty-eight people and has sixteen 2-foot viewports (eight on each side) and one 52-inch viewport on the bow. With a group of friends and a few cocktails, this could be lots of fun. Costs will run about $139 BDS per person.

Other activities of interest: cricket (the Bajan national sport) at the Kensington Oval in Bridgetown. The season usually runs from May through December, though cricket is played locally year round (check the local papers for current matches or ask at the Tourist Board). Crop Over, held in July and early August, celebrates the completion of the sugar-cane harvest. This is Barbados' version of Carnival, with calypso bands, tons of food, and a grand finale called "Kadooment Day." There are also tours of Bajan Great Houses sponsored by the Barbados National Trust that feature weekly "open houses" of private estates as well as five permanent-trust properties. The Trust also sponsors day-hikes every week.

Barbados, unlike most other islands its size, does have nightlife. The place to go for live music and dancing is an old converted house on the beach in Christ Church called Harbour Lights (there *is* a dress code: no shorts). A younger, more rambunctious crowd frequents the Warehouse in Bridgetown, which also has live music and dancing. For a publike atmosphere that's hardly mellow, you can crawl into the St. Lawrence Gap and slug down a few Banks at The Ship Inn. Don't miss the house band, Axis, on Tuesday and Friday nights. Next door to the Ship Inn is After Dark, playing reggae music and catering to a more local crowd. Probably the most fun is visiting the eateries on Baxter Road in the wee hours of the morning. There are always people awake and they will keep you in stitches. Pop into Enid's and ask for "pot hot"—some tasty local chicken.

THE BRIEFEST HISTORY

Originally settled by Amerindians from South America, the island was uninhabited when the Portuguese discovered it in the early sixteenth century (the name comes from the Portuguese *los Barbados*, "the bearded ones"—the explorers found bearded fig trees on the shore). The first settlers were British, who arrived in 1627. The island remained British until it achieved independence in 1966—one of the few islands to escape the power struggles so typical of the other Caribbean islands. Probably Barbados' location, about 90 miles east of the "chain," and its flatness (making it hard for navigators to sight), saved it. Due to its agreeable terrain, sugar plantations blossomed and prospered into this century. Barbados is now a sovereign state within the British Commonwealth of Nations.

BARBADOS: KEY FACTS

LOCATION	13°N by 59°W
	100 miles east of St. Vincent
	2,200 miles southeast of New York
SIZE	166 square miles
HIGHEST POINT	Mt. Hillaby (1,116 ft.)
POPULATION	280,000
LANGUAGE	English
TIME	Atlantic Standard Time year round (1 hour ahead of EST)
AREA CODE	809
ELECTRICITY	110 volts AC, 60 cycles
CURRENCY	The Barbados dollar, Bds (Bds$1.99 = $1 U.S.)
DRIVING	On the *left*; a temporary permit is needed if you do not have an International Driver's License; there is a fee for the permit
DOCUMENTS	Proof of citizenship with photo for U.S. and Canadian citizens and ongoing or return ticket; British citizens need a valid passport

DEPARTURE TAX   Bds$25 ($12.50 U.S.)
BEER TO DRINK   Banks
RUM TO DRINK   Cockspur
MUSIC TO HEAR   Dancehall

GETTING THERE

You know Barbados loves tourists when you arrive at the sparkling
Grantley Adams International Airport—the best in the Caribbean.
All the major carriers fly nonstop or direct here: AMERICAN and
BWIA from the States, BWIA, AIR CANADA and CANADIAN
HOLIDAYS from Toronto and Montréal. LIAT and AIR MAR-
TINIQUE provide service to and from the other islands. BRITISH
AIRWAYS flies nonstop from London.

GETTING AROUND

With excellent roads and road signs, there's no reason not to rent
a car. Minimokes are abundant here, so why not have some fun
while you tool around the island. There are no major international
car-rental agencies on Barbados (I guess the government is protect-
ing local businesses), however, try NATIONAL ([809] 426-0603)—
(not affiliated with the one operating in the U.S.), SUNNY ISLE
MOTORS ([809] 435-7979), and AR ([809] 428-9085). COURTESY
([809] 431-4160) is the only firm with a desk at the airport.

FOCUS ON BARBADOS: WINDSURFING

With everything else Barbados has to offer, the fact that it is also
one of the windsurfing capitals of the Caribbean is almost lost in the
shuffle. Steady strong wind and surf conditions on the southern tip
of the island combine to make optimal boardsailing. Add to that
sunny skies, warm water, and Barbados' other amenities, and it's
easy to understand why so many vacation here, or even spend a
season hanging ten.
    Most activity centers around Club Mistral in Maxwell (809) 428-
7277. The beach here has some coral cobble and reefs to dodge and

is not the best that Barbados has to offer. But the Barbados Wind-surfing Club's bar next door is a fun place to hang out and watch the action. If you're not on your board, you're at the bar. If the Bajan bartender has his way, and he usually does, reggae music is on the stereo. The bar is open on two sides to the ocean, providing the best vantage point for viewing the action on the high seas. There is always a breeze to ventilate the accommodations and wiggle the bar glasses from the overhead rack to a crashing demise. People come and go constantly. Yet it's very common just to hang out all day and not even bother getting wet.

Club Mistral is *not* for the windsurfing novice. This is dictated more by wind and surf conditions than by club policy. It's just too hard to learn with the wind ripping the boom out of your arms and the waves shaking your board like an earthquake. There are calmer places on the island better suited for beginners. The prerequisite for Club Mistral is that you can make a beach start in moderate condi-tions—the point being that if you can make it through the breakers you'll be okay. This loosely translates to a classification of interme-diate—those who have windsurfed before and made it back to the starting point in a good breeze without assistance.

Club Mistral is sponsored by Mistral of Switzerland, one of the leading manufacturers of equipment. It provides state-of-the-art equipment and top-notch instruction for intermediates to experts. This solves the serious windsurfer's problems in regard to trans-port, customs officials, and spare parts. And Mistral has designed its equipment to meet the challenge of the local wind and surf conditions.

Mistral has two facilities on Barbados that correspond to each location's level of difficulty. The Mistral operation at Maxwell offers several different kinds of boards and three different sail rigs. The staff can tailor a board and rig to accommodate both your abilities and the day's weather. The conditions at the Silver Sands shop (located on the southern tip of the island and the site of the Suzuki Fun Board Championships), (809) 428-6001, are strictly for experts (the equipment provided reflects that). Here you'll find shorter boards that are big on speed, surf jumping, and wave riding. The instruction offered at the Sands focuses on improving the highly developed skills of boardsailors who want to make the leap to expert.

But for the majority of windsurfers who want to improve, the Mistral shop at Maxwell is the best place to get instruction. It offers a weekly program that covers the essential elements of the sport. Classes usually have up to five people. Lessons for tacking and use of the harness are available on request as is private instruction. Rates at press time are by no means cheap, starting at BDS $50 ($25 U.S.) per hour. Larger instructional packages are negotiable.

If all you want to do is rent a board, they have many combinations that will suit individual abilities and current conditions (you won't be stuck with a light-air sail when it's blowing a gale). Rates at press time are as follows:

one hour $17.50 U.S.
two hours $30 U.S.
half-day $35 U.S.
full day $50 U.S.
one week $200 U.S.
two weeks $340 U.S.
three weeks $420 U.S.
four weeks $480 U.S.

There is a crash boat poised at the ready should any equipment—or you—break down.

For those with the competitive spirit, Club Mistral will set up races for any group that shows interest. With Club Mistral's encouragement, resident experts often give advice or on-the-spot seminars at almost any time. So don't be surprised if someone approaches you with helpful hints. There is usually someone around to offer repair and breakdown tips should you bring your own board.

What about the beginner? What does he or she do? Club Mistral will gladly put them in touch with Mark Hurdle who operates Sandy Beach Watersports (435-8000, ext. 270) out of the calm Sandy Beach Lagoon near the Carib Beach Bar at Worthing. This is actually where windsurfing started on Barbados. The water is shallow and very flat—ideal for learning.

WHERE TO STAY

Most accommodations are on the south coast. Almost all the high-end resorts are on the west coast, which has the calmest water. With more than 65 hotels and 12 guest houses on the island, there are a wide variety of places to stay. Try to book a land/air package that includes one of my recommended establishments—it will save you a lot of money.

GINGER BAY BEACH CLUB (809) 423-5810, fax (809) 423-6629
St. Philip, Barbados, W.I.

This small property, with only 16 suites, has one of the most wonderful beach settings I have seen (and believe me, I've seen a lot of 'em). Situated on a small point, the sea has carved out grottos and caves and has created three distinct beaches for the hotel: and they are all basically empty—only hotel guests and occasionally some Bajans use them. Best of all is the entrance to the beach—down a winding staircase into a huge cavern with several passageways to the sea—Madonna should have filmed her "erotica" video here. Talk about a place to have sex in the afternoon! It's also a great place for parties—I'd recommended a group renting out the entire club and just enjoying a wild week. The accommodations are pleasant, each is a one-bedroom suite that sports a lanai with a hammock on it for those afternoon naps. The units face the trades so they are comfortably breezy. The décor is on the simple-basic-hotel-tropical-side, and there are cracks in the paint here and rust stains there, but I'd still highly recommend it for the *fabulous* beach. There is a small pool, bar, and restaurant. Rates are cut in half during the off-season—a good value.

Rates are VERY PRICEY for singles and doubles (EP).

BARBADOS HILTON INTERNATIONAL (809) 426-0200, fax
    (809) 436-8946
Stateside: (800) HILTONS
(P.O. Box 510), Needham's Point, St. Michael's Parish, Barbados,
    W.I.

Hilton International is a class act (not to be confused with the not-so-classy Hiltons in the U.S.—a totally different company and league). Hilton International Hotels throughout the Caribbean are leaders in providing superb accommodations for businesspeople and travelers alike with standards you learn to expect. This Hilton is no exception—it is a hubbub of local business activity (government and corporate meetings, etc.) as well as a haven for weary tourists. I like seeing what goes on in local life.

Set on fourteen landscaped acres on the site of the old Fort Charles at the edge of Bridgetown, this sixties architecturally inspired hotel of arches and concrete has its own protected lagoon beach and another adjacent to it with surf. There are 185 rooms surrounding an atrium lobby with palm trees growing in the middle. The rooms are spacious and have the standard Hilton amenities. There is a pool, four lighted tennis courts, a restaurant (the Verandah), and two bars.

Rates are WICKED PRICEY for singles and doubles (EP).

THE FAIRHOLME (809) 428-9425, no fax
Maxwell, Christ Church, Barbados, W.I.

A five-minute walk from Club Mistral, the Fairholme is a clean, quiet, and cheap alternative. While the common rooms are very spartan in their faded, fabulous-fifties furnishings, the rooms in the main house are surprisingly comfortable and attractive. All have private baths, ceiling fans, and firm double or twin beds. There are newer efficiency apartments in a separate wing, but they lack the main house's character and style. The garden and pool in the back are pleasant. The Fairholme is very popular with Europeans, especially the Dutch and Germans.

Rates are NOT SO CHEAP for singles and doubles (EP). *No credit cards.*

CASUARINA BEACH CLUB (809) 428-3600, fax (809) 428-1970
St. Lawrence Gap, Christ Church, Barbados, W.I.

A large resort with spacious grounds surrounded by casuarina pines in the midst of the heavily developed south coast. The atmosphere is relaxed and there are some real perks that make this typical-looking beach hotel a value, including an Olympic-sized swimming pool, air-conditioned squash courts, tennis courts, and a very nice beach. The rooms have balconies with standard big-hotel décor.

Rates are VERY PRICEY to WICKED for singles and doubles (EP).

GLITTER BAY (809) 422-4111, fax (809) 422-3940
Stateside: (800) 283-8666
Porters, St. James, Barbados, W.I.

This stucco Moorish-style luxury resort, while a tad out of character with Bajan architecture, is still a very deluxe place to stay should comfort and service be your first priority. Built on the grounds of the former Cunard estate (the Great House is now the reception and administration area), the beach/pool/bar area is terrific, as is the service. Two night-lit tennis courts and complimentary water sports complete the facilities.

Rates are RIDICULOUS for standard rooms and OUTRAGEOUS for one-bedroom suites on up (singles and doubles—EP). Add $60 per person for MAP.

CRANE BEACH HOTEL (809) 423-6220, fax (809) 423-5343
Crane Beach, St. Philip, Barbados, W.I.
Stateside: c/o Robert Reid Assoc., 845 Third Avenue, New York, NY 10022 (800) 223-6510/(212) 832-2277
Canada: c/o Robert Reid Assoc., 12 Redstone Path, Etobicoke, Ontario M9C 1Y7 (416) 622-8813

The first thing you notice on entering Crane Beach is the redesigned entrance, aimed at steering the onslaught of tourists that visit directly over to the restaurant and away from hotel guests. Set on a bluff overlooking one of the nicest hotel beaches in the Caribbean (and there are great waves for bodysurfing, too), the hotel and its white-columned pool are stunning. The Estate Mansion, or main building, has some magnificent high-ceilinged suites in its old wing that overlook the Atlantic (the hotel is on the Atlantic or windward side). There is also the Crane Beach Mansion, down the beach, which is a fully staffed, four-bedroom luxuriously decorated mansion on the beach available to you for only $1,300 per day.

Rates are VERY PRICEY to RIDICULOUS for singles and doubles (EP) in the main hotel.

SANDY LANE HOTEL & GOLF CLUB (809) 432-1311, fax (809) 432-2954
St. James, Barbados, W.I.
Stateside or Canada: (800) 225-5843

While golf may be your *raison d'être* for staying at the Sandy Lane, there are other reasons why the Sandy Lane may appeal to you. This is particularly true if you're into luxury, as it is considered one of the Caribbean's poshest resorts. Made of white coral stone and set on 380 acres in the chichi parish of St. James, this elegant hacienda-style hotel has one of the best and most elegant designs of any resort in the tropics. Its focal point is an extraordinary building where a double balustrade embraces an open-air terrace adjoining the Sandy Lane's stunning beach. What a place for a party! The beach is partially shaded by stately trees and beach umbrellas. There are chaises for comfort and white-jacketed waiters to ensure a steady flow of piña coladas. Waterskiing, windsurfing, sailing, and snorkeling are available at the beach for a fee.

Off the beach, the Sandy Lane has an excellent tennis program with five all-weather courts (two floodlit) and instruction. It also has a reputation for excellent service and a friendly staff. There are 82 recently refurbished double rooms, 27 suites, and three penthouses—all furnished in a Romanesque white-and-gold motif and with balconies overlooking the Caribbean. The gardens are beautifully planted and maintained. Of course, this place isn't cheap!

Rates are BEYOND BELIEF for singles and doubles (MAP).

For those on a tight budget, this is an expensive island. However, I have scoured the coasts and have found some choices which are clean, very simple, and, to a certain extent, have that facet people love, character. Remember though, you get what you pay for! They are:

SUMMER PLACE/HOME BY SEA (809) 435-7417 or 7424, no fax
Worthing, Christ Church, Barbados, W.I.

F-U-N-K-Y! This is the only way to describe it. Actually, this might take the funky award for all the Caribbean. This is truly unique, as is the gentleman who owns it, George De Mattos. However, it is on a very nice beach, all rooms have private baths and it costs only $20 U.S. for a single and $30 U.S. for a double. I recommend only rooms 6 and 7, which have kitchens and face the beach (room 6 gets better breezes). These are slightly more expensive at $35 apiece, but the extra $5 is worth it. The other rooms tend to be claustrophobic. Believe it or not, it is very popular, so book ahead. But remember, I warned you!

Rates are DIRT CHEAP for singles and CHEAP for doubles (EP).

ABBEVILLE HOTEL (809) 435-7924, fax (809) 435-8502
Rockley Beach, Christ Church, Barbados, W.I.

Situated just down the road from Accra Beach, this is a fine value.
Set in an old Bajan house, the upstairs rooms are the biggest and
have the most character (high ceilings, eclectic and simple old furnishings, etc.). All have baths, but only the downstairs rooms have
air conditioning—and these cost $5 more. I'd recommend the up-
stairs, particularly room 3, which faces east and is cooled by the
breezes. Avoid the rooms directly on the road because they are
noisy. The hotel also has two motel-style rooms in the back which
are quiet, bigger, but more expensive and lacking in character.

Rates are CHEAP to NOT SO CHEAP for singles and doubles
(EP).

WHITE SANDS BEACH APARTMENTS (809) 428-7484, no fax
St. Lawrence Gap, Christ Church, Barbados, W.I.

This is a very basic and funky waterfront accommodation with a
very pleasant little beach in front and a kind of groovy young crowd
as guests. If you want a studio with kitchenette on the beach for
around $50, this might be the ticket. Remember, it's very basic/
funky.

Next door is the SALT ASH BEACH APARTMENTS, (809)
428-8753, which is about the same price, well-tended, and caters to
a more middle-aged clientele, but worth a try if you want a self-
contained unit and are on a tight budget.

Rates are NOT SO CHEAP for singles and doubles (EP).

WHERE TO EAT

The more upscale hotels and restaurants of Barbados offer gourmet
international dishes, but the native Bajan cuisine offers an entirely
different dining experience.

ILE DE FRANCE, Windsor Arms Hotel, Hastings, Christ Church,
435-6869

Classic French cuisine served in a garden atmosphere. Reservations
are recommended. $$$$

DAVID'S PLACE, St. Lawrence Main Road, Worthington, Christ
Church, 428-2708

Good Bajan cuisine (Baxter Road chicken, flying fish, pepperpot,
etc.) at very reasonable prices. Reservations are suggested. $$

BROWN SUGAR, Aquatic Gap, St. Michael, 426-7684

A popular lunch place for businesspeople due to its fixed-price
Planters Buffet, you'll find good Bajan cuisine here. Also open for
dinner. Reservations are recommended. $$$

FATHOMS, Paynes Bay, St. James, 432-2568

This is an excellent and stylish seafood restaurant on the beach on
the west coast, a ten-minute drive south of Holetown. Reservations
are recommended for dinner. $$$$$

BAGATELLE GREAT HOUSE, Highway 2A, St. Thomas, 421-
6767

Set in a beautiful 300-year-old Bajan plantation house a 15-minute
drive north of Bridgetown, the cuisine here is Bajan/continental.
Reservations are recommended. $$$$$

CARAMBOLA RESTAURANT, Derricks, St. James, 432-0832

Acclaimed as one of the best restaurants on the island, Chef Paul
Owens serves up French/Créole cuisine atop a dramatic perch overlooking the sea. Reservations are a must. $$$$$

WATERFRONT CAFE, The Careenage, Bridgetown, 427-0093

The Bajan/continental food here is quite good, the prices are very
reasonable and the setting by the fishing boats is very pleasant. $$$

ATLANTIS HOTEL, Bathsheba, St. Joseph, 433-9445

This is a Bajan institution and a great and funky place to stop for
lunch en route to Cattlewash Beach. Owner-chef Enid Maxwell's
Bajan buffet has everything Bajan and otherwise that you would
ever want to eat. $$ *No credit cards accepted.*

Don't Miss

THE MT. GAY DISTILLERY TOUR—Located about five minutes from Bridgetown, you can finally see where the Mt. Gay of your Mt. Gay–and–tonics comes from. Open Monday through Friday from 9 A.M. to 5 P.M. and on Saturdays from 10 A.M. to 1 P.M. Admission is BDs$8. Call 425-8757 for more information.

THE BARBADOS NATIONAL TRUST—They offer open houses of historic Bajan houses and weekly hikes. Call 436-9033.

AXIS AT THE SHIP'S INN—This is a great cover band and a fun night out.

A DRINK AT THE SANDY LANE, St. James, 432-1311—Be fabulous for one drink at this incredibly expensive but pretty hotel.

A BIKE HIKE—Rent a bike and explore the backroads of this relatively flat terrain. M. A. Williams Rentals (427-3955) rents 12-speed cross-trainers for $12.50 U.S. per day.

CRANE BEACH—Gorgeous turquoise water, great body-surfing waves, and a pretty beach make it a must stop.

JOLLY ROGER, Bridgetown Harbour—It's a tourist thing, but people have a great time on their sunset cruises and get blotto on the open bar while they're at it. For information, call 436-6424.

BAXTER ROAD, LATE AT NIGHT ON A WEEKEND—A fun scene of still-too-awake-to-go-to-bed-Bajans and good, cheap food too.

BEQUIA

TOURISTO SCALE 📷 📷 📷 3

Sitting at the bar at Frangipani enjoying a "Happy" Hairoun, the Vincentian brew, on my first visit to Bequia in 1987, I unwittingly revealed to the woman next to me that I was a travel writer. She stiffened and brusquely requested that I not write anything about Bequia. "We don't need or want any more tourists," she said with conviction. It's a typical response of a seasonal resident who wants to slam the door in the face of any new arrival. But as I got to know Bequia, I began to agree with her. This island is extraordinary—I would hate to see it spoiled. So it was with great reluctance and profuse apologies that I brought Bequia (pronounced *"Beck-wee"*) to light in the first edition of *Rum and Reggae*. And after six years, it still has its magic.

The best way to describe Bequia is that it is the quintessential Caribbean experience—a harmony of all the elements that make the islands special. It is pretty, clean, and small enough to get to know intimately. The local residents are very friendly and responsive. There are handsome beaches, good restaurants, lots of bars, shops, and accommodations that are very reasonably priced. A sea orientation and yachty element add the perfect touch to the island's ambience.

For such a small place it's surprisingly lively. It's easy to spend a week here and not be bored. The action revolves around the waterfront of Port Elizabeth, starting at the ferry dock and winding around the Harborwalk to Princess Margaret Beach (also known as Tony Gibbons Beach). Here you can browse in a small but intelligent bookshop, buy some fresh fruit and vegetables from Rastas, have a few drinks, check out the brown coral jewelry from sidewalk

vendors, dance to pan music, eat lobster pizza, go scuba diving, buy
clothes and T-shirts, have more drinks, and go for a swim at a very
pretty beach—all in a half-mile stretch.

Bequia has a great mix of people too. In addition to the welcoming locals, there are all kinds of interesting visitors. The island has
always attracted an artsy element. People like Sanford Meisner, the
famed acting teacher, who maintains a house here and often conducts classes and seminars on Bequia. Many artists winter here,
finding more than enough inspiration from the surroundings.
There are lots of Europeans, especially Germans, who seem to love
the island's mellow pace. The North Americans who visit are much
more sophisticated than, say, the average tourists who go to Barbados. Bequia appeals to independent travelers (readers, that's you)
who are looking for a low-key yet stimulating environment to shake
off and forget whatever pressures they have in their everyday
worlds. Finally, there are the boat people—the cocktail cruisers
who come in on their yachts or charter boats and love to have a
good time. They add a little zip and glamour to the mix. I'm telling
you, you'll meet more interesting people here in a week than you
would being co-host with Linda Richmond on "Coffee Tooawk."

There have been some changes on Bequia over the last six years.
The most dramatic was the opening of the airport near Paget Farm
in May 1992. It's huge for Bequia, built on landfill to accommodate
the largest prop planes and small private jets. There is a large and
attractive terminal to greet you. Built with a grant from the European Community, now you can get here in one day from the mainland as there are several flights a day from Barbados on Air
Mustique. So far, the airport hasn't dramatically flooded the island
with new arrivals, although everyone's kind of nervous about it.
The convenience is wonderful. The residents of Moon Hole aren't
pleased, as the planes often fly overhead when making their approach. Other changes on the island are the building of a new
pavilion for the rastas selling their veggies (a welcome addition) and
the building of two mini-shopping arcades—the Bayshore Mall and
the Harbour Centre—to accommodate the dreaded but periodic
cruise ships. These are small and unobtrusive and don't ruin the
island's ambience, but please, no more. And the final change to date
is the island schooner *Friendship Rose*'s retirement from her routine
ferry schedule to St. Vincent. However, she has been refurbished
and given a facelift and now sails day excursions to Mustique, the
Tobago Cays, and other Grenadines.

Can you tell yet that Bequia is my favorite getaway island in the
Caribbean?

THE BRIEFEST HISTORY

The island of St. Vincent was first settled by the Ciboney before
Christ and then the Arawaks. Not much is known about Amerindian settlements on Bequia (the northernmost of the Grenadines)
until the 1600s, when the Caribs inhabited an island they called
"Becouya," which means "island of the clouds" (a strange name for
this rather dry island—perhaps it was rainy on the fateful day it was
named). There is no record of Columbus sighting either St. Vincent
or the Grenadines on any of his voyages. Bequia was left in peace
to the Caribs by the warring European navies in the region. Then,
in 1675, the slave ship *Palmira* sank off the island, and some of the
slaves on board escaped to the island and were welcomed by the
Caribs. As a result of the intermarriage between Caribs and runaway African slaves, the tribe became known as Black Caribs. They
used Bequia as a war-staging port for attacks on the Yellow Caribs
of St. Vincent. Meanwhile, back on St. Vincent, the Yellow Caribs
were getting nervous about their neighbors on Bequia and permit-
ted the French to build a settlement on the island in 1716. The
French claimed the island and all of the Grenadines. Previously, no
Europeans were able to conquer the island and, given the resistance
and its mountainous terrain, focused on the more attractive islands
for sugar plantations—Barbados and St. Lucia, for example. The
French also imported slaves, many of whom escaped and went into
the mountains and joined the Black Caribs. The result was too
many headaches and battles for the French with the Black Caribs,
so the island was declared neutral between France and Britain in the
Treaty of Aix-la-Chapelle in 1748. But, of course, treaties were
meant to be broken, and the two battled it out until finally, in 1783,
the Treaty of Versailles deeded St. Vincent and the Grenadines to
the British. One last gasp by the allied forces of the Black Caribs and
the French failed to dislodge the British, and most of the Black
Caribs on the islands were shipped off to Honduras and Belize. In
1871, St. Vincent and the Grenadines became a part of the British
Windward Islands colony. But it wasn't until 1979 that St. Vincent
and the Grenadines achieved independent statehood within the
British Commonwealth.

BEQUIA: KEY FACTS

LOCATION	13°N by 61°W
	9 miles south of St. Vincent
	2,050 miles southeast of New York
SIZE	7 square miles
	5 miles long by 3 miles wide
HIGHEST POINT	Belle Pointe (881 ft.)
POPULATION	4,874
LANGUAGE	English
TIME	Atlantic Standard Time (1 hour ahead of EST, same as EDT)
AREA CODE	809
ELECTRICITY	Electricity is 220 volts AC, 50 cycles, so you'll need an adapter and transformer
CURRENCY	The Eastern Caribbean dollar, EC$ (EC$2.70 = $1 U.S.)
DRIVING	On the *left*; you'll need a temporary permit—just present your valid U.S. or Canadian driver's license and pay the fee
DOCUMENTS	Proof of citizenship and a return or ongoing ticket
DEPARTURE TAX	EC$20 (about $7.50 U.S.)
BEER TO DRINK	Hairoun
RUM TO DRINK	Any Vincentian brand
MUSIC TO HEAR	Dancehall

GETTING THERE

With the brand-new airport now open, getting to Bequia is a helluva lot easier than it used to be. Now you can fly to Barbados on AMERICAN, BWIA, AIR CANADA, or BRITISH AIRWAYS and connect with regularly scheduled service or charter on MUSTIQUE AIRWAYS. (The last flight is at 4 P.M.) SVGAIR also runs an air taxi/charter service. LIAT flies in from Grenada and St. Vincent. If you still want to arrive by boat, the motor ferries *Admiral I* and the *Admiral II* leave Kingstown, St. Vincent, at various times from 9 A.M. to 7 P.M. For schedules, call (809) 458-3348. If you want to trek through the Grenadines (to Union Island) on a mail boat, the *Snapper* has twice-weekly departures from St. Vincent on Mondays and Thursdays (at 9:30 A.M.) and returns from Union Island on Tuesdays and Fridays. Call the Department of Tourism at (809) 457-1502 for the latest schedules.

GETTING AROUND

Bequia is a small island, and you could walk everywhere if you like exercise. However, there are some substantial hills to climb to get to the other side, so you may want to take a taxi, which your hotel can call for you (I use Gideon's or Noah). You can take the mini-vans which travel the main roads or you can easily hitchhike. There are no car-rental agencies on the island, but you can rent a scooter or bike from Handy Andy's (458-3722). Some locals may also rent you their car for a price to be negotiated. You will also find water taxis that will take you from town or the Frangipani dock to Princess Margaret Beach or Lower Bay for EC$10.

FOCUS ON BEQUIA: EXPLORING THE MAGIC

It's easy to become possessive about Bequia because it is a small island which can easily become familiar in a week's time. After discovering the magic of this island, you begin to feel that it's your own. So you should definitely get out and see it.

There are walks that will take you to just about anywhere on the island in an hour or less. Port Elizabeth, where the recommended hotels are, is not only the island's hub but its center as well—all roads lead to town. The walks are fairly easy, up over the hills to the other side.

My favorite walk is to Industry. Leaving town on the road to Spring, you will climb and descend the hill and come upon an old sugar-mill ruin overgrown with hibiscus and bougainvillea on the left—a good photo opportunity. It is then a very pleasant walk through tall coconut trees, acres of them, with the usually deserted Spring beach off to the right. The road follows the curve of a bluff offering terrific views of Petit Nevis and Mustique. It quietly descends into more coconut groves and Industry beach. There is a bar at the beach to quaff a rum punch before heading back, and the swimming is also quite good. For the industrious, there is a hike from there to Bequia Head on cowpaths. This should be attempted only with ample daylight. People do get lost, so be sure of the way back and wear good walking shoes.

Another area worth exploring is "Moon Hole," an interesting and innovative development on the western end of Bequia. Designed by Tom Johnson, it strives to blend with its natural surroundings and to a great degree it succeeds. The stone used in the walls matches the cliffs and gullies where they are built. At first sight it looks as though the developer ran out of money. The complex looks unfinished; there is no glass where windows should be, no color except for gray stone and metal. Yet that is the architect's intention—to achieve harmony with the striking natural setting. The centerpiece of this creation is Moon Hole, a huge natural arch that, it is said, frames the full moon. Underneath the arch is a terraced, Victorian-style house. It is all gray and adorned with bright white whalebones and other marine accents. It's a bit odd, but still stunning. To get there, take the road to Friendship and at the top of the hill follow the right fork (the left takes you down to the Friendship Bay Hotel—noteworthy for its swinging bar chairs). The road will hug the coast through La Pompe and Paget Farm, where it seems every house is painted powder blue. Here you'll pass Bequia's new airport. Keep going and you'll eventually reach Moon Hole. Be as discreet as the designers were—this is *not* meant to be a tourist attraction.

A third walk takes you to Hope Bay and a totally deserted beach which is perfect for nude sunbathing. For this one, you'll want to take a taxi to the Old Fort Country Inn (and arrange for a pickup later on). Bring water and refreshment as it is a long way down the mountain and a hot way back up. The friendly folks at the Inn will direct you to the path. Sit and have a rum punch to get ready for the trip and off you go. The trail is not difficult, but you will sweat a little. Once at the beach, be careful swimming as the water can be rough. If you want privacy, there is the ruin of an old mill on the north side of the beach, which is perfect for some hanky-panky, if you are so inclined. When you return, be sure to have another rum punch as your reward for a job well done.

If you want to explore what's under the water, there is Dive Bequia, P.O. Box 16 (809) 458-3504, in the U.S. (800) 351-DIVE. This is a very laid-back operation in the most "for sure" Southern California style. Run by Bob Sachs, Dive Bequia offers anything from snorkel trips, resort courses, and PADI certification to night dives and underwater videos of yourself doing a Lloyd Bridges imitation. Bob has great T-shirts for sale too. The other dive shop on the island is Sunsports (809) 458-3577, in the U.S. (800) 525-3833, which offers boat dives, equipment rental, NAUI or PADI certification, snorkeling and sailing trips, and even tennis. Certainly both will satisfy your "Sea Hunt" urges.

WHERE TO STAY

There are several *very* reasonable places to stay that are quite satisfactory. Prices on Bequia are still much lower than the more tourist-oriented islands. Who's complaining?

THE PLANTATION HOUSE (809) 458-3425, fax (809) 458-3612
Stateside: (800) 223-9832/(212) 599-8280
Admiralty Bay (P.O. Box 16), Bequia, St. Vincent, W.I.

Ideally situated between a stellar beach and the diversion of the waterfront, this is the most expensive place to stay on Bequia. The establishment is a symphony of pink and turquoise. Make a point to stay in the cabanas, particularly those that border the coconut-tree-studded common. Each cabana has a small veranda, comfortable and attractive furnishings, ceiling fan, mosquito netting, and hot water (a luxury here). You also get a fridge (of the dorm-room mold) in your cabana if desired. The main house is all pink with a wraparound, arched veranda. Meals are served here and are very good (the MAP route is standard here). There is a small but attractive raised kidney-shaped pool and the standard beach bar. Dive Bequia is located on the grounds, too. A small beach is tucked in front of the bar with chaise longues, but it's worth the five-minute walk over the point to HRH Maggie's Beach.

Rates are WICKED PRICEY for singles and RIDICULOUS for doubles (MAP). Dive packages are available.

THE FRANGIPANI (809) 458-3255, fax (809) 458-3824
(P.O. Box 1), Bequia, St. Vincent, W.I.

If you like being the center of attention, especially with the yachty set, then the Frangipani is for you. It sits on a point in the middle of the Harborwalk and has people marching by all day long. The main house, with its trademark red roof, has several shared-bath rooms furnished with mahogany antiques (room 4 has a majestic four-poster, its own bath and a corner view of the harbor but the floor and your bed will bounce if someone walks down the hall. If you want more privacy, the newer "garden" rooms are made of stone and wood, are much larger and more spacious and have sundecks. On Thursday nights there is a barbecue and buffet with decent pan bands for jumping. Get there early; the music stops around 11 P.M., as does most activity on Bequia. The Frangipani is owned by the P.M. of St. Vincent—Pat "Son" Mitchell.

Rates are CHEAP to NOT SO CHEAP for singles and NOT SO CHEAP to PRICEY for doubles (EP).

JULIE'S GUEST HOUSE (809) 458-3304, fax (809) 458-3812
Port Elizabeth (P.O. Box 12), Bequia, St. Vincent, W.I.

Julie's is still the best deal in the Caribbean. For $33 U.S. single, $54 U.S. double, you get a room *and* breakfast and dinner. The rooms are very simple with firm platform double beds, mosquito nets, blond wood, bright wall colors, and private baths (no hot water). The food is good West Indian fare, again, very simple. You really enjoy eating because the whole place is such a bargain that the food seems *free*.

Julie's is not on the beach but one block in from the harbor in a residential neighborhood. You'll hear dogs barking and roosters crowing at all times (especially as you try to fall asleep). The "lulla-by of Bequia" usually starts with either an all-dog or all-rooster chorus. They sing a duet which builds to a cacophony and then, spent, gradually winds down. You get used to it.

The people who stay here are an interesting bunch and are usually repeaters. This is *not* a place to be antisocial. There is a bar where a bunch of Julie's friends listen to the cricket matches. The staff is courteous and very friendly, especially when you introduce your-self.

Rates are CHEAP for singles and NOT SO CHEAP for doubles (MAP).

THE OLD FORT (809) 458-3440, fax (809) 458-3824
Mount Pleasant Beach, Bequia, St. Vincent, W.I.

Situated on the top of the very breezy mount, the Old Fort commands the best views of any establishment on Bequia. Created from the remains of an old mill, Sonja and Otmar Schaedle have achieved a wonderfully peaceful environment. Both the common and guest rooms have the original stone walls and natural woods. The parlor even has a fireplace for those cool nights on the hilltop. The rooms are simply but comfortably furnished, and the lanai of room 5 is one of the best places to read a book while the view and the breeze provide welcome distraction. The Old Fort has an excellent Mediterranean-Créole restaurant, with Chef David (one of the nicest and most athletic chefs you'll ever meet) presiding. The Old Fort is also a great site for small groups and conferences.

Rates are PRICEY for singles and WICKED PRICEY for doubles (MAP). *No credit cards accepted.*

SPRING ON BEQUIA (809) 458-3414, same for fax
Spring Bay, Bequia, St. Vincent, W.I.
Stateside agent: Spring on Bequia, P.O. Box 19251, Minneapolis,
    MN 55419 (612) 823-1202

If you want real quiet (i.e., seclusion) in an extraordinary setting, stay at Spring. Situated on rising ground amidst the ruins of an old sugar mill and acres of coconut palms, this is one of the most peaceful (some might call it dead) places to stay anywhere. The airy design of stone and wood blends wonderfully with the surroundings. This is a reader's and meditator's heaven. The rooms are simply, almost minimally furnished, yet they're comfortable and consistent with the tranquility theme of this inn. Most have views of Mustique from their lanais. There is a restaurant serving all meals, including a very popular Sunday curry brunch (reservations necessary). A pretty pool and a clay court are on the grounds for your leisure and the wonderful walks and beaches of Spring and Industry are steps away.

Rates are VERY PRICEY for singles and WICKED PRICEY for doubles (MAP). Spring on Bequia is closed from mid-June to November 1.

KEEGAN'S GUEST HOUSE (809) 458-3530, no fax
Lower Bay, Bequia, St. Vincent, W.I.

Another great Bequia deal, this is your best bet if you want cheap accommodations at the beach *with meals*. Keegan's is an 11-room guest house less than 100 yards away from a great and really fun beach, Lower Bay. Being a guest house, all rooms are very simple but they do have private baths and fans. Keegan's restaurant serves good West Indian fare, and De Reef Bar & Restaurant is right at the beach.

Rates are CHEAP for singles and NOT SO CHEAP for doubles (MAP).

WHERE TO EAT

Since the last edition, there has been an explosion of restaurants. If you're staying in town (Port Elizabeth), don't choose the hotel MAP plan unless there is no other option, since there are a number of good restaurants to explore. If you're staying at Spring or the Old Fort, the MAP plan makes sense since traveling for meals would be inconvenient (and you would have to spend a lot on cab fare). Here are my dining choices:

DAPHNE'S, Port Elizabeth, 458-3271

This is a great place in town for West Indian/local-style food. Reservations are suggested. $$

DAWN'S CREOLE GARDEN, Lower Bay, 458-3154

Located on a hill at the far end of Lower Bay, Daphne's serves excellent West Indian/Créole cuisine and seafood specialties. Open for breakfast, lunch, and dinner. Dinner reservations a must. $$$ *No credit cards.*

DE REEF, Lower Bay, 458-3447

As you're already on the beach, this is a convenient and casual place for lunch and cocktails. Dinners here are surprisingly good. $$ *No credit cards.*

THE FRANGIPANI, Hotel Frangipani, Port Elizabeth, 458-3255

At the hub of the Harborwalk, the Frangi has consistently served good Caribbean cuisine at very fair prices as long as I've been coming here. Reservations are suggested, especially for dinner. $$$

LE PETIT JARDIN, Port Elizabeth, 458-3318

Probably Bequia's most expensive restaurant, Le Petit Jardin is located off the beaten path on Back Street. But the cuisine, French with Créole flourishes, is excellent, as is the service. Reservations are suggested. $$$$$ *No credit cards.*

MAC'S PIZZERIA & BAKE SHOP, Harborwalk, 458-3474

This is an institution on Bequia—don't miss Mac's mouth-watering lobster pizza. Open for breakfast, lunch, and dinner, no stay on Bequia is complete without a pit stop here. $$$ *No credit cards.*

THE OLD FORT, the Old Fort Hotel, Mount Pleasant, 458-3440

Chef David serves some delicious Créole and continental dishes in a very romantic and serene setting. And an after-dinner stroll to star-gaze is an added bonus that makes it worth the taxi ride up and back. Reservations are suggested. $$$$ *No credit cards.*

THERESA'S, Lower Bay Beach, 458-3802

Her Monday night international buffet is becoming an island event not to be missed. $$$ *No credit cards.*

DON'T MISS

BEQUIA BOOKSHOP—Located on the waterfront across from the park, it features an excellent collection of West Indian writers and a good general selection. And if it's maps and charts you're into—this is the place. Bequia Bookshop is owned by a very knowledgeable and polite ex-Bajan named Ian Gale, a good person to talk to about Caribbean authors. The store's logo T-shirt is an intelligent collector's item (as are books).

MAC'S PIZZERIA (see entry above)—They have lobster and fish pizza that is unusually good—it's been made almost world famous by the yachty set.

Perched on the Harborwalk with a breezy veranda, it features a healthy array of food, from pita-bread sandwiches and quiche to banana bread and homemade yogurt. Tuesday nights Mac's throws a barbecue and jump-up with live bands.

EASTER REGATTA—This is a great time both on and off the race course, as the racing is meant to be fun rather than competitive. Always held in April.

INDUSTRY BAY—Be sure to see this part of the island. It boasts lofty palm groves, a secluded beach, and a spectacular view of several nearby islands.

FOR DRINKS

- THE HARPOON SALOON—for sunset cocktails and a great view of the harbor. Also, their Saturday jump-ups are a blast.
- DE REEF—in Lower Bay; go on Sunday afternoons.
- FRANGIPANI—the hub. Also, Thursday-night jump-ups.

ST. VINCENT DIVERSIONS

There is a St. Vincent day trip that will both please and exhaust even the most energetic—a hike up the Soufrière volcano on the northern end of the island. Be sure to bring good walking shoes, water, energy snack, and a windbreaker or sweatshirt. It's cool and windy at the top and after the sweaty hike it will make your teeth chatter.

You leave at 6:30 A.M. on a ferry that will get you to Kingstown by 8 A.M. On arrival in Kingstown, you will be met by an onslaught of cab drivers. This is the time to be a shrewd and hard-nosed negotiator. Talk to several drivers, finding one whom you won't mind spending the day with, whom you can understand, and who seems to know what he's talking about. By speaking to many drivers, you'll get a good idea of the going rate and a mutually agreeable price range. At press time this was about EC$300 (about $110 U.S.), which should be all-inclusive and *not* per person.

Reconfirm the price and what's included at least two or three times. It'll sound stupid but it will prevent the driver from sneaking in hidden charges. You may also want to see the vehicle; it's a long drive to the starting point over roads that aren't in the greatest shape.

The drive itself will take about one hour. You'll have to switch to a Jeep for the half-hour bounce up to the trailhead. (The cab driver will have the Jeep connection arranged.) It is then a three-hour, fairly strenuous hike to the crater rim and summit. And rim is no exaggeration. You actually crawl up to the edge of the crater and peer over about a 1000-foot sheer drop to the floor of the volcano. There used to be a rather large crater lake that is now only a semblance of its former self. If you carefully walk, or crawl, along the rim to the right from the top of the path, you will find a rope pegged into the ground. It was put there by researchers who go down to take measurements on the activity of this very active volcano (it last erupted in 1979). You can climb down via the rope (with some sort of protection for your hands) to roam around the crater. *Before* doing this, tug on it a few times to make sure it's still in good shape. Otherwise you'll end up as a postscript on the hometown eleven o'clock news. Obviously, the climb back up to the crater rim will be very tiring—make sure you are strong enough and have the energy to do it.

After you've taken your pictures and refueled, the return climb will be easier. Leave no later than 1 P.M., allowing two hours for the descent. If you keep to this timetable, you should be able to make the 4:15 P.M. boat back to Bequia. If you don't, there's always the Umbrella Beach Apartments (see below) and the superb Botanical Gardens. The gardens are among the oldest in the Western hemisphere and this is where Captain Bligh of *Mutiny on the Bounty* fame planted the Caribbean's first breadfruit tree.

St. Vincent Accommodations

If you decide to come to Bequia by boat, or if you can't make air connections for some reason, here are some suggestions for St. Vincent accommodations:

PETIT BYAHAUT (809) 457-7008, same for fax
Petit Byahaut Bay, St. Vincent, W.I.

If you want to stay in a 50-acre valley that is accessible only by boat, this is a granola-type establishment where your rooms are 10 × 13-foot floored tents with screened windows, queen-size bed, solar-heated shower, and hammock.

Rates are PRICEY for single and doubles (AP).

THE UMBRELLA BEACH APARTMENTS (809) 458-4651, fax (809) 457-4930
P.O. Box 530, St. Vincent, W.I.

Lovely accommodations and a favorite of those on the guest house circuit, this establishment has private baths, all water sports, and a location on the beach. The French Restaurant is next door (see below).

Rates are CHEAP (EP).

KINGSTOWN PARK GUEST HOUSE (809) 456-1532, no fax
P.O. Box 41, Kingstown, St. Vincent, W.I.

Located on a hill overlooking the town and Bequia beyond, this converted old plantation house gets raves from guests. The quarters are clean, cheap, and there is good West Indian cuisine served. It's only about a ten-minute walk to town and is less than three miles from the airport.

Rates are DIRT CHEAP for singles and doubles (EP).

HERON HOTEL (809) 457-1631, fax (809) 457-1189
P.O. Box 226, Kingstown, St. Vincent, W.I.

An easy walk from the ferry dock, this is a great spot to stay if you want to catch the early boat. The comfortable rooms—in pale tones with wood floors surrounding a courtyard—provide refuge from the not-very-scenic neighborhood.

Rates are CHEAP for singles and NOT SO CHEAP for doubles (CP).

YOUNG ISLAND (809) 458-4826, fax (809) 457-4567
Stateside: (800) 223-1108
P.O. Box 211, Young Island, St. Vincent, W.I.

If it's luxury you want and spending lots of money proves it, there's Young Island. Billing itself as "an exclusive, private island resort," it's hardly that. A Chappaquiddick-sized swim and you're practically in downtown Kingstown. But it is one of those service-and-sunshine places that are la mode for some. I'd rather be on Bequia.

Rates are OUTRAGEOUS for singles to BEYOND BELIEF for doubles (MAP).

NOTE: Be sure to dine at THE FRENCH RESTAURANT (458-4972) in Villa. The food and atmosphere are great. $$$

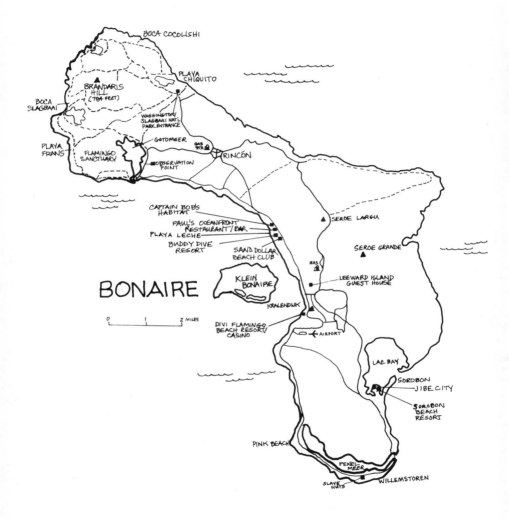

BONAIRE

BOCA COCOLISHI

PLAYA CHIQUITO

BRANDARIS HILL (784 FEET)

BOCA SLAGBAAI

WASHINGTON/ SLAGBAAI NAT'L PARK ENTRANCE

GOTOMEER

GAS STA.

RINCÓN

PLAYA FRANS

FLAMINGO SANCTUARY

OBSERVATION POINT

CAPTAIN BOBS HABITAT

PAUL'S OCEANFRONT RESTAURANT/BAR

PLAYA LECHE

BUDDY DIVE RESORT

SAND DOLLAR BEACH CLUB

SEROE LARGU

SEROE GRANDE

GAS

KLEIN BONAIRE

LEEWARD ISLAND GUEST HOUSE

KRALENDIJK

DIVI FLAMINGO BEACH RESORT/ CASINO

AIRPORT

LAC BAY

SOROBON JIBE CITY

SOROBON BEACH RESORT

0   1   2 MILES

PINK BEACH

PEKEL- MEER

SLAVE HUTS

WILLEMSTOREN

BONAIRE

Pink flamingos. You thought they only existed on suburban front lawns, the Hialeah racetrack, and in a John Waters movie starring Divine. But these shy and gangly birds flock to Bonaire, a gem of an island off the coast of Venezuela. So do divers, as Bonaire is one of the top dive destinations in the Caribbean and the world. Pink flamingos and divers, what a combination! If you are a diver like me, however, it's wonderful.

Bonaire is a very dry, even arid island, like the other islands in the Lesser Antilles (although is not quite the desert that is Aruba). It has a few nice beaches on the southern end of the island and one on the northern tip. It has a big park (Washington/Slagbaai National Park), on its northern end. It has big iguanas, parrots (both of which I saw), lots of cactus, and huge salt ponds (the major industry besides diving). It is almost always sunny, breezy, and hot on Bonaire. Even without the incredible reefs on the western side of the island and all around Klein Bonaire—an islet off the center of the island—this would be a very pleasant, low-key and quiet place to spend a week. The ambience on Bonaire is wonderfully relaxed, casual, and very friendly. Locals are very hospitable and accommodating. But the diving makes it heaven for those of us who go down and is why the license plates say "Diver's Paradise." You'll notice a very strange language being spoken here which sounds a lot like Spanish but is not—it's Papiamento, a native dialect which is a combination of Spanish, Dutch, and Portuguese with some African and Arawak words thrown in. If you understand Spanish, you should get the jist of it. Most locals here speak at least four languages: Papiamento, Dutch (the official language), English, and Spanish.

THE BRIEFEST HISTORY

Amerindians from nearby Venezuela first settled on Bonaire (the name is Amerindian for "low country") hundreds of years before its discovery by Amerigo Vespucci in 1499. The Spanish were the first Europeans to settle here and established a colony in 1527. They remained for almost a century until a war with the Netherlands caused the Dutch to seize control of the island in 1636 from their base on Curaçao. They set up shop and began producing salt from the vast salt ponds. This became big business. Slaves were imported to work the ponds. Evidence of their existence can be seen in the tiny stucco slave huts by the salt ponds. In the early 1800s, there were periodic seizures of the island by British and French pirates, but the Dutch regained final control in 1816. When slavery was abolished by the Dutch in 1863 (twenty-nine years after the British!), the profitability of salt plummeted without the slave labor, and the island sank into a sixty-year-long depression. The advent of oil refineries on Aruba and Curaçao in the 1920s caused many residents to move to those islands to work. They would then send the money back to their families. The beginnings of tourism in the 1950s also made the economy look up—as did union and autonomy of the Netherland Antilles within the Kingdom of the Netherlands. This brought in much needed outside aid. Diving now is the big business, and continues to thrive.

BONAIRE: KEY FACTS

LOCATION	12°N by 68°W
	50 miles north of Venezuela
	1,720 miles southeast of New York
SIZE	112 square miles
HIGHEST POINT	Brandaris Hill (784 ft.)
POPULATION	11,150
LANGUAGE	Papiamento plus Dutch (the official language), English, and Spanish widely spoken
TIME	Atlantic Standard Time (1 hour ahead of EST, same as EDT)
AREA CODE	Bonaire *is not* part of the 809 area code that applies to most of the Caribbean; to call Bonaire from the U.S. dial 011 (the international

access code), then 599 (the Bonaire country code), then 7 (the area code) and the four-digit local number

ELECTRICITY   127 volts, 56 cycles (slightly different from North America—be sure to ask before plugging in or recharging diving equipment)

CURRENCY   The Netherlands Antillean florin (NAf), sometimes called a guilder (1.77 NAf = $1 U.S.)

DRIVING   On the *right*; a valid U.S. or Canadian driver's license is accepted

DOCUMENTS   Passport or proof of citizenship with photo for U.S. and Canadian citizens, plus an ongoing or return ticket

DEPARTURE TAX $10 U.S.

BEER TO DRINK   Grolsch

RUM TO DRINK   Mt. Gay

MUSIC TO HEAR   Salsa

GETTING THERE

Bonaire has Flamingo International Airport, which receives daily direct flights from Miami (via Curaçao) on ALM. AMERICAN flies daily from New York and San Juan to Aruba, where you connect with an AIR ARUBA or ALM flight to Bonaire. AIR ARUBA has direct flights from Newark and Miami (touching down briefly in Aruba before continuing to Bonaire).

GETTING AROUND

You should definitely rent a car to explore the island. The roads are good, fairly well marked, easy to drive, and you'll appreciate the mobility. A few of the majors are here, including AVIS ([800] 331-1084), BUDGET ([800] 527-0700), and DOLLAR ([800] 800-4000). Be sure to make reservations in advance to ensure availability and the best rate.

FOCUS ON BONAIRE: THE DIVING EXPERIENCE

ALWAYS BREATHE. That's the first rule of diving. Even when there is a six-foot barracuda staring you in the face, maintain your composure and breathe regularly. If you don't, your lungs could explode. Besides, air costs about $1 for every minute you're underwater, so you're paying for it anyway!

NEVER RISE FASTER THAN YOUR BUBBLES. That is cardinal rule number two. If you do, you could very likely experience the "bends," which is not at all pleasant—not to mention that it can also paralyze and kill you.

BE PREPARED TO BECOME A SCUBA ADDICT. With 80-degree water, 100-feet-plus visibility, and an abundance of exotic tropical marine life to contemplate, chances are once you start, diving here will become an essential part of your life—right up there with your therapist and the Sunday *Times*. It is an equipment-intensive sport, much like skiing, so soon you'll be shelling out tons of money for the latest in BCs, regulators, and fog-free face masks. Then there is the cost of transportation, accommodations, and the diving itself. This is very definitely, if you'll pardon the expression, an "upscale" sport.

There is no better reason to come to the tropics than to explore its tremendous marine resources by scuba (self-contained underwater breathing apparatus). You'll find some of the best diving in the world here and certainly the most accessible to the many potential divers on the Eastern Seaboard, Midwest, and Canada. Hundreds of programs and packages are available for all levels of divers—from total neophyte to the status levels of dive master and instructor.

What is it like to sink slowly to the bottom and look up and see the surface 60 feet above your head? It's wild—like being in a giant aquarium. What do you feel when you're neutrally buoyant and floating past fabulously colored fish and coral? Fantastic. It's another dimension, like being in a 3-D movie. The best word to describe the experience is "Nirvana."

For those in search of a real mind-blowing experience, try diving at night. Imagine the thrill of jumping into total darkness with only the glow rings on the other divers' tanks and flashlights to guide you. Turn around and it's pitch black. Is the great white lurking somewhere behind you? This is the time when strict imagination control is in order. But don't worry, chances are Jaws is resting, waiting for the dawn feeding frenzy. Once you get to the bottom (which won't take long as night dives regularly don't go beyond a depth of 40 feet), you will observe the ocean asleep. Fish are so docile you can touch them. Coral comes alive, sending out delicate feelers to feed on plankton. Shine a light on a coral head and you'll see it close up within seconds. Colors become more brilliant than daytime, as the artificial white light brings out reds and yellows you can't see in sunlight. (As the water gets deeper, it "eats" the red and yellow light waves—giving everything a bluish cast.)

To keep up with the latest info on the sport, a subscription to *Skin Diver* magazine is considered a prerequisite for serious divers. It reports on dive spots around the world and has a special Caribbean issue every year. It features dive operations and reports on the newest trends in equipment.

For novices, or those who don't want to be scuba-exclusive, there are some attractive options. The sensible choice is to first do a Resort Course, which allows you to complete a shallow dive (to 40 feet) in one day without any previous experience. It is the scuba sampler, will cost around $50 U.S., and is available on most islands. After this you'll know whether you'll want more, which is likely. Then you can sign up for certification—about five full days (four to five dives)—or just take more Resort Courses in between golf and the beach.

For those interested in doing some serious diving, it is imperative that you are certified or have completed your classwork for certification. In order to get tanks filled with air (or to rent scuba equipment), you must be a card-carrying (with photo) diver. Your certification is in effect your underwater driver's license—you must have one to dive. The course lasts about four to five full days if you wait to take it on your vacation. It's no fun paying lots of money to sit in a room for a week listening to lectures, while the sun and sea beckon. There are certification courses up north that will allow you to do your open-water dives down here—far preferable to the wet suits, cold water, and limited visibility of the Atlantic. Any dive shop in your area will be able to tell you about certification courses (usually given by PADI or NAUI—the two largest professional diving organizations) and where to find them. Many local YMCAs also offer a course that is widely recognized by most dive operators.

There are four reasons why diving on Bonaire is so superb. The first is the reef profile of the island. Bonaire is not part of the continental shelf of South America, so depths plummet not far out from shore. This means that a reef wall exists only about 100 feet from the beach. At the start of the reef, the depth is about 20–30 feet. The wall is steep, allowing the diver lots of areas to peek into and explore. It levels off at about 130 to 150 feet for another 100 feet before taking another plunge to about 600 feet. With knowledge of the reef profile, the diver knows not to go farther than the level-off, and probably won't go below 100 feet anyway. There are over 60 designated dive sites along the west coast of Bonaire and Klein Bonaire, if you get tired of the one in front of your hotel.

The second reason is the marine life here and its protection. Because the entire coastline of Bonaire and Klein Bonaire is a Marine Park, nothing—dead or alive—can be touched or moved. Stiff fines await the diver who takes even a sand dollar from below the surface. While that may be bad news for your shell collection, it's great news for the incredible hard and soft corals and, of course, the animals. And great news for your viewing pleasure! On my first dive on Bonaire, I saw two mammoth moray eels, a huge grouper, an octopus, and schools and schools of all kinds of colorful fish. I had only been in the water for 15 minutes!

Number three on the Bonaire superlative list is the visibility of the water. It doesn't get better than this. Visibility ranges of between 80 and 120 feet are awesome. This way you can see the 20-foot tiger shark heading toward you, giving you time to decide not to panic. Water temperatures range between 78° and 86° Fahrenheit, making only a light wetsuit skin or top necessary.

The final reason why diving is so fabulous here are the facilities. There are at least eight full-service dive operations on the island, offering every conceivable kind of dive, instruction, certification, equipment, and accommodation/dive package. To be able to jump off the dock, go down and know that your dive outfit is only a few hundred feet away, is a great convenience and assurance for the novice. There is also a state-of-the-art decompression chamber on the island.

With all these options, how do you decide who to choose. Well, I dove with Sand Dollar (Sand Dollar Beach Club, tel. 8738) and was very impressed with their professionalism and service. I highly recommend them—you don't have to stay at the Sand Dollar to buy a dive package with the dive operation. Of course, there are several other very competent dive operations. You should choose the one that offers you the package and program that fit your needs.

WHERE TO STAY

The decision of where to stay on Bonaire is a little more complicated than just finding a lodging that appeals to you. This is because
dive operations are affiliated with or own the hotels where they are
located. So you're choosing a dive shop too. Usually, you get both
in a package, which lowers your cost and just makes everything
easier—from storing or renting equipment to paying the bill. Do a
package, unless you're on the island for just a few days. If you're
not a diver, any of the hotels below would love to have you. One
of them has nothing to do with diving—it's a nudist resort.

SAND DOLLAR BEACH CLUB (011-599-7) 8738, fax (011-599-7)
   8760
Stateside: (800) 766-6016/(617) 821-1012
P.O. Box 262, Kaya Gouverneur Debrotweg 79, Bonaire, N.A.

The dive shop here is top-notch—a full-service, five-star PADI
facility run by Andre and Gabrielle Nahr. It offers every scuba
course known to man as well as photo and video courses and the
Nikonos Shootout contest. Next to the shop is the Green Parrot
restaurant. This is a pleasant place to use up some surface time
while you sip a Grolsch.

   The accommodations are condos that come in studio apartments
and one-, two-, and three-bedroom configurations. While not at all
fancy, the units are spacious and comfortable. All have lanais where
you can hang your wet suit out to dry, as well as air conditioning,
fully equipped kitchens, and cable TV. There's a small market on
the property for those who like to cook. A pool and two lighted
tennis courts round out the facilities.

   Rates are VERY PRICEY for singles and doubles (EP—not inclusive of diving). Add $250 per person for six days of unlimited boat
dives and unlimited use of tank and air.

CAPTAIN DON'S HABITAT (011-599-7) 8290, fax (011-599-7)
   8240
Stateside: (800) 327-6709
P.O. Box 88, Kaya Gouverneur Debrotweg 103, Bonaire, N.A.

Captain Don was the original dive pioneer and dive operation on
Bonaire. He runs a full-service, five-star PADI facility and also runs

certification for NAUI and SSI. He has eight dive boats and a full photo/video program.

The environment here is real nice. The villas are an attractive Mediterranean-stucco style and come in all sizes and costs to meet your needs. Captain Don even has a package for singles. All units have air conditioning and many have kitchens. There is a pretty pool area and a cool restaurant/bar area.

Rates are PRICEY to VERY PRICEY for singles and doubles (EP). Packages run between $800 and $1,600 per person for eight days/seven nights accommodation and unlimited diving (CP).

BONAIRE DIVI FLAMINGO BEACH RESORT & CASINO
(011-599-7) 8285, fax (011-599-7) 8238
Stateside: (800) 367-3484/(607) 277-3484
J. A. Abraham Blvd., Bonaire, N.A.

This is the island's biggest resort. It is also the home of Dive Bonaire I and II, at opposite ends of the beachfront, the largest dive operation on the island. It too is a full-service dive facility, offering all levels of certification. Photo Bonaire offers underwater photo and video courses as well as equipment rental.

The resort has 145 guest rooms, all with lanais, air conditioning, ceiling fans, tropical décor, phones, and cable TV. There are two pools with Jacuzzis, several lighted tennis courts, and all water sports. The beach here is tiny, though. There is a casino, two restaurants, and several bars.

Rates are PRICEY to WICKED PRICEY for single and doubles (EP—not inclusive of diving). Several dive packages are available.

SOROBON BEACH RESORT (011-599-7) 8080, fax (011-599-7) 5363
P.O. Box 14, Lac Bay, Bonaire, N.A.

Moving away from wearing lots of gear to wearing nothing at all, this is Bonaire's "clothing optional" (read—nude) resort. Situated on a pretty, shallow, and protected bay open to the trade winds, this is a very pleasant establishment with a fine private beach. Next door to the resort is Jibe City, the windsurf operation (this is also Bonaire's best spot for windsurfing). Accommodations consist of 20 one-bedroom chalets. There is a bar, restaurant, library, water sports, and a dive affiliation with the Dive Inn.

Rates are VERY PRICEY for singles and doubles (EP).

LEEWARD INN GUEST HOUSE (011-599-7) 5516, fax (011-599-7) 5517

Kaya Grandi 60, Kralendijk, Bonaire, N.A.

The Leeward Inn is a newly renovated guest house owned by a delightful couple from upstate New York. All rooms are simple and clean, with private bath, ceiling fans, and daily maid service. The Inn is within easy walking distance of downtown Kralendijk. The folks here also run the Harthouse Cafe next door and have a dive operation called Blue Divers in the back.

Rates are CHEAP to NOT SO CHEAP for singles and doubles (EP).

WHERE TO EAT

The choices are fairly easy in this department because there just aren't that many. The local specialties are fresh-caught fish, an occasional *rijstaffel*, and such dishes as keshi yena. Your best bet is to rent a villa or efficiency with kitchen facilities. But if you don't feel like cooking, try PAUL'S OCEANFRONT (phone 5580), RICHARD'S WATERFRONT DINING, 60 Abraham Blvd. (phone 5263), RAFFLES', Kaya C.E.B. Helmund 5 (phone 8617), DEN LAMAN, Gouverneur Debrotweg 77 (phone 8955) and MONA LISA, Kaya Grandi 15 (phone 8718).

DON'T MISS

WASHINGTON/SLAGBAAI NATIONAL PARK—Occupying 15,000 acres; there are lots of trails and a cute two-part deserted black sand beach called Boca Cocolishi.

JIBE CITY—Located at Lac Bay next to the Sorobon Resort, this is a great place to windsurf, as the bay is thigh-deep, sandy, and has an on-shore breeze—so you won't be blown out to sea. There is a little bar to quaff a few while you rest or watch. Jibe City carries a variety of custom Dutch boards called Wave Warriors. For more info, call (011-599-7) 5363 and ask for Ernst.

SLAVE HUTS—Located at the salt ponds on the southern end of the island, these tiny, whitewashed, thatch-roofed huts look like kids' play-houses, yet they housed the salt workers during the week while they worked; on weekends they walked to their homes in nearby Rincón.

THE FLAMINGOS—These stunning pink flocks hang out at the southern salt ponds and at the Goto Meer in the north by the park.

BRITISH VIRGIN
ISLANDS

To some people, sailing is torture. Visions of ice-cold water flying over the bow into your face, or that salt-caked skin sensation without a hot water shower antidote, or the queasy feeling that rises when your vertigo gets Osterized from the constant motion, and that insipid dampness that permeates everything, especially your towels and sheets—who needs it! Fortunately, these images should keep the crowds on the beach and off the high seas because for many, sailing is sheer bliss. The art of moving very slowly but expensively is for some the ultimate therapy. It causes you to focus on getting from point A to point B. And all the variables that constantly surface—like wind, seas, breakdowns, mutinies, and so on—keep your thoughts on sailing, allowing all other disturbing thoughts and anxieties to float away in your wake. It's no wonder that so many high-stressed movers and shakers have sailboats.

The British Virgin Islands offer some of the best sailing waters in the world. They rival the Mediterranean and the South Pacific for steady winds and warm, clear water, providing superb opportunities for swimming and snorkeling as well as eyeball navigation for those unfamiliar with the waters.

There are over 50 British Virgin Islands, or BVIs, from the big (24-square-mile) island of Tortola to the teensy Sandy Cay—most are uninhabited. If you're not into sailing—after all, sailing is torture—there are many islands where you can stay and never have to set foot on a boat. Landlubbers can rejoice in Tortola, Virgin Gorda, Jost Van Dyke, Peter Island, Guana Island, Mosquito Island, Marina Cay, and the incredibly expensive Necker Island (you rent the whole thing). Of course, a boat is the ultimate waterfront

VIRGIN ISLANDS

ANEGADA

ATLANTIC OCEAN

Prickly Pear Is.
Necker Is.
VIRGIN GORDA
VIRGIN GORDA YACHT HARBOUR
NORTH SOUND
Fallen Jerusalem
Mosquito Is.
Great Camanoe Is.
Scrubb Is.
The Dogs
Beef Is.
Guana Is.
The Baths
Ginger Is.
Cooper Is.
Salt Is.
Peter Is.
Marina Cay
Channel Tunnel + Dead Chest Is.
TORTOLA
Cane Garden Bay
West End
Norman Is.
The Bight
Sandy Cay
Drake's Channel
Sir Francis Drake
Jost Van Dyke
Soper's Hole
Columbia Bay
Cruz Bay
Coral Bay
St. John
Great Tobago
Little Tobago
Great Thatch Is.
West Gregoric Gate
Thatchcap Gate
Two Hook
Charlotte Amalie
St. Thomas
Water Is.
Buck Is.
St. Croix

CARIBBEAN SEA

N

0   5
    MILES

accommodation, and you can see so much more. But tomatoes for some are tomahtoes to others, so you have your choice.

With such great sailing territory, most visitors to the BVIs are sailors on a week-long charter. This explains why Jost Van Dyke, with a population of under 100 people, has six major bars. Tortola is the charter-boat headquarters and is where all the outfits in the BVIs are based. These people are obviously mobile and migrate daily to different anchorages. Landlubbers have plenty of options, however (see "Where to Stay," pages 119–20).

THE BRIEFEST HISTORY

Like the U.S. Virgin Islands, the British Virgins were first populated by Amerindians from South America. First came the Arawaks and the Caribs, then Columbus sighted them on his second voyage in 1493. The Dutch, however, were the first Europeans to settle the islands. But Britain took control in 1666 and has ruled the islands ever since. Until the recent tourist boom, sugar and fishing were the economic mainstays. Today, the BVIs are still a Crown Colony of the British Commonwealth, although they are fairly self-governing and the U.S. dollar is the official currency. (I love these uncomplicated histories.)

BRITISH VIRGIN ISLANDS: KEY FACTS

LOCATION	18°N by 64°W
	1,650 miles southeast of New York
SIZE	59 square miles total (including the water)
HIGHEST POINT	Mt. Sage, Tortola (1,720 ft.)
POPULATION	12,000
LANGUAGE	English
TIME	Atlantic Standard Time (1 hour ahead of EST, same as EDT).
AREA CODE	809
ELECTRICITY	110 volts AC, 60 cycles
CURRENCY	The U.S. dollar
DRIVING	On the *left*; a Canadian or American driver's license is accepted, but in addition you must pay $10 for temporary BVI permit, valid for three months

DOCUMENTS	Passport or proof of nationality with photo is acceptable for U.S. or Canadian citizens up to six months; an ongoing or return ticket or boat charter is also required
DEPARTURE TAX	$5 U.S. by air, $4 U.S. by boat
BEER TO DRINK	John Courage
RUM TO DRINK	Cruzan
MUSIC TO HEAR	Dancehall

GETTING THERE

Both Tortola and Virgin Gorda have airports, although most flights come into Tortola. You'll have to fly into San Juan or St. Thomas/ St. Croix from the mainland to make connections. From San Juan, AMERICAN EAGLE, AIR BVI, SUN AIR EXPRESS, and LIAT fly several times daily. From St. Thomas and St. Croix, it's SUN AIR EXPRESS. From St. Maarten, St. Kitts, and Antigua, it's LIAT.

There are also numerous ferries from St. Thomas and St. John to Tortola and Virgin Gorda. From St. Thomas and St. John, SMITH'S FERRY SERVICE ([809] 494-4430) and NATIVE SON INC. ([809] 495-4617) have scheduled service to both West End and Road Town. From St. Thomas to Virgin Gorda, SPEEDY'S FAN-TASY/SPEEDY'S DELIGHT ([809] 495-5240) has service three times a week. From Tortola to Virgin Gorda, SPEEDY'S (see above), SMITH'S (see above), and NORTH SOUND EXPRESS ([809] 494-2746) have daily service.

GETTING AROUND

Well, the best way is by sailboat (see "Focus on the BVIs—Sailing and the Charter Experience," which follows). If you're a landlubber, only three islands—Tortola, Virgin Gorda, and Anegada—are big enough to have rental cars. The other islands are just about small enough that you can walk everywhere. BUDGET ([800] 527-0700), HERTZ ([800] 654-3001), NATIONAL ([800] 227-3876/[809] 494-3197), and AVIS ([800] 331-1084) have outposts on Tortola; HERTZ has an agency on Virgin Gorda and D.W. JEEP RENTALS is it on Anegada. Be sure to make reservations in advance to ensure availability and the best rate.

FOCUS ON THE BVIs—
SAILING AND THE CHARTER EXPERIENCE

WHAT COLOR IS YOUR SPINNAKER?

Don't let the idea of being on a sailboat for a week lead to angst, because you *can* do it. For sure, sailing is certainly more rigorous than cruising on an ocean liner. But there are all kinds of options open to you depending on your experience and motivation. A word of caution here—pay careful attention to the personalities being assembled. A boat provides little refuge from others.

THE CREWED BOAT

If you just enjoy lying on the deck and having someone *else* do the work, or if your sailing experience was a Sunfish at camp, then a crewed boat is for you. In this situation, the degree of effort, from hoisting the sail to hoisting a drink, is up to you.

So you want the easy way out? No problem. There are two major considerations: where and how much. Let's talk about the latter first. Costs can run you on average for four adults from $4,500 to $20,000 per week during the winter season. Of course, the "mega" boats are higher, such as the *Endeavor*, a j-boat—yours to love for the base price of $50,000 a week. Once you've decided your budget, the choice becomes simpler. With over 300 boats to choose from, here are some carefully considered suggestions (prices quoted are for the number of people the boat sleeps and for the winter season):

CREWED CHARTER BOATS

- *Anne Marie II*—Sparkman & Stevens, 47 ft./2 crew/sleeps 2/ $4600
- *Ambiance*—Beneteau, 51 ft./2 crew/sleeps 6/$6,400
- *Emily Morgan*—A very comfortable performance boat/57 ft./2 crew/sleeps 6/$7500
- *New Spirit*—Little Harbor, 75 ft./3 crew/sleeps 6/$12,000
- *Titan V*—Irwin, 65 ft./3 crew/sleeps 8/$12,000

- *See Flo*—A Swan, the Ferrari of sailboats, 65 ft./2 crew/sleeps 4/$9,600

- *Southern Cruz*—The *Architectural Digest* of boats, 68 ft./2 crew/ sleeps 6/$8,500

- *Rhapsody*—A custom ketch with a parrot mascot, 72 ft./3 crew/ sleeps 8/$10,500

- *Sweptaway*, Windship sloop, 72 ft./3 crew/sleeps 6/$14,500

- *Harbinger*—Classic ketch, 93 ft./3 crew/sleeps 6/$20,000

- *Whitehawk*—The most beautiful sailboat ever built, 105 ft./5 crew/sleeps 6/$16,000

Generally, these boats are not limited to one region and will consider guest preferences when scheduling their itineraries. Keep in mind that the laziest time will be in the Virgins and the most invigorating in the Grenadines.

How does one get set up with his dreamboat? As with just about everything else in life, you call a broker. And we all know how we feel about brokers—they're pretty far down the list. Where there's money to be made, there's a broker. However, there are some that are very good and very reliable, but the best is:

- SWIFT YACHT CHARTERS, 26 Summer Street, Hingham, MA 02043, (800) 866-8340/(617) 749-8340, fax (617) 749-1120

Hope Swift will be able to send you brochures on the boat of your choice as well as others that are in the same ballpark. She will also help you make captain contact. Since you will be spending a week with him and his crew in very close quarters, this is a crucial step to follow through on before laying out cash. Don't be shy to ask pertinent questions like "Do you mind more than two unmarried people sleeping together?" or "Is it okay to sunbathe topless or au naturel?" Bad chemistry between captain and guests can ruin your vacation. Using our recommendations later in the chapter, hash out an itinerary with the captain before you embark. Because he is more familiar with the waters and because he is the captain, be flexible and defer to his judgment. What might be a serene little harbor one day will look like Coney Island the next due to the migratory habits of bareboaters. The captain will know these things.

THE BAREBOAT

While the bareboat doesn't have all the amenities of the crewed yacht, it still has some significant advantages. The privacy (among friends) is hard to beat, the freedom to go wherever your charter agreement permits will allow you the spontaneity that makes vacations great, and it's a helluva lot cheaper. You'll have to work harder, but you will get off on the accomplishment, and deservedly so. However, there must be at least one person on board who has a thorough understanding of, and experience in, big-boat sailing. He or she should be somewhat mechanical and very patient with those who don't comprehend the arcane language of sailing nomenclature. You will have to pass a proficiency test before you set sail— and failure could be very embarrassing to all involved (not to mention inconvenient). It is also a good idea to have a first mate who has been sailing before and can absorb unfamiliar maneuvers and territory very quickly. The rest can learn through osmosis.

Chartering a bareboat is different from chartering a crewed boat in that more emphasis should be placed on the composition of the crew and the size of the boat. With no objective authority figure like a professional captain, some friends become unnerved when a peer commands them to do something. When you're sailing, there often is not enough time to follow Miss Manner's rules of asking nicely. So use extra care in the crew selection—these are people you will be intimate with for at least a week. Directly related to the success of this fragile coexistence is the size of the boat. Since most charter operations have a wide range of boats available, consider the amount of privacy you'll need (from your friends) and don't be cheap here—the additional space is worth it. I recommend a center-cockpit boat, generally 35 feet or longer, as it creates two distinct staterooms fore and aft—each with its own head (bathroom). There's nothing worse than listening to a couple go at it all night long (when you're not able to) because all that separates you from them is a wafer-thin, louvered door. There is a general rule of thumb here: under 30 feet—one couple, 30 to 40 feet—two couples, over 40 feet—larger groups.

Once you've sized up your crew and boat, you're ready to contact a broker. Due to the intense competition among bareboat charter companies, especially in the Virgins, most boats are comparably equipped. Many boats used are designed for the charter business, and have options available for more money, such as a sail board or an inflatable dinghy (recommended for its stability

and comfort) with an outboard on it. Again, the best broker to
talk to is:

• SWIFT YACHT CHARTERS, 26 Summer Street, Hingham,
  MA 02043, (800) 866-8340/(617) 749-8340, fax (617) 749-1120

Call or write for brochures and then compare the pros and cons
of the specific designs and features of the boats available and weigh
them with the cost. Also check out packages offered: some include
a hefty discount on airfare, provide ground transportation to the
dock, strap a windsurfer on the deck, and have options for fully or
partially provisioned (food and booze) boats. If you like eating
ashore, then the latter is recommended. Costs for a 35-foot boat for
a week run anywhere from $2,000 to $4,000. Plan on $15 to $20 per
day per person for full provisioning. If you're unsure about your
sailing expertise, an additional $75 per day will give you the services
(sailing related only) of a professional skipper.

SAILING THE BVIs

The British Virgin Islands are the islands best suited for the sail-
charters. The area's well-protected waters, abundance of sheltered
harbors, and short distances between islands will show off sailing's
best side. You will also find a surprising number of seasoned sailors
who relish the relative calm of the waters and the immense variety
of sailboat options available to them. Unfortunately, the near-per-
fect conditions contribute to a less than perfect overpopularity—
translating into crowded anchorages. Virgins they *once* were, but
alas, the past twenty years have taken their toll on the old girls.

But for even well-versed old salts, these islands are among the
favorite sailing waters in the world. This sheltered sea of 35 miles
by 10 (the Sir Francis Drake Channel), is still magnificent despite
the *explosion* of cruising boats here. Charters begin in either St.
Thomas or Tortola, the major gateways, both within easy distance
of the choice spots to visit.

If you are starting out from St. Thomas, the name of the game is
to get out as fast as you can. St. Thomas, especially the main port
of Charlotte Amalie, is overcrowded with cruise-ship tourists on a
bargain shopping frenzy. The roads around town resemble L.A. at
rush hour—all day long—we're talking major bumper-to-bumper
traffic. The harbor is polluted and is jammed with boats of all sizes.
Now St. Thomas does have some redeeming qualities. It's just that

compared to where you will be going, why bother? If you must stay, be sure to lock your boat—*really*—and take the Oldport Launch (thus avoiding traffic and the sometimes nasty cab drivers). It costs $3 and monitors Channel 9 on your boat's VHF radio. At night it's a pleasant trip to Frenchtown, where you'll find Famous—renowned for its delicious stir-fry and Créole dishes at affordable prices. You'll be able to get out of there for about $25 a head, which in the Caribbean is rare for a good meal.

If you're starting out from Tortola, stop at Road Town (also known as Hot Town because the mountains block the cooling breezes); there are some places worth checking out before you leave. Right in the town is the Pusser's Rum Shop. This savory name is the "official Drink of the British Royal Navy." Some people think it tastes like it sounds although I think it's worth a

CRUISING GUIDE TO RESTAURANTS

RESTAURANT	CUISINE	COMMENTS
FAMOUS/St. Thomas	Stir-fry/Créole	Good, healthy food/funky décor
STANLEY'S/Tortola	Barbecue/Fish	The lobster + T-shirt = tops
HARRIS'/Jost	Barbecue (Mon./Thurs.)	On the beach w/Peace and Love
BRANDYWINE BAY/Tortola	West Indian	Tortola's Famous
SKY WORLD/Tortola	Continental	Sour Sop daiquiri and the view
BITTER END Y.C./Virgin Gorda*	Continental	Overrated but good lobster
DRAKE'S/Virgin Gorda*	Continental	Very romantic/food's okay
MARINA CAY/Marina Cay	Continental/ Barbecue	Like a VFW Banquet
PETER ISLAND Y.C.*/Peter Island	Continental	Dressy and expensive/great buffet
COOPER ISLAND BEACH CLUB/Cooper Island	West Indian	Small but popular

*Make reservations as far in advance as possible.

shot. The shop has some great souvenirs with the Pusser's name on them, including mugs, hats, and a wristwatch that spells out Pusser's Rum in code flags. Nearby is the Caribbean Marketplace, which sells some terrific spices in tasteful mahogany that make great gifts for friends back home. For provisioning, there is a well-stocked and reasonable supermarket called RITE WAY. It has a small gourmet section and a great selection of wines.

For an incredible view overlooking Road Town and the Channel, take the free shuttle for a hair-raising ride up the mountain to the Cloud Room. Have a drink and go for dinner to Brandywine Bay outside of Road Town, or continue on to Sky World for cocktails at sunset—the best spot in the Virgins for viewing. (Observant passengers will notice a beautiful fungus growing in the cow patties along the roadside. These can be obtained from any Rasta on the beach in Cane Garden Bay or at the Bomba Shack.) Once arrived, sop up a Sour Sop Daiquiri, a Sky World specialty. Sour Sop is a local fruit that resembles a cross between a mango and a pineapple.

Once you've left the hustle-bustle of the major home ports, plan to sail as much to windward (east in this instance) as possible during the first days out. This will allow for leisurely exploration of the islands worth seeing, with the winds in your favor. Start with North Sound, Virgin Gorda, and work your way west through the southern string of islands and the fringes of Tortola and Jost Van Dyke.

If you head over to St. John, you will have to deal with customs in the U.S. and then again upon your return. In the BVIs, this means it will take forever to wait in line and fill out forms. (All they really want is your $4 pleasure-boating tax. So why not just have a cash register at the dock?) To minimize this inconvenience, stay in the BVIs until you leave it for good.

One of the nicest features of Virgin Gorda is Gorda Sound (called North Sound by locals), a splendidly protected bay near the northeast end of the island. The mountains to the south are a national park, which accounts for their pristine state. When you enter the Sound, there is a massive reef to the right that boats are *always* hitting. There are markers so just be prudent and leave plenty of room to starboard (the right). That reef, called Colquhoun Reef, offers some super snorkeling when sea conditions are calm. Most people head for a mooring ball at the Bitter End Yacht Club. It really isn't a yacht club in the proper sense but a nice resort with a marina and launch service. I prefer a mooring near Biras Creek, a very pretty inlet with a nice hotel/resort sitting on a promontory overlooking the Atlantic on one side and the Sound on the other.

I'd stay here for some discreet rendezvous. There are two resorts in the area that comprise the "Bitter End": Biras Creek and the Bitter End Yacht Club. If you can, take a hike out to the real Bitter End along the trail and be sure to *bring your camera*. It's a healthy hike so wear the appropriate footwear. There's also a good reef off Prickly Pear Island for snorkeling. On land, the Quarterdeck Bar has some high-octane cocktails and a very "You watch me, I'll watch you" crowd. The Dining Room is a standard stop, the most popular on Virgin Gorda. The Caribbean lobster is good here though, and it's only slightly more than the prix fixe for dinner so you might as well have it, especially if you're splitting the bill. There are two free movies shown in the Sand Palace outdoor pavilion. Popcorn is served. In front of the Main Pavilion, there is a shark pen with a startlingly low fence around it (someone is eventually going to fall in or get thrown in) with real-enough-looking sharks lurking in the water. A must stop is the Pirates Pub on Saba Rock. Happy hour is from 4 to 5 P.M. This is a great place to get smashed and watch the sunset. Careful getting back into your dinghy—those drinks are strong.

Across the Sound is Mosquito Island, a privately owned 125-acre resort called Drake's Anchorage. Moor here to avoid the Bitter End hubbub. The island is really worth exploring as it has trails all over its hilly terrain. Wear sneakers and hike to the eastern end, just beyond the last cottages of the hotel. There are underwater caves on Rocky Beach for snorkeling. Over to the west is Honeymoon Beach, a cozy cove that is just right for two people. On the other end of the island is Long Beach, which touts one of the best snorkel/dive spots in the Virgins. Jean-Michel Cousteau brings his students here. Getting to the reef, however, can be tricky. The Drake's Anchorage resort is very low-key, with weathered cottages, a solid restaurant, and a dining room that looks like it was built for the set of *South Pacific*.

When leaving North Sound, get out the binoculars and check out the palace of the founder of Virgin Atlantic on Necker Island. It is also the occasional home of Princess Di and her kids.

DROPPING OUT TO DROP ANCHOR

Are you fed up with the corporate yuppie scene, a disillusioned child of the sixties who has lost interest in the next trend in cuisine? Try crewing on a charter boat. There are a lot of drop-outs floating around the American Paradise and many ex-execs being everything from cooks to deckhands to captains. It is hard work—there is little time for private life, especially during high season, and virtually no chance for extended quality time. The pay is low, on average about $1,000 per month plus room and board.

So why bother? Leaving behind competitive pressures and phone bills is a major reason. It's therapeutic—manual labor in a very pleasant environment. It is also a good way to save money, something that current metro rents and mortgages don't allow. With no time or department store to spend your money in, it's easy to save.

Rebecca was one of these refugees. She left a lucrative ad sales job and Garden District condo in New Orleans to work aboard *Rangga*, a gorgeous 73-foot French-built schooner. She was the cook, meal planner, and provisioner. It's tough planning and stocking a boat with seven days' worth of food and drink for three meals a day—all within twenty-four hours. But despite the long hours and the loss of privacy, she enjoyed the independence and the low-pressure environment of her position.

Author's Note: Rebecca was on *Rangga* for 12 months. Then she went up north to study holistic healing and massage at an institute in the Berkshires. Today she is a full-fledged masseuse with a thriving business. *Rangga* was destroyed in Hurricane Hugo.

The Virgin Gorda Yacht Harbor, in Spanish Town on the southern end of Virgin Gorda, is a good port to call on if you want to disembark at will. It's a cramped but well-run and clean marina managed by Rockresorts (Little Dix Bay is around the corner). The Bath & Turtle is a good bar to hang out in and sip a cold beer. On Wednesday nights it holds a "jump-up" party. Dinner at Chez Michelle down the road is quite good and there are a few interesting shops to throw money around in, including a tiny record store if you're tired of your tapes.

Early the next morning, stop in for lunch at the Baths just south of Spanish Town. This stretch of gigantic boulders creates hundreds of caves and caverns with cool, clear saltwater pools in many. Because "it's special," an armada of boats descends to its shore and it gets very crowded here, particularly in the afternoon, so come early (7 to 10 A.M. is ideal). There are now clearly marked trails through the boulders as well as ladders to make climbing the rocks easier and safer. Restrooms are located at the beginning of the trail.

The snorkeling is fantastic in *calm water*. Unfortunately, the surge (swells) prevents comfortable overnight anchoring. For privacy, take the walking trails to the Atlantic side of the point.

After the Baths, there's a fork in the road. You can head over to Marina Cay with a well-protected but not overly scenic anchorage. By all means, avoid Trellis Bay and The Last Resort. Trellis Bay is noisy from the airport it borders and The Last Resort puts on a painful comedy routine only your parents would appreciate. Or you can stop for another swim and explore Fallen Jerusalem—a rarely visited jumble of rocks named because it reminded someone of Jerusalem after one of its bad days. There's a small, private beach and lots of rocks to scramble over and under. Continuing on, you can really only sail by Ginger Island and wave; there is no suitable anchorage. Also, it has become a haven for drug runners. If the authorities see you've stopped there, chances are you'll be searched. Stay clear! Cooper Island doesn't offer much improvement except for good dining at the Cooper Island Beach Club. The next island west, Salt Island, has a protected spot on the south to throw out the hook. On the island there is an old black woman who sits on the beach and will barter bags of sea salt for anything you might have; a bottle of rum or, of course, cold hard cash. On the west side of the island is the site of the wreck of the R.M.S. *Rhone*, lost in the Hurricane of 1876 when she was loading cargo. The wreck is best suited for scuba divers as it's down between 30 and 85 feet. But when there are divers, the air bubbles create shimmering columns that are actually more interesting to look at from the surface than the wreck itself. The story of its demise is worth mentioning. Apparently, the captain knew the weather was going to turn real bad, so he threw out both anchors and rode out the first half of the tempest running the engines at full throttle, sheltered from the sea by the island. During the eye of the hurricane, when the sun came out and it was dead calm, he tried to hightail it for the open water because he knew the new wind direction would blow him right against the rocks. Of all times for the anchor to get snagged! The wind and seas roared in, pushed the *Rhone* up on the reef, demolished the boat, and took 125 lives. One last piece of lore: This is the wreck that Jackie Bisset swam around in *that* T-shirt in the film *The Deep*.

Next down the chain is Peter Island—home of the Peter Island Yacht Club (like the Bitter End, another pretender). This private little island is one of the Caribbean's most expensive resorts, so definitely go ashore to see if you think it's worth it. The buffet is good—expensive ($35) for a buffet, but good. Men will need a jacket.

From Peter Island, head directly west for the Bight off Norman Island. This is one of the finest protected harbors in the Virgins, and one of the prettiest, too. There are no man-made structures on the island, but there are wild goats of which you should steer clear. There are some caves around the western entrance, reputed to have held major treasure troves and provided Robert Louis Stevenson with the inspiration to write *Treasure Island*. I don't know about that, but you *can* pilot your dinghy right inside one of the caves—now that's inspiration. When you've had enough, go for a snorkel around the reef off the center shore in the Bight. Then hit the floating bar, the William Thornton, for a "Nelson's Blood" (grapefruit juice, orange juice, cranberry juice, and Pusser's rum). The bar, a former Baltic Sea Trader, serves burgers and similar fare. Around 9 P.M., the "locals" (crew from the charter boats) flock to the bar, which makes it interesting. The Thornton stays open until the "lights go out."

CRUISING GUIDE TO SNORKEL SPOTS

LOCATION	COMMENTS
THE INDIANS, Norman Island	lots of fish, nice wall
THE BIGHT, Norman Island	good snorkeling in the middle by the shore
WHITE BAY, Guana Island	when visibility is good, some great corals
LONG BAY, Mosquito Island	Cousteau's students go here, tricky access
WHITE BAY, Jost Van Dyke	excellent Elkhorn coral
SANDY CAY, Sandy Cay	nudie snorkeling
BREWER'S BAY, Tortola	several reefs in harbor
THE DOGS, The Dogs	sea turtles
ANEGADA, Anegada	the island is a huge reef/lobster
THE BATHS, Virgin Gorda	early in the A.M./visibility sometimes murky

Now it's time for some sailing as you head across the Sir Francis Drake and around the West End of Tortola to Jost Van Dyke (named after some semilegend of a Dutch pirate, although I think it must mean "cheers" in Dutch). Jost is rather an unusual place. There can't be more than a hundred people living on the island, yet there are six bars. Obviously, such a situation demands a fitting response, that is, time to do some serious drinking. Keep those islanders in business, that kind of thing.

Great Harbor is the home of Foxy's, now world famous. It would be called a dive anywhere else but it's a sailor's mecca in the Virgins. There's really nothing to it—it's like something you'd expect to see deep in Appalachia. Be careful not to step on the chickens but be sure to hit the new Foxy's Boutique. The bartenders are real nice guys, and Foxy Caldwell will occasionally play some tunes on his guitar. Foxy's also has a D.J. who spins reggae and calypso. There are some well-worn hammocks on which to lounge and sway. But the real attraction is the crowd and the Painkiller Punch sold in plastic milk cartons for three bucks a pop (no wonder there are six bars). Next to Foxy's is Happy Larry's, another dive, but with pool tables. To the west of the Customs House is Club Paradise and down past the church is Rudy's, which is actually quite nice. Here you'll find jump-up to the reggae beat until 2 A.M., if you haven't already passed out. Both have dance floors with disco balls.

Over at Little Harbor, a healthy and very beautiful couple of miles up and down the high road, is Sidney's Peace and Love Bar, where you're on the honor system to make your own drinks and write down how many you've had. Sidney apparently collects business cards; the walls are covered with them. Next door is Harris' Place, a cute little place with gusto-guzzling ice-cold beers and lobster-mania (all you can eat for $29.95) on Mondays and Pig Roast Buffet on Thursdays and Saturdays with live reggae. And across the harbor is Abe's, more of the same with a tiny marina. Before leaving Jost, White Bay to the west offers a quiet, secluded spot with a beautiful beach to help ease you out of your hangover. The same goes for Sandy Cay, a small, deserted island with trails and plenty of privacy for nude sunbathing (if there are no other boats).

Just to the east of Sandy Cay is Cane Garden Bay on Tortola, with its gorgeous palmed beach, the old Caldwell Distillery where you can imbibe a wicked rum (if they feel like opening), and Stanley Hodge's Welcome Bar & Restaurant—one of the best bars in the Caribbean. At Stanley's, you can pig out on the lobster, get bombed on the one-two punch, and dance barefoot on the beach to the steel band. Before you leave, make sure you buy a T-shirt with its trademark tire on a rope. Also be sure to visit the Rhymer complex, including Rhymer's and Quito's. Both have happy-hour specials. Keep an eye out for Rastas, they sell "magic" mushrooms to help you laugh the night away.

THE SAILING TROUSSEAU

While the emphasis on sailing is "less is more," there are a few items that the wise crew member should stow away in his or her duffel bag before leaving home. Generally, a bathing suit (at times optional) and a T-shirt are all you'll need. But there are a few other things you should think about packing. Periodically, sunny skies become mean, and ominous-looking clouds can drop a torrent of cool water on you after you've just lotioned up. For these occasions, and for when the seas are sizable and the going gets wet and rough, the items below will be much appreciated.

• FOUL-WEATHER JACKET—Even though the water temperature hovers around 80 degrees year round, the combination of cool rain, constant spray, and gusty winds can be bone-chilling. Foul-weather gear—the lighter the weight the better—keeps you dry, doubles as a windbreaker, and looks great in pictures. Some boats may provide this, so ask ahead of time.

• WATERPROOF SUNSCREEN—You'll be in and out of the water so much that this will save you a lot of effort. Don't use suntan oils—they get all over the boat, smudging and smearing everything in sight.

• TRANSDERM—This antiseasickness medicine is a miracle of modern science. Worn as a small circular Band-Aid behind your ear, it releases a drug through the skin that essentially dulls the nerve endings in the inner ear—the area that motion effects. It doesn't make you as drowsy as Dramamine and other oral medications and lasts for three days.

• TWO PAIRS OF BOAT SHOES—One invariably is wet so if you like dry feet bring an extra pair.

• MUSIC—Almost all of the crewed boats have decent sound systems but not a preferred selection of good party tapes. And some of the smaller bareboats don't even have a sound system. As dancing on the deck can be great fun, a boom box, a Walkman or CD player with portable speakers will do the trick. Get a hold of the *Jaws* soundtrack and play it loud while others are having a late-night skinny dip.

- CAMCORDER—A video memory of your cruise will be treasured forever. The antics of a loved one struggling with the winch or helm will provide infinite pleasure.

- WATERPROOF TROPICAL REEF GUIDE—A laminated card or small book attached to your suit that allows you to know what those pretty fish are called.

- A HAT AND/OR VISOR—Common sense dictates this.

WHERE TO STAY

If you don't plan to be on a boat, there are plenty of options for you in the BVIs. On Tortola, most people stay on the island's pretty west coast. Here you'll find the LONG BAY BEACH RESORT, (800) 729-9599/(809) 495-4252, fax (809) 495-4677, a 62-room complete resort on Tortola's best beach; rates are VERY PRICEY to OUTRAGEOUS (EP). Up the coast on Apple Bay is SEBASTIAN'S ON THE BEACH, (800) 336-4870/(809) 495-4212, an attractive surfer hangout (the surf here is the best in the Virgin Islands); rates are PRICEY to VERY PRICEY (EP). In Little Apple Bay, there is THE SUGAR MILL HOTEL, (800) 462-8834/(809) 495-4355, fax (809) 495-4696, a bungalow hotel on the beach carved out of the ruins of an old plantation; rates are VERY PRICEY to WICKED PRICEY (EP). If you need to be by the airport, BEEF ISLAND GUEST HOUSE, (809) 495-2303, is on the beach and very comfortable; rates are PRICEY (CP).

Virgin Gorda has several deluxe resorts, including LITTLE DIX BAY HOTEL, (800) 223-7637/(809) 495-5555, fax (809) 495-5661, as a Rockresort with the same subtle elegance as Caneel Bay; rates are OUTRAGEOUS to BEYOND BELIEF (EP). The BITTER END YACHT CLUB, (800) 872-2392/(809) 494-2746, fax (809) 494-4756, is a full-service resort located on North Sound which now includes the former Tradewinds complex; rates are RIDICULOUS to OUTRAGEOUS (FAP). BIRAS CREEK ESTATE in my opinion needs a facelift, so skip it this time. DRAKE'S ANCHORAGE, (800) 624-6651/(809) 494-2254, fax (809) 494-2254, on Mosquito Island is a wonderfully romantic place with private cottages and an island to yourself—I highly recommend it; rates are WICKED PRICEY to OUTRAGEOUS (AP).

Moving down the island chain, the PETER ISLAND YACHT CLUB, (800) 323-7500/(809) 494-2561, fax (809) 494-2313, is a luxury resort and not a yacht club. It IS Peter Island, there is nothing else on this 1,800-acre island; rates are RIDICULOUS to OUTRAGEOUS (EP). The GUANA ISLAND CLUB, (800) 554-8262/(809) 494-2354, has its own island too and is a *very* remote and *very* expensive private spot; rates are BEYOND BELIEF (AP). Jost Van Dyke has SANDY GROUND ESTATES, (809) 494-3391, fax (809) 495-9379, eight deluxe villas in a remote location on the eastern end of the island available for weekly rental at $1,200 double per week. Also on Jost is the SANDCASTLE HOTEL in White Bay, (809) 771-1611, fax (809) 775-5262, a four-cottage beach hotel on a deserted beach; rates are WICKED PRICEY (FAP). Finally, there's Anegada, a low-lying coral island off Tortola with *phenomenal beaches* out on its own. It has the pleasant and isolated ANEGADA REEFS HOTEL, (809) 495-8002, fax (809) 495-9362, with twelve rooms; rates are VERY PRICEY to WICKED PRICEY (AP).

DON'T MISS

A FULL-MOON PARTY AT THE BOMBA SHACK—Located in Cappoon's Bay on Tortola, this is Tortola's best reggae club and the site of the monthly Full-Moon Party, an event that draws people from as far as Antigua. It starts at 6 P.M. and ends at 6 A.M. the next day. Call 495-4148 for more details.

A DRINK AT: Sky World, Tortola (sunset cocktails); the Thornton, Norman Island; Pirate's Pub, Saba Rock, Virgin Gorda; Foxy's, Jost Van Dyke.

DINNER AT DRAKE'S ANCHORAGE—It's très romantic.

CARRIACOU

TOURISTO SCALE 📷📷📷 3

A friend of mine told me once that just as her plane touched down on Carriacou, it suddenly lifted up with jarring swiftness. When she looked out the window, she saw a cow on the runway.

That's Carriacou. It's on its own wavelength. Everyone—and everything—moves at it's own pace, as did the runway keeper. If you're an efficiency freak or into deluxe accommodations, this island isn't for you. What makes Carriacou special—besides its natural beauty—is a special sense of detachment and the resulting preservation of some unique African/Caribbean customs. Regrettably, tourism has begun to intrude in the last few years; a few of the smaller cruise ships now stop here regularly, and several guest houses are being built in and around Hillsborough. But at this writing you can still get away from it all on Carriacou. There are enough people around to keep your sensibilities alive, and yet a mind-your-own-business philosophy bred by the big business of smuggling allows you to socialize only when you want to. There are few activities designed for tourists.

Located 20 miles north of Grenada, Carriacou is the largest of the Grenadine chain—but it's still pretty small at 8 miles long, 5 miles wide, and with only 6,000 inhabitants, most of them in the main town of Hillsborough. It gets extremely dry, almost parched, as the winter progresses. It then begins to look like autumn in New England—give or take a few palm trees and other tropical props. There are several uninhabited "satellite islands" with gorgeous white sand beaches, although lately the best of these—Palm and White islands—have been overrun by passengers from the cruise ships on certain days of the week.

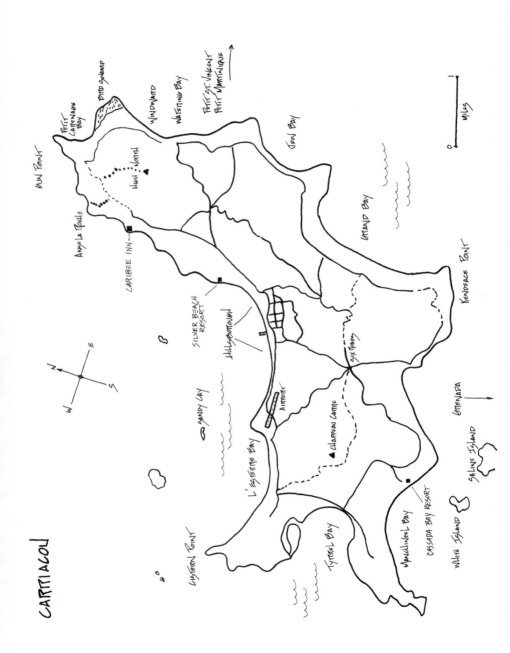

CARRIACOU

THE BRIEFEST HISTORY

Carriacou is part of the country of Grenada, which achieved independence from Great Britain in 1974. During the eighteenth century the island was divided up into estates for raising sugar cane, and the lovely stone ruins of those plantations can be found around the island. The Kayaks (natives of Carriacou) are proud of their African heritage and take pains to preserve it, yet both the English and French colonialists left their marks in ways remarkable for so small an island: most of the inhabitants of the town of Windward bear Scottish names, while those who live only a few miles away in L'Esterre have French names and still maintain a group, led by world-famous artist Canute Caliste, to play and dance the quadrille. Boat-building is still a major occupation, and Carriacou's sloops are among the best in the Caribbean.

CARRIACOU: KEY FACTS

LOCATION	12°N by 61°W
	23 miles northeast of Grenada
	2,175 miles southeast of New York
SIZE	13 square miles
	8 miles long by 5 miles wide
HIGHEST POINT	High North (955 ft.)
POPULATION	6,000
LANGUAGE	English
TIME	Atlantic Standard Time (1 hour ahead of EST, same as EDT)
AREA CODE	809
ELECTRICITY	220/240 volts AC, 50 cycles
CURRENCY	The Eastern Caribbean dollar, EC$ (EC$2.70 = $1 U.S.)
DRIVING	On the *left*; a local permit is needed and will be provided for a charge (about EC$60) with a valid driver's license
DOCUMENTS	Valid passport or proof of nationality (with photo) and an ongoing or return ticket
BEER TO DRINK	Heineken
RUM TO DRINK	Jack Iron
MUSIC TO HEAR	Dancehall

GETTING THERE

There are daily flights from Grenada on LIAT, HELENAIR, and AIRLINES OF CARRIACOU. On Wednesdays and Saturdays wooden schooners (*Alexia II* and *Adelaide*) come up from St. George's, taking about four hours.

GETTING AROUND

From early morning to sundown buses (minivans, in reality) criss-cross the island for EC$1 or EC$2. The drivers will be more than happy to throw out all the other passengers and charge you EC$10 or EC$15 for a "private taxi." For special and nighttime trips you will have to go private; we always use "Danny Boy."

FOCUS ON CARRIACOU: WALKING

The northern and eastern sides of the island are almost entirely uninhabited and traversed by an old plantation road. Spectacular views, eighteenth-century stone ruins, secluded beaches, and solitude will be your reward for braving the tropical sun and heat. Bring along plenty of water and some sandwiches and pastries from the bakery in Hillsborough. Should you decide to bushwack, following the cow pastures down the hillsides and into the woods, and then come upon a mysterious cultivated field of wacky weed, it is definitely *not* a good idea to explore further in that particular direction or to accost any mysterious passersby to inquire about local agricultural practices.

WALK 1—Anse la Roche (half to full day)

Take the road north out of Hillsborough to Bogles. At the end of Bogles take the dirt branch to the left, which climbs up past the Caribbee Inn (formerly the Prospect Lodge). Continue on this James Taylor country road shaded by manchineel trees until you come to a large tree on the right leaning out over the road. Take the cowpath to the left through the woods past calabash trees to the ruins of an old plantation. In front is a huge sloping pasture that opens out to a magnificent vista with Union Island looming in the distance. This view is so enjoyable you may not want to proceed further, but by all means do. Follow the trail down to the right until you reach a black rock with a shell on top; then take the steep path down the hill and into the woods again until you get to the beach. It is usually deserted, or with only a few people from the Caribbee or from boats. Snorkeling is good along the rocks on the north (far) end, but save some energy for the hot climb back up.

WALK 2—Windward (half to full day)

You can continue past the cutoff to Anse la Roche on the same plantation road around High North to Gun Point, and Petit Caren-age Bay, where there is a very nice deserted beach and reef for snorkeling. At the right end of the beach is a mangrove swamp called the "bird swamp." Directly across the bay is Petit St. Vin-cent—better known as PSV—the "trop chic et cher" resort on its own island and Petit Martinique. The latter is part of Grenada's Grenadines, although its residents hardly think so. It supposedly has a much higher standard of living than its neighbors due to its proudly held position as the smuggling capital of the West Indies. It is common to see Carriacou-built trading boats laden with VCRs and French wine. Forget St. Thomas, Petit Martinique is where the *real* bargains can be found—although recently the government in Grenada has been trying to crack down. Supposedly there is a guest house on Petit Martinique, but nobody I know has stayed there; if you manage to, write and let us know for future editions.

Continuing on your walk, the road leads into Windward. This is still a major West Indian boatbuilding center. Brightly colored wooden boats can be seen everywhere in the Grenadines, and they are particularly photogenic here on the beach, under construction or repair. As mentioned above, most of the residents of Wind-ward are of mixed Scottish and West Indian descent—the Scots came here to build a merchant fleet when Britain ruled the is-lands.

There are several rum shops and minimarkets to get some re-freshment, as it can be very hot and dry in Windward. You can hire a boat here to take you to Petit Martinique or sail up the Grena-dines to the Tobago Cays or Canouan. We had a very good experi-ence sailing with Zev MacLaren on his hand-built boat, the *Sweetheart*. You can get back to Hillsborough by continuing to follow the road around across the island to Bogles.

Walk 3—Grand Bay–Kendeace Point–Sabazan–Six Roads (all day)

This is a serious walk for the more dedicated stroller, but it is well worth the effort. You must take a bus or taxi over to Grand Bay—it is too steep and too far to walk. At the bus stop, walk down to the right until you discover the old plantation road that leads south and then west. You will reach Kendeace Point fairly quickly, but don't bother to bushwack out on the point; instead follow the cowpaths down to the spectacular and totally deserted beach just to the north of the point. As you follow the road around to Sabazan, you won't see a single sign of human habitation, except some old stone ruins. Up on the hill at Sabazan, you'll see some fairly spectacular ruins peeking above the treeline. Getting to them is not as easy as it looks, and is recommended only for the determined archeologist or historian. At Great Breteche Bay, there is a beautiful beach, with a lovely little cove for swimming on the north side, and some weirdly wonderful wind-sculpted trees on the south end. At Dumphries make sure you take the cutoff up to the right past the lime factory ruins to Six Roads or you'll be in for a very long hike indeed. There is a rum shop at Six Roads for refreshment, and at that point you'll be glad to know it is only a short and easy walk back into Hillsborough.

Don't Miss

SANDY CAY—About a half-mile offshore, this tiny island of creamy sand and palm trees offers a beautiful spot for a day's outing. There is also a fantastic reef for snorkeling off the northern end of the cay with huge coral heads and a large variety of fish. Anyone at Silver Beach or the Caribee can arrange for a boat to get you there. Unfortunately, the odds are you won't be alone on the beach. This is a regular pit stop for the yacht and cruise contingent. Try to arrange your trip on a day when no cruise ships are slated to visit.

CANUTE CALISTE—Canute Caliste, the most famous painter in the lower Caribbean, lives in L'Esterre, out past the airport. His folk paintings feature such traditional Kayak subjects as Big Drum, the Quadrille, Carnival, boatbuilding, and fishing—and also such supernatural characters as mermaids and jagluars (Carriacou's version of the vampire). The British publishing firm of Macmillan has even published a book of Caliste's paintings. You'll have no trouble finding his house/gallery—just ask anybody or follow his handpainted signs in L'Esterre. In his nineties, Caliste is very lively, and you will be amply rewarded with tales from Carriacou's daily life and folklore if you take a little time to discuss his paintings with him. You might also want to visit another island painter, Frankie Francis, who lives in L'Esterre and works in Hillsborough at the telephone company. In his twenties, he is as handsome as a movie star and paints charming island scenes.

CARNIVAL—Either because people got too rowdy for the tourists or because there was too much competition from Carnival in Trinidad, Carnival on Grenada was moved to August. But on Carriacou it still takes place during the traditional week before Ash Wednesday. Here it is a lovely and charming small-town celebration with an intricate structure rooted in tradition. Each town spends the weeks preceding making elaborate costumes for their queen (a young woman chosen for looks, talent, and style) and her court, called a band. Each queen and her band illustrate a theme, such as "the solar system" or "back to nature." On the Saturday a week and a half before Ash Wednesday the festivities kick off with a parodistic competition—the choosing of a male "queen" and female "king." The real competition occurs a week later when the genuine Carnival queen and the band of the year are chosen. Other features include a "dirty mas" when everybody gets totally tanked and smears everybody else (including you! Dress accordingly!) with mud and ashes, a "clean mas" when everyone parades around in their Sunday finest, a calypso contest, a parade on Shrove Tuesday, and an extraordinary custom peculiar to Carriacou—the "fighting mas," in which the men dress up as Pierrots and wander around reciting Shakespeare and beating each other with sticks (I'm not kidding). If the thought of Carnival in Brazil or Trinidad has always intimidated you, Carriacou's Carnival is the one for you. The people are warm and welcoming, and if you get tired of celebrating, just get out of Hillsborough.

BIG DRUM—Another custom unique to Carriacou is Big Drum, also known as "nation dances." It is an all-night celebration featuring percussive music that stems from African tribal drumming. There are three drums made of rum kegs and goatskins, and the music is accompanied by a highly intricate and beautiful dance. Big Drum is played at most important island occasions—boat launchings, house blessings, and tombstone dedications, among them. You will be fortunate indeed to be invited to one.

REGATTA—Featuring boat races and even more onshore fun, Regatta is the big hoo-hah of the Grenadines. The racing is really secondary to the drinking and shenanigans characteristic of all Caribbean sailing regattas. It lasts for four days (around the first week of August) and features such frolicking summer-camp activities as greased-pole, tug-of-war, and donkey races. For more information, contact the Grenada Tourist Office, 820 Second Avenue, Suite 900D, New York, NY, 10017, (800) 927-9554/(212) 687-9554, fax (212) 573-9731.

WHERE TO STAY

CARIBBEE INN (809) 443-7380, fax (809) 443-7999
Prospect, Carriacou, Grenada, W.I.

In its former incarnation as the Prospect Lodge, this was everyone's ideal of a Caribbean inn; it was run by the legendary Lee and Ann Katzenbach—artists and hippies—who provided a truly stimulating atmosphere for dirt-cheap prices. The new owners, Robert and Wendy Cooper, have jacked up the prices considerably—but who can blame them? No one could figure out how Ann and Lee were doing it.

The Caribbee still has the best location on Carriacou, perched high over the ocean, in the woods on the island's northern coast. It is just a short walk away from Anse la Roche and a longish, though manageable walk to Hillsborough. The food is excellent, although expensive at $30 U.S. per person for breakfast and dinner. The Coopers—who somehow remind me of pioneers from the days when the sun never set on the empire—have brought their own brand of English charm. Robert is a former London actor and theater manager and is said to arrange impromptu readings of Shakespeare when fellow actors visit. The compound includes two rooms in the main building and two in an adjacent building, which also has an "apartment." The latter has its own pretty terrace and a largely useless kitchen with a noisy icebox. Out back there is a detached "villa."

Rates are PRICEY to VERY PRICEY for doubles.

SILVER BEACH RESORT (809) 443-7337, fax (809) 443-7165
Stateside: (800) 223-9815/(212) 545-8469
Silver Beach, Beauséjour Bay, Carriacou, Grenada, W.I.

This is a West Indian–owned and –run hotel on the northern edge of Hillsborough. It is on the water, but since it is adjacent to the town wharf, it's not a place for swimming. The rooms are comfortable and modern and there are semi-detached efficiency units out back. The food in the restaurant is good and the bar is the place to meet locals. Say hi to Mary and Uvi if you stop by. Recently the place has become affiliated with a German-owned dive shop, so you are apt to find yourself surrounded by fiercely sunburned Aryan blonds in wet suits with lots and lots of extremely complicated, state-of-the-art diving equipment.

Rates are NOT SO CHEAP to PRICEY for doubles and cottages.

CASSADA BAY RESORT (809) 443-7494, fax (809) 443-7672
Belmont, Carriacou, Grenada, W.I.

A former Canadian school for marine biology, Cassada Bay has Carriacou's most spectacular view—on a high hill, looking south to Grenada. The weathered-wood rooms are extremely charming. For swimming they will ferry you over to nearby White Island, a Caribbean idyll, when you're not sharing it with several hundred cruise-ship passengers (this doesn't happen often, though, and they don't stay very long). Cassada Bay is inconveniently located for the rest of the island, however, so this is definitely *not* the place to stay if you plan on attending Carnival because getting back and forth to Hillsborough will be a nightmare. When Mary and Faithina ran the hotel, it was the best place to stay on Carriacou. Recent management shake-ups make it difficult to recommend at this present writing.

Rates are NOT SO CHEAP for doubles.

WHERE TO EAT

Basically you eat at your hotel on Carriacou—especially dinner. In Hillsborough the bakery is a good place to get breakfast or light lunch. TALK OF THE TOWN on Hillsborough Road has delicious, cheap food, but seems to be open for lunch only. CALLALOO looks enticing, but never seemed to be open for any meal, even when we had reservations. The only place you can count on for dinner is the ROOFTOP, which serves excellent chicken or fish and chips after 7 P.M. Before you go anyplace else for dinner, make sure to call first for a reservation (if the place you want to go has a phone!), and arrange transportation to and from, although in Hillsborough you will usually be able to find a taxi. THE GREEN BOULEY, right next to the wharf, is a popular place for drinking and socializing.

GOING OUT

No visit to Carriacou would be complete without a visit to the island's hot spot, the HILLSBOROUGH BAR AND RESTAURANT ([809] 443-7932). You'll know it because it sports Hillsborough's only neon light. The reason for all the excitement is owner/bartender Edward Primus, a bodybuilder who was born in Carriacou but raised in England. Bring your own group to dance on the postage-stamp-sized disco floor. If you are especially nice, Eddie might arrange a private screening of *Soul Man* or make his world-famous West Indian barbecue chicken for you.

CULEBRA

We had just missed the last plane from Fajardo to Culebra. A split-second decision to charter a plane, and off we went on a six-seater Britten Islander. It was a dramatic entrance. But that was nothing compared to what greeted us upon our arrival. Our "limo" was a beat-up old VW van, with no door and two plastic deck chairs for seats. Our hostess was an American woman with twelve children who lived in a trailer where goats came and went through it and had eaten most of the upholstery. Welcome to Culebra—the land of the very laid-back.

Culebra is a small and simple island. Politically part of the Commonwealth of Puerto Rico, it is light-years away from the fast pace of San Juan. Although Spanish is the primary language here, English is spoken everywhere. The main village on the island is Dewey, named for Admiral George Dewey, an American hero of the Spanish-American War. This is where the ferry docks and where the post office and most of the commerce are located. There are only 150 guest/hotel rooms on the island, a few restaurants, and no nightclubs, discos, or casinos. The pace is slow, slow, slow! Overall, one gets the impression that this is what the Caribbean used to be like. Indeed, Culebrans are very covetous of their way of life and are very suspect of any change, or "progress." Their attitude is one of "leave us alone." So far, they've been successful. Actually, Hurricane Hugo in 1989 helped out their cause tremendously by wiping out the flourishing tourist tide both in ruined accommodations and bad publicity.

Culebra is not a lush, verdant island. Rather, it's very dry and brownish. But its star attraction, besides its unspoiledness, is its

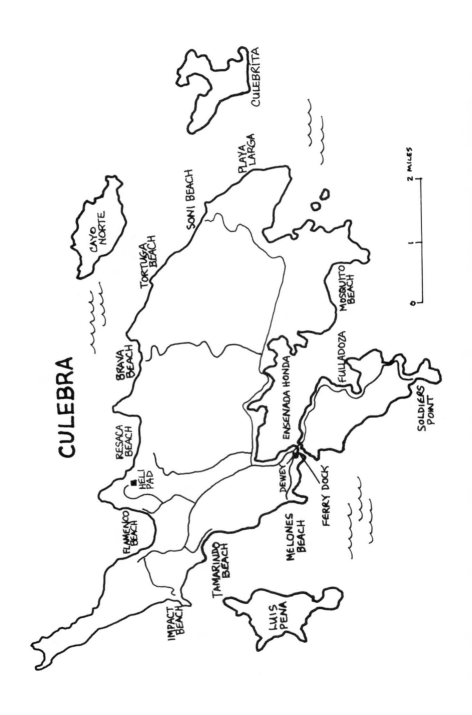

CULEBRA

FLAMENCO BEACH

RESACA BEACH

BRAVA BEACH

CAYO NORTE

TORTUGA BEACH

SONI BEACH

PLAYA LARGA

CULEBRITA

HELI PAD

IMPACT BEACH

TAMARINDO BEACH

LUIS PEÑA

MELONES BEACH

DEWEY

ENSENADA HONDA

FERRY DOCK

FULLADOZA

MOSQUITO BEACH

SOLDIERS POINT

2 MILES

beaches—some of the most beautiful in the Caribbean. One of my
top ten Caribbean beaches, Soni, is here on Culebra. On a busy day,
there may be ten people on this huge stretch of white sand.

Culebra is not for everyone. It's rustic, and if you expect to be
pampered or entertained, forget it, it's not for you. But if you don't
mind simple accommodations, cooking for yourself a lot or eating
at very simple restaurants, and tons of quiet, then you'll love it.
Probably the best analogy is a town somewhere in the boonies—
that's Culebra. It is the Caribbean's best-kept secret—an island
where the pace is that of yesteryear and the beaches are gorgeous.

THE BRIEFEST HISTORY

Culebra was uninhabited by Europeans until the very late date of
1886, when it was settled by the Spanish (it was part of the Spanish
Virgin Islands). It was ceded to the U.S. as part of the settlement of
the Spanish-American War. The U.S. incorporated it in the Commonwealth of Puerto Rico, where it has remained ever since (see
Puerto Rico, pages 309–43).

CULEBRA: KEY FACTS

LOCATION	18°N by 65°W
	17 miles east of Fajardo, Puerto Rico
	12 miles west of St. Thomas
	1,660 miles southeast of New York
SIZE	7 miles long by 3 miles wide
HIGHEST POINT	Mt. Resaca (650 ft.)
POPULATION	1,600
LANGUAGE	Spanish and English
TIME	Atlantic Standard Time (1 hour ahead of EST, same as EDT)
AREA CODE	809
ELECTRICITY	110 volts AC, 60 cycles
CURRENCY	The U.S. dollar
DRIVING	On the *right*; valid driver's license okay
DOCUMENTS	U.S. citizens do not have to have a passport or visa. Canadians should have a passport or proof of citizenship with ID; U.K. visitors need a passport and visa

DEPARTURE TAX   None
BEER TO DRINK   Medalla
RUM TO DRINK   Don Q or Bacardi
MUSIC TO HEAR   Salsa

GETTING THERE

San Juan is the primary gateway to the Caribbean and is AMERI-
CAN's Caribbean hub (see Puerto Rico, "Getting There," p. 314).
From San Juan and Fajardo, FLAMENCO AIRWAYS ([809] 725-
7707 or [809] 863-3366) has regularly scheduled service. ALAS DEL
CARIBE ([809] 742-3777) also has scheduled service from Fajardo.
Both airlines are available for charter flights. If you don't want to
fly, there is ferry service from Fajardo daily. Call (800) 462-2005 or
(809) 863-0705 or (809) 863-0852 for the latest schedules.

GETTING AROUND

As there is virtually no public transit, you'll need a car (or a good
mountain bike) to get to the best beaches and the grocery store.
There are no major rental companies here, but there are several
people and outfits who do rent cars. Try PRESTIGE CAR
RENTAL ([809] 742-3546) or CULEBRA CAR RENTAL ([809]
742-3277). For bikes, try DICK & CATHY ([809] 742-0062); JU-
NIOR'S ([809] 742-3372); or LA LOMA ([809] 742-3565).

FOCUS ON CULEBRA: THE BEACHES

For such a small island, there are some amazing beaches on Culebra.
The lack of development here has saved most of them too from the
usual Caribbean resort blight. Two of the beaches, Resaca and
Brava, are nesting sites for leatherback turtles and are off-limits
from April 1 to August 30. They are also hard to get to (the best way
is by boat). Since shade is minimal at all Culebra beaches, *be sure to
bring a beach umbrella* so you don't get burned to a crisp.

The best beach on the island is Soni, at the eastern end of the
island. It is a wide stretch of wide sand with calm surf and no

people. There are great views of the islets of Culebrita and Cayo Norte across the bay, and, far in the distance, St. Thomas. To get there, take the eastern road as far as it will go. You will see cars parked where the road gets really bad. Park here, and walk the remaining 100 yards down to the beach. There are no facilities at the beach, so be sure to bring water.

The most popular beach, especially with day-trippers from Puerto Rico, is Flamenco. A two-mile arc of white sand, this is also a beautiful beach (although I think Soni is prettier). At the parking area, there are restrooms and picnic tables. If you walk to the left, you'll come to a very secluded part of the beach—especially if you go around the rocky/corally point. Here people camp out for free and for long periods of time in the Hugo-destroyed remnants of an old army post. We met a woman from Massachusetts who was camping for a month. There are no facilities, but she loved it. While this is not officially sanctioned, camping here seems to be tolerated. To get to Flamenco, take the road that passes the airport (the runway will be on your right) and follow it to the end.

Other beaches to explore on the island are Tamarindo (rocky), Impact Beach (great snorkeling), and Tortuga Beach (very private). There is also a wonderful little beach on the islet of Luis Peña and two gorgeous beaches on Culebrita. The latter can easily be reached by hiring a boat (*Muff the Magic Fun Boat*—talk to Jack or Pat [809] 742-3516).

WHERE TO STAY

Ah, there aren't many options here. In Dewey, there are three guest houses, Posada La Hamaca, Mamacita's, and Villa Fulladoza. There are several condos/villa properties which may be the best way to go since you'll have a kitchen. One place to avoid is Club Seaborne, where the service I received was rude and nonexistent.

POSADA LA HAMACA (809) 742-3516
P.O. Box 388, Culebra, PR 00775

Located right in Dewey on the canal by the drawbridge, this wonderfully clean and comfortable guest house is the best in-town accommodation. Situated in a simple Spanish-style house, there are six double rooms and three efficiency units (i.e., with kitchenettes/

kitchens). Each room has a private bath and ceiling fan. But the best thing about Posada La Hamaca are the managers, Pat and Jack, who are very friendly and helpful and seem to know more about the island than anyone else.

Rates are CHEAP to NOT SO CHEAP for singles and doubles (EP).

MAMACITA'S GUEST HOUSE (809) 742-0090
P.O. Box 818, Culebra, PR 00775

This is a small guest house located right next door to Posada La Hamaca. Mamacita's is also *the* place to have breakfast on Culebra. There are only three rooms, located above the restaurant in renovated and decked spaces. The room on the top floor has the best views, including a sweeping vista of the harbor. All rooms have private baths, lanais, and ceiling fans.

Rates are CHEAP to NOT SO CHEAP for singles and doubles (EP).

VILLA FULLADOZA (809) 742-3576
P.O. Box 162, Culebra, PR 00645-0162

Situated right on the water with nice views of Enseñada Honda, this is an interesting and somewhat eclectically decorated apartment complex within a ten-minute walk of town. Each unit has a kitchenette and private bath. There are a boat dock and moorings available to those who have boats.

Rates are CHEAP to NOT SO CHEAP for singles and doubles (EP).

BAYVIEW VILLAS (809) 742-3392
Culebra, PR 00775-0775

Situated on a hill overlooking Enseñada Honda and within walking distance of town, these are the best villa accommodations on the island. Units are multileveled, with lots of Brazilian hardwood, sloped ceilings, large windows, and tiled floors. The fully equipped kitchens have a dishwasher, a gas grill, and a clothes washer. The baths are spacious and tiled, and ceiling fans keep the breeze moving should the trades die down. Each unit has a large deck with hammocks and chaises.

Rates are NOT SO CHEAP TO PRICEY for singles and doubles (EP).

HARBOR VIEW VILLAS (809) 742-3855
P.O. Box 216, Culebra, PR 00775

These rather space-age–looking villas-on-stilts sit just outside of Dewey on the road to Melones Beach. Large lanais, lots of wood, high ceilings, big windows and French doors, and views of Bahía de Sardinas are the main features here. There are fully equipped kitchens and air-conditioned suites.

Rates are NOT SO CHEAP to PRICEY for singles and doubles (EP).

WHERE TO EAT

The choices here are slim. For breakfast, it's MAMACITA'S (742-0090). For lunch, try the CAFE CULEBRA. For dinner, it's the DINGHY DOCK BARBEQUE on Friday and Saturday nights, or EL BATEY (742-3828) or the HAPPY LANDING. The best idea is to cook your own meals. Avoid Club Seabourne, as it took me a half an hour to get a drink AT THE BAR, and there weren't many people there.

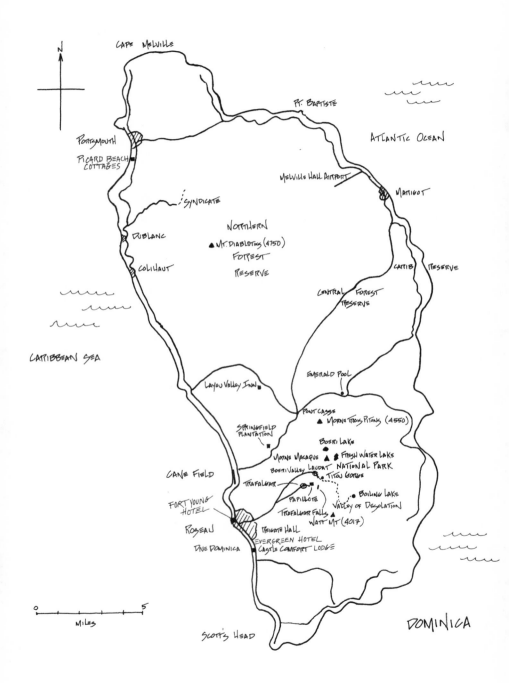

DOMINICA

Everyone here has a hurricane story. On August 29, 1979, a mega-tempest named David pummeled the southern half of Dominica for six hours. Winds up to 200 mph left 40 dead, 60,000 homeless (that's 80 percent of the island's population), and removed up to six feet of topsoil in places. It was total devastation. But a visitor today would be hard-pressed to see any signs of this.

That's because everything grows in Dominica. This is the lushest, most verdant island in the Caribbean. When David wiped out square miles of trees, Nature grew back at a rate that is hard to believe. We're talking full-grown vegetation, not saplings or up-starts. What nature couldn't restore was replenished by aid from the U.S., France, Venezuela, and other countries. Housing was replaced and roads rebuilt—many are in better shape than before the hurricane.

Much of Dominica (pronounced Dom-in-ee-ka) is rain forest. Its volcanic, mountainous topography traps moisture from the trade winds and converts it into 200 to 300 inches of rain a year. The color green takes on a whole new meaning here, with so many shades it puts even Ireland to shame. Dominica does have beaches, but is not for beach freaks. The beaches here are mostly of the black-sand variety and the prettiest are on the windward side and have dangerous undertows. Quite frankly, there are better beaches on other islands. Dominica's unique beauty is in its mountains. This is where the rain forest thrives, where waterfalls and thermal springs abound, and where walking and hiking are the best in the Caribbean.

Dominica is for nature lovers, those who like being in the rain forest; who like hiking in wilderness areas; or who like the idea of lush, leafy thickets, raging rivers, waterfalls, hot springs, and so on. If you want big resorts, forget Dominica. The people who come here like nature and simple things. Room service is not an m.o. here; splashing around in the sulfur pools is. Get the picture?

Dominica is also quintessentially West Indian. Roseau, the capital, is not pretty, cute, or charming. Rather, it's hot, crowded, and fairly clean—with architecture that is more functional than attractive. This is part of its special character and is decidedly Caribbean. Roseau is very market-oriented, geared to satisfy the needs of islanders not tourists. This is particularly refreshing, as is the friendliness and openness of its people, especially those in the small mountain villages.

I am concerned for Dominica, however. In an effort to increase tourism, the government is openly courting the cruise-ship business. This is a misdirected effort in my opinion. All cruise passengers do is buy T-shirts and ice-cream cones, and use the bathrooms. At the same time, the government has been slowly ruining some of the primary natural tourist attractions as part of its hydroelectric development program. This is a crime. Energies should be spent on the wonderful natural splendor of the island and how to *preserve it*. Many of the things that made me love this place six years ago have been spoiled, like the Titou Gorge and the Fresh Water Lake, all due to the hydroelectric projects, which don't seem to work and are far less cost effective than importing oil. Come on, Dominica, get it together.

THE BRIEFEST HISTORY

Dominica was first settled by Indians from South America in 3000 B.C., later by the Arawaks, and finally the Caribs. Columbus sighted the island in 1493 on his second voyage and named it Dominica (Spanish for Sunday Island). Unfortunately, his brother Diego gave the same name to part of the island of Hispaniola at about the same time (no faxes or cellular phones available then to avoid such a faux pas), so there has been 500 years of confusion since. Officially, Dominica is called the Commonwealth of Dominica, whereas the Spanish country on Hispaniola is called the Dominican Republic. Mail is always getting mixed up, as well as the true identity of those who call themselves Dominican. Since Columbus, the French settled the island, imported slaves from West Africa and eventually ceded things over to the British. Independence was granted in 1978 and today Dominica is a member of the Commonwealth of Nations and is governed by a prime minister, currently Mrs. Eugenia Charles.

DOMINICA: KEY FACTS

LOCATION	15°N by 61°W
	30 miles south of Guadeloupe
	26 miles north of Martinique
	1,924 miles southeast of New York
SIZE	300 square miles
	29 miles long by 16 miles wide
HIGHEST POINT	Morne Diablotin (4,747 ft.)
POPULATION	75,000
LANGUAGE	English
TIME	Atlantic Standard Time (1 hour ahead of EST, same as EDT)
AREA CODE	809
ELECTRICITY	220 to 240 volts AC, 50 cycles, so both adapters and transformers are needed for U.S.-made appliances
CURRENCY	Eastern Caribbean dollar, EC$ (EC$270 = $1 U.S.)
DRIVING	On the *left*; a local permit is needed with your valid drivers license—$12 U.S.
DOCUMENTS	U.S. and Canadian citizens must have proof of citizenship, such as a passport or a voter registration card or birth certificate and a photo ID, plus an ongoing or return ticket
BEER TO DRINK	Carib
RUM TO DRINK	Macoucherie
MUSIC TO HEAR	Dancehall

FOCUS ON DOMINICA—NATURE

There are several ways to enjoy the natural splendor of Dominica. If you aren't terribly mobile, you can traverse the island by car and get a sense of the rain forest. You can hang out at Papillote (see

"Where to Stay" below) and sip Cuthbert's killer rum punch while you soak up the gardens and hot springs around you. Or you can hike, which for me is the only way to really experience Dominica. It's simple, it doesn't cost much (a taxi ride to the trailhead, a guide if necessary) and brings you up close and personal with the natural forces of Dominica. So bring a good pair of hiking sneakers/shoes (ones that can and will get muddy and wet), and choose among the following hikes.

TRAFALGAR FALLS

Located about 25 minutes due east from Roseau, up a fairly rough road and virtually next door to Papillote, Trafalgar Falls is a series of *huge*, narrow, vertical waterfalls. A 20-minute walk and a moderately easy rock scramble will bring you to the base of "Papa" falls ("Mama" is the medium-sized one on the right and "Baby" is the smallest one way up on the left). You'll need to ford the river once, which, at the right place, is wet but not difficult. (Remember, if it's raining hard, the river rises swiftly, so be advised.) Once at the base of "Papa," you can carefully slip into a pool of cool mountain water and work your way against a slight current to the left of the falls. Here you'll see mustard-orange–colored rocks, which is where the hot springs flow into the stream. Maneuver your way under this water—it's not too hot—and enjoy a natural Jacuzzi. The farther up you climb, the hotter it gets. Basking in hot water, while tons of water gush and tumble by five feet away, you'll think you've found a bit of heaven. Before you leave Papillote, you will be asked a dozen times if you want a guide to the falls. You don't need one. There's a trail leading up to it, though you will come to the stream and think you've come to a dead end. You haven't—just ford the stream and follow the rocks and "path" to the left. You'll have to climb a little, but it's not very hard. Unfortunately, the beauty of the falls and their proximity to Roseau and Papillote's restaurant have made this destination popular with tourists. Best advice: Go early in the morning or late afternoon (light's best then, too) for more solitude and privacy.

THE BOILING LAKE

Trafalgar Falls is really just kid's stuff. The real hiking is farther up the valley. Here you'll find Caribbean wilderness in the National Park. There are several hikes that should appeal to serious walkers.

The best is the hike through the Valley of Desolation to the Boiling Lake. It sounds Dante-esque and indeed there are places along the way that seem right out of the *Inferno.* But there are also intensely green mountains, lush rain forest, and fabulous vistas that take you through several climate zones in one day. If you only have one hike in you, do this one. It's very strenuous, as you'll be walking for at least six hours at a fast pace. But if you are in decent shape, you'll never forget the hike. There aren't cliff faces to climb—just several mountains to go up and down. The trail is very narrow and can get very muddy, so the going can be tricky. You won't recognize your Reeboks after this one—hiking boots are better.

You will need a guide for this hike. While the trail can be followed, it's just too long and isolated to risk getting disoriented. A guide will cost about EC$80–$100 (about $35–$40 U.S.) and can be found in the villages of Laudat and Trafalgar. Two guides who are particularly good are Irvin and Kerwin Charles from Trafalgar—they can be reached by contacting Papillote.

You must bring water. I recommend at least a 1.5-liter plastic container of Eau Erté (available at any store in Dominica) per person. Also take along some high-energy food to replace the thousands of calories (wishful thinking) that it feels like you're burning. The starting point for the Boiling Lake hike is the village of Laudat. This is about as high and as close to the park as you can go. From here you will have stunning views of Trafalgar all the way down to Roseau and the sea. It's also a very scenic twist-and-shout drive up to this pretty little spot. (You'll want to be driven, as you'll need your strength for the walk ahead.) You used to have to hike in from Laudat and balance-beam your way along an aqueduct to the Titou Gorge. Now you just drive right up to the Gorge. You can park here (leave no valuables in the car, of course) or be dropped off here by the taxi (MAKE SURE to arrange a pickup time—about seven to eight hours later—your guide will be the best judge so defer to his wisdom).

Just before the gorge there is a trail of stone steps going up to the right. This is the trailhead to the Boiling Lake. Once you leave the gorge it's a pretty steady uphill climb, not terribly difficult but very steady. At this point, the trail is in good shape and fairly clear—some roots and rocks to step over but it's obvious it has been well trodden. After about forty-five minutes of this you will arrive at what is called the "Breakfast River" by the locals (so named because

it's a good place to rest and fuel up. The hard stuff begins on the
other side). Here is where you will hear the mountain siffleur—one
of the most exotic-sounding birds I've ever heard—which only lives
at these elevations. A tiny, grayish-blue bird that's almost impossible to see, it trills a beautiful, symphonic five-note song that ends
on a high note.

After the pit stop, get ready to climb stairs for the next hour. It's
a very steep trek up a narrow trail to the summit. This ascent/
descent is the real kicker in the hike—and you have to do it twice!
You will arrive at the top dripping with sweat, only to almost suffer
hypothermia from the stiff breeze. The view is reminiscent of vistas
afforded by the Rockies or Cascades, except that the ocean in the
distance is that incredible light blue. Now you're ready to go down
into the Valley of Desolation (sounds like a Joni Mitchell song).
The descent is slow, muddy, and slippery. But when you look up,
the view is unbelievable: a massive green sweep of valley with high,
jagged mountain peaks and thermal vents sending wisps of steam
into the air. Off in the distance and hidden by a peak, the Boiling
Lake's giant caldron bubbles away, sending a huge plume of white
vapor several hundred feet into the air. The wonderfully fragrant
smell of sulphur is everywhere. Talk about sensory overload!

Once in the valley, you'll go along a rocky river bed with a
hot-water stream flowing down it. The color of the water will
change as you get farther into the valley (due to the mineral content
and how it has stained the rock below). You'll see water that's
black, gray, white, green, and light blue. Where it's open to the sky
and elements, it's cool and breezy. But at the bottom, the vegetation
is dense and it's hot and humid.

When you finally reach the Boiling Lake, after a few more ups,
downs, and a traverse across a rock-strewn slope, you will feel very
remote and isolated. You *are*. The lake itself is situated in a crater.
It's fairly large, about 100 yards across, and very round. It is the
second largest of its type in the world (the biggest is in New Zea-
land). The water is a milky white and it *is* boiling. The rising steam
combines with the cool ocean breeze to create a warm mist that
envelops you. This is a good spot to rest and eat lunch, but don't
get *too* comfortable because it's an equally long and arduous hike
back.

To cool off once you've begun the return journey, take a dip in
the first stream you encounter. There are several warm-water pools
upstream of light blue warm water (from the mix of minerals) with

little waterfalls and other touches of Nature's kitsch that make swimming very pleasant. Since it's unlikely you'll encounter anyone, whip off your clothes for a fun skinny-dip and splash around.

You return to Laudat the same way you came. But the different perspective allows you to see things you might have missed before. One thing you will definitely notice is the fatigue in your legs, so take it slow and hit the brakes. The descent down the muddy trails can be treacherous. But you have the Titou Gorge to look forward to—a wonderful reward for a hard day's work.

The Titou Gorge lies at the base of the trail and used to go almost unnoticed before they put in the road and parking lot. Progress marches on. Far worse than these additions is the tampering with water levels in the gorge by the hydroelectric company in order to power the turbines. It used to be a guaranteed beautiful experience. Now it all depends on the whims of the company. That said, hopefully you will encounter something wonderful. Assuming this, jump into the cool-but-oh-so-very-refreshing-after-walking-and-sweating-for-seven-hours water and swim into the gorge. What you see at water level is truly beautiful. Deep-light-blue or medium-green water—depending on the amount of sunlight—rock walls that rise up at least 50 feet creating natural halls and chambers, and a roaring waterfall at the gorge's end. Unfortunately, this fall is hard to photograph unless you have a waterproof camera or play water-polo and are used to propelling yourself upright with your feet. The waterfall does create a strong current, particularly as you get closer to it. Once you enter the waterfall room, it's fun to walk up the right side of it about five feet—it's not at all difficult—and sit behind the fall in the space Mother Nature has thoughtfully provided. The vantage point here is one of total hydration—memorize it for the next time you're stuck on a rush-hour subway in mid-July. Swimming out is anti-climactic, so I turned around and made a second approach—it's pretty difficult to get tired of this one.

OTHER OPTIONS

There are several other hikes in the National Park as well as in the National Forest Reserve in the north of the island. In the National Park, an easier walk than the Boiling Lake journey will take you along a road to the Fresh Water Lake, a once pristine and very tranquil lake that was swimmable, but is now a reservoir. For those who would rather let their fingers do the driving, a four-wheel-drive vehicle like a Suzuki Samarai (which are available all over the Carib-

bean) can take you right up to the lake. A little more remote is the
Boeri Lake, where the water is very heavy and hard to swim in. The
Boeri Valley, downstream from the lake, is still an essentially uninhabited wilderness area that's ideal for orienteering and bushwack-
ing. Before attempting it, check with the Forestry Department to
make sure you won't get lost for days. Fortunately, there is nothing
poisonous on Dominica to worry about. The Boeri Valley can be
reached by a forty-five-minute climb from the Middleham Falls to
Stinking Hole. This window to the Boeri Valley is located about
halfway between the junction of the Laudat–Trafalgar road and
Laudat. It is now well marked and maintained.

To the north of the island, the National Reserve offers hiking up
Dominica's highest mountain, Morne Diablotin (4,747 ft.). The
trailhead begins in Syndicate, which is also the place to view the
imperial parrot (also known as the Sisserou) and the red-necked
parrot. There aren't many of these species left and the ones that are
are protected and under study by a team of British birders. Fortunately, their efforts seem to be helping as the parrots seem to be on
the rebound. The birders have built a viewing platform over a gorge
that should only be scaled by those with no fear of heights (it's
precariously perched on a tree that leans several hundred feet over
the gorge). The best time to see the birds is early in the morning or
around dusk. They are loud squawkers so you will be able to tell
them from other large birds. To reach the viewing area and the trail
to Morne Diablotin, take the west coast road north from Roseau.
Go four miles north of the town of Colihaut. As you pass a school
on your left and then, just around a bend, a white house with red
trim, take a sharp right and follow this road until you come to a
grapefruit orchard on your right (there will be a small house on the
left). Turn left on the dirt road and right again at the next junction.
You are now on a banana plantation road that borders the National
Forest Reserve. Go for about one-half mile until you pass a tiny
concrete bridge and a little banana shed on the left just beyond the
bridge. Park your car before the bridge and well out of the way of
the occasional banana trucks that pass by. Walk past the shed for
about 300 yards until the road bends to the left. At this point you
will notice a trail on the right through banana trees. This will lead
you to the parrot viewpoint and the trail to Morne Diablotin.
When you're on this trail for about ten minutes, you will notice a
trail on the right—this is the trailhead to Morne Diablotin. Continuing straight for another ten minutes, you will reach the gorge and
the small platform for the parrots. There are plans to build an

information center about the birds and the Forest Reserve, which will make finding your way around a lot easier. It is both a good idea and island etiquette to contact the Forestry Department before venturing inland. They also have detailed maps and information that are very helpful. They can be reached by phoning 448-2401 or stopping by at their headquarters in the Roseau Botanical Gardens.

Finally, there are the sulphur springs at Wotten Waven (sounds like Baba Wawa). These are a short taxi ride from either Papillote or Roseau and an equally short (thirty-minute, if that) walk to the springs. They can be muddy, so be prepared. And remember that sulphur smells a lot like hard-boiled eggs.

AUGUST 29, 1979

No one has a better hurricane story than Anne Gray Jean-Baptiste, the owner (along with husband Cuthbert) of Papillote—a very simple and naturalist accommodation surrounded by waterfalls in the mountains east of the island's capital, Roseau. When hurricane David struck, Anne was two weeks away from opening a supper club—one of four buildings on her property. Reports indicated a severe hurricane was expected to make landfall on Martinique or St. Lucia, Dominica's neighbors to the south. But around nine A.M., the winds began to roar. As Anne and Cuthbert were listening to the latest update, the roof blew off. Within an hour, all four buildings were leveled. The Jean-Baptistes found themselves lying in two inches of water under a crawl space created by the collapsed roof and the only remaining upright wall. To make matters worse, dozens of help-less baby bats from the eaves were screaming and drowning in the water. Because Papillote is located high up at the rear of a box canyon, all during the hurricane the winds bouncing off the canyon walls created periodic tornados that literally tore up the valley. Each time one hit, the cracks in the remaining wall grew wider and longer. Had one more come up the canyon, the wall would have collapsed and it would have been curtains. During those six hours, Anne thought she would never survive. Even after such a harrowing event—and the destruction of every last bit of Papil-lote—Anne found the experience absolutely thrilling. Being subject to the sheer force of nature is one of the risks—rewards—of living in an environ-ment such as this.

GETTING THERE

Dominica is still not the easiest place to reach. Neither of the two airports can accommodate commercial jets (there are plans to enlarge Canefield Airport—the most convenient—for bigger prop planes), so you will have to make connections from San Juan on AMERICAN EAGLE or St. Maarten/Antigua on LIAT. Both LIAT and AMERICAN EAGLE fly from other islands with stops in Dominica. Check with your travel agent if you are coming from another island besides those above. AIR GUADELOUPE flies from the French islands to Dominica and BWIA flies from Antigua and Trinidad. Try to fly into Canefield, as the Melville Hall Airport is way over on the other side of the island. While it's a very scenic drive, it will take you about an hour to an hour and a half to get to Roseau and cost you about $45 U.S. for the taxi. Canefield Airport is only five minutes north of Roseau and will cost you about $8 U.S. for a taxi ride. For the real adventurous, there is a high-speed catamaran ferry between Dominica, Guadeloupe, and Martinique called the *Emeraude Express* operated by CARIBBEAN EXPRESS. It brings you to Roseau from Pointe-à-Pitre, Guadeloupe, or Fort-de-France, Martinique. It is helpful to *parlez français* when choosing this option.

GETTING AROUND

If you want to really explore the island, you should rent a car. There are several outfits on the island to choose from, including BUDGET ([800] 527-0700/[809] 449-2080). Ask your hotel hosts about getting the best deal—they should steer you in the right direction. If you don't feel like driving, you can hire a van to take you around. Again, ask your host—they usually have someone they work with who will give you a fair price. As always, be sure to agree on a price, inclusive of everything, before you go. It is not necessary to tip unless you think your driver really deserves it. One outfit which really has it together is KEN'S HINTERLAND ADVENTURE TOURS ([809] 448-4850 days, 448-3517 eves), with trips to all points on the island and hiking expeditions as well.

WHERE TO STAY

Since the last edition six years ago, the tourist industry has blossomed . . . er, proliferated, with the addition of many new hotels, guest houses, and lodging compounds. Most places to stay are along the west coast of the island around the two major towns, Roseau and Portsmouth. My recommendation is still the same: to stay in the rain forest, which is what makes this island unique. Tops on my list again is Papillote in Trafalgar. With this in mind, my recommendations are as follows:

PAPILLOTE (809) 448-2287, fax (809) 448-2285
Trafalgar Falls Road (P.O. Box 67), Morne Macaque Roseau, Dominica, W.I.

This is still my first choice for those who want to be at one with nature. The place is geared to the outdoors, located high up in the mountains where the air is noticeably cooler. It combines the island's natural beauty with the warmth and friendliness of the locals. Sitting suspensefully under the perfect cone of a dormant volcano known as Morne Macaque, it is truly integrated into its surroundings; from the hot-water springs running through the compound and the painstakingly planned and cultivated botanic gardens to the exotic fowl and the ever-present residents of Trafalgar (the village down the road). The eight rooms are simple and comfortable. With the sound of rushing water everywhere, time here is meant to be spent outdoors. There is a pavilion where meals are served and where it's wonderfully pleasant to sit anytime. Two hot-water pools constructed by a Canadian artist out of indigenous stone feature sculptures of iguanas and fish that spew hot mineral water, which feels orgasmic after a day of hiking. Staying here will also give you a good chance to meet Dominicans from all walks of life, as the Jean-Baptistes are very popular among the locals. Papillote is conveniently located next to a vast wilderness area and the best hikes on the island (Trafalgar Falls are a short 20-minute walk away) and Anne Grey Jean-Baptiste is very enthusiastic about showing plant lovers around. She has also built a separate restaurant and center at the base of the property to steer away the day-tourist traffic from the hotel so they won't interfere with the guests' privacy, a definite plus. Plans are also in place to add another hot-water pool by the guest accommodations. Since you are miles away from the nearest restaurant, the MAP plan makes sense. The food is good West Indian fare and the menu is more varied than before, but the lime delight they serve for dessert is unfortunately still around (I think I'll send them some new dessert recipes!).

Rates are NOT SO CHEAP for singles and PRICEY for doubles (MAP).

LAYOU VALLEY INN (809) 449-6203, fax (809) 448-5212
(P.O. Box 196), Roseau, Dominica, W.I.

Not to be confused with the Layou River Hotel (not recommended), this is a great place for those who want solitude or for "stay-at-home" types. It is really in the middle of the island and, consequently, in the middle of nowhere. It's very clean with several tastefully furnished rooms that have private baths. Sitting 1,500 feet up on the backbone of Dominica, there are great views and access to hiking and nature. Like Papillote, the management is into nature and will help you with hikes, walks, and so on. The cuisine is country French, which makes the Inn very popular with French tourists.

Rates are NOT SO CHEAP for singles and PRICEY for doubles (MAP).

EVERGREEN HOTEL (809) 448-3288, fax (809) 448-6800
(P.O. Box 309), Castle Comfort, Dominica, W.I.

Situated on the beach south of Roseau, this is a highly regarded lodging for those who want to be on the water and have friendly service, clean and comfortable rooms, a swimming pool and diving nearby. There are 16 rooms with air conditioning, cable TV for CNN addicts, private bath, and phone. New waterfront units have just been added with the completion of a new building in front of the old one. The Evergreen's restaurant serves excellent West Indian cuisine.

Rates are NOT SO CHEAP for singles and doubles (MAP).

SPRINGFIELD PLANTATION GUEST HOUSE (809) 449-1401,
   fax (809) 449-2160
(P.O. Box 41), Roseau, Dominica, W.I.

Built in the English colonial style, this hotel features big rooms and antique furnishings. There are nine guest rooms and cottages available to guests, and a river-fed pool. It is located near the entrance to the National Park at an elevation of 1,200 feet, so there are great views and cool, mountain air. Now owned by Clemson University, there can be students visiting and service is known to be spotty, if not totally lacking. The previous owner, an American, gave the property to the university and still lives on the premises. Well into his years, he occasionally descends from his quarters to chat with guests.

Rates are NOT SO CHEAP for singles and doubles (EP).

FORT YOUNG HOTEL (809) 448-5000, fax (809) 448-5006
Victoria Street (P.O. Box 519), Roseau, Dominica, W.I.

This is by far the most deluxe accommodation on the island. It grew from the ruins of Fort Young, which is right in the heart of Roseau on the water. Businesspeople like this hotel because of its proximity to government offices and other commercial establishments, plus its amenities—including room service, air conditioning, CNN and direct-dial phones *in each room*. There are 33 accommodations and all are very comfortable and nicely appointed. While there is no beach, there is an outdoor pool and a restaurant/bar on premises.

Rates are NOT SO CHEAP for singles and PRICEY for doubles (EP).

REIGATE HALL HOTEL (809) 448-4031, fax (809) 448-4034
Mountain Road (P.O. Box 356), Roseau, Dominica, W.I.

Once the *ne-plus-ultra* of Dominica hotels, this resort overlooking Roseau features a pool, sauna, tennis court and gym, along with pleasant rooms carved out of an old plantation house. Recently sold and under new management (the company also purchased the Sissirou Hotel, which is now called the Reigate Waterfront Hotel), Reigate Hall could use a facelift.

Rates are NOT SO CHEAP for singles and doubles (EP).

PICARD BEACH COTTAGES (809) 445-5131, fax (809) 445-5599
(P.O. Box 34, Roseau) Portsmouth, Dominica, W.I.

Located on the beach south of Portsmouth on 16 acres of an old coconut plantation, there are several nicely furnished Caribbean-

style cottages with kitchen, veranda, bedroom, bath, and living/
dining area. This is a great place to be away from it all, on the beach
and yet accessible to the rain forest. There is also a restaurant, Le
Flambeau, on the grounds. The facilities include a pool and a dive
center.

Rates are PRICEY to VERY PRICEY for the cottages (they can
sleep four people).

HUMMINGBIRD INN (809) 449-1042, fax (809) 448-5778
(P.O. Box 20), Roseau, Dominica, W.I.

Situated conveniently close to Canefield Airport and Roseau (each
are five minutes away), this new establishment sits up on a hill
called Morne Daniel and has wonderful views and a quiet, private
setting. It's pleasant, still fresh, and very reasonably priced. Local
and continental cuisine is available.

Rates are CHEAP for singles and CHEAP to NOT SO CHEAP
for doubles (EP).

CASTLE COMFORT LODGE (809) 448-2188, fax (809) 448-6088
(P.O. Box 63, Roseau), Castle Comfort, Dominica, W.I.

Popular with divers because it offers several dive packages, this is
also the home of Dive Dominica (call toll free from the U.S. for
information—[800] 544-7631). It is very informal and a great place
for diver camaraderie. Located on the water south of Roseau,
rooms are basic, are air-conditioned and some have TV.

Rates are NOT SO CHEAP for singles and doubles (MAP). Ask
about packages here if you are a diver.

POINTE BAPTISTE (809) 445-7322
c/o Ms. Geraldine Edwards, Calibishi, Dominica, W.I.

A restored big house and cottage on the north coast just east of
Calibishi, it has both a black- and a white-sand beach. This is a good
alternative for a large group that wants to be on the sea and still have
access to the mountains. You will need a car and should fly into
Melville Hall Airport, not Canefield. The price for the house is
negotiable.

Two other places are worth mentioning. The CHERRY LODGE
([809] 448-2366), located in the heart of Roseau, is old-world, deca-

dent, and brothel-like—a definite trip to another time—and a possibility for those on a tight budget; rates are DIRT CHEAP. The other place, RED ROCK HAVEN ([809] 448-2181, fax [809] 448-5787), offers very nicely appointed one- and two-bedroom chalets with maid service and is in Calibishi Village on the remote northeast corner of the island (where the few white-sand beaches are located). You'll definitely want a car here (be sure to fly into Melville Hall). Rates are NOT SO CHEAP to PRICEY (sleeps four to six).

WHERE TO EAT

In most cases, you will elect to use the MAP plan at your hotel or guest house. But you may want a night out in Roseau, so here are the best choices:

LA ROBE CRÉOLE, 3 Victoria Street, Roseau, 448-2896

Still reputed to be the best restaurant on the island, it is also Dominica's most famous. It's small and attractive, made of gray stone and heavy wood. Their specialties include shrimp in coconut, mountain chicken (frog) in beer batter, land crab, fresh fish, and local squash and pumpkin soups. Service can be slow, but who's in a rush? Reservations are advised. $$$$

THE ORCHARD, corner of King George V and Great George streets, Roseau, 448-3051

A spacious West Indian restaurant with typical Créole cuisine, the Orchard is basically a large room with a high, sloped, squared-off ceiling replete with swirling fans. The menu changes daily but always features a local fish and meat dish. Specialties include vegetarian delights, rôti, callaloo soup, and black pudding. $$

WORLD OF FOOD, Vena's Hotel, 48 Cork St., Roseau, 448-3286

This restaurant should actually be called the World of Créole because of its excellent West Indian cuisine and atmosphere. If you want real local-style specialties—curried goat, rôti, crab backs, conch, and tee-tee-ree—this is the place to go. $ *No credit cards.*

BREAKFAST AND LUNCH ONLY

GUIYAVE, 15 Cork Street, Roseau, 448-2930

This is another typical West Indian–Créole restaurant set on the second floor of an old wood-frame house. It's popular with the business-lunch set, so you know it's good. Guiyave serves a mean rum punch, as well as fresh tropical juices. $$

MOUSE HOLE SNACKETTES, 3 Victoria Street, Roseau, 448-2896

Located downstairs from La Robe Créole and owned by it, this is a great place to get West Indian take-out or a quick lunch. $

DON'T MISS

MAC'S GYM, 10 Old Street, 3rd floor (opposite the Old Market), Roseau, 448-8050

For those of you who just can't let those pecs, bis, and tris go for a week, Mac's is a new facility with free weights, aerobics, instructors, and a health bar.

THE DOMINICAN
REPUBLIC

TOURISTO SCALE   📷 📷 📷 📷 📷   5

Third World—and I don't mean the reggae band—these are the first two words that come to mind as soon as you leave the Customs area of Santo Domingo's Las Américas International Airport. The initial entrance into this country is deceiving. You exit the jetway to a very modern terminal and you think, hmmm, this is pretty nice, although the kids in uniform standing by security—who are no more than ten and whose function is unbeknownst to me—make you wonder. Then, after going through immigration (and paying $10 U.S. for a "tourist card"), you start to hear a din which gets louder and louder. Then you enter the Customs area and you see the reason for all the hubbub—about 100 porters vying for the attention of those leaving Customs. But that is nothing compared to the mass of people waiting for you when you exit through the Customs doors. And then you know, "Wow, I'm in the Third World."

Welcome to the Dominican Republic. As I was walking out the door, an American Airlines flight attendant said to me, "What's a nice white boy like you doing here?" I said, "I'm here on business and I want to be here." He said, "Be very careful, you really will stand out." I replied, "Yeah, well obviously, but not to worry, I'm a veteran Caribbean traveler." "Do you speak Spanish?" he asked. "*Un poco*," I replied. He just gave me a look and was off into the crowd. Oh great, I thought, I haven't been here two minutes and I've already been told to be nervous.

This is a poor country. I mean very poor, so keep that in mind when you walk out the Customs door. It's shocking at first. My hosts kept saying, "You'll get used to it." And to a certain extent

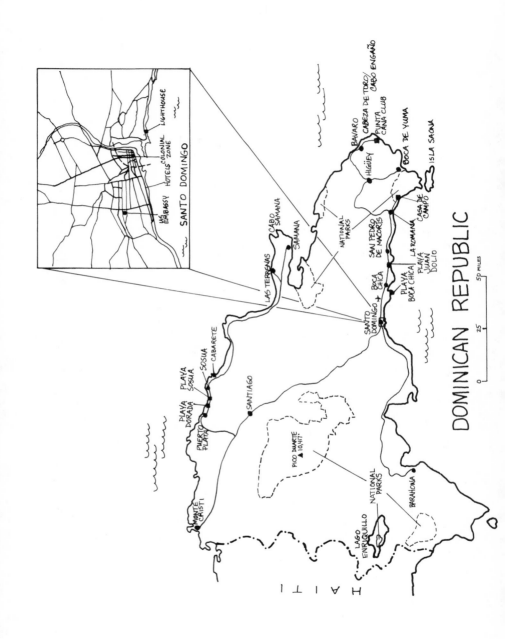

LIGHTHOUSE

COLONIAL ZONE

HOTELS

SANTO DOMINGO

U.S. EMBASSY

CABO SAMANA

SAMANA

LAS TERRENAS

CABARETE

PLAYA SOSUA

SOSUA

PLAYA DORADA

SANTIAGO

PUERTO PLATA

MONTE CRISTI

PICO DUARTE ▲ 10,417'

LAGO ENRIQUILLO

NATIONAL PARKS

BARAHONA

SANTO DOMINGO

BOCA CHICA

PLAYA BOCA CHICA

PLAYA JUAN DOLIO

SAN PEDRO DE MACORIS

LA ROMANA

CASA DE CAMPO

NATIONAL PARKS

HIGÜEY

BAVARO

CABEZA DE TORO/ CABO ENGAÑO

PUNTA CANA CLUB

BOCA DE YUMA

ISLA SAONA

HAITI

DOMINICAN REPUBLIC

0   25   50 MILES

you do—like seeing homeless people on the street in the States, after a while you don't even notice them. Here, when you first see the poverty, it's really a slap in the face. But after a while you see so much of it, you realize that's the way it is. Not that it doesn't bother you, you just don't see it as much.

Most people will come here and stay in a resort and won't leave the grounds. If they do leave they will most likely be on a tour bus, which is fine because there are those who just want to go someplace that has what they want and just stay put. But if you are intrepid (which my readers are, I hope), and want to explore this fascinating and beautiful country, you should rent a car.

Renting a car will be your first venture into what it's like to feel really different, to stand out, as the flight attendant said. You'll marvel at how many people are employed by the rental agency and are just waiting on you (I ended up giving the father of one of them a ride out of the airport, and the only mode of communication was my elementary Spanish and lots of hand gestures). But the most refreshing and wonderful thing you realize as your first impressions are gelling is how friendly and courteous the Dominicans are. They may be mostly poor, but they are polite. The man at the rental desk, his name was Francisco, was very friendly. He shook my hand, which threw me a bit. We Americans are not used to such intimate contact from service people. I would encounter this throughout my stay. Dominicans always shake hands before speaking to you. It's just done.

This is a country of striking contrasts. You can be in a car next to a man and donkey laden down with wares and then walk into a very nice restaurant, which would be at home in New York. You see contrasts like this all the time. Or you can be driving to a resort and will see incredibly poor people living in hovels just outside the entrance and then find yourself in a sumptuous resort with buffet tables loaded with food. It blows you away.

Driving into Santo Domingo on the Avenue of the Americas is your second most memorable impression. It's a trip, and I'm not talking about the 30km distance either. You really think you are in a banana republic. It's a little unsettling. What if I get thrown in jail for no reason? Who will help me? At that point, you squelch the paranoia and focus on the task at hand, which is driving. The road is a four-lane parkway, with the Caribbean to the left. By itself, it is pretty and could be anywhere. But once you look to the right, you see the difference: men herding cattle along the side of the road, people walking everywhere, and that pervasive poverty. This contrast of modern versus primitive, rich versus poor, will hit you again and again as you experience the Dominican Republic. The story of this road is a classic example. The much despised former dictator—Rafael Trujillo—built this parkway for his son, so he could have a place to race his sports car.

As you get closer to the city, the Third World scenario gets more intense. You'll come to traffic lights, where some work and some don't, and where driver anarchy will reign when the lights don't work. There are people everywhere, on foot, on bikes and mopeds. All headed for the bridge into town. It gets more congested the closer you get. I came in at rush hour. Fortunately, once in town, a brigade of traffic cops somehow keeps traffic moving. Be sure you have your directions down before you leave the airport. With all the things requiring your attention, the last thing you'll need to do is try to figure out where you're going. You *must be very alert* behind the wheel. Three lanes will often be created where only two exist.

The Dominican Republic is a big country for the Caribbean, second only to Cuba in size. At 18,712 square miles, it's about as big as the states of New Hampshire and Vermont combined. It occupies about two-thirds of the island of Hispaniola, which again is second in size only to Cuba. (The other third is occupied by Haiti, which is physically and culturally very different). There are incredibly beautiful beaches among its 870 miles of coastline, high mountains (Pico Duarte reaches 10,414 feet—the highest in the Caribbean), lush vegetation, desert, and the urban sprawl of the capital, Santo Domingo. And throughout it all there are over seven million people.

Dominicans are a mix of races. Most of the ruling class are Latino-white and, at least the ones I saw in the capital, are heavy (I guess they have plenty to eat). Most Dominicans are racially shades of brown, with a real mixture of Latino, Indian, and black features. However Santiago, the commercial center of the country, is much whiter and more Latino than other parts of the country. The blackest people are from the southwest and closest to Haiti. One thing you notice about all Dominicans is that even though most people are very poor by our standards, they are surprisingly well dressed. Also, men *always* wear pants everywhere in the country except at the beach, even when it's scorching outside.

The Dominican Republic attracts lots of European tourists, particularly Germans. I visited many resorts where 80 to 90 percent of the guests were German (almost all on package tours with Lufthansa or a German charter company). Next in line after the Germans are the Italians, then the Brits. Americans are a rare breed here, except in Puerto Plata, Casa de Campo, and the Club Med in Punta Cana, where you will see and hear some. Most Dominicans thought I was Italian, which was different for me as everywhere else I go it's like I have the word "American" stenciled on my forehead. Because most of the tourists who come purchase package deals and stay at big resorts—and are terrified to venture far away from them—most of the country is totally untourited. If you are adventurous, this is a great county to explore and discover—if you speak Spanish.

Few people speak English once you leave the hotels. If you don't speak Spanish, you can hire a guide. Arrangements can be made through your hotel, or, if you know anyone who lives here, through that person. It's easy, cheap (between $20 and $50 per day), and your guide will take you places you normally wouldn't see. This is big money to these people, so you should be able to get the best.

THE BRIEFEST HISTORY OF A COMPLICATED PAST

The island of Hispaniola was first settled by Amerindians, who gradually migrated up the island chain from South America. There were several variations of the Arawak tribe present on the island when Columbus landed on his first voyage in 1492, including the Taino. They called the island Quisqueya, "Mother Earth." With the discovery of gold (gifts from the Arawaks), Columbus sent his brother Bartolomé to establish a settlement, which he did in Santo Domingo. Founded in 1496, it was to become the capital of the Spanish colonies. From here expeditions and conquests were launched to Puerto Rico, Cuba, and Mexico.

But the Spanish were never able to get a grip on the island they renamed Hispaniola ("Little Spain"). Sir Francis Drake and the British sacked the capital in 1586. Then the French laid claim to what was eventually to become Haiti. By 1795, they had control of the entire island. When the Haitian slave uprisings began in the early 1800s, revolt spread into the Spanish side, causing major instability. When Spain regained control in 1809, it largely ignored the country. This triggered the "Ephemeral Independence" led by José Nuñez de Cáceres, who proclaimed the "Independent State of Spanish Haiti" in 1821. The new independent slave republic of Haiti, however, objected to the idea of two countries on one island, invaded, and ruled the country for the next twenty-two years. It was at this time that the seeds of the deep animosity between Haitians and Dominicans were planted (Trujillo's killing of about 10,000 Haitians in the next century fanned the flames).

The 19th century was really a mess for the Dominicans. After the founding fathers of Dominican independence—Juan Pablo Duarte, Francisco del Rosarío Sánchez and Ramón Matías Mella—formed the new country of the Dominican Republic, there were long periods of instability and uncertainty. Factional bickering and territorial and economic fighting among the ruling class led to many civil wars. More invasions by Haiti and a four-year occupation by Spain didn't help matters at all.

In 1916, the U.S. invaded the island to quell major unrest and the Marines occupied the country until 1924. When the U.S. left, they had established a formidable army, under the command of Rafael Leónidas Trujillo Molina. Six years later, he overthrew the President and began one of the most corrupt and evil dictatorships in the history of the Americas. It lasted until his assassination in 1961. But the bumpy ride wasn't over, as a succession of quick presidencies (including one by the current president, Dr. Joaquin Balaguer), and military coups caused tremendous instability. Civil war broke out again in 1965, and with Castro now entrenched in Cuba and seemingly menacing, the U.S. quickly dispatched troops to establish order. Democracy was restored in 1966 under the leadership of President Balaguer, who served until 1978. He was re-elected in 1986 and is currently well into his eighties and blind but is still going strong. Whew!

DOMINICAN REPUBLIC: KEY FACTS

LOCATION	19°N by 70°W (at its center)
	50 miles west of Puerto Rico
	1,600 miles southeast of New York
SIZE	18,712 square miles
HIGHEST POINT	Pico Duarte (10,414 ft.)
POPULATION	7,200,000

LANGUAGE	*Spanish!*
TIME	Atlantic Standard Time (1 hour ahead of EST, same as EDT)
AREA CODE	809
ELECTRICITY	110 volts AC, 60 cycles (in most places)
CURRENCY	The Dominican peso, RD$ (about RD$12 = $1 U.S.)
DRIVING	ONLY FOR THE EXPERIENCED, ASSURED DRIVER On the *right;* a valid American or Canadian driver's license and a valid credit card or a substantial cash deposit is needed to rent a car
DOCUMENTS	U.S. or Canadian citizens need a passport or proof of citizenship; a Tourist Card ($10 U.S.) must be purchased at airport when you arrive (don't lose it)—or purchase it at the airport counter at your point of embarkation
DEPARTURE TAX	$10 U.S.
BEER TO DRINK	Presidente
RUM TO DRINK	Barcelo Gold
MUSIC TO HEAR	*Merengue!*

GETTING THERE

There are two international airports in the Dominican Republic—Las Américas International in Santo Domingo and La Unión International in Puerto Plata. Both Santo Domingo and Puerto Plata can handle jumbo jets. In addition, La Romana takes smaller prop planes and private jets. AMERICAN, CONTINENTAL, and DOMINICANA all have nonstops to Puerto Plata, Santo Domingo, or both from New York. AMERICAN and DOMINICANA also have nonstops from Miami. AMERICAN EAGLE flies from San Juan to La Romana. LIAT flies to Santiago from San Juan.

GETTING AROUND

It's a big country, with over 10,000 miles of roads. The best way to see it is by car. However, driving in this country is absolutely

nerve-wracking! Renting a car, and worse, driving a car, is an experience only for good, confident, and aggressive drivers. This is not a
place for the meek—you will wind up a basket case before you leave
the airport.

If you arrive in Santo Domingo, the first task is to find the rental
desk, which is tucked away to the left of the main entrance, where
the concessions are located. As you're walking out of Customs, it
will be about 300 feet to your right—keep walking, you'll find it.
What you'll probably see first is a man holding a sign with the
rental agency's name on it. He ends up carrying your bag to the
counter (maybe 150 feet—give him 10 pesos), where you wonder
how the hell they can work in these tiny shoeboxes.

Renting a car is very expensive in the Dominican Republic. It will
cost you *at least* $300 per week, likely more. This is because cars
cost twice as much here as in the U.S. (import duties double the
price) and because the accident rate is so high. One look at your
rental car will tell the tale. It will have several dents, broken lenses
on the lights, ripped interior, etc. My college car was in better
condition (and my mother and two brothers had used it before me)!
They make Rent-A-Wreck cars look brand new.

Most of the major international players are here, including BUD-
GET ([800] 527-0700), AVIS ([800] 331-1084), THRIFTY ([800] 367-
2277), DOLLAR ([800] 800-4000), HERTZ ([800] 654-3001 or [809]
688-2277), and NATIONAL ([800] 227-3876/[809] 562-1444). Be
sure to make an advance reservation in the U.S. before you arrive—
you will get a better rate. In addition, be sure to check with your
credit card company when it comes to the Collision Damage
Waiver. Some may not provide you with coverage here. Understand *all* your liabilities before you get on the road.

If you decide to drive on secondary roads, be sure to ask about
the road's condition before you go (unless you have a Jeep). It's easy
to get stuck in the middle of nowhere, which here can be a scary
experience. We drove from Sosúa (on the north coast near Puerto
Plata) to Santiago on a secondary road over the mountains. While
the primary roads are in surprisingly good shape, the secondary
ones can be horrific. Some are being improved, but most are not.
On our drive, we hit the bad roads. We drove very slowly, the
bottom scraping rocks on our loaded-down '83 Honda Accord,
through these tiny mountain towns where people looked at you as
if they had never seen a tourist before in their lives. Then they
would smile and wave. It was fascinating.

A driving alert: *Avoid driving at night outside of urban areas.* Many cars don't have taillights, and some cars and trucks don't have headlights. The roads are narrow (mostly two-lane), trucks pass uphill and they sometimes don't have lights, and there are pedestrians on the sides of the roads you cannot see. 'Nuff said.

FOCUS ON THE DOMINICAN REPUBLIC: MERENGUE

You hear it everywhere. On the car radio, at the corner bodega, from loudspeakers on the sidewalk, at the airport, at the baseball stadium, at the hotel clerk's desk, in the nightclubs—there's no escaping the national pride of the Dominican Republic: merengue. This music is the national pulse of the country, and it's a racing (and racy) one at that. As the tempos of the popular merengues get faster and faster every year, the lyrics become more loaded with naughty double entendres—all about sex of course—so much so that some can't get air play here. Unlike rap, which can be very explicit and vulgar, merengue prides itself in masking risqué ideas in the lyrics. The result makes you gasp and laugh and is definitely part of the fun of this music.

Dominicans rule merengue. Several bands from this country top the U.S. Tropical Latin charts with their music. Probably the hottest Dominican band in the country is Rokabanda. Their first album/CD was a huge hit here. During an all-day merengue festival in Santo Domingo in November 1992, held in the Plaza de Espagna, the crowd of at least 100,000 went beserk for Rokabanda. Everyone knew the lyrics to every song and were literally jumping in the air. Also very popular, especially in the U.S. and Puerto Rico, is Jossie Estebán y La Patrulla 15. Their hit, "El Tigeron," about a man called "the tiger" who seduces the narrator's wife while he is at work (the refrain *"Fue a la nevera y se comió mi salchichón"* literally translated means "He ate my sausage in the fridge," but figuratively in Spanish means "He screwed my wife"), is now a classic. Las Chicas del Can, "The Fun Girls," are very successful and popular both in and out of the country. Other bands of note are Johnny Ventura, Wilfredo Vargas, the Hermanos Rosarios, Tono Rosario, Victor Roque, Coco Band, Los Sabrosos del Merengue, Carlos Alfredo, and the Puerto Rican bands of Cana Brava and Zona Roja.

The Miami Band—many of the band members are Dominicans living in Miami—hit gold with their first album/CD and the song "Ponte el Sombrero"—which literally translated means "Put on

Your Hat," but figuratively means "Put on Your Condom." It's about a girl who spurns the sexual advances of her date because he won't wear a condom (it's not macho). The refrain goes, *"Ponte, ponte, ponte el sombrero, papi—ponte el sombrero."* Another song of theirs, "El Bigote," is a great example of the double entendre. The singer opens the song by stating, "They come in all sizes and colors. Big and fat, small and thin, black or white," and then she reveals she is speaking of mustaches (*bigotes* in Spanish) and not the male sex organ.

All Dominicans seem to be born knowing how to dance to this music. I marvel at the way they move. With merengue, you have to feel the music deep down in your hips. It's a very fast-paced but erotic dance, with lots of hip-grinding body contact. It's kinda like a combo of swing meets the slow-dance of the sixties, but at warp speed. My advice to novices: Watch the Dominicans dance it for a while; venture onto the dance floor with a Dominican or Latin only when its crowded; try to feel the music deep "down there"; follow your partner's lead and then gaze into his/her eyes—it'll come to you.

For those who are interested in seeing and hearing merengue performed live, there is a Merengue Festival held every July in Santo Domingo from the last week of the month until the first week in August. This is done in conjunction with the celebration of the founding of Santo Domingo on August 4, 1496.

There is also a smaller festival held in Puerto Plata every October. If you live in a major metro area with a Latino population (Miami, New York, Chicago, etc.), check your local listings—these bands tour all the time. Most major record stores, like Tower, HMV, and Spec's, all have Latin music sections where you can find some of the above artists.

WHERE TO STAY

SANTO DOMINGO

Santo Domingo is a sprawling city of over two million people. When you first arrive, one breath will indicate that pollution controls are nonexistent. Diesel engines rule here, and the amount of exhaust (and dust) on the road will prompt you to turn on the air conditioning and push the lever over to recirculate. One look at the cars will tell you that car inspections also don't exist. You expect some to fall apart before your very eyes. Many cars are without doors, fenders, windows, or lights and are carrying about three times as many people as was intended by the designer.

The city core is the Colonial Zone, the sight of the original settlement and some of the oldest buildings in the Hemisphere. Located at the western juncture of the Caribbean and the Río Ozama, this will be the focus of your stay in the Capital, as Santo Domingo is called by everyone who lives here. You don't live in Santo Domingo, you live in the Capital. The area between the Colonial Zone and the Avenida Máximo Gómez to the west is the best residential area of the city. It is here where all the good hotels are: the Jaragua, the Sheraton, the Hotel V Centenario, the Lina, the Hispaniola, the Continental, and the Santo Domingo. Many of these hotels are on the Malecón (the waterfront drive) and offer ocean views. It is also the district where most of the government buildings, the Presidential Palace, the U.S. Embassy, the many neoclassical public buildings built by various dictators and the political party headquarters are located (even the Communists are in this fashionable neighborhood).

RAMADA RENAISSANCE JARAGUA RESORT, CASINO AND SPA (809) 221-2222, fax (809) 686-0528
Stateside: (800) 228-9898; Canada: (800) 268-8998/(416) 485-2610; UK: 01-235-5264
Avenida George Washington 367, Santo Domingo, Dominican Republic

Built on the site of the old hotel of the same name and opened in 1988, this massive property on 14 acres of landscaped gardens is a modern/deco mélange of design and décor. It is, in my opinion, the best place to stay in Santo Domingo. It has a great location adjacent to the Colonial Zone, yet the spacious grounds offer an oasis of retreat from the bustle of the city. There are 293 very comfortable rooms and suites, all with the accoutrements you'd expect from a luxury hotel. A huge pool with cabañas, a European-style spa, tennis courts, casino, nightclub, restaurants—you'll find the whole shebang here.

Rates are VERY PRICEY to WICKED PRICEY for singles and doubles (EP).

HOTEL SANTO DOMINGO (809) 221-1511, fax (809) 535-1511
Stateside: (800) 877-3643/(305) 856-5405
Avenida Independencia, corner of Abraham Lincoln, (P.O. Box
2112), Santo Domingo, Dominican Republic

This is probably the most stylish and elegant hotel in the Capital.
A rambling, modern, stucco and tile-roofed complex set on 14 acres
of gardens, it's located next to the Centro de los Héroes and the
Malecón. There are 220 rooms and suites decorated by Oscar de la
Renta, many with lanais and ocean views. All the amenities of a
luxury hotel are here, including 24-hour room service, Olympic-
sized swimming pool, three lighted tennis courts, a spa, three restaurants, and a piano bar. A casino and other facilities are available
at the Santo Domingo's sister hotel next door, the Hispaniola.
You'll need to cab it to the Colonial Zone from here.
      Rates are PRICEY to VERY PRICEY for singles and doubles
(EP).

HOTEL V CENTENARIO (809) 221-0000, fax (809) 686-3287
Avenida George Washington 218, Santo Domingo, Dominican Republic

This is the new deluxe hotel in Santo Domingo. Recently opened to
mark the 500th anniversary of the Columbus landing, this high-rise
palace has 200 rooms, all facing the Malecón and the water. All the
amenities you'd expect from a luxury hotel are here, including
24-hour room service, business services, pool, tennis, nightclub,
casino, and spa.
      Rates are WICKED PRICEY for singles and doubles (EP).

SHERATON HOTEL & CASINO (809) 221-6666, fax (809) 687-
8150
Stateside: (800) 325-3535
Avenida George Washington 365, Santo Domingo, Dominican Republic

This is a big complex with a high-rise tower located right on the
Malecón and adjacent to the Colonial Zone—a great location. It's
also a hubbub of activity. There are 260 comfortably furnished and
pleasant rooms, many with lanais overlooking the sea and all with
24-hour room service. There is a pool, two lighted tennis courts, a

health club with sauna and Jacuzzi, three restaurants, a casino, a nightclub and bar.

Rates are PRICEY for singles and doubles (EP).

GRAN HOTEL LINA & CASINO (809) 563-5000, fax (809) 686-5521

Stateside: (305) 374-0045

Avenida Máximo Gómez, Corner Avenida 27 de Febrero, Santo Domingo, Dominican Republic

Located near the American Embassy, this high-rise, all-suite hotel is another good value when staying in the Capital. It's got everything: two swimming pools, two tennis courts, a casino, sauna, nightclub, restaurants, shopping arcade, 24-hour room service, etc. There are 218 standard but comfortable rooms, all with air conditioning, cable TV, and refrigerators. You'll need to cab it to the Colonial Zone from here.

Rates are NOT SO CHEAP for singles and doubles (EP).

HOTEL CONTINENTAL (809) 689-1151, fax (809) 687-8397

Avenida Máximo Gómez 16, Santo Domingo, Dominican Republic

Located across from the Palacio de la Cultura, a pretty beaux-arts complex, the Continental is a good value. With 100 simple, standard hotel rooms, this high-rise hotel has a lot of the amenities of a more expensive hotel, including room service. While it is a tad far to walk from the Colonial Zone, the money you save by staying here will pay for the cabs. There is a pool, restaurant, and bar on the premises.

Rates are NOT SO CHEAP for singles and doubles (EP).

HOTEL DAVID'S (809) 685-2270, fax (809) 685-9121

Arzobispo Nouel 308, Zona Colonial, Santo Domingo, Dominican Republic

This is a very small but cute two-story hotel in the Colonial Zone. It's run by a very friendly staff who keep it purring. The lobby, on the second floor, has a terrace overlooking the street and a garden/rooftop bar and café. The rooms all have private bath, cable TV, phones, refrigerators, and air conditioning. All the Zone's attractions are a few minutes' walk away.

Rates are NOT SO CHEAP for singles and doubles (EP).

WHERE TO DINE

Santo Domingo has a surprisingly sophisticated restaurant scene. There are some excellent restaurants serving delicious and exotic cuisine, with attentive and courteous service. All of the hotels recommended, except the David's, have at least one restaurant. These tend to be good but overpriced. If you're in the mood, it's best to venture out and discover how interesting the dining is.

CAFÉ ST. MICHEL, Avenida Lope de Vega 24, Naco, 562-4141

This café is highly regarded by the local Capitalinos, who adore its award-winning French/Continental cuisine. Reservations are recommended. Dressy. $$$

EL BODEGÓN, Arzobispo Merino y Padre Billini, Colonial Zone, 682-6864

Set in a beautiful old house in the Colonial Zone, this restaurant serves excellent Spanish cuisine. Reservations are suggested. $$$$

IL BUCO, Arzobispo Merino 152-A, Colonial Zone, 685-0884

Serving delicious Northern Italian cuisine, this perfectly attractive restaurant has excellent cuisine and very attentive service. This restaurant could easily flourish in New York. $$$

LA BAHÍA, Avenida George Washington 1, 682-4022

This is a very casual restaurant serving excellent fresh fish and the best seafood in town. It's popular, it's not expensive, and it's open late. $$ *No credit cards.*

LA FROMAGERIE, 27 de Febrero, Plaza Ciolla, 567-9430

A mix of Continental and local food, plus great prices, make this restaurant popular with locals. $$

LA MEZQUITA, Avenida Independencia 407, 687-7090

Very good Spanish cuisine and a pleasant, attractive atmosphere are the hallmarks of this conveniently located restaurant. $$$

LINA, Gran Hotel Lina, Avenida Máximo Gómez, 563-5000

The best paella in Santo Domingo comes out of the kitchen of this hotel. Reservations are a must. Dressy. $$$$

MESÓN DE LA CAVA, Mirador del Sur, 533-2818

This is an institution in the Capital, since it's the only restaurant set up in a real underground cave. While the food is not exceptional, there's nightly entertainment and dancing to merengue, so why not? Reservations are a must. Dressy. $$$$

VESUVIO, Avenida George Washington 521, 221-3333

This is a very good Italian and Continental restaurant that is very popular with locals. Dressy. $$$$

GOING OUT

As it is a big city, there are a number of choices to dance the night away with merengue or the latest disco as well as fun cafés and pubs. Please note that most of the clubs require jackets for men and dressy clothes for women. Jeans are iffy here, unless you're gorgeous. Among the best:

BARS AND DISCOS

CAFÉ ATLÁNTICO, Avenida México, Corner 27 de Febrero, 565-1841

This is a rather hip spot where the Santo Domingo "movida" hang out. Young and fun.

GRAND CAFE, Avenida Lope de Vega 26 (next to Café St. Michel), 541-6655

Another trendy café in an interesting space where the Capitolino swells like to gather.

GUACARA TAINA, Mirador Park, 530-2666

This is a fun place located in a real cave featuring live music, disco, and shows.

ALEXANDER'S, Avenida Pasteur 23, 685-9728

The latest dance hits from the U.S. are the mainstay here. Open real late.

BELLA BLUE DISCO, Avenida George Washington 165, Malecón, 689-2911

This is a popular disco playing a good mix of music.

DRAKE'S PUB, Plaza de España, 320-3660

One of the most fun bars in town, and certainly in the Colonial Zone, it draws a real interesting mix of people. A must.

EXODUS, Malecón, 687-3054

This is a hot spot for young locals and is open very late.

LA RÉGINE, Avenida George Washington 557, Malecón, 689-1978

This is more of a Euro–New York/flashy disco with the crowd and music to match.

OMNI DISCO, Sheraton Santo Domingo, Avenida George Washington 361, 686-6666

This is very popular with both tourists and locals, and they do play merengue.

GAY BARS AND DISCOS

FREDDIE, Calle Polvorin 10, Colonial Zone, 688-7905

This is a tiny bar where the locals are all for hire for less than a good meal. Be sure to chat with the owner (he's British), and, of course, be careful.

LE POUSSEE, Calle 19 de Marzo, 682-5189

Open mainly on weekends, this is a small, hot, and very crowded club with merengue dancing.

EL PENTHOUSE, Calle 20, corner of Seybo Altos, no phone

In a bad neighborhood (the bouncer greets you with a baseball bat), the Dominicans at this firetrap are also all for rent. There is a disco and floor show.

PERO SEÑOR POLICIA! (BUT OFFICER!)

When driving anywhere in the country and especially on major routes, be prepared to be stopped by the police. They hang out at the side of the road and will flag you down. Then they will tell you that you were speeding, even though you weren't (and despite the fact they don't have radar). Universally what they want is a payoff—forty pesos (about $3.50) will do. I was warned by some friends in Santo Domingo to expect this.

Sure enough, I was only a few kilometers out of the capital when a cop flagged me down. I was advised to pretend that I knew no Spanish, as they do not speak English. Since I already knew what would happen, I was curious to see how they actually go about extorting the money from a tourist (they regularly extort money from residents too). Ah corruption, thy name is Latin America. The cop, a sergeant, told me I was speeding, which I pretended not to understand. "No hablo español," I said. I handed him my Florida driver's license and the car-rental papers, which he superficially perused and stood at the car window just shaking his head and smiling. We were obviously at a stalemate and I wanted to continue my trip. So I pulled out my wallet, a bigger smile from the cop, and pulled out twenty pesos. He breathed in through his teeth, shook his head and let out a sigh, then mumbled something in Spanish which I think reiterated that I was speeding. I gave the grinning maniac a "yeah, right" look and pulled out another twenty pesos. Ah, the nod of approval and several " 'ta bien, 'ta bien" affirmations. He then proceeded to tell me that he had a sister he wanted me to meet! I was speechless. As I would quickly learn, Dominicans think all Americans are rich, rich, rich. So why not marry off your sister to one so the whole family will benefit.

After that incident, I was told that if you flash your headlights twice when you see a cop at the side of the street, it's a "secret code" of the ruling class and they won't pull you over. They also probably won't chase you on their mopeds if you don't stop, and they don't have radios. But I wouldn't advise doing this unless you speak fluent Spanish or if you have a Dominican with you, just in case they somehow catch you (I can envision the letters from irate readers: "But you wrote that I didn't have to stop . . ."). Stop and pay the bribe.

BEYOND SANTO DOMINGO

BOCA CHICA/JUAN DOLIO

These two little beach towns are only 10 and 20 minutes east of Las Américas International Airport, respectively, and are very popular with German tourists. The town closest to the airport, and only 30 minutes from Santo Domingo, is Boca Chica. This is where Capitalinos go to the beach, particularly on weekends (except the really wealthy ones—they have villas at Casa de Campo). The beach here is wide and pleasant, with all kinds of activity both on (water sports, volleyball) and off (restaurants, bars, shops) it. If you're single and want to meet others, particularly Dominicans, this is a reasonably priced destination.

The beach town of Juan Dolio is funky, small, and cheap. There is a nice but rather narrow beach and a lot of little eateries, shops, and beach bars (the latter to get shiffahst at), which will appeal to those who despise big resorts and want to mingle with the locals. Of the two, I prefer Juan Dolio just because it's smaller. Don't miss the Magica disco, near Villas del Mar, and the Taino Bar, right on the beach.

DON JUAN BEACH RESORT (809) 687-9157, fax (809) 688-5271
Boca Chica, Dominican Republic

With a good location and a casual, relaxed ambience about it, this is a good choice when staying in Boca Chica. It's also easy to zip into Santo Domingo from here. There are 124 rooms, both in suites (with kitchenettes) and rooms—all with air conditioning, TV, and phone. There are a pool, beach bar, tennis courts, water sports, a disco, and a restaurant.

Rates are NOT SO CHEAP for singles and doubles (EP).

HAMACA BEACH HOTEL (809) 562-7475, fax (809) 566-2354
Boca Chica, Dominican Republic

An imposing stucco structure on the edge of town, this is the most deluxe resort in the area. There are 256 comfortable and attractive rooms, all with air conditioning, lanais, cable TV, and phones. Hamaca has two restaurants, a disco, a spacious lobby and several sitting areas, as well as a beach, water sports, pool, gym and sauna, and lighted tennis courts.

Rates are PRICEY to WICKED PRICEY for singles and doubles (EP).

RAMADA GUEST HOUSE (809) 526-3310, fax (809) 526-2512
Juan Dolio, Dominican Republic

This is a cute and very cheap guest house. It has its own little beach and restaurant. There are 30 air-conditioned, simple rooms, a tiny swimming pool and Jacuzzi, and even a disco overlooking the beach!

Rates are DIRT CHEAP for singles and doubles (EP).

TAMARINDO SUN CLUB RESORT (809) 567-9575, fax (809) 567-9577
Stateside: (212) 681-5694
Juan Dolio, Dominican Republic

Another alternative in tiny Juan Dolio is the Sun Club, which is a pleasant little complex, has its own beach bar, and has a clientele base which is 85 percent German (the rest are Canadian). If the latter appeals to you, go for it. Be sure to ask for a room away from the road.

Rates are NOT SO CHEAP for singles and doubles (AP).

LA ROMANA

La Romana is the home of Casa de Campo, the 7,000-acre resort that is the biggest and most reknowned resort in the Dominican Republic. While the resort is huge, rich, and pretty, the town of La Romana is something that you want to get through quickly. Again, the land of contrasts. You drive through muddy side streets with goats, donkeys, barefoot people—it screams p-o-v-e-r-t-y—and then, a few kilometers away, you can ensconce yourself at a sumptuous patio bar with servants left and right, and you wonder, What is wrong with this picture. The sixties bleeding-heart liberal in me,

which is basically my political identity if you haven't figured that
out yet, was uncomfortable here. Yet the nineties pragmatist that I
am often forced the thought that, yes, there certainly are inequities,
but just think of how many people this place employs. What would
happen if it wasn't here? The Third World traveler's dilemma presents itself once more.

CASA DE CAMPO (809) 523-3333, fax (809) 523-8548
Stateside and Canada: (800) 8-PREMIER or (305) 856-5405 in
   Florida
La Romana (Box 140), Dominican Republic

Undoubtedly, the most impressive feature of this huge resort to be
noticed first is the security. "Was President Clinton here on vacation?" I wondered. Uniforms were everywhere, with guards and
gates on every possible road and entrance. I later learned that this
was just a normal day. Since the resort is often home to many
famous people, including Julio Iglesias, Oscar de la Renta, and
Frank Sinatra, the resort wants to ensure their safety and, hey, labor
is cheap here.

   The second most impressive feature is the size of the resort, 7,000
acres (that's seven times as big as the Dorado/Cerromar complex in
Puerto Rico). It is sprawling, with acres and acres of one- and
two-story stucco and red-corrugated tin-roofed villas, casitas, and
hotel-condo–looking buildings. There are 950 rooms in casitas
and villas; two championship Pete Dye 18-hole golf courses, including "The Teeth of the Dog"—which is ranked number 1 in the
Caribbean by Golf Magazine and has seven oceanfront holes (the
third most impressive feature); three polo fields and 200 polo po-
nies; a complete equestrian center with 2,000 horses; trap and skeet
shooting facilities; 14 swimming pools; 13 tennis courts; a health
and fitness center; beaches; a marina; and Altos de Chavón (see
below).

   The atmosphere here, considering the above, is surprisingly casual. The main lobby is a series of covered walkways connecting the
various hotel desks with the patio bar, main pool, boutiques, etc.
A big plus is the American Airlines ticket counter in the lobby—a
major convenience. The main pool is fairly large, with a pool bar
(the kind with the stools in the water). The rooms are very nice,
with all the deluxe amenities and were decorated by Oscar de la
Renta.

But golf seems to be what makes Casa de Campo a major destination. Golfers come from all over to play The Teeth. When I was
there, there were many Japanese on the course, which, given their
fananticism about the game, is testimony to the fame of these links.
For more about the course, see the "Don't Miss" section.

There is also another roadside attraction, if you will, at Casa de
Campo which, while contrived, is certainly unique. It's called Altos
de Chavón (the fourth most impressive feature)—a very thorough
reproduction of a sixteenth-century Tuscan village. The site is
perched on a promontory overlooking the Río Chavón. The attention to detail, making columns look like the remnants of a Roman
temple, and the weathered look of the stucco, is almost convincing
and probably does convince some tourists. This is an "artists'
colony," with an art school affiliated with the Parsons School of
Design in New York and galleries exhibiting their work, along with
many high-priced restaurants and boutiques. There is also a Regional Archeology Museum (open daily) with a good collection of
Taino artifacts. While parts of it are pretty, I couldn't help but
wonder, why create a Tuscan village in the Dominican Republic?
What were they thinking—or what were they on: let me have some!
Well, it's there, and if you're in the ballpark, you should see it. It's
interesting, period. Also part of the complex is an amphitheater,
modeled after the Greek ruins at Epidaurus, which was dedicated
by The Voice himself, Frank Sinatra.

The final most impressive feature is the price. Rates here are
about half of what they would be for similar luxury resorts on other
islands. Rates are VERY PRICEY for singles and doubles (EP).
Three- and four-bedroom villas are available in the BEYOND BE-
LIEF category.

PUNTA CANA

With an unbroken 20-mile stretch of white sand strand, this area
has one of the longest and nicest beaches in the Caribbean. Located
on the eastern tip of the country, this area has only recently been
developed, with several large resorts, including a Club Med, strung
out along the beaches. Not to despair, it's easy to find deserted
beaches here. The closest town is Higüey, about 48 kms away (29
miles), home of the Basilica of Higüey (the site of a series of miracles
by Our Lady of Altagracia, the patron saint of the Dominican

Republic). There is a huge modern shrine in her honor in the center of town and it is a major pilgrimage destination. There is also a neat little village, called La Otra Banda, just east of town on the road to Punta Cana. Here you'll find lots of brilliantly painted, well-tended houses, which provide ample photo ops.

PUNTA CANA BEACH RESORT (809) 686-0084, fax (809) 687-8745
P.O. Box 1083, Santo Domingo, Dominican Republic

Of all the resorts in the area, this is the best. Located on 105 acres on a nice-sized beach, this Dominican-owned establishment has a very pleasant and relaxed atmosphere about its attractive, coconut-palm—studded surroundings. It's bigger than it looks, with 350 rooms dispersed throughout the property in three-story buildings and villas. But what's best about it is the concerted effort to use Dominican materials and artisans in the construction and décor of the resort, which creates a definite local feel to the place. Both rooms and villas are comfortable with a Caribbean décor and all the amenities. There are five restaurants and five bars, a pool, disco, four lighted tennis courts, and all water sports. Most of the guests who vacation here are European, especially German.

Rates are PRICEY to VERY PRICEY for singles and doubles (MAP).

CLUB MED–PUNTA CANA (809) 687-2767, fax (809) 687-2896
Stateside: (800) CLUB-MED/(212) 750-1670
Apartado Postal 106, Punta Cana, Higüey, Dominican Republic

This is one of the few resorts outside of Puerto Plata where there is a sizable American contingent (about 50 percent of the guests). It's a Club Med, so it's all-inclusive. The physical campus looks just like a college campus, say in Florida. But the beach is gorgeous and there are all those water sports and activities which have made Club Med famous. And of all the Club Meds in the Caribbean, this would be my first choice.

Rates are PRICEY for singles and WICKED PRICEY for doubles (all-inclusive).

BÁVARO BEACH RESORT (809) 686-5773, fax (809) 686-5859
Stateside: (800) 876-6612
Bávaro Beach, Apartado Postal 1, Punta Cana, Higüey, Dominican
Republic

With the best beach of any resort in the country right in front, it is probably enough reason to stay at this sprawling resort. Another Dominican-owned property (it is owned by the Barcelo family, of the Dominican rum Barcelos), there are almost 1,400 rooms here, making it the biggest resort roomwise in the Dominican Republic. There are four distinct parts to the resort—Hotel Playa Bávaro, Hotel Jardín Baváro, Aparthotel Golf Bávaro, and the Hotel Casino Bávaro. Since the beach is the raison d'être to be here, I'd recommend staying at Playa Bávaro. Then you can just jump out of your bed and hit the beach. If you want separate bedrooms, then the Aparthotel is your best bet. All rooms have such standard amenities as air conditioning, phone, TV, refrigerator, and private balcony or terrace. There are several pools, tons of tennis courts, volleyball, and all water sports.

Rates are PRICEY for singles and WICKED PRICEY for doubles (MAP).

FROM SANTO DOMINGO TO PUERTO PLATA

The road between Santo Domingo and Puerto Plata is the heaviest traveled in the country. It is exhausting to drive. There are lots of trucks, spewing out their diesel fumes and dust, along with all kinds of vehicles and pedestrian traffic. You'll want to use the air conditioning here. We had the windows down and my face was covered in soot (half my face looked like it had been blasted with black charcoal dust). My skin and lungs felt as if I had been sitting in the Lincoln Tunnel for hours. Along the way, there are several pit stops (called *paradas*) which cater exclusively to the north–south travelers, particularly when you are about halfway. You can't miss them. For some reason they are all on the west side of the road and are worth the stop, if only to use the bathroom. There are rows of food stalls, most hawking fried food—there goes your no-fat diet—beer, as well as merengue music and a general hubbub around mealtime.

PUERTO PLATA/SOSÚA

I really wouldn't bother staying in Puerto Plata—it's just too tour-isty and not really very attractive. I'd much rather be in Sosúa. Puerto Plata is really a cruise-ship stop, a-not-so-pretty town with several resorts and a cable car. (Regarding the latter, if you ski, what's the big deal about a cable car—the view from the top? I'd rather be on the beach myself!). If you want a cheap place to stay, there's the LONG BEACH HOTEL, which is under $10 per night and is across the street from a good beach. It's funky and clean. Period. I don't like Bayside Hill, so I'd recommend that you bypass it.

Sosúa is a much wiser choice. It has a very pretty beach with a variety of things available to you: chaises, tiny restaurants offering all manner of cuisine—Italian, German, Québecois, French, Do-minican—and are really cool and really good. There are also lots of little shops with tons of groovy souvies and even a tape/CD shop where you can get bootleg Latin tapes for $3 to $4. There are lots of Dominicans hanging out, so it's easy to meet them. It's a fun place to spend the day. You'll have a great time. Probably the best place to stay is the CASA MARINA BEACH CLUB ([809] 571-3690, fax [809] 571-3110). This full-service hotel has its own beach and a convenient location close to the main beach.

CABARETE

Just down the street from Sosúa, well, a few miles away, is Cabarete. It's the windsurfing capital of the Dominican Republic—and one of the top windsurfing destinations in the Caribbean. The beach is over two miles long, and the trade winds blow onshore, so you won't get blown out to sea. When the trades rage in the winter, the surf really gets big as the beach is totally exposed to the swells coming in off the Atlantic. During the summer, the trades blow but the seas are calm. There are a couple of resorts and several cheap and decent places to stay here while you hang ten to the waves and the wind. Puerto Plata International Airport is only a ten-minute drive away.

CAMINO DEL SOL (809) 571-0894, fax (809) 571-0892
Camino del Sol, Playa Cabarete, Dominican Republic

With 136 rooms and villas on the beach and all the amenities of a big resort, this is one of the best places to stay in Cabarete. The resort has windsurfing facilities, as well as tennis, other water sports, plus two restaurants and three bars.

Rates are NOT SO CHEAP for singles and doubles (EP).

PUNTA GOLETA (809) 571-0700, fax (809) 571-0707
Stateside: (800) 874-4637
Playa Cabarete, Dominican Republic

Windsurfing is the name of the game in this town and at this resort. Situated on 100 acres across the street from the beach, there are 126 comfortable and pleasant rooms with the standard amenities. As it is a resort, there are lots of other diversions here—like tennis, volleyball, horseback riding, etc.—should you want a rest from the boards.

Rates are NOT SO CHEAP for singles and doubles (EP).

BURN, BABY, BURN

There are a lot of discos and nightclubs in the Dominican Republic. And not just in the major cities and towns. Dominicans like to party, so you'll see huge nightclub complexes in the most unlikely places. On the road to Puerto Plata from Santo Domingo near Santiago, is "Las Vegas," a mega-disco that brings in big-name merengue bands. But one of the best places to party is on a Saturday night on the Malecón in Santo Domingo. This is where you will usually find at least one merengue band playing and a constant party. It's the music—you can't help but move—and it's free.

CURRENCY CHANGING

Be sure to use the bank at the Customs area to change your currency. You'll get the best rate of exchange among banks. You must have pesos, as it is illegal to deal in dollars (although people and hotels do do it).

A LEFTOVER SOLUTION

If you go out to a restaurant and have leftover food, have it wrapped and give it to some child on the street who looks hungry (you won't have a hard time finding one). Often these kids, mostly boys, have a little shoeshine kit. We picked out a kid and were rewarded with a big smile. Try it.

DON'T MISS

THE COLONIAL ZONE, SANTO DOMINGO—This is the oldest city in the Western Hemisphere and the Zone is the oldest part of the city. The architecture and the buildings themselves are wonderful to see and have been recently restored for the Columbus Quincentennial. This is the original part of Santo Domingo, founded by Bartolomé Columbus, Christopher's bro', in 1496. As I said earlier, some of the oldest colonial buildings in the Western Hemisphere are here, including the oldest church in North and South America: La Catedral de Santa María La Menor, Primada de América. This was the first cathedral of the New World, begun in 1514 and completed in 1540. And there's plenty more to see, including El Alcázar de Colón (Diego Columbus' palace), el Convento de los Jesuitas, the Torre del Homenaje, the Casa del Cordón, the Puerta de la Misericordia, the Casa de Nicolás de Ovando, and the Iglesia del Carmen. That list will keep you busy! The entire Colonial Zone is about the size of Central Park. So, once there, you can walk everywhere. One of the pleasures of the Colonial Zone is walking around in the evening. Residents leave windows and doors open for the breeze and are all sitting around watching TV. Families, friends all gathered around the tube and chatting—I found it a real glimpse into the day-to-day lives of Dominicans.

EL FARO A COLÓN—Built at a cost in the hundreds of millions of dollars (which certainly could have been used for better purposes—like food and housing for the poor), this coffinlike behemoth is Balaguer's tribute to Christopher Columbus. Here, underneath the beacon and under military guard, rests the remains of Columbus. It takes so much power to operate the lights that there are blackouts and brownouts in "other"

COLONIAL ZONE

Santo Domingo

MAP KEY

1. PARQUE COLON (COLUMBUS PARK)

2. CATEDRAL DE SANTA MARIA LA MENOR (CATEDRAL PRIMADA DE AMERICA) SANTA MARIA LA MENOR CATHEDRAL/ PRIMATE CATHEDRAL OF THE AMERICAS

3. FORTALEZA OZAMA (OZAMA FORTRESS)

4. CASA DE BASTIDAS (BASTIDAS HOUSE)

5. RELOJ DE SOL (SUNDIAL)

neighborhoods while it's turned on. (It is something to see at night—the hundreds of lights along the edifice project a cross into the sky along with the superpowered beacon—which is visible for 100 miles at sea.

THE TEETH OF THE DOG, LA ROMANA—Rated the toughest and best golf course in the Caribbean by *Golf Magazine*, this 6,888-yard links has seven oceanfront holes. It's rated 74.1 and has a slope rating of 140. There are four par-5's over 500 yards.

DOMINICAN DIVORCES—Remember on "Dynasty" when Fallon flew to Santo Domingo to get her divorce from Jeff, because it only takes 24 hours here? With a legal separation of mutual consent, one spouse can come to the Dominican Republic, hire a Dominican attorney to present the case to court, and be on his or her way the following day—a single person again.

SAMANÁ—The still rather undeveloped peninsula on the northeast coast, this is where some of the nicest beaches in the country are located. The drive from Sosúa to Samaná is a great trip along the coast with lots of beaches to explore on the way. If you decide to stay, EL PORTILLO BEACH CLUB ([809] 688-5749, fax [809] 685-0457), is on a wonderful beach called Las Terrenas and is an all-inclusive resort. Rates are PRICEY for singles and doubles.

BARAHONA—The "Pearl of the South," this city on the southwest coast, recently discovered by the tourism industry, is known for its dramatic cliffs and dry weather. There are also some nice cove beaches. Barahona is the home of the Magnetic Pole, where cars actually roll uphill.

SOSÚA BEACH—The beach here is a fun place to hang out. The sand is soft and white and the water is crystal clear and calm.

BASEBALL—This is a national obsession. There are ballparks in every town but the capital of Dominican baseball is San Pedro de Macorís. It produces more Major Leaguers than any other town in the world. Catch a game at the stadium here.

MERENGUE—Just listen, you'll hear it. Turn on the car radio and hit the clubs and experience the rhythym.

GRENADA

TOURISTO SCALE 📷 📷 📷 📷 📷 5

Grenada is an evocative country. Its tranquil natural assets of lush tropical vegetation, gushing rivers, scenic mountains, and coast are very powerful. The memory of political turmoil and an American invasion have faded, and Grenadians seem much more confident and outgoing today than on my last visit six years ago.

The island is a wonderful place to visit if you want to hike and immerse yourself in its people and past. Outside the primary tourist areas of Grand Anse, L'Anse aux Epines, and St. George's—all on the southwest corner of the island—you begin to experience the real Grenada. Vivid images come to mind of women washing clothes in a river, potholed roads, spice stations, rich hues of green, and the ever-watchful eyes of the people.

Nicknamed the "Isle of Spice," Grenada is a very popular destination for Europeans, particularly Germans, Brits, and Italians. Americans and Canadians do come, but they are a minority. Most people who visit here rarely venture into the island, which is a shame for them. Grenada will appeal to the adventurous traveler (my readers, I hope) as they discover so much more than what you'll see around the hotels.

THE BRIEFEST HISTORY

Grenada was first settled by Amerindians from South America. First came the Arawaks and then the Caribs. By the time Columbus sighted the island on his third voyage in 1498, the Caribs were firmly entrenched thus inhibiting European settlement until the

GRENADA

N

CARIBBEAN SEA

ATLANTIC OCEAN

SUGAR LOAF
LEVE RA BAY
GREEN ISLAND
BATHWAY BEACH
SANDY ISLAND

SAUTEURS
PROSPECT
MORNE FENDUE
BETTY MASCOL'S

VICTORIA
LOOP
GOUYAVE
NORTHERN

TIVE ANTOINE
LAKE ANTOINE
ANTOINE BAY

MT. ST CATHERINE
(2757)

PEARL'S AIRPORT

DAVIDALL ESTATE
CONCORD FALLS
GRAND ETANG FOREST PRESERVE
GRENVILLE

HALIFAX HARBOR
GRAND ETANG
SOUTHEAST MT.
(2348)
SEVEN SISTERS
MT. SINAI
(2306)

ST. GEORGE'S
RAMADA RENAISSANCE
GRAND ANSE (THE BEACH)
SOUTHERN LOOP
LA SAGESSE
LITTLE BACOLET BAY
WESTERNHALL PT.

PT. SALINEY INT. AIRPORT
HOG ISLAND
CALIVIGNY ISLAND

PRICKLY BAY
L'ANSE AUX EPINES

MILES

1600s, when the French defeated the Caribs in 1651. This is a famous battle, as the last band of Caribs tossed their women and children into the sea, and then, in a suicide leap, plunged to their own deaths off Leapers' Hill (Le Morne de Sauteur), onto a rocky beach below rather than be conquered.

After this conquest, Grenada, like so many other islands in the West Indies, became a pawn in the constant tug-of-war between the two chief rivals of the region, France and Britain. The island changed hands several times. Finally, in 1783, the Treaty of Versailles deeded the rights to Britain. Independence was granted almost 200 years later, when Grenada became an independent state in 1974—with Sir Eric Gairy at the helm.

Now Sir Eric is a weird fellow (he believes in UFOs and says he's communicated with them) and a demagogue. In 1979, his chief rival both politically and ideologically, Maurice Bishop, staged a coup d'état while Sir Eric was out of the country. Bishop was a Marxist and wanted closer relations with both Castro (his mentor) and the Soviet Union. He ruled for four years, trying to institute socialist reforms in the country. It was when Bishop started making overtures to the U.S. that a rival faction in his New Jewel (Joint Endeavor for Welfare, Education and Liberation) Movement, led by Bernard Coard, staged another coup d'état in 1983 and had Bishop and his close advisers arrested and executed. When news of this spread throughout St. George's, the capital, widespread unrest occurred. The U.S. and several Caribbean island nations—led by Eugenia Charles of Dominica—viewed the alliance of Grenada and Cuba with great suspicion; both felt that Castro wanted to use Grenada as a new base of menace. Indeed, he was rebuilding the airport to receive jet aircraft. So under the pretext of rescuing about 100 American medical students at the school on Grand Anse Beach, the U.S. invaded Grenada, expelled the Cubans (who did put up armed resistance), and restored order. Most of the inhabitants of St. George's fled to the mountains while the manuevers were happening. But Grenadians were very happy that the "troubles" were over, and appreciative of the American effort and especially of all the aid money that poured in afterward (there were a lot of new cars around a year after the intervention). Elections were held in 1984 to elect a new government and prime minister, and since then things have been back to normal on the Isle of Spice. The current prime minister and government are U.S.- and tourist-friendly.

GRENADA: KEY FACTS

LOCATION	12°N by 61°W
	90 miles north of Trinidad
	2,200 miles southeast of New York
SIZE	133 square miles
HIGHEST POINT	Mt. St. Catherine (2,756 ft.)
POPULATION	120,000
LANGUAGE	English
TIME	Atlantic Standard Time (1 hour ahead of EST, same as EDT)
AREA CODE	809
ELECTRICITY	220/240 volts AC, 50 cycles, so transformers and adapters will be necessary for U.S.-made appliances
CURRENCY	The Eastern Caribbean dollar, EC$ (EC$2.70 = $1 U.S.)
DRIVING	On the *left*; a valid U.S. or Canadian driver's license okay with a local permit (EC$30)
DOCUMENTS	Passport or proof of nationality with photo ID and an ongoing or return ticket
DEPARTURE TAX	EC$25 (about $9 U.S.)
BEER TO DRINK	Carib
RUM TO DRINK	Jack Iron
MUSIC TO HEAR	Dancehall

GETTING THERE

The Point Salines International Airport is conveniently close to most tourist accommodations on the island. At this writing, there is no nonstop service to Grenada from the States but you can fly direct from the States on AMERICAN (connections in San Juan) and BWIA. AIR CANADA will also route you there with connections. LIAT flies to Grenada from most islands in the West Indies chain.

GETTING AROUND

There are plenty of taxis at Point Salines International Airport. A taxi to the hotel area will cost between EC$25 and $30 (about $10 to $12 U.S.). Be prepared to be ambushed by cabbies when the Customs door slides open. Do haggle—the competition is fierce and you should win. Don't let anyone grab your luggage until all financial matters are settled. There are also minivans or minibuses, which charge next to nothing (about EC$1.25, .45¢ U.S.) that ply the major roads from the Grand Anse Beach into St. George's. These are an easy and fun way to travel. They blast reggae music and the names of the vans are names like "Ruff Xample," "X," "Oo-la-la," or "Tight Clothing." It's a great way to meet Grenadians.

There are plenty of rental cars available too, although the roads outside of the tourist area aren't very good and are poorly marked. AVIS—SPICE ISLAND RENTALS ([800] 331-1084) and BUDGET ([800] 527-0700) have outposts here. Be sure to make your reservations well in advance to ensure the best rates.

The best way to see the island is with Dennis Henry and HENRY'S SAFARI TOURS ([809] 444-5313, fax [809] 444-4847). He'll show you the real Grenada (in an air-conditioned, comfortable van) and take you on some great hikes too. One of his best is to "Honeymoon Falls." It's a 3½-hour hike that is no honeymoon (you must climb up a river for a ways), but once you get there, ahhhhhhh. Dennis leads a number of other safaris too. Better still is Dennis himself. He has such a wealth of knowledge about his island and is a great, athletic, and fun guy. Dennis also provisions sailboats, so if you're chartering out of Grenada, give him a call.

FOCUS ON GRENADA: GRENADA PHOTO SAFARI

Grenada's physical beauty makes it a natural for the camera. But getting to your subject matter can prove difficult. I wouldn't recommend renting a car to explore the north of the island unless you hire a guide. The roads are bad and there are no directional signs. For those who know the territory (and have a sense of adventure), there is the bus—an experience in itself. This is a fine way to get to know Grenadians. The buses, really minivans, play reggae music and squeeze in as many people as possible as they zip around the island.

If that isn't what you had in mind, a great way to see the island is with Dennis Henry. His company Henry Safari Tours ([809] 444-5313), will take you for an all-day tour leaving at 9 A.M. from your hotel or guest house and will return you there at around 5 P.M. for $90 U.S. for one person; $110 U.S. for two people. Dennis, who goes by at least five names, will design a photo safari that will let you put the best of Grenada on film. The tour features frequent stops for photo opportunities as well as a tasty lunch at Betty Mascol's Plantation House. The vehicle is an air-conditioned, comfortable van with good visibility and height to let you take in as much as you can. Dennis is also an avid hiker and conducts mountain walking tours (see "Getting Around," page 187).

CAMERA ETIQUETTE

Many people get irritated when you snap a picture of them without permission (just look at Sean Penn). To show courtesy and to avoid unpleasantness, it is wise to ask before clicking the shutter. Sometimes a friendly gesture and a smile will do the trick. With group shots, use your judgment. A group of women washing clothes in a river may not mind as much as a group of Rastas who may end up taking the film—and your camera—from you.

PHOTO SAFARI 1—ST. GEORGE'S

St. George's is best seen on foot. The town, built on steep hills around a small harbor, has many stair accesses and roads too narrow for cars. It's easy to get to St. George's from your hotel as you are never more than five miles away by taxi, minibus, or thumb.

Plan on doing the walk in the morning as it gets too hot by lunchtime. (Also, the bright light bleaches the color and life out of your subjects until about 3 P.M.) The best place to start is at the Carenage. You'll find a Grentel office for overseas calls, a LIAT office to reconfirm your return flight, the tourist board to buy a good map, and Fed Ex—all in a row. Across the street to the right, the mailboats *Alexia II* and *Adelaide* and sailing schooner *Alexia III* depart Wednesdays and Saturdays for Carriacou. These wooden boats with sails, mast, and so on may not inspire much confidence either as a form of public transport or especially as pleasure craft. But it's possible to secure passage on one—which is, in fact, a great experience.

Moving along, you'll pass the Nutmeg—a good spot for lunch

later on and a rum punch now. If you need the Post Office, it's
farther down the Carenage past Rudolf's restaurant. Otherwise,
turn right on Young Street (Rudolf's will be on the corner). Walking up Young Street, you'll pass the National Museum on the left.
Admission is $1 U.S. and will take you about fifteen minutes to
scour. Far more interesting is the Rasta who is sometimes in front.

At Church Street, take a right and follow it all the way past
several good examples of both English- and French-influenced island architecture—including the Anglican church and the cathedral
that dominates the top of the hill. Then cruise down the Market
Hill to Market Square, where tables are set up and anyone can come
in and sell their wares. Be friendly and open here as you may be the
only nonlocals in sight. This is a good place to strike up a conversation, especially in one of the surrounding rum shops.

When you're ready to move on, head up Halifax Street and turn
right on Cross Street to the Yellow Poui Art Gallery. This is a
legitimate gallery, not a tourist joint. There are several Grenadian
and West Indian artists on display. Prices are not too high and it's
worth a look. Owner Jim Rudin is very knowledgeable and will
show you the latest Calistes (a hot primitive painter).

You're in the homestretch now. Take a left on Church Street,
right on Simmons, and down the steps to Scott Street and the
Carenage. That should put you right at the Nutmeg for lunch and
a much-needed rum punch.

PHOTO SAFARI 2—NORTHERN GRENADA

For this expedition, you need a guide. The roads aren't marked and
are in bad shape—your AAA card won't work here. The guide will
show you places you could never find on your own.

This is an all-day affair. Your guide (I'd recommend Dennis
Henry—phone 443-5313) will pick you up at your hotel and whisk
you through St. George's to the western road. As soon as you leave
St. George's you'll know you're entering the real Grenada.

- LAUNDRY
  Never did laundry look so photogenic. Several times along the
  west coast you will encounter women doing laundry in the rivers.
  The light is muted from the green canopy and the subjects are
  almost always interesting from any angle.

- CONCORD FALLS
  A one-lane road snakes up the hill past countless nutmeg trees to

the falls. Get out of the car and walk up to the Fontainebleu Falls (which takes about 30 minutes)—it's much prettier. There are heavy lush greens with peaked hills as background.

- RUM SHOPS
One thing that becomes clear as you drive around Grenada—and most other West Indian islands—is that just about every house has a liquor license. These shops sell sundries as well as drinks, so you can have a rum punch while looking at the eggs. Now that's progress.

- DAVIDALL ESTATE
This is a spice-processing station near Concord. Outside, there are several drying racks on rollers. Should it rain, they are swiftly pushed into the workhouse and rolled out when the sun shines again. Inside, women separate the mace from the nutmeg seed as well as prepare cocoa beans, cinnamon, and bay leaves. The faces of the workers alone are worth the trip.

- GOUYAVE (pronounced guave)
Here is a large nutmeg-processing station (the next step after Davidall). Gouyave is notorious for its looney citizens, who seem to burn the midnight oil more here than anywhere else on the island. There is a sizable fishing community whose odd hours may add to the general wackiness. Every Sunday evening, there is a crazy "jump-up" in the street with reggae music.

- WOMEN WITH THINGS BALANCED ON THEIR HEADS
You won't see this on the streets of New York. These women have strong necks. It's astonishing what they can balance. Brownie points if you can snap a woman carrying a case of Coke or Carib on her head.

- PROSPECT
If the bridge is out, or just for the fun of it, take the road through this area. It's real Grenadian back country with fine examples of rural dwellings.

- SAUTEURS
Past Prospect, the road will suddenly end on a beach with a commanding view of Sauteurs and its cathedral on top of Leapers' Hill (Le Morne de Sauteur). The town itself is picturesque and worth a brief tour with camera in hand. The drive up to the cathedral will bring you to Leapers' Hill, where the last remaining Carib Indians leaped to their deaths rather than be captured by

their French pursuers. At the church, a workshop of the Young
Grenadians United Crafts Workers Association busily makes
candles or batik that can be bought on the spot. These are teenag-
ers trying to make a cooperative succeed—a worthy effort. In
front of the workshop is an old cemetery and beyond an excellent
view of Carriacou.

• MORNE FENDUE
Home of Betty Mascol's Morne Fendue Plantation Great House,
where you should plan on having lunch. The great house was built
of gray stone and wrought iron by Betty's father in 1908. There
are several varieties of brilliant flowering shrubs featuring the
biggest red poinsettias I've ever seen.

• RIVE ANTOINE
Several miles outside of Morne Fendue, the road will emerge
from the hinterland onto a windswept, palm-studded beach that
curves around to some gigantic cliffs to the north. This is a good
place to sit, cool off, and enjoy the view. If you swim, beware of
the undertow.

Right up the road from the beach is the Rive Antoine rum
distillery. After driving through fields of sugar cane—many
charred from the annual harvest burning—you'll arrive at some
old stone buildings and the distillery's huge waterwheel. This is
one of the few remaining distilleries that looks and operates the
way it did over 150 years ago.

There are four stages in the Rive Antoine distilling process. The
first is the crushing station. It uses the big waterwheel and
squishes the juice from the cane stalks, then sluices the juice into
the next stage—the boiling room. In this cavernous barn, five
different tanks bubble the juice at different temperatures while
birds fly in and out of the rafters adding their "seasoning" to the
batch. It is then sluiced off again to the fermenting and storage
room. After aging, it goes to the still to be boiled to its clear white
state. Unfortunately, you can't sample it here due to strict Grenada laws regarding liquor taxes (the VAT). Only the Customs
man has the key. However, it's sold in just about any rum shop
by the glass and in a few liquor stores in St. George's under the
Rive Antoine label.

• PEARL'S AIRPORT
This rock-strewn strip with cattle grazing on the side used to be
the international airport. Noteworthy here are the burned-out

remains of an Aeroflot and a Cubana Airways airplane. A re-
minder of what used to be.

• GRENVILLE
A fishing and boat-building center with good waterfront/boat
photo potential. Get out of the car and check it out. Then head
south through the basket-weaving district. It seems like everyone
is weaving. Stop and ask about the craft, maybe buy something,
and ask to take a picture.

• GRAND ETANG NATIONAL PARK
It's been a long, hot day but you're almost home. Don't worry,
you won't be hiking—just driving through Grenada's rain forest.
There will be points along the snaking road from Grenville to St.
George's with nice vistas of both the forest vegetation and St.
George's in the distance.

WHERE TO STAY

Almost all the available accommodations can be found on the
southwestern corner of the island from St. George's to the tip of
L'Anse aux Epines. I found prices about average here. Many of the
accommodations are within walking distance of Grenada's most
popular beach, Grand Anse. An exception is Betty Mascol's Morne
Fendue Plantation Great House, which has several interesting
rooms for those who like being in the middle of nowhere (see pages
191 and 196 for more information).

THE FLAMBOYANT HOTEL (809) 444-4247, fax (809) 444-1234
P.O. Box 214, St. George's, Grenada, W.I.

The name alone is reason to stay here (it's actually the name of a
brilliant flowering tree found in these parts). The Flamboyant is a
complex of 30 cottages on a hill with a terrific view of Grand Anse
and St. George's. They are functional in design and come with one
or two bedrooms, kitchen, living/dining room, and front porch to
enjoy the view. The grounds are nicely landscaped and a footpath
takes you on a five-minute walk to the beach. There is a supermarket about a mile down the road.
    Rates are NOT SO CHEAP to PRICEY for singles and doubles.

ST. ANNE'S GUEST HOUSE (809) 444-2727
Paddock, St. George's, Grenada, W.I.

Very popular with the seasoned international travel set (not to be confused with jet set), St. Anne's is the best deal on the island. Located in the hills of St. George's near the Botanical Gardens (it is *not* a ritzy neighborhood), there are 12 clean and simple rooms, very good West Indian cuisine, and an interesting clientele. The beach is not close, there is no view, and assorted stray chickens and goats abound. Nevertheless, some people will stay only at St. Anne's so make your reservations early.

Rates year round are DIRT CHEAP for singles and CHEAP for doubles (CP).

CALABASH (809) 444-4334, fax (809) 444-4804
L'Anse aux Epines (P.O. Box 382, St. George's), Grenada, W.I.

You can rent a suite with its own private pool for $475 U.S. a night. The 27 other suites are cheaper and have a maid who will serve you breakfast in your room. Located on eight acres on L'Anse aux Epines Beach, the upstairs units of these attractive, West Indian–style buildings have the most spacious and comfortable rooms. The atmosphere here is casual and the grounds and beach are very pleasant. The staff, however, doesn't know too much about the "real" Grenada, so be sure to call Dennis Henry (see "Getting Around," p. 187). For the money, you also get a lighted tennis court.

Rates (excluding the pool suite) are WICKED PRICEY for singles and RIDICULOUS for doubles (MAP).

L'ANSE AUX EPINES COTTAGES (809) 444-4565, fax (809) 444-2802
P.O. Box 187, St. George's, Grenada, W.I.

With beautiful coconut-palm–studded grounds and a nice beach out front with lots of shade (it shares the beach with Calabash), this property offers some very pleasant stone and wrought-iron green tin-roofed cottages. All cottages are screened and have fully equipped kitchens, ceiling fans, air-conditioned bedrooms, and TV. Also included is full maid service—she'll clean, cook, and do light laundry: a definite plus. Don't stay in the apartments, though, they look like prisons.

Rates are NOT SO CHEAP for singles and doubles (EP).

VILLAMAR HOLIDAY RESORT (809) 444-4716, fax 444-4847
L'Anse aux Epines (P.O. Box 546, St. George's), Grenada, W.I.

This is a cute little property located behind the Calabash resort and is a good, cheap alternative for accommodations in this area. There are 20 clean and simple one- and two-bedroom suites, with air conditioning, lanais, kitchenettes, phone, TV, maid and room service. There is a bar, restaurant, and pool on the property. The beach is a short walk away.

Rates are NOT SO CHEAP for singles and doubles (EP).

CORAL COVE COTTAGES AND APARTMENTS (809) 444-4422, fax (809) 444-4847
L'Anse aux Epines (P.O. Box 487, St. George's), Grenada, W.I.

This is a quiet little place on the water and another wonderfully cheap alternative. Guests have a choice of 18 simple but comfortable cottages or apartments, all with fully equipped kitchens, lanais, maid service and ceiling fans. The beach is small but private (with good snorkeling in front), and there is a tennis court and pool for your leisure.

Rates are NOT SO CHEAP for singles and doubles (EP).

RAMADA RENAISSANCE HOTEL (809) 444-4371, fax (809) 444-4800
Stateside: (800) 228-9898; in Canada: (800) 268-8998/(416) 485-2610; in the UK: (01) 235-5264
P.O. Box 441, Grand Anse Beach, Grenada, W.I.

If you want a big, comfortable, and deluxe resort, this is your only choice on Grenada. Located in the middle of Grand Anse Beach—the best location on the best beach in Grenada—this 184-room, 20-acre resort is the largest on the island. As big resorts go, it's not bad looking. Rooms, situated in two-story wings, are spacious and attractive, with air conditioning, balcony or veranda, phone, cable TV, and room service. There's a big pool, two tennis courts, all water sports (Dive Grenada is located here) and an activities desk. There are two restaurants and two bars.

Rates are VERY PRICEY to WICKED PRICEY for singles and doubles (EP).

LA SAGESSE NATURE CENTER (809) 444-6458, fax (809) 444-4847
Stateside: (800) 322-1753
P.O. Box 44, St. David's, Grenada, W.I.

If you're looking for a very quiet place to stay that's well off the beaten path, La Sagesse may be for you. It is set on a 77-acre former banana plantation with a pretty beach in front. All three simple apartments are situated in an old manor house and have kitchenettes, private bath, ceiling fans, and screened windows. There is a bar and a seafood restaurant on the premises. A nature sanctuary and hiking trails border the property.

Rates are NOT SO CHEAP to PRICEY for singles and doubles (MAP).

WHERE TO DINE

There is not a huge selection of great restaurants, but there are some good places to eat. My favorites are:

MAMMA'S, Old Lagoon Road, 440-1459

Mamma's is the Whitman's Sampler of West Indian restaurants. There is no menu—just small plates that start arriving at breakneck speed and don't stop. As the plates start piling up, you're reminded of Lucy and Ethel trying to eat all the chocolates on the conveyor belt. There are all kinds of delights: callaloo soup, conch fritters, armadillo, manicou (possum), fish stew, breadfruit, tannia fritters, christophene, and on and on. The dishes change nightly. The décor is funky at best and the food is good, not great. The hand-painted shirts are a must buy. $$ *No credit cards.*

LA BELLE CREOLE, Blue Horizon Cottage Hotel, Grand Anse Beach, 444-4316

Reputedly one of the best restaurants in Grenada, it features what could be called upscale West Indian food (local dishes with a Continental flourish). Reservations are required for nonhotel guests. $$$$

THE BOATYARD, Spice Island Marina, L'Anse aux Epines, 444-4662

The only reason I mention this haunt of the yachty set is that when I was there the first time, Ted Kennedy sat at the next table. I found the food dreadful, but liquid dinners are the vogue among boaters anyway. $$

THE NUTMEG, on the Carenage, St. George's, 440-2539

Their rum punch is fantastic, which may be the best reason to go here. The food is decent, the place clean, and the second floor offers pleasant views of the harbor. Their fish specials and lambi (conch) are recommended. A great spot for breakfast and lunch in town. Locals eat here—a good sign. $$

MORNE FENDUE PLANTATION GREAT HOUSE (BETTY MASCOL'S), Morne Fendue, St. Patrick's Parish, 442-9330

A classic old plantation house located in the heart of Grenada's north country that's made of gray stone with wrought-iron grill-work and huge poinsettia plants in the circular driveway. A woman greets you and sends (orders) you to the washroom to freshen up. Then Betty Mascol—the proprietress—places an outstanding rum punch (the best in the Caribbean) in your hand as she introduces herself and the other guests at the table. The cuisine is West Indian: callaloo soup, ox tail and tongue, seasoned rice, chicken, christo-phene, and a papaya custard and cream are usual fare, although Mrs. Mascol changes her menu when it suits her. The lunch is not cheap, but it's the only place in this town for sit-down. $$ *No credit cards.*

TABANCA, Grand Anse Beach, 444-1300

Located on a hill at the southern end of the beach (look for the huge pink banner), this is a great spot for a few cocktails and dinner. $$$

THE FOUNTAIN, next to Island Center, Grand Anse, 444-4235

The place for burgers, rôti, and sandwiches at cheap prices.

BIRD'S NEST, Grand Anse, 444-4264

Great service, dreadful Chinese food—you decide. $$

CANBOULEY, Morne Rouge, St. George's, 444-4401

This is a very highly regarded, if pricey, nouvelle Caribbean restaurant located in St. George's. Reservations are suggested. $$$$

FISH & CHICK, Old Sugar Mill Building, Grand Anse, 444-4235

With such a great name, this is fast food with, duh, fish & chicken. Take-out or eat-in. $

PORTOFINO RISTORANTE ITALIA, the Carenage, St. George's, 440-3986

Serving Italian food with a pretty view of the harbor, this is the only Italian restaurant on the island. It's also a good place to get pizza (available to go, too). $$$

SUGAR & SPICE, Grand Anse Shopping Plaza, 444-4597

This place is very popular with locals for both pizza and 'scream. $

COCONUT'S BEACH (aka THE FRENCH RESTAURANT), Grand Anse, 444-4644

Located on the beach in an old, funky house, this establishment features excellent French/Créole cuisine in a very romantic and casual setting. Reservations are suggested. $$$

GOING OUT

There are some fun things to do here at night. COT BAM, on the beach in Grand Anse (no phone), gets some jammin' reggae bands on weekends. The BOATYARD at L'Anse aux Epines Beach in the Marina has a popular Friday-night party with a steel band and a loco and local DJ. FANTAZIA 2001, in the Gem Apartments on Morne Rouge Beach (444-1189), is the island's hot disco and is very popular with locals (no shorts). LE SUCRIER, in the Old Sugar Mill by the Grand Anse roundabout, has live jazz bands on Thursdays and DJs on Fridays and Saturdays.

Don't Miss

HENRY'S SAFARI TOURS—You won't be disappointed (see "Getting Around," page 187).

FOODLAND—If you have an efficiency, this is a great supermarket located in the Grand Anse Shopping Center.

CARRIACOU—Grenada's sister island (see Carriacou, pages 121–30)

A RUM PUNCH AT BETTY MASCOL'S MORNE FENDUE PLAN-TATION GREAT HOUSE—The best in the Caribbean (see page 196).

THE OTHER GRENADINES

There are several other Grenadines besides Bequia and Mustique (re-
viewed elsewhere in this book). Heading south from Mustique, there is
Canouan, Mayreau, the Tobago Cays, Union Island, Palm Island, and Petit
St. Vincent. Then you cross the border into Grenada, when you reach
Carriacou (see pages 121–30) and Petit Martinique (the reputed smuggling
capital of the West Indies—don't even think about setting foot on this
island). But what about the other islands? Can you stay on them? Are they
worth visiting? Yes and yes; yet they are so petite that all the essential info
you need to know can be included here.

Of the bunch (Canouan, Mayreau, the Tobago Cays, Union Island, Palm
Island, and Petit St. Vincent), Union Island is the most "developed."
While there is some hiking that can be done here, the island is very arid
and just not all that interesting (and the beaches are lacking). Rather,
Union is a launching pad for Palm Island, Petit St. Vincent, and the
Tobago Cays. Both Palm Island and Petit St. Vincent are very small islands
that are also resorts. Palm Island sits just off Union and is the labor of love
of the Caldwell family. It is a very casual, relaxed place and is not outrageously expensive, considering its location. Petit St. Vincent is a super-
royal-deluxe luxury resort with a price tag of over $500 a day. Like Palm
Island, PSV, as it is called, is the kind of place that appeals to the traveler
who wants to be quiet, pampered, and sequestered with someone else (I
wouldn't advise going to these places alone or you'll have lots of dates with
your hand). Both islands have good beaches, although if you want to be
nudie, Palm Island won't work but PSV will.

The third destination from Union, the Tobago Cays, are actually uninhabited. They are, however, a standard stop on the cruising circuit so don't
be surprised is you find 50 other boats in the harbor when you take an
excursion to the islands. Fantasies of your own deserted beach where you
can reenact *Swept Away* just won't play here, at least during the high
season. But the snorkeling is excellent, and I highly recommend going here
if you can.

The other two islands on the chain, Mayreau and Canouan, are at the
cusp of being discovered. Indeed, a 200-room hotel is in the works for the
northern part of Canouan, where its best and most pristine beaches, Ma-
hault Bay and The Pool, are located. Obviously, this will overwhelm the
little island. At the moment, there are four places to stay on Canouan—

The Canouan Beach Hotel, The Crystal Sands Hotel, Villa le Bijou, and the Anchor Inn Guest House. Of the lot, the Canouan Beach Hotel is by far the most deluxe and expensive; it's also an all-inclusive resort. Adding to my foreboding, the island now has a rebuilt airport which allows night landings, so it is poised to handle more traffic. I'd hurry if you want to see the island before it explodes—or at least the nice beaches are spoiled. On Mayreau, there are two places to stay—Salt Whistle Bay and Dennis' Hideaway. The former is another deluxe resort and the latter is a funky guest house with a real personality as proprietor. Mayreau's best beach is Salt Whistle Bay, but you'll be sharing it with the resort and visiting yachts. (So there may be 10 people on the beach on a busy day. Can you handle it?) Mayreau is right next door to the Tobago Cays, so they are easily reached (Dennis will take you).

WHERE TO STAY, DINE, ETC.

Palm Island

PALM ISLAND BEACH CLUB (809) 458-4804, fax (809) 458-8804
Stateside: (800) 776-PALM
Palm Island, The Grenadines, St. Vincent, W.I.

The resort and its privately owned villas have full roam of this 130-acre island. There are 24 spacious and comfortable cottages all along Casuarina Beach (the island's best). A restaurant set in a South Seas Island pavilion and a circular beach bar complete the facilities. All water sports and tennis are available. The resort has its own private launch from Union Island, the *J & J*. Rates are WICKED PRICEY for singles and RIDICULOUS for doubles (FAP). Here FAP even includes afternoon tea.

Petit St. Vincent

PETIT ST. VINCENT RESORT (809) 458-8801, fax (809) 458-8428
Stateside: (800) 654-9326/(513) 242-1333
Petit St. Vincent, The Grenadines, St. Vincent, W.I.

If you want a luxury resort and your own island to boot—and you have lots of money—then PSV is for you. There are 22 totally loaded cottages spread about the island. Room service is summoned by raising colored flags: Yellow—please come, I want service; red—please, please stay away.

P.S. You should be able to find an empty beach here for whatever you want to do.

Rates are BEYOND BELIEF for singles and doubles (FAP).

Canouan

CANOUAN BEACH HOTEL (809) 458-8888, fax (809) 458-8875
Stateside: (508) 788-0306
Sandy Glossy Bay (P.O. Box 530), Canouan, The Grenadines, St. Vincent, W.I.

Built on a peninsula with beaches on both sides, this 43-cottage resort catering to a French clientele is the biggest hotel in the country. This is an all-inclusive resort, so everything from soup to nuts is included in the price. Tennis and water sports are also available.

Rates are WICKED PRICEY to OUTRAGEOUS for singles and RI-DICULOUS to BEYOND BELIEF for doubles (FAP).

VILLA LA BIJOU (809) 458-8025, no fax
Friendship, Canouan, The Grenadines, St. Vincent, W.I.

This is a ten-room guest house on the top of a hill with great views and an obvious French influence. The beach is a short walk away.

Rates are PRICEY for singles and doubles (MAP). *No credit cards.*

CRYSTAL SANDS BEACH HOTEL (809) 458-8015, fax (809) 458-8309
Grand Bay Beach, Canouan, The Grenadines, St. Vincent, W.I.

This is a small ten-unit motel-like accommodation. Fishing, sailing, and snorkeling can be found off the very fine beach.

Rates are PRICEY for singles and doubles (MAP). *No credit cards.*

ANCHOR INN GUEST HOUSE (809) 458-8568, no fax
Canouan, The Grenadines, St. Vincent, W.I.

A tiny guest house close to the beach featuring three simple rooms with baths. This is the cheapest place to stay on Canouan.

Rates are NOT SO CHEAP for singles and doubles (MAP).

Mayreau

SALT WHISTLE BAY CLUB (809) 493-9609, no fax
Stateside: (800) 263-2780; Canada: (613) 634-1963, fax (613) 384-6300
Mayreau, The Grenadines, St. Vincent, W.I.

Located on the most beautiful beach on Mayreau (and some say the Grenadines), this deluxe property of 22 acres and 10 bungalows is a very tranquil
retreat. It's also a popular stop for the yachty set. The accommodations
were built by local craftspeople using as many indigenous materials as
possible. The result is very satisfying.

Rates are RIDICULOUS for singles and OUTRAGEOUS for doubles
(MAP). *No credit cards.*

DENNIS' HIDEAWAY (809) 458-8594
Mayreau, The Grenadines, St. Vincent, W.I.

What was once a famous restaurant among the yachty set has expanded
into a guest lodging as well. Dennis, the glue that attracts all kinds of
visitors because he is a party animal, has added some small, rather spare
but affordable rooms. The restaurant still serves excellent Créole fare, and
the establishment is the hub of activity on the island (Dennis plays guitar).
Its central location makes access to all of the island very simple. Beware of
barking dogs, however.

Rates are CHEAP for single and doubles (CP).

GUADELOUPE

TOURISTO SCALE   📷 📷 📷 📷 📷 📷 📷   7

It's morning and I'm hungry. Stepping out into the streets of Gosier, I almost swoon from the smell of freshly made baguettes. I follow my nose. I see several Guadeloupeans coming down the street with several baguettes in hand. I must be getting close. Just the thought of a fresh, flaky croissant is making me mad. I reach the pâtisserie, order my café au lait and croissant. I take this marvelous French creation in my hand and take a ravenous bite. Heaven. And this is only the beginning. Guadeloupe is a culinary paradise in the tropics. There are more restaurants here than you can imagine—it seems like there is one on every block. So if you love French food with a Créole twist, you'll love Guadeloupe.

Guadeloupe is very French. It is a full-fledged *région* of France. Paris is the cultural and political capital of the island (the Guadeloupe *région* also includes St. Barts and St. Martin). Just off the coast of Guadeloupe are the Îles des Saints and Marie-Galante, which are small islands and just as French. The island of Guadeloupe is actually two islands (Grande-Terre and Basse-Terre) separated by a seawater channel, the Rivière Salée. These island names, in French literally meaning "Big Land" and "Low Land," are really misnomers as Basse-Terre is the mountainous, volcanic part of the island and Grande-Terre is fairly flat. There are several theories as to why this is so. Probably the most likely explanation is that they are named for wind velocity—the flatter island having stronger winds, thus being named Grande-Terre.

Guadeloupe, like Martinique, is highly developed (although Martinique is considered more sophisticated and affluent). Often you will feel more like you're in some part of continental France than

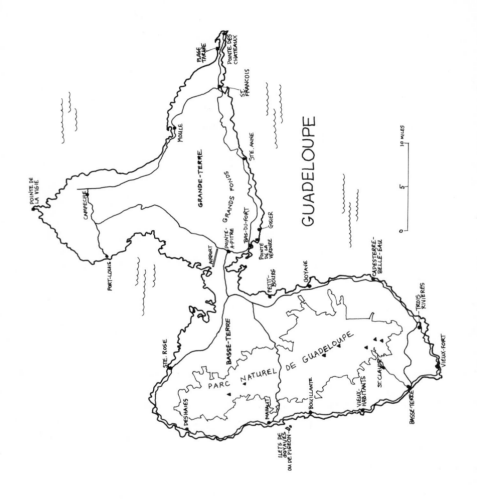

GUADELOUPE

POINTE DE LA VIGIE
PORT-LOUIS
CARPECHE
GRANDE-TERRE
MOULE
PLAGE TARARE
POINTE DES CHATEAUX
ST-FRANCOIS
STE-ANNE
POINTE-À-PITRE
AIRPORT
GRANDS FONDS
BAS-DU-FORT
POINTE LA VÉDURE
GOSIER
STE-ROSE
BASSE-TERRE
PARC NATUREL DE GUADELOUPE
PETIT-BOURG
GOYAVE
CAPESTERRE-BELLE-EAU
DESHAIES
MAHAUT
BOUILLANTE
ÎLETS DE GOYAVES OU DE PIGEON
VIEUX-HABITANTS
ST-CLAUDE
TROIS-RIVIÈRES
BASSE-TERRE
VIEUX-FORT

0   5   10 MILES

in the Caribbean, especially in Pointe-à-Pitre. There are high-rise apartment buildings, shopping centers, huge supermarkets, billboards galore, and freeways. But there are wonderful Caribbean elements too—like open-air markets and West Indian–style houses—and the contrast between the two is striking. When you venture into the countryside, the balance tips more toward the Caribbean flavor, yet you have the great French road system to help you see the sights. The smaller out islands, like the Îles des Saints, are much less developed.

Almost all the hotels and tourist areas are on Grande-Terre and are concentrated on the south coast stretching from Pointe-à-Pitre to Pointe des Châteaux. This is where the best beaches are located. Along this coast, are three major towns: Gosier, Ste-Anne, and St-François. Of the three, St-François is the most desirable. It is the least developed and has the nicest beaches nearby, including Plage Tarare—the official nude beach. Ste-Anne is also pleasant and the home of good windsurfing and the Club Med (which also has a small, not terribly private, nude beach). Gosier is the most developed, with big resorts and lots of tourists (but also some great restaurants and the best nightlife). Basse-Terre doesn't really have a tourist area per se, as its black sand and often rocky beaches aren't a draw. But there are a few options here, including two places near Pigeon Island on the West Coast—a popular snorkel and dive spot—and the Parc Naturel, a 74,100-acre preserve of waterfalls, rain forest, lakes, mountains, flora and fauna.

While there are some Americans and English Canadians who come here, the overwhelming majority of visitors to Guadeloupe are French. Almost all of them come on package tours. If you are a Francophile, you'll love it. But you should note that English is not spoken widely here. As a matter of fact, it's rarely spoken except at a few major resorts. If you don't speak French, you will have a difficult time understanding and communicating. I consider my French to be passable, and even I had difficulty when something out of the ordinary occurred. For example, my room didn't have a shower curtain and I needed a voltage converter for my laptop. The front desk staff didn't speak English. Trying to explain these problems in French was hard enough. I can't imagine trying to explain them without knowing the language. But if you do speak French, you will have a ball.

THE BRIEFEST HISTORY

Like almost all the other Caribbean islands, Guadeloupe was settled by the Caribs, who called the island *Karukera*, or "Island of Beautiful Waters." Columbus sighted the island on his second voyage in 1493 and named it after Santa Marie de Guadeloupe de Estremadura. The Caribs, fierce fighters that they were, kept the Spanish off the island. But the French landed a party in 1635 and eventually drove the Caribs off. Sugar became the major money-maker and the French imported lots of slaves from Guinea to make it work. The island was officially annexed by the King of France in 1674 and remained under French control, except for 1759–1763, when the British occupied the island. It went back to France under the terms of the Treaty of Paris, in which French Canada was ceded to Britain. The French Revolution brought instability to the island; there was a short reign of terror and then the abolition of slavery. This was reversed with the advent of Napoleon; slavery was reestablished in 1802 and remained in force until the efforts of Alsatian Victor Schoelcher permanently abolished the abomination in 1848. To keep the plantations running, indentured labor (another form of slavery) was imported from Calcutta. For a century, Guadeloupe remained in the backwater of French politics until it became an overseas *départment* in 1946 and finally in 1974 became a *région*. The *région* is governed by a prefect, appointed by the French Minister of the Interior, and by two locally elected legislative bodies, the Conseil General and the Conseil Régional (a third group, the Economic and Social Committee, acts as a consultant). Guadeloupe has two senators, four deputies, and two members of the Economic Committee representing it in the French Parliament. There is a strong independence movement that has gained momentum in recent decades. Tourism and agriculture (bananas and sugar) are the primary engines driving the economy.

GUADELOUPE: KEY FACTS

LOCATION	16°N by 62°W
	38 miles south of Antigua
	30 miles north of Dominica
	1,845 miles southeast of New York
SIZE	530 square miles

Basse-Terre—312 square miles
Grande-Terre—218 square miles

HIGHEST POINT	La Soufrière Volcano (4,813 ft.)
POPULATION	360,000
LANGUAGE	*French!*
TIME	Atlantic Standard Time (1 hour ahead of EST, same as EDT)
AREA CODE	To call from the U.S. dial 011 (the international access code), then 590 (the country code), followed by the six-digit local number
ELECTRICITY	220 volts AC, 50 cycles, which means you'll need a transformer and an adapter
CURRENCY	Legal tender is the French franc (F); the rate of exchange fluctuates a bit, so check before your trip
DRIVING	On the *right;* your valid driver's license will suffice for up to 20 days, after which you'll need an International Driver's License
DOCUMENTS	For stays of less than 21 days, U.S. and Canadian residents need only proof of identity (a voter registration card or birth certificate with photo ID), plus an ongoing or return ticket; for longer stays a passport is necessary
DEPARTURE TAX	None
BEER TO DRINK	Corsaire
RUM TO DRINK	Rhum Bologne
MUSIC TO HEAR	Zook

GETTING THERE

Guadeloupe's La Raizet International Airport accepts jumbo jets from all over. AMERICAN flies nonstop from New York and Miami; AMERICAN EAGLE flies nonstop from San Juan; AIR CANADA flies nonstop from Montréal; AIR FRANCE has Sunday flights from Miami; AIR GUADELOUPE has Thursday and Saturday flights from Miami and daily flights from neighboring islands; and LIAT has several flights daily into Guadeloupe from neighboring islands, including Antigua—a major hub. By boat, the

Emeraude Express, a high-speed catamaran, has several trips weekly from Martinique, Dominica, Antigua, and Montserrat.

GETTING AROUND

With 1,225 miles of good roads, among the best in the Caribbean, you should definitely rent a car. Driving is on the right, which makes it easy, too. Roads are clearly marked (a rarity in these latitudes) and the European sign system is very helpful and easy to use. All of the major international companies are here, including AVIS ([800] 331-1084/[590] 82-02-71), BUDGET ([800] 527-0700/[590] 82-95-58), HERTZ ([800] 654-3001/[590] 82-00-14), THRIFTY (800) 367-2277, and NATIONAL's affiliate, EUROPCAR ([800] 468-0008/[590] 82-50-51). Be sure to reserve well in advance, as the cheapest cars will be booked if you arrive without a reservation. You will also be able to lock in a better rate. If you don't want to drive, there are plenty of taxis (they're expensive) or the public bus system, which is excellent here and a great way to meet the locals.

FOCUS ON GUADELOUPE: AN EXCURSION TO THE ÎLES DES SAINTES

If you remember what St. Barts used to be like before the advent of super-luxury hotels and all those fabulous New Yorkers and Los Angelenos, you will love the Îles des Saintes, a small cluster of islands about eight miles south of Basse-Terre. There are actually five islands (which physically look a lot like the smaller Virgin Islands), of which two are inhabited and one is available for travelers, Terre-de-Haut. The latter is a very picturesque and hilly island, with several good places to stay, lots of good restaurants and some nice beaches—including a nude beach.

Terre-de-Haut is small, I believe the French call it *petite*, so it's very easy to explore, discover, and feel a sense of possessiveness about. The town is a symphony of red roofs and brightly colored West Indian houses and buildings. It is very clean and decidedly French (it was settled by immigrants from Breton). Above all, it is very picturesque (your cameras will eat it up). The climate here is

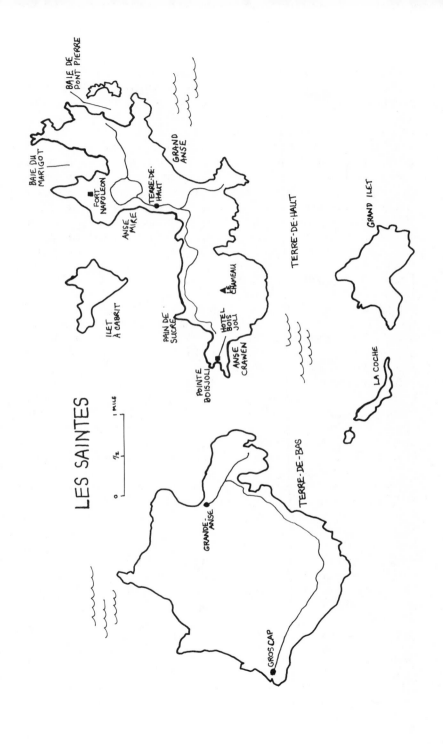

LES SAINTES

BAIE DE PONT PIERRE

BAIE DU MARIGOT

GRAND ANSE

FORT NAPOLÉON

TERRE-DE-HAUT

ANSE MIRE

ÎLET À CABRIT

PAIN DE SUCRE

LE CHAMEAU

HOTEL BOIS JOLI

POINTE BOIS-JOLI

ANSE CRAWEN

TERRE-DE-HAUT

GRAND ÎLET

LA COCHE

TERRE-DE-BAS

GRANDE ANSE

GROS CAP

0   ½   1 MILE

dry and sunny. The focal point of town is the ferry dock, and there is a little square at the foot of the dock which is a fun place to people-watch. On the south side of the square is a café on the second floor with a veranda overlooking the activity. Time out for a ti punch, made with fresh coconut milk and lots o' rum. Floating down the stairs, you can explore the whole town with a few hours' stroll. The town is also in the middle of the island, so all points elsewhere are not far away. With a Peugeot scooter, you can go just about anywhere. Be sure to rent one (about 80F per day) as soon as you get off the ferry, or have your hotel make arrangements. Many of the recommended accommodations are out of town, which is no big deal, but it's nice to have a fun means of transportation. In addition, the nicest beach, Anse Crawen (which is also the nude beach), is at the southern end of the island—a long walk from town. There are several big hills, if not mountains, on Terre-de-Haut. These are particularly fun with scooters, especially the extraordinarily steep and hairpin road up Le Chameau (988 ft.), with the reward of great views and a hair-raising ride down awaiting you.

Once you have a map, it's easy to explore. If you're just in on a day trip, get your scooter and head for Fort Napoléon, which sits almost 400 feet high overlooking the entrance to the harbor and bay with commanding views. It closes at noon, so this is a good first stop. Fort Napoléon was called the "Gibraltar of the Caribbean" (not to be confused with Brimstone Hill on St. Kitts, the "Gibraltar of the West Indies"). The fort is interesting for about twenty minutes, then take in the view, and off you go to explore the various beaches. There aren't many roads, so it's easy. I recommend finishing your exploring by noon so you can have a leisurely lunch. Everything here closes for lunch; even scooter traffic (except for residents) is banned from town between the hours of 12:30 and 2 P.M. (so townspeople can have some peace and quiet). After lunch, hit the beach—the best one being Anse Crawen. If you eat lunch at Bois Joli, it's just over the hill. The best thing about the beach, besides being so remote, is that there are plenty of shade trees for relief from le soleil. Note that there are lots of day-trippers who come here from Guadeloupe, which is very unfortunate but a reality, as are the flies which seem to be everywhere.

GETTING THERE

While there is an airport, most people arrive by boat. If you are prone to seasickness, I strongly suggest flying in and out or taking a heavy dose of Dramamine and finding yourself a spot on the outside deck. The voyage can be rough (and wet on the top deck). I saw more than a few people hurl over the side. CARIBES AIR TOURISME flies to Les Saintes twice a day from La Raizet and both BRUDEY FRÈRES and TRANS-ANTILLES EXPRESS make the high-speed boat trip from Pointe-à-Pitre as well as St-François and Trois-Rivières on Basse-Terre. Of the two, I recommend Brudey Frères, as Trans-Antilles Express left me stranded on Les Saintes by canceling regularly scheduled service without any notice. Fortunately, I was able to catch the last boat out to Trois-Rivières on Brudey Frères. I was livid, as my car was in Pointe-à-Pitre, an hour-and-a-half-drive away. These situations often have a silver lining, as I met a very nice trumpet player who, upon overhearing my story, offered me a ride and gave me lots of great info about the island (and he spoke English).

WHERE TO STAY

If you are going to be on Guadeloupe, you should definitely plan to stay on Les Saintes for a few nights. Actually, I think a week here would be superb, quiet but superb. Be sure to make reservations well in advance as this is a petite place. There are a few good places to stay, and here are the best bets:

HOTEL BOIS JOLI (011-590) 99-52-53, fax (011-590) 99-55-05
Terre-de-Haut, 97137 Terre-de-Haut, Les Saintes, Guadeloupe, F.W.I

Located on the western end of the island in a small cove, this is the best place to stay on Les Saintes (and a must). Stretching out along the beach, there are tastefully furnished, air-conditioned pink bungalows overlooking the water, Ilet-à-Cabrit, Terre-de-Basse, and Guadeloupe's Basse-Terre in the distance and clouds. There are also 25 hotel rooms. The hotel has a huge open-air dining pavilion with views of the beach, bay, and swimming pool immediately below. A bridge straddles the pool, which seems to be more popular with guests than the beach. A rather hip crowd stays here, so it could be fun (and the food is the best on the island). There are water sports available, including sailing, waterskiing, and plongee (scuba).

Rates are PRICEY for singles and VERY PRICEY for doubles (MAP). Bungalow suites are WICKED PRICEY (MAP).

LE KANAOA (011-590) 99-51-36, fax (011-590) 99-55-04
Anse Mire, 97137 Terre-de-Haut, Les Saintes, Guadeloupe, F.W.I.

A compact hotel on the north end of the harbor, Le Kanaoa is a good and cheaper alternative if Bois Joli is booked or above your budget. It has its own very tiny sandbox as beach, a boat dock, and a comfortable but small pool and patio. Fishing and waterskiing are available at the hotel. Rooms are simple and pleasant, with knotty pine furniture, private bath, and air conditioning. There is a central bar/restaurant area for meals and gathering. Best of all, Le Kanaoa is run by some very nice people.

Rates are NOT SO CHEAP for singles and PRICEY for doubles (CP).

LE VILLAGE CREOLE (011-590) 99-53-83, fax (011-590) 99-55-55
Pointe Coquelet, 97137 Terre-de-Haut, Guadeloupe, F.W.I.

Right next door to the Kanaoa, this property is a series of duplex units stacked together. All 22 units have kitchens, so if you want an efficiency, this is the place. Rooms are rather basically furnished with bath and washer/dryer and offer maid service. There is only a rocky beach, but the views and breezes are great. Note that there is no pool, although you may be able to make an arrangement with the Kanaoa.

Rates are PRICEY to VERY PRICEY for singles and doubles (EP).

LES PETITS SAINTS AUX ANACARDIERS (011-590) 99-50-99,
fax (011-590) 99-54-51
La Savane, 97137 Terre-de-Haut, Les Saintes, Guadeloupe, F.W.I.

Right in town a few blocks up the hill sits the Anacardiers, a ten-room hotel set in a pretty Créole house. There is a good view of the bay from both the rooms and the pretty restaurant. All rooms have air conditioning, telephone, TV, and minibar. A patio and pool complete the picture.

Rates are NOT SO PRICEY for singles and doubles (CP).

JEANNE D'ARC (011-590) 99-50-41
Anse du Fond Cure, 97317 Terre-de-Haut, Les Saintes, Guadeloupe, F.W.I.

If you're on a tight budget, this is a simple and clean place right in town on the water. There are ten rooms in a rather nondescript-looking building.

Rates are NOT SO CHEAP for singles and doubles (CP).

WHERE TO EAT

For a petite isle, there are some great restaurants. Among the best are:

BOIS JOLI, 99-50-38

This is the best restaurant on the island, serving three meals a day. Specialties include fish pancakes, clams in Créole sauce, stuffed burgots (sea snails), and barbecued fish steaks. Reservations are suggested. $$$$

LA SALADERIE, 99-54-23

Located on a point just north of town, this is a wonderful place for lunch or dinner with fab views overlooking the harbor. Prices are very reasonable too. $$$

LES PETITS SAINTS AUX ANACARDIERS, 99-50-99

More of a bistro, this Créole/French restaurant is worth the stop. $$$

DON'T MISS

- ANSE CRAWEN—the nude beach
- A SCOOTER RIDE UP LE CHAMEAU
- LUNCH AT BOIS JOLI—call 99-50-38
- CLUB NAUTIQUE FOR DIVING—call 99-54-25

WHERE TO STAY ON GUADELOUPE

As I said earlier, almost all of the hotels and tourist areas are on Grande-Terre and are concentrated on the south coast stretching from Pointe-à-Pitre to Pointe des Châteaux. Most are in the three major towns—Gosier, Ste-Anne, and St-François. Of the three, St-François is the most desirable, Ste-Anne is quite pleasant and the home of good windsurfing and the Club Med, and Gosier is the most developed, with big resorts and lots of tourists but also some great restaurants and the best nightlife. Basse-Terre doesn't really have a tourist area per se but there are two places to stay if you want to try something different and stay here. Both are close to diving on Pigeon Island and the Parc Naturel. This area is very untouristed, so it may be worth checking out. When booking, try to get a package, it will save you a lot here.

ST-FRANÇOIS

HAMAK (011-590) 88-59-99, fax (011-590) 88-41-92
97118 St-François, Guadeloupe, F.W.I.

With the reputation as the best hotel on Guadeloupe, a reputation which many on the island say has gone south, this is certainly one of the most expensive. Situated on a small, protected beach and with 250 acres of tropical gardens to roam around on, there is also a Robert Trent Jones II, 18-hole, 6,755-yard, par-71 golf course with a full-service clubhouse and snack bar for duffers. Other recreational possibilities include a spa, Jacuzzi, pool, tennis courts, windsurfing, and other water sports. There are 56 suites with kitchenettes situated in villas scattered about the property.

Rates are WICKED PRICEY to RIDICULOUS for singles and doubles (EP).

PLANTATION STE-MARTHE (011-590) 88-72-46, fax (011-590) 88-72-47
Stateside: (800) 223-9815/(212) 251-1800
97118 St-François, Guadeloupe, F.W.I.

A four-star hotel (all hotels in France are rated by the government), this is one of the best places to stay in St-François. Built with a New Orleans–style look, this 3-story, 120-room hotel sits up on a hill overlooking the sea. There is a large pool, tennis and golf available nearby. Rooms are attractive and tastefully furnished and all have air conditioning. The beach is down the road.

Rates are PRICEY to VERY PRICEY for singles and doubles.

LE MÉRIDIEN ST-FRANÇOIS (011-590) 88-51-00, fax (011-590) 88-40-71
Stateside: (800) 543-4300
97118 St-François, Guadeloupe, F.W.I.

This is a big, rather plain-looking hotel on the beach owned by Air France, so check out packages here. There are 265 rooms and all the amenities of a large four-star hotel, including 24-hour room service and several restaurants and bars on the premises. There is a pool, tennis, and most water sports on the beach. Golf is available next door at the Hamak.

For those who want to spend even more money on luxury, the Méridien has added a 52-suite luxury wing called LA COCOTE-RAIE. Each room has a view of the sea, a private balcony, a round tub and separate shower in each bathroom, etc.

Rates are WICKED PRICEY to OUTRAGEOUS for singles and doubles (CP). For La Cocoteraie, rates are OUTRAGEOUS to BEYOND BELIEF.

STE-ANNE

HOTEL LA TOUBANA (011-590) 88-25-78, fax (011-590) 88-38-90
Stateside: (407) 777-2207
Durivage (B.P. 63), 97180 Ste-Anne, Guadeloupe, F.W.I.

Perched high up on a bluff overlooking the sea and the Club Med, this reasonably priced hotel is your best bet in Ste-Anne, unless you want the Club Med. Accommodations are scattered about the hillside in 32 bungalows in both standard and superior classes (the latter have better views and furnishings). All have a kitchenette, air conditioning, phone, a private garden and lanai. Units are nicely done in pastels. There is a pool and a deck with great breezes and views. Down the hill, there is a small man-made beach that is protected from the surf. Other activities available are tennis, billiards, and Ping-Pong. The restaurant here is quite good and English is spoken here—a plus.

Rates are PRICEY to WICKED PRICEY for singles and VERY PRICEY to WICKED PRICEY for doubles (CP).

CLUB MED–CARAVELLE (011-590) 88-21-00, fax (011-590) 88-06-06
Stateside: (800) 258-2633, fax (602) 948-4562
97180 Ste-Anne, Guadeloupe, F.W.I.

One of the original Club Meds (it opened in 1973), this is an extensive complex of 310 rooms with a wide variety of sports and activities, which is a Club Med hallmark. This is an all-inclusive resort, which in the land of extraordinary cuisine and restaurants, is a drawback—unless you forgo the buffets and head out on your own. The place is big, with a pretty if somewhat crowded beach. Inside, there is a theater, nightclub, several bars and restaurants, health club, video room, billiards, and a card room. Rooms have private baths and a king- or two full-sized beds, but not all have balconies. Outside, there are six tennis courts, volleyball, basketball, archery, trapeze, and every water sport you can imagine. The beach here has a small but very busy nudie section adjoining the main beach.

Rates are VERY PRICEY to WICKED PRICEY for singles and doubles (AP).

LE ROTABAS (011-590) 88-25-60, fax (011-590) 88-26-87
Durivage (B.P. 30), 97180 Ste-Anne, Guadeloupe, F.W.I.

Located right on the beach next to Club Med and L.C.S. Windsurfing, this is a somewhat cheaper and good accommodation for those who are here to windsurf. There are 44 air-conditioned rooms in several small buildings wedged around the property. It's a relaxed place and the rooms are pleasant.

Rates are PRICEY for singles and doubles (CP).

GOSIER

LA CRÉOLE BEACH HOTEL (011-590) 90-46-46, fax (011-590) 90-46-66
Stateside: (407) 777-2207
Pointe de la Verdure (B.P. 19), 97190 Gosier, Guadeloupe, F.W.I.

If you're going to be in Gosier, this is your best bet. Located just west of town on Pointe de la Verdure, it's a medium-sized resort, with 156 rooms spread out among several attractive Créole-style buildings. It has a large pool (good for laps), it's own man-made beach, lots of water sports (the Hobie 16 Worlds were held here in 1993), and a poolside bar area that is a very pleasant spot for a cocktail. Guests have privileges at the adjacent SALAKO (owned by the same company), which has a decent gym for keeping up with your workouts. Rooms are comfortable and furnished in what might be called tropical/French moderne. All rooms have air conditioning, balcony, TV, bath (European-style with the hand-held shower), and direct-dial phone. The staff is helpful, even if communicating takes some imagination.

Also operated by the same company is MAHOGANY HOTEL and LES RESIDENCES YUCCA, which are next door and share many facilities with La Créole Beach (as well as the same address and phone). Mahogany offers suites (with Jacuzzi), duplexes, and rooms—all with kitchens or kitchenettes. This is a good option for those looking for an efficiency situation. Yucca offers studios with kitchenettes. Of the two, choose Mahogany for this option.

Rates are PRICEY to WICKED PRICEY for singles and VERY PRICEY to WICKED PRICEY for doubles (full breakfast included). Look for packages. For Mahogany and Yucca, rates are PRICEY to VERY PRICEY (CP).

PULLMAN AUBERGE DE LA VIEILLE TOUR (011-590) 84-23-23, same for fax
Stateside: (800) 221-4542
Montauban, 97190 Gosier, Guadeloupe, F.W.I.

This is the grande dame of the Gosier hotels, built around an eighteenth-century windmill and set on a six-acre bluff just steps away from town. Steps down from the main building, which houses the restaurant and bar, are a series of two-story buildings stretched along the shore. All rooms are air-conditioned and overlook the sea with their own lanais. Rooms are pleasantly decorated in the tropical motif (the hotel was refurbished in 1990). On the grounds is a pool, a private beach, and tennis courts.

Rates are WICKED PRICEY for singles and WICKED PRICEY to RIDICULOUS for doubles (CP).

BASSE-TERRE

There are three accommodations here that I would recommend. Two are close to Pigeon Island and Guadeloupe's best diving. All three provide easy access to hiking and the rain forest.

HOTEL PARADISE CRÉOLE (011-590) 98-71-62, fax (011-590) 98-72-08
Route de Poirer-Pigeon, 97132 Bouillante, Guadeloupe, F.W.I.

This is a small hotel set up in the hills that features great sunset views. There are 10 air-conditioned rooms with lanais, a pool, and a restaurant serving Créole cuisine. The hotel will help you arrange diving, waterskiing, hiking, deep-sea fishing, and other activities.

Rates are NOT SO CHEAP for singles and doubles (CP).

ROCHER DE MALENDURE (011-590) 98-70-84, fax (011-590) 98-89-92
97125 Bouillante, Guadeloupe, F.W.I.

If you're looking for a place with kitchenettes on the western side of Basse-Terre, this is it. Situated on a hilly point overlooking the sea, there are nine white-roofed bungalows (actually rondavels) marching up the hill in formation. One of the nicest black-sand beaches on the island is just down the road—it sports several restaurants—and Pigeon Island is just offshore (excursion boats run from the beach).

Rates are NOT SO CHEAP for singles and PRICEY for doubles (EP).

HOTEL RELAIS DE LA GRANDE SOUFRIÈRE (011-590) 80-01-27, fax (011-590) 80-18-40
97120 St-Claude, Guadeloupe, F.W.I.

Located in the semi-fashionable town of St-Claude, which is northeast of Basse-Terre in the mountains, this hotel is an old governor's mansion that was built in the 1860s. There are 21 simply furnished rooms, each with private bath and air conditioning. The hotel is very close to the Bains Jaunes and La Soufrière volcano (and hiking) and is only 15 minutes to the sea. Its perch in the hills affords great views and its restaurant serves *cuisine gastronomique*.

Rates are NOT SO CHEAP for singles and doubles (EP).

WHERE TO EAT

This is the land of *cuisine gastronomique et Créole*, so eating out here is a pleasure. There are hundreds of restaurants, from grand expensive affairs to little dives that serve great food. Part of the fun on Guadeloupe is discovering these, and I urge all of you to follow your nose and your instincts. I'll give you some suggestions, but if you discover other or better establishments let me know. Be sure to pick up a copy of *Ti Gourmet*, a free restaurant guide, when you arrive. Among the best I found:

GREATER GRANDE-TERRE

LE CHÂTEAU DE FEUILLES, Campêche, Anse Bertrand, 22-30-30

This is the best restaurant on Guadeloupe and a special must for lunch (they are not open for dinner). Set out in the middle of nowhere (nine miles from Le Moule on the Campêche road—nowhere, right?) in an old colonial house, you dine on a patio overlooking the pool. Specialties include sea-egg pastries, kingfish pavé with garlic cream, and passionfruit crème brûlée. Reservations are a must. $$$$

ST-FRANÇOIS

LE ZAGAYA, St-François, 88-67-21

An expensive but excellent restaurant for sit-down in St-François. The cuisine is Créole/Continental. Reservations are required. $$$$$

LE VIEUX CARRÉ, Ste-Marthe, St-François, 88-58-64

Set in an old Créole house, this is an informal yet great restaurant that won't break the bank for dinner. It also serves dinner until midnight, a plus for night owls. The large bar features jazz and old Créole songs for entertainment and is a fun place to hang out after dinner. $$$

PLAGE TARARE, no phone

Situated at the end of a dirt road where you park your car for the nudie beach, this is a great place for wine and lunch (and after lunch you can step down to the beach and peel off your clothes). $$

STE-ANNE

LE RELAIS DE MOULIN, Châteaubrun, Ste-Anne, 88-23-96

Crayfish raviolis, fricasseed octopus, and accros de morue are just some of the Créole delights of this restaurant by the windmill. Open for lunch and dinner. Reservations are recommended. $$$$$

FOOD STANDS, Caravelle, Ste-Anne

Wedged on the beach between the Club Med and Le Rotabas (and next to L.C.S. Windsurfing, these little lunch stands prepare heavenly sandwiches on fresh baguettes for under $5, a steal on any French island. $

GOSIER

PESCATORE, Gosier, 84-35-13

This is a funky place with a major hip demeanor. They play cool music, have a youngish crowd and reasonable prices. Cuisine is pastas, pizzas, and salads. There is a tiny front porch and inside it's real Caribbean-style down to the bamboo roof. $$

LE BAOULÉ, 36 Boulevard Amede Clara, Gosier, 84-29-41

If you love grilled Caribbean lobster, look no farther—you've found the place. Le Baoulé is set on a hillside, and you dine while overlooking the sea. A fixed-price dinner at 120F includes a three-course meal. For an additional 40F, you can have lobster. Reservations are suggested. $$$$

LE MEDICIS, Gosier, 84-02-83

This is a very good crêperie and pasta place on the main street of Gosier. There is a big veranda with tables—a great place to sit and watch the activity. Open from 8 A.M. to 11 P.M. $$$

CHEZ DEUX GROS, Route de la Riviera, Gosier, 84-16-20

Furnished with an eclectic mélange of antiques, this restaurant serves excellent *cuisine français et Créole*. Try the queen's necklace, or *la sympathie*. Open only Wednesday through Saturday nights. $$$$$

LA MANDARINE, Rue Simon Radeguonde, Gosier, 84-30-28

Sylvette and Patrick run a fine Créole/français restaurant in the heart of Gosier. Open for lunch except Sundays, and dinner every night until midnight. Try the lobster profiteroles or the sole filet with coconut champagne. $$$$$

L'ENDROIT, Face Ecotel, Gosier Montauban, 84-46-57

If you feel like pizza, there are over 30 varieties served here in a garden setting. It's open until 2 A.M. (they serve until 1 A.M.). A bar and pool table make this a fun late-night spot. $$$

POINTE-À-PITRE

COTE JARDIN, La Marina, Pointe-à-Pitre, 90-91-28

If you're in the mood for *haute cuisine français* and don't mind spending a few chips to have it, this restaurant provides delicious food and nice atmosphere. Open for lunch and dinner except Sundays. Reservations are advised. $$$$$

GREATER BASSE-TERRE

LA TOUNA, Galet, Pigeon, Bouillante, 98-70-10

Right on the beach, this is where seafood comes in fresh every day from the restaurant's own fisherman (swordfish, kingfish, or dolphin). Open for lunch and dinner (during high season) and closed every Monday. Reservations are suggested. $$$$

GOING OUT

Want to shake your groove thang? Well, head for Gosier/Bas-du-Fort and try these establishments out. Check with your hotel host or concierge for which night is hot where (it changes constantly), as well as any special "do's" worth hitting.

• ZENITH, Bas-du-Fort—local music
• LE VICTORIA, Bas-du-Fort—disco
• NEW-LAND, Route Riviera, Gosier—disco
• CARAIBES II, Gosier—cabaret and topless follies
• LE GRAND-LARGE, Gosier—club and disco
• LE SHIVA 2, Gosier—the place to begin the beguine, popular with locals
• AU QUAI DES ETROITS, Gosier—the only gay bar between San Juan and Caracas (90-93-28)

DON'T MISS

MARIE-GALANTE—This is a very untouristed and very French-speaking island off Guadeloupe which is bigger in area (60 square miles) than many popular Caribbean islands and is shaped in an almost perfect circle. It's easy to take a day-trip here from Guadeloupe on either the Trans-Antilles ferry (83-12-45) from Pointe-à-Pitre or the Amanda Galante car ferry (83-19-89)—you can take your rental car—or on a short Air Guadeloupe flight (27-61-90). While here, hit the beach at Petite Anse or Plage de la Feuillere and have lunch at LE NEPTUNE, in the town of Grand-Bourg. If you want to stay overnight, three simple and clean places are AUBERGE DE SOLE-DAD (97-75-45), which is just out of Grand-Bourg, LE SALUT (97-02-67) in the town of St-Louis, and HAJO (97-32-76), which is on the beach near Capesterre. Rates are CHEAP to NOT SO CHEAP for singles and doubles. Make sure you have reservations before you arrive if you want to stay over!

PLAGE TARARE AND LES SALINES—The buff beach near Pointe des Châteaux and the pretty beach next to it—both are local favorites.

ÎLES DE LA PETIT-TERRE—Take a catamaran sail from St-François for great snorkeling.

BASSE-TERRE—Worth at least a day-trip or two. Be sure to take the traverse road (La Route de la traversée) right through the Parc Naturel. On the way, check out the town of Basse-Terre and, if you feel like it, go diving off Pigeon Island.

L.C.S FUNBOARD—With locations in Ste-Anne (for beginners and intermediates) and in Le Moule (for advanced and wave jumpers), this is Guadeloupe's best windsurfing school and facility featuring Fanatic/Copello and Gaastra equipment (88-15-17, fax 88-15-21).

ESPACE SANTE DE RAVINE CHAUDE—A new spa in Basse-Terre with all kinds of thermal spring water therapies (25-75-92).

PARC NATUREL—Lots of great hiking opportunities are available here. For detailed info, contact the Parc Naturel de la Guadeloupe, Habitation Beausoleil, Monteran, Sainte-Claude 97120, (80-24-25, fax 80-05-46). For professional guides, contact Gerard Berry at the Organisation des Guides de Montagne, Maison Forestière, Matuba 97120 (81-05-79).

DIVING OFF PIGEON ISLAND—One of the top ten on Jacques Cousteau's dive-spot favorites, there are three dive centers that will take
you there: Les Heures Saines (98-86-63), Chez Guy (98-81-72), and the
Nautilus Club (98-85-69). They offer resort courses for noncertified
divers too.

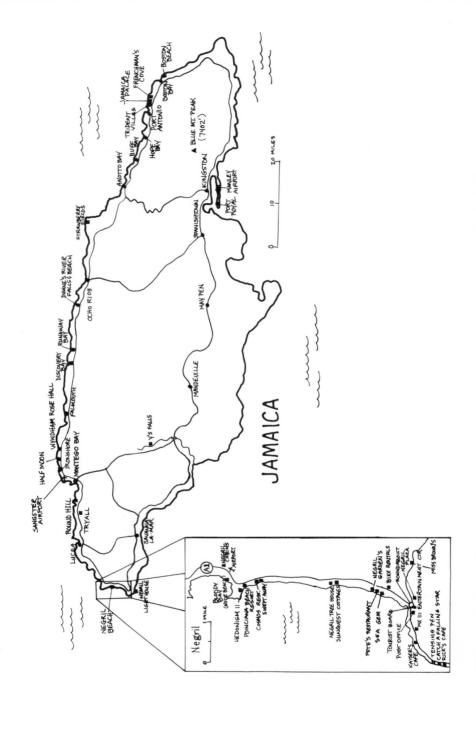

JAMAICA

Negril

Negril Beach
Negril Light House

(A1)

Negril Gardens
Negril Airport

Brandy Bay (nude beach)
Hedonism II
Poinciana Beach Resort
Chaos Rest
Sweet Amar

Negril Tree House
Sundaywest Cottages

Pete's Restaurant
Sea Gem
Tourist Board
Post Office
Kaiser's Cafe

Negril Gardens
Negril Bike Rentals
Round Robin
Negril Plaza
Miss Brown's
MK III Easter Pann Meat Ctr.
Tensing Ten
Catch A Falling Star
Rick's Cafe

Sangster Airport
Round Hill
Lucea
Half Moon
Tryall
Wyndham Rose Hall
Ironshore
Montego Bay
Savanna La-Mar
Ys Falls
Falmouth
Discovery Bay
Runaway Bay
Ocho Rios
Mandeville
May Pen
Strawberry Fields
Dunne's River Falls & Beach
Anotto Bay
Buff Bay
Port Antonio
Trident Villas
Jamaica Palace
Freachman's Cove
Boston Beach
Boston Bay
Hope Bay
▲ Blue Mt. Peak (7402')
Spanishtown
Kingston
Port Royal
Manley Airport

0   10   20 MILES

JAMAICA

TOURISTO SCALE 📷 📷 📷 📷 📷 📷 📷 7

One love, one heart
Let's get together and feel alright . . .
One love, one heart
Come to Jamaica and feel alright.

Thus exults a recent television commercial for Jamaica, based on the historic Bob Marley song, "One Love/People Get Ready." And if there is one place in the Caribbean to feel alright, it's Jamaica. The incredible beauty of this island, the dynamism of the Jamaican people, and the power of Jamaica's world export, reggae music, will blow you away. You'll return home from Jamaica with the feeling that you have been to another world and another culture. And you will be relaxed.

Since it is a big country—the island is the third largest in the Caribbean after Cuba and Hispaniola—there are many different destinations for the traveler: Montego Bay, the North Shore, Ocho Rios, Negril, Port Antonio, and Kingston. Your Jamaican experience will vary dramatically with each destination. You will be subjected to tourist hordes in Ocho Rios, be sequestered away in the large all-inclusive resorts on the North Coast, and experience more tourist swarms in Montego Bay. With a few exceptions (Round Hill and Tryall), I recommend avoiding Ocho Rios, the North Shore, and Montego Bay entirely. Rather, you should go to Negril, which is fun, mellow, and what you think the Jamaican experience should be. Or you should try Port Antonio, which is quiet and incredibly verdant. Kingston is worth a trip for the Reggae Sunsplash Festival and various cultural institutions, including the Bob Marley Museum.

All kinds of people go to Jamaica, reflecting its size and diverse appeal. Package-tour groups go to the all-inclusive resorts, which I loathe and which are plentiful in Jamaica. These are resorts where everything—room, meals, drinks, tips, and all kinds of activities—is included in one price. All-inclusives are, with a few exceptions, just a muddle of mediocrity, down to the last buffet dinner. The clientele here is generally not terribly sophisticated, easily satisfied, and very budget-conscious. Their attitude is, Why should I go out for a lunch, dinner, or drinks when it's free here (it really isn't—they already paid for it). But this thinking locks them in, and all-inclusive tourists rarely leave the front gates unless it's on a tour bus—isn't that sad. Even worse, are the couples-only all-inclusive resorts, like the Sandals empire. The very thought of staying at one gives me hives! Can you imagine being stuck with hundreds of other couples gathered around the buffet table? I'd rather die. At least Swept Away, in Negril—a couples/all-inclusive resort, allows same-sex couples, which provides a little relief. And then there is Hedonism II, which is a trip in itself (see pages 241–42). But the all-inclusives are really just adult summer camps with double rooms instead of bunkhouses and aerobics and crab races replacing arts and crafts. They are great for people for whom luxury is a fiberglass hot tub, an open bar, or "ethnic night" in the dining room. If you are traveling alone to an all-inclusive, there's a good chance you will have to share a room with someone of the same sex—this could be disastrous if you do not hit it off. *A word to the wise:* Make sure you can get your own room, or look elsewhere.

The younger, more with-it crowd heads for Negril. This is where Jamaicans go to unwind, and unwound it is. Situated on the west coast of Jamaica with a seven-mile-long golden beach, Negril is a constant beehive of laid-back activity. A very good mood prevails here, probably because everyone is so high. The very relaxed atmosphere is reflected by the laissez-faire attitude of the government toward *ganja* (marijuana) and "magic" mushrooms (the ones that make you laugh hysterically and sometimes give you mild hallucinations), which, while still illegal and technically punishable with stiff fines and prison sentences, are both easily available in Negril. At many local (i.e., Jamaican) restaurants, you can order a spliff for desert (it's not on the menu, however) or a steaming cup of mushroom tea.

Those seeking a quiet and wonderfully lush setting will head to

Port Antonio. This was Jamaica's first resort area, made famous by Noël Coward and Errol Flynn—both of whom had residences here—and their well-known and fabulous guests. There are some magnificent cove beaches here, hidden by really tropical vegetation. Many films requiring an idyllic tropical location were shot here, including *The Blue Lagoon, Cocktail, Club Paradise, Lord of the Flies, Return to Treasure Island, Clara's Heart,* and *The Mighty Quinn.* Ironically, Port Antonio is the least-touristy part of the Jamaica destinations. This is one of the reasons why I like it a lot.

Finally, for reggae and art lovers, there is Kingston. Now the home of Reggae Sunsplash (although it might soon be moved back to Mo Bay), it is also the home of the Bob Marley Museum—a must stop if you are here. There are numerous art galleries where you can buy Jamaican art. There is also the Institute of Jamaica and the National Gallery, which is the best showcase for a lesson in Jamaican art, past and present. As the largest English-speaking city south of Miami, Kingston is big (pop. 700,000), so a couple of days is all you'll need here, unless you like big cities.

THE BRIEFEST HISTORY OF A COMPLEX COUNTRY

Jamaica was settled by the Arawaks, who had a peaceful, agrarian society. The name Jamaica comes from the Arawak name Xaymaca, which means "Land of Wood and Water." Unlike most Caribbean islands, the fierce Caribs never made it here. But the Spanish did, beginning with Columbus's sighting of Jamaica on his second voyage in 1494. They established a capital in 1509 near Ocho Rios and named it New Seville, which today is being excavated by archeologists. They began sugarcane cultivation and introduced slavery, first with the Arawaks. It didn't take long for the Arawaks to be wiped out (there were about 100,000 when the Spaniards arrived) and then they imported Africans. Many of the slaves escaped into the mountains, and later became known as the Maroons, from the Spanish word *cimarrones* for "runaways."

In 1655, the English drove out the Spaniards and proceeded to take the production of sugar and the importation of slaves to new heights. The English also encouraged pirates (such as Henry Morgan) to operate out of Port Royal on the Kingston peninsula. They plundered Spanish and French ships and established Port Royal as "the richest, wickedest city in Christendom." The honeymoon ended in 1692, when a catastrophic earthquake caused most of the city literally to fall into the sea. Divine intervention, perhaps? Today, there are still some buildings left and it is an interesting stop if you are in Kingston a-ree.

Meanwhile, the Maroons were giving the British major headaches, as they would periodically stage rebellions and attract more runaway slaves. *Fehklempt*, they granted the Maroons autonomy in 1739, which they still have today, although the Maroons are full-fledged Jamaican citizens. And the planters, following the lead of the American Revolutionaries, were getting restless. However, the presence of Lord Nelson, who was the commanding admiral of the British Navy in the West Indies and a towering presence, squelched the discontent.

In 1834, slavery was abolished in the British Empire. Economic turmoil followed, but with the importation of Indians (from India) and Chinese as indentured servants, sugar and rum production prospered. Intermarriage created the mixed racial makeup you find in Jamaica today, hence the national motto "Out of Many, One People." Other products were developed and exported, including bananas, ginger, allspice, coffee, and bauxite.

In the twentieth century, the current political scene emerged, with the creation of rival parties in the 1930s: the Jamaica Labor Party (JLP) by Alexander Bustamante and the People's National Party (PNP) by Norman Manley. They were cousins by the way. Jamaica was one of the first British West Indies to gain independence, which was granted in 1962 with these two parties in control of the government. Rivalries between the parties became very bitter and continue to this day, although elections aren't as violent as they used to be. At issue is patronage and jobs, and each party seems to control a large army of thugs who stir things up and occasionally get violent when intimidating the other side and the voting populace at large. The worst of this occurred in the late seventies and early eighties, when hundreds were killed in the year before an election. This precipitated the historic Bob Marley "One Love" concert held in Kingston in 1978, where he got the two rival leaders to hold hands on stage. Bob's song "One Love/People Get Ready" was written for that occasion. Today, the PNP is in power but Bob's legacy for harmony seems to have caught on. Ya, mon!

If all the political strife wasn't bad enough, Jamaica was ravaged by Hurricane Gilbert in September 1988. One of the most powerful hurricanes on record (a Category Five storm—the strongest, with sustained winds of over 140 mph), Gilbert went from the east end of the island right down the center to the west end, leaving nothing untouched. But today you have to really look hard to see traces of the devastation Gilbert caused.

JAMAICA: KEY FACTS

LOCATION	18°N by 77°W
	90 miles south of Cuba
	1,450 miles south of New York
SIZE	4,411 square miles
	146 miles long by 22 to 51 miles wide
HIGHEST POINT	Blue Mountain Peak (7,388 ft.)
POPULATION	2.4 million
LANGUAGE	English
TIME	Eastern Standard Time all year
AREA CODE	809
ELECTRICITY	110 volts AC, 50 cycles, 220 volts in some places—ask for a transformer and adapter if necessary
CURRENCY	Jamaican dollar (at press time J$22 = $1 U.S.)
DRIVING	On the *left*; a valid driver's license from back home is acceptable for short-term visits
DOCUMENTS	U.S. and Canadian citizens need proof of citizenship with a photo ID, plus an ongoing or return ticket; other visitors need passports
DEPARTURE TAX	$J200
BEER TO DRINK	Red Stripe
RUM TO DRINK	Wray & Nephew Overproof
MUSIC TO HEAR	Reggae/Dancehall—ya mon!

GETTING THERE

Although there are two international gateways, Montego Bay (Donald Sangster) and Kingston (Norman Manley), most people come into the country via Montego Bay due to its proximity to Negril, the North Coast, and Ocho Rios. If you're going to Port Antonio, you'll want to fly into Kingston. AIR JAMAICA flies from New York, Baltimore/Washington, Philadelphia, Miami, and London. It usually offers the best rates from these destinations too. AMERI-CAN flies from New York and Miami, NORTHWEST from Tampa, CONTINENTAL from Newark, the JAMAICA SHUT-TLE from Orlando, the JAMAICA EXPRESS from L.A., AIR CANADA from Toronto and Montréal, and BRITISH AIRWAYS from London. BWIA and ALM serve Jamaica from other Carib-bean destinations.

GETTING AROUND

Since Jamaica is a big country, you'll want to rent a car if you plan to venture far. If you're based in Negril, you probably won't need a car if you plan to just stay there. There are plenty of cabs to take you around in Negril (average cab fare is $5 U.S.). But if you really want to explore, rent a car. The roads are in surprisingly good shape by Caribbean standards, but watch out for the local drivers—they go very fast. Most of the major car-rental agencies have outposts here, including AVIS ([800] 331-1084), BUDGET ([800] 527-0700), and HERTZ ([800] 654-3001). As rentals here are among the most expensive in the Caribbean, be sure to reserve and call around well ahead of your trip to get the best rate.

There used to be a train from Montego Bay to Kingston which took five hours and was an amazing trip that I highly recommended in the last edition of Rum and Reggae. However, it runs no more—a real shame.

FOCUS ON JAMAICA

NEGRIL—ALL YOUR BRAIN AND BODY NEEDS

There is a resort in Negril called Hedonism II—one of the all-inclusives—which has established itself as the premier party place in the Caribbean. The tales emanating from here are mind-boggling, if they are indeed for real. Stories abound of people going at it in public. And not only in the usual places like hot tubs, but in the middle of the dining pavilion—while dinner is being served. Maybe it's the name that makes everyone feel naughty. Whatever, this is adult summer camp at its raunchiest.

There is also a place in Negril called Miss Brown's, where you can get "magic" mushroom tea and "special" cake (not unlike the brownies we used to make in college), as well as more down-to-earth fare. There are two strengths of tea, regular and double. May I suggest the regular-strength tea (about J$125), as it will give you quite a buzz. For those of you who still don't get it (I had a reader tell me she didn't know what "special" cake was, tried it, and was surprised and unhappy that she got high—I mean, c'mon, coffee— smell it!), "special" cake is cake made with marijuana and "magic" mushrooms will make you laugh hysterically and sometimes will be mildly hallucinogenic. Now you know, dweeb! I'm sorry, I digress. Miss Brown's is really a must stop. A visit here will definitely put a smile on your face. Located about a half-mile east of the round-about that separates the Beach from the West End, it's a typical small Jamaican restaurant (although they have expanded with a covered patio in front since the last edition) with more on the menu than jerk chicken. It is run by warm and modest country folk who are most comfortable with inquisitive travelers who seek out their "café." So it's somewhat surprising when Ms. Brown hands out attractive business cards describing her place as "World Famous," although maybe by now it is. The logo on the card is, of course, mushrooms. She even sells T-shirts with the same logo.

Sex and drugs—all that's missing is rock 'n' roll. As Ian Dury (of the Blockheads) once sang, "It's all me brain and body needs." If you replace rock 'n' roll with reggae, you should be very happy in Negril, the land of anything goes. Now don't get me wrong—Negril is not one huge bacchanalia (unless you stay at Hedonism II). It's just an extremely mellow place where rules and regulations seem to evaporate in the tropical heat. The quintessence of laid-back, the ambience here is not some developer's contrivance but its own natural karma. I've never experienced anything quite like it. This is where Jamaicans go to relax, and they're already a helluva lot more relaxed than we are. So if you need to cool out at your own pace (without feeling programmed), this is the place to do it. Or if you're a believer in sunbathing in the buff, it's no problem here.

There are actually two parts to Negril, the Beach and the West End. The Beach is a seven-mile arc of sand, calm turquoise water, and palm trees. It is highly developed, but in Negril fashion. There are no high-rise hotels or condos and few large resorts. One of the

few rules in Negril that is followed is a strict building code that
dictates no building can rise higher than the trees, although a few
crafty developers brought in very tall trees from elsewhere in order
to build an extra story. Shame on them! The Beach itself is very
public, making Negril one of the few destinations in Jamaica where
tourists and Jamaicans can mingle freely without security gates,
guards, and the heightened racial consciousness which accompanies
such barriers. The Beach is also a moving bazaar, with all kinds of
goods (especially cigarettes) and services brought to your beach
towel or chaise for scrutiny. You will never really want for anything. Fresh fruit, sodas, beer, nuts, *ganja*—all the refreshments
that make for a great beach day—are available cheaply with a simple
wave of the hand. If you are already taken care of, then a pleasant
"no thank you" will keep the traffic moving. Despite all of this
human commotion, the Beach's beauty is mostly intact. And the
sand extends way out, creating a natural swimming pool of very
clear water. The shoreline is shallow, which allows you to go far out
before you're over your head.

The West End is a rocky peninsula that juts out from the southern end of the Beach. It is the funkier, hippyish section of town.
Here you'll find lots of Rasta/vegetarian restaurants, bars and rum
shops, as well as local arts, crafts, some excellent accommodations,
and a fantastic reggae showplace called MXIII. Rick's Café, located
well down the West End Road, is very popular for sunset cocktails
and is probably the biggest *tourist* attraction in Negril. It is also
where local boys dive off the cliffs to the clicks of scores of cameras.

KINGSTON—RASTAMAN VIBRATIONS, YEAH (POSITIVE)

> *You're going to lively up yourself and*
> *don't be no drag,*
> *You're going to lively up yourself 'cause reggae is*
> *another bag.*
> *You lively up yourself and don't say no,*
> *You're gonna lively up yourself 'cause I said so.*

Thus spake Bob Marley. As the undisputed king of reggae, his 1974
song "Lively Up Yourself" was a call to action on behalf of
Jamaica's biggest export—his music. At the peak of his career, his
record sales accounted for about 10 percent of the country's gross
national product. Even after his premature death in 1981 at the age

of thirty-six, he is still considered the prime mover in popularizing reggae in North America and throughout the world.

Bob Marley is a national hero. His statue stands in the middle of a square across from the National Arena in Kingston, a tribute to his contribution not only to Jamaican music, but to his country's cultural identity. But as reggae music goes, he is certainly not the only Jamaican to leave his or her mark. There is Bob's son, Ziggy, with the Melody Makers and Judy Mowatt—a former member of the Wailers female vocal backup, the I-Threes. The late Bunny Wailer and the late Peter Tosh, both former members of the Wailers, were known worldwide. So are Jimmy Cliff, Gregory Isaacs, Freddie "Toots" (of the Maytalls), Sister Carol, Burning Spear, Nadine Sutherland, Terror Fabulous, Shabba Ranks, John Holt, and the bands Third World, Black Uhuru, and Chalice. There are countless more. A visit to a Kingston record shop will reveal more artists you've never even heard of, and a huge selection of 45s (from local talent and labels) that I haven't seen since the sixties. Surprisingly, two of the most popular reggae bands today are not Jamaican—UB40 and Steel Pulse are British, although many of these groups' band members trace their roots to Jamaica.

Reggae now has a strong following around the world and recent reggae bands like Ziggy Marley and the Melody Makers, Shabba Ranks and UB40 have been hugely successful. Bob Marley's *Legend* album, a collection of his work first released in 1984 and recently re-released on CD, has gone platinum and is still selling like crazy. There is also a CD box set of all his work which is also very popular. Final proof of reggae's popularity is its offspring, dancehall—a reggae/rap hybrid—which has swept through the Caribbean and is on it's way up the charts in the U.S. and Europe.

It didn't used to be that way, even when Bob Marley was king (many say he still is). Reggae's success was a long time coming. The music first hit the charts in 1969, when Desmond Dekker reached number twelve on the Billboard chart with "The Israelites." Jimmy Cliff then had a hit in 1970 with "Wonderful World, Beautiful People." Bob Marley and the Wailers' 1976 album, *Rastaman Vibration,* reached number eight on the Billboard album charts—which at the time was unprecedented for both Marley and reggae musicians in general.

On the other hand, "mainstream" musicians have made it big with reggae. Paul Simon led the way when he wrote "Mother and Child Reunion" back in 1972. About the same time, Johnny Nash took Bob Marley's song "Stir It Up," made it a hit, and followed shortly thereafter with the reggae-influenced "I Can See Clearly Now." Then came Eric Clapton's blockbuster version of "I Shot the Sheriff"—another Marley tune. After that, a number of groups jumped on the reggae bandwagon, from The Police with songs like "Roxanne" and "Walking on the Moon" and Blondie ("The Tide Is High"), to Kool and the Gang ("Let's Go Dancin' [Ooh, La La La]"), Club Nouveau ("Lean on Me"), to such all-time greats as Bonnie Raitt ("True Love is Hard to Find," "Have a Heart," and "Come to Me"), and Mick Jagger with Peter Tosh ("Don't Look Back"). Snow had a number one hit, "Informer," which is in the reggae dancehall format. Finally, UB40 recently reached number one on the charts with a reggae version of the Elvis Presley hit "Can't Help Falling in Love."

REGGAE'S ROOTS

Reggae evolved from a variety of Jamaican musical styles. Its roots can be heard in the traditional Jamaican music called "mento." It has a slow beat and rather lewd lyrics—much like the Béguine of Martinique. Like the "wine" and calypso music, it was danced very intimately, with two people joined at the hips simulating intercourse.

The advent of rhythm-and-blues in the U.S., coupled with the spread of transistor radios, doomed mento. The powerful AM broadcasts out of Miami brought the R & B sound home to Jamaica. So did the growing popularity of "sound systems"—traveling DJs with PA systems and the hottest singles from the U.S. American music soon influenced Jamaica's own, resulting in a fast-paced synthesis called "ska."

While ska was not tremendously popular elsewhere, Millie Small's 1964 song, "My Boy Lollipop" was a worldwide hit. By the late sixties, ska gave way to yet another music called "rock steady." It was much slower, with a more evenly paced beat—reggae's forerunner. Rock steady delivered an increasingly more serious message than its lighthearted predecessor. The music soon expressed the heightened sense of black pride brought on by the U.S. civil rights movement.

It was rock steady's growing lyrical consciousness that gave birth to the slower, more powerful reggae. Reggae became the vehicle of discontent, rooted in the shantytowns of West Kingston and Trenchtown. Bob Marley and the Wailers became the stewards of this new music, formulating the now-familiar guitar rythyms and timing. In 1970, Marley founded the Tuff Gong Studios, and by 1971 he and his band were on their way with the hit "Trenchtown Rock." At the time of his death in 1981 (of brain cancer), Marley had produced over twenty albums and had made reggae a dynamic force worldwide.

While reggae is still popular on the Jamaican music scene, dance-hall now reigns supreme. Terror Fabulous, Buju Banton and Nadine Sutherland are three of the most popular dancehall artists at the moment.

THE BOB MARLEY MUSEUM, (809) 927-9152
56 Hope Rd., Kingston

This is a must stop in Jamaica for any reggae fan. Run by Rastas, it occupies the former Tuff Gong Studios, where most of Bob Marley and the Wailers' best music was recorded. It's located in a well-heeled neighborhood near Jamaica House (the official residence of the Prime Minister). When you pull up to the gate, you are greeted by a security guard who announces that the only pictures allowed are of the Marley statue inside. After that, all cameras and recording devices must be checked at the gatehouse. A guide will then take you inside to view an hour-long video presentation that shows Bob Marley in concert, recording at the studio (which is where you are sitting), and out and about. The rest of the tour includes the grounds, notably murals, herb gardens, Marley's statue, a beehive, and a real, live *ganja* plant.

Back inside the museum, which originally was an old Victorian house, there are two floors of memorabilia. They include two rooms of news clippings pasted to the walls, a replica of Bob's first record shop in Trenchtown called Wail 'n Soul Records, his bedroom preserved intact (it looks like a hippie den—with pillows on the floor and a large smoking pipe), as well as a wax statue à la Madame Toussaud that will eventually move to simulate him singing. When you finish the tour, you'll want to check out the Bob Marley Museum Souvenir Shop for T-shirts and jewelry.

Admission is J$70 (about $3.50 U.S.) for adults and hours are 9:30 A.M.–5 P.M. on Mondays, Tuesdays, Thursdays, and Fridays. The museum is open from 12:30–6 P.M. on Wednesdays, Saturdays, and holidays, and is closed on Sundays.

JAMAICAN ART

There are few places in the Caribbean where the art scene is as dynamic or impressive as it is in Jamaica. This can readily be seen in Kingston, the capital and largest English-speaking city (pop. 700,000) south of the U.S. The average tourist may think that the crafts markets of Ocho Rios or Montego Bay, with their wood carvings and amateur paintings, encapsulate the Jamaican art scene. But this is hardly true.

For a true perspective on Jamaican art, you must visit the National Gallery on 12 Ocean Boulevard, Block 3, Kingston Mall (809) 922-1563/8544/8540. Since 1982, the gallery has occupied two floors of a new building it has already outgrown. Its 18 galleries house various collections of paintings, prints, and sculptures from different eras and artists of Jamaica. The gallery also has an international collection that focuses on Caribbean works.

Of particular interest at the gallery is the magnificent sculpture collection of Edna Manley, one of the primary forces in modern Jamaican art. Her work is truly moving, from the reflection on recent political violence called *Ghetto Mother* (1982) to such timeless pieces as *Negro Aroused* (1935), *The Beadseller* (1922), *The Diggers* (1936), and *Horse of the Morning* (1943).

There are other prominent artists whose works should not be missed. These include Mallica Reynolds (known as Kapo), Barrington Watson, Christopher Gonzalez, Karl Parboosingh, and Albert Huie. Kapo is probably Jamaica's most prolific primitive sculptor, with evocative pieces like *All Women Are Five Women* (1965). He is also a renowned painter. Barrington Watson's neorealist oil paintings of the human form are outstanding, including *Conversation* (1981) and *Mother and Child* (1968). Christopher Gonzalez' mahogany sculpture titled *Man Arisen* (1966) explodes with emotion. *Ras Smoke I* (1972), by Karl Parboosingh, and *The Constant Spring Road* (1964), by Albert Huie, both oils, are powerful documentations of the lives and times of the Jamaican people. The Gallery is open Monday through Saturday, 11 A.M.–4:30 P.M.

If you are in the mood to buy or browse, check out: the Contemporary Arts Centre at 1 Liguanea Ave. (926-4644); The Edna Manley School of the Visual Arts at The Cultural Training Centre, 1 Arthur Wint Dr. (926-2800)—works in progress and student exhibition during the last week in June and the first week of July; the Bolivar Bookshop and Gallery, 1-D Grove Rd. (926-8799); Chelsea Art Gallery, 12 Chelsea Ave. (929-0045); Mutual Life Gallery, 2

Oxford Rd. (929-4302); The Palette Gallery, 21 Haining Rd. (929-2820); The Upstairs Downstairs Gallery, 108 Harbour St. (922-1260); Frame Centre Gallery, 10 Tangerine Place (926-4644); Makonda Gallery, The Wyndham Hotel, 77 Knutsford Blvd. (926-5430); and finally the Institute of Jamaica, 12 East St., (922-0620)—exhibitions of student work of all ages.

No art adventure in Kingston would be complete without seeing the monumental wall murals on the campus of the University of the West Indies. While there, pick up a catalog. Who knows, the Jamaican art experience may arouse new interests that demand further study.

REGGAE SUNSPLASH

Now here is an event for hard-core reggae fans. Held in August each year (there have been more than 16), this is a 5-day festival which always features the best talent in the field—a mini-Woodstock of reggae music. Usually held on Mo Bay, the venue was moved in 1993 to Kingston because the land in Montego Bay where the newly built Bob Marley Centre sits has been slated for public housing—a worthy and needed cause. Now it is being held at the JAMWORLD Entertainment Centre, located about 15 minutes from downtown Kingston. The Centre, to be eventually renamed the Jamaica Festival Village, is on 80 acres of land and has an amphitheater that can accommodate 40,000 people as well as restaurants, nightclubs, water sports and the whole shebang. This event regularly draws over 120,000 people during the course of the festival.

Tickets for the week are $100 U.S., which includes special entry and unlimited access to all Sunsplash events, a Sunsplash T-shirt and souvie 'zine, and access to the backstage hospitality area and parking. Packages are also available which include lodging, airfare, etc. For more info, call (800) 93-SPLASH/(212) 206-8907.

WHERE TO STAY, EAT, AND MORE

In my book, and this *is* my book, there are only certain destinations in Jamaica worth visiting for the aforementioned reasons: Negril; Round Hill, Tryall, and Half Moon near Montego Bay; Port Antonio; and Kingston. These options are plenty and the best of scores. Trust me.

NEGRIL

WHERE TO STAY

In Negril there are more options for lodging, from rustic/funky to deluxe, than in practically any other part of Jamaica. You can choose according to your style and budget, though the offbeat type of accommodation is a Negril specialty. If you stay on the West End, there is no beach, but you get to dive into turquoise water from rock platforms—lots of fun and no sand stuck to your legs. Here's the scoop on accommodations in Negril:

TENSING PEN (809) 957-4417, same for fax
West End Road (P.O. Box 13), Negril, Jamaica, W.I.

Situated on a rocky bluff on the West End amid several acres of beautiful landscaped grounds, Tensing Pen is my favorite place to stay in Negril. The accommodations are really fabulous for their uniqueness, privacy, and setting. Looking like primitive thatched huts, they are actually quite elegantly, if simply, furnished inside with four-poster beds, polished wood floors, and private bath. There is a lanai with rocking chairs, most looking out over the water facing west. I couldn't think of a better place in Negril to sit and read or watch for the green flash. Many of the huts are elevated, called the Pillars, giving the impression of a tree house. Two of my favorites are Middle Pillar and Cove Cottage. All the units have privileges in a well-equipped communal kitchen attached to a very comfortable and pleasant dining and sitting area. For large groups, there is a three-bedroom great house with a huge living room and basically open to the sea and the views. Managers Dave and Bernice are very friendly and willing to help with any special needs.

While Tensing Pen doesn't have a beach, it has a craggy coastline with all kinds of places to jump or dive into the crystal-clear tur-quoise water and strategically placed ladders to easily get out. On most days, the water is very calm, making it fun and safe to do so. There are also sunning patios carved out of the rock with chaises for your tanning pleasure. A cove bisects the property and a footbridge connects the two points, although it is not necessary to use the bridge. It doesn't have any railings and is sort of like walking a wide plank over the water—easy but a tad scary. Small children would not agree with Tensing Pen.

Rates are PRICEY for singles and doubles (CP). For the Great House, rates are WICKED PRICEY (CP). Rates go down 30 percent during the off-season (May 1–December 1).

CATCHA FALLING STAR (809) 957-4446
West End Road (P.O. Box 22), Negril, Jamaica, W.I.

Located next door to Tensing Pen, Catcha Falling Star is a place to try if you can't get into Tensing Pen. While it lacks Tensing Pen's charm and specialness, Catcha Falling Star is still very comfortable and pleasant. There are six attractive one- and two-bedroom cottages with maid service and breakfast served in your cottage. As with its neighbor, you can swim off the rocks and sun on their specially built patios.

Rates are PRICEY to VERY PRICEY for singles and doubles (includes full breakfast).

NEGRIL CABINS (809) 957-4350, fax (809) 957-4381
Rockland Point (P.O. Box 118), Negril, Jamaica, W.I.

Located on the north end of Negril across the road from the Bloody Bay Beach (Negril's nude beach), this tree-house–like accommodation sits in a shady grove of Jamaican royal palms and bull thatch. There are 24 units in 10 timber cottages. All units are simply but comfortably furnished and are very airy and open with lots of wood. Each unit has a balcony or patio, ceiling fan, and private bath. Windows are louvered with screens. The beach across the road is mostly undeveloped, a definite plus. When making reservations, ask for a unit as far away from the road as possible (Units 12-1 and 12-2)—these will be the quietest.

Rates are PRICEY for singles and doubles (EP).

SEA-GEM (809) 957-4318, same for fax
Norman Manley Boulevard, Negril, Jamaica, W.I.

If I was on a tight budget, this is where I would stay. Located on the beach, this is a very charming small property with several gingerbread cottages that are simple and comfortable. Owned by the Williams family, manager and son Ralph is a great guy and tries to use as much local wood, brick, and stone as possible when renovating units. He has also built a patio and barbecue area out of large stones originally handmade by slaves and is constantly trying to make his place better for his guests. Ralph will negotiate a very fair price if you plan an extended stay.

Rates are NOT SO CHEAP for singles and doubles and CHEAP during the off-season (EP).

NEGRIL GARDENS HOTEL (809) 957-4408, fax (809) 957-4374
Stateside and Canada: (800) 223-9815/(212) 251-1800
Norman Manley Boulevard (P.O. Box 58), Negril, Jamaica, W.I.

If you want to stay at a small resort on the beach with a beach bar and restaurant, this is the place. Located right in the middle of the Beach and just steps away from Pete's restaurant, this is an attractive hotel with 54 comfortable rooms and a friendly staff. Negril Gardens spans both sides of the road, with the pool on the side not on the beach (these rooms are also slightly cheaper). All rooms have air conditioning, verandas or balconies, and private baths. There is a water-sports shop on the beach, as well as chaises and the constantly moving beach parade. The beach bar is the home of the best banana daiquiri in Negril.

Rates are PRICEY for both singles and doubles (EP).

NEGRIL TREE HOUSE RESORT (809) 957-4287, fax (809) 957-4386
Stateside and Canada: (800) NEGRIL-1
Norman Manley Boulevard (P.O. Box 29), Negril, Jamaica, W.I.

One of the original hotels on the beach, the resort has 58 rooms and 12 suites and favors a younger clientele. I recommend a room on the second floor, which is more private and airy. Each unit has a balcony, air conditioning, ceiling fans, telephone, full bath, and all are pleasant and comfortable. The resort has a restaurant and two bars, and lots of hammocks for an afternoon snooze. Water sports are a specialty here as well as volleyball. There is a small pool and Jacuzzi on the beach. Cooking facilities are available to guests.

Rates are PRICEY to VERY PRICEY for singles and doubles (EP).

SUNQUEST (809) 957-4470
Norman Manley Boulevard, Negril, Jamaica, W.I.

If you're really, really on a tight budget and the Sea-Gem is not available, this place might be the ticket. Looking like a "cozy cabins" lakeside cottage retreat in New Hampshire, there are cute, simple, and clean cottages. There is a restaurant serving Jamaican food on the premises.

Rates are CHEAP for singles and doubles (EP).

HEDONISM II (809) 957-4201, fax (809) 957-4289
Stateside: (800) 858-8009; Canada: (800) 553-4320
Negril Beach Road (P.O. Box 25), Negril, Jamaica, W.I.

The name of this resort couldn't be more appropriate, though I'm not too clear on what the "II" means (there was never a Hedonism I). This place was founded on the pleasure principle and has built its reputation on sophomoric play. Personally, you'd have to pay me to stay here. This is not because I disapprove of its philosophy. It fills a valid need for many people. I simply don't find the clientele terribly sophisticated or attractive. I felt this way the first time I visited and still do six years later. But who needs culture and class when it comes to bodily pleasures anyway? The management tries to sell Hedonism II with the line "Pleasure comes in many forms: the mind, the body, the spirit, and the soul." Judging from what I witnessed here, I'd say the overwhelming focus was a spirited and mindful effort to enhance the pleasures of the body to the point of selling one's soul.

The buildings and grounds are not very exciting. Frankly, I think the blocks of rooms look like a suburban medical center. The rooms themselves are relatively nice in a contemporary sense, with lots of mirrors, including one over the bed, and have private bath, air conditioning, but no balcony or patio. On the grounds, there is a rather small free-form pool that adjoins the main bar and entertainment and dining amphitheater. The bartenders there are kept very busy, often by shouting, drunken men and women who could easily be cast in My Cousin Vinny, down to the gold chains around their necks and the Ozone Park accents. At the other end of the pool is the disco roof. The throbbing beat of the music penetrates the poolside air. The disco bar has windows that look into the pool, much the same as you would find in a public aquarium. You'll see lots of dangling feet, legs, and torsos—the effect is quite provocative. There are stories of some very explicit happenings—a true exhibitionist/voyeur's dream. Down the slope from the disco is the beach, which is nice if you want to get away from the main staging area. They have also installed a trampoline and trapeze (with safety net), for those with fantasies or fears of flying. The management does pull in some superb entertainment, especially on Saturday nights. The staff, in the mode of camp counselors, is very friendly and very up.

Rates at Hedonism II fall in the WICKED PRICEY range per day. There is a minimum three-night-stay requirement.

SWEPT AWAY (809) 957-4061, fax (809) 957-4153
Stateside: (800) 545-7937/(305) 666-2021
Norman Manley Boulevard (P.O. Box 77), Negril, Jamaica, W.I.

While this is a couples-only all-inclusive resort, the idea of which I loathe, this is a good one in a good location (and it allows same-sex couples, so you could go with a friend or a significant other). [The name, I assume, comes from the Lena Wertmuller classic film.] The accommodations here are very attractive. Rooms have tiled floors, lots of wood, louvered windows, ceiling fans, air conditioning, and spacious lanais. What makes Swept Away really different is its incredible sports and health club facility (also available to nonguests for a fee). There is an Olympic-sized pool with separate lanes (a rarity in any resort), a complete gym, ten lighted tennis courts—five of which are clay, racquetball, squash, basketball, yoga, saunas, steam rooms and Jacuzzis. Swept Away even includes complimentary weddings, down to the wedding cake and champagne (all you need is the ring).

Rates at Swept Away fall into the RIDICULOUS to OUTRA-GEOUS categories per couple. There is a minimum three-day stay requirement.

WHERE TO EAT

There are scores of restaurants here, from small beach shacks to big hotel restaurants. Undoubtedly, new ones will pop up, so be sure to ask around. But don't miss these:

COSMO'S SEAFOOD RESTAURANT & BAR, Norman Manley Boulevard, 957-4330

This is a very popular restaurant with both locals and hip tourists (we saw one table where everyone was wearing black—in the tropics). It's so cheap and good too. There are two sections, the larger on the beach—which the tourists like—and a smaller section around the bar—which the locals seem to prefer. Whatever, the food's the same in both places. Be sure to try the escovitched fish and get a T-shirt as a souvie. Open until 10 P.M. $$

MR. NATURAL, West End Road (across from Kaiser's), 957-9181

The is "de best" veggie restaurant, serving all kinds of vegetarian dishes, pasta, and seafood and featuring a juice bar. It is open for breakfast, lunch, and dinner from 7:30 A.M. till midnight. $$

PETE'S ON THE BEACH, Norman Manley Boulevard, still no phone

Located just a little south of the Negril Gardens Hotel on the Beach, Pete's is the ultimate in eating on the beach local-style. There are picnic tables set up about 20 feet from the water, and Pete, the chef, will grill up some mean red snapper, lobster, or chicken for you and the DJ/dub music will keep your feet tapping in the sand. For dessert, there is some strong *ganja* cake, just ask for the "special cake." $

CARIBBEAN DELIGHT, Norman Manley Boulevard, no phone

This is another local-style restaurant, but it is slightly fancier than Pete's. Located just south of Negril Gardens, they serve an excellent and very cheap breakfast. $ *No credit cards.*

PARADISE YARD CAFE/CAFE LA RASTA PASTA, Sheffield Road, 957-4005

This is the home of the original Rasta Pasta—red and green "dreadlocks" pasta served with ackee, peppers, and tomatoes. A very casual place, they also serve veggie dishes, seafood, curried chicken, quesadillas and enchiladas. Located just beyond the new police station on the way to Miss Brown's (or the way back). Open daily from 8 A.M. to 11 P.M. $$ *No credit cards.*

NEGRIL JERK CENTRE, West End Road, 957-4847

No, this is not a club for jerks but the best place in Negril for jerk chicken and pork, the very spicy, grilled meat that is one of the

Jamaican national dishes (along with ackee and codfish). You must try it. Located just past the tiny Negril Library. Hours are daily from 10 A.M. till 11 P.M. $ *No credit cards.*

RICK'S CAFÉ, West End Road, 957-4335

The place is totally tourist and expensive to boot, so why bother? If you must, just go at sunset and have a drink. $$$$ *No credit cards.*

DON'T MISS

MXIII, West End Road, 957-4818—This is a great outdoor venue to see reggae and dancehall. Live music happens every Thursday and Saturday. MXIII brings in the tops in reggae talent. I saw Burning Spear here. There are two bars and a bazaar of local crafts where you can get your rasta-colored beads and accessories.

KAISER'S, West End Road, 957-4450—Located on the cliffs, this is a Negril institution. Kaiser's also brings in big talent, like Third World, Frankie Paul and Yellowman. There is live music on Wednesdays and Fridays. A Jamaican and seafood restaurant is on the premises.

MISS BROWN'S, Sheffield Road—see write-up on page 231.

SWEPT AWAY SPORTS COMPLEX, Norman Manley Boulevard, 957-4040—This is an excellent health club and sports center. For $12 U.S. per day, anyone (you don't have to be staying at the resort) can work out with free weights, machines, aerobics, play squash and racquetball, play tennis on 10 courts (five of which are clay), play basketball, swim laps in a superb lap pool, take yoga classes, play pool, or take a steam or sauna. This is a great place to keep those bis and tris in tone and work off the hangover from the previous night.

Y.S. WATERFALL—What Dunn's River Falls used to be, i.e., untouristy, is what Y.S. (pronounced wyess) is today. Located about two-thirds of the way from Negril to Mandeville and about ten miles north of the town of Black River, this is a good day-trip for waterfall lovers and will let you see the untraveled part of Jamaica. Just take the road to Savanna-la-Mar and then route A2 through Black River to Y.S. If you want to go with a guide, call South Coast Safaris at (809) 962-0220/3551.

AROUND MONTEGO BAY

WHERE TO STAY

I would avoid staying right in Montego Bay, as it is a city and is rather crowded and hot. There are, however, two wonderful but very expensive luxury resorts to the west that are the finest in Jamaica, Round Hill and Tryall. If you are into *golf*, then this area is definitely the place for you. Besides the beautiful Tryall 18, there are three 18-hole courses just east of Montego Bay: Half Moon, Wyndham/Rose Hall, and Ironwood.

ROUND HILL HOTEL AND VILLAS (809) 952-5150, fax (809) 952-2505
Stateside: (800) 972-2159
On the A1 (P.O. Box 64), Montego Bay, Jamaica, W.I.

Located about 10 miles west of Mo Bay on a 98-acre peninsula, Round Hill is one of the grandes dames of Caribbean resorts. Since its inception in 1953, it has hosted more than its fair share of the Hollywood and jet set. There are pictures in the bar of Grace Kelly in the buffet line, and a score of other celebs, from Noël Coward and Queen Elizabeth to Rockefellers, Paleys, Kennedys, Andy Warhol, and Paul McCartney. This is an old-school resort, where flash is looked down upon and understatement is the name of the game. Under the recent stewardship of Josef Forstmayr, who used to run the Trident in Port Antonio, Round Hill has had a much-needed face-lift. And a lot of help in the design department came from Ralph Lauren, who has owned a villa here since 1979. His influence is apparent, especially in the bar, which looks right at home with the New York Yacht Club. There is a staff of 250 to attend to your needs; over 40 have been with Round Hill for more than 30 years—now that's loyalty.

There are 27 privately owned villas (really bungalows), painted white with green trim and nestled among the hibiscus and bougainvillea. Seventeen of the villas have their own swimming pools and all are fully staffed with maids (who cook you breakfast in your villa) and gardener. All the villas are cut up into suites (two, three, or four units each—65 in all). While each of the suites has its own entrance, this means that you will be sharing a house with someone else unless you rent the entire villa—my suggestion. Just get some friends together. That way, you won't have to share the pool or deck with anyone you don't know. Try to get villa 15—it sits on the top of the hill and has three bedrooms, a great pool, and fab views.

There are also 36 rooms in the seaside building known as the Pineapple House, affectionately called "The Barracks" since the beginning. All these rooms have been refurbished and look great. The best are on the second floor, with cathedral ceilings, large, louvered windows overlooking the sea, bright-colored walls; all are tastefully furnished. In front of "The Barracks" is a new communal pool and a small beach with water sports. Guests can play golf at Tryall for a fee.

Rates are WICKED PRICEY to OUTRAGEOUS for singles and VERY PRICEY to RIDICULOUS for doubles (EP). MAP costs $60 U.S. per person per day. Villas are BEYOND BELIEF (includes breakfast). Villa 15 rents for $7,000 per week. You must prepay before you stay here.

TRYALL GOLF, TENNIS & BEACH RESORT (809) 956-5660, fax (809) 956-5673
Stateside and Canada: (800) 336-4571
St. James (P.O. Box 1206), Montego Bay, Jamaica, W.I.

Just two miles west and down the road from Round Hill, this sprawling resort is really like a huge, very deluxe country club. Situated on the site of a 2,200-acre former sugar plantation and tumbling down to the sea from a far-away hilltop, this is a magnificent property, especially for those of you who love golf.

Let's talk about golf—the raison d'être for Tryall. This is Jamaica's best course, and one of the finest and prettiest in the Caribbean. Superbly maintained and a very scenic par-72, it was recently redesigned to accommodate the Johnnie Walker World Championship. The course is a hilly 6,680 championship yards long and is full of water hazards on the last holes, especially the tricky 15th, a par-3. There are two par-5s that are well over 500 yards each. This "new" course is definitely tougher and more challenging. But it's still scenic—signs of the property's glory days are everywhere, including the plantation's 200-year-old water wheel. Views of the turquoise Caribbean can be seen at every divot. Tryall also conducts a three-day VIP Golf School, held in March, to improve your game.

The resort itself is very grand, and very expensive. The U-shaped main building, the Great House, is a symphony of pink, light blue, white, parquet, and chintz. It commands expansive views of the grounds and the sea beyond. There are 52 guest rooms and all have been attractively redecorated. They are very bright and airy, with air conditioning, marble floors, sumptuous and fluffed chintz furnishings, and French doors. But if you really want to go first class, rent one of the 42 villas, each distinctively decorated and furnished. All have a private swimming pool and a full-time staff (including cook, chambermaid, laundress, and gardener). The larger villas also come with a butler and bartender. To help decide which is the best for you, the resort publishes brochures on all the villas, with photos and layouts for your perusal. Down at the beach, there is a beach club and water-sports center.

Rates are WICKED PRICEY to OUTRAGEOUS for singles and doubles (EP). Add $66 U.S. per person for MAP. Villa rates are BEYOND BELIEF. A three-bedroom villa will run you $6,500 per week (EP). You pay extra for the food the chef will cook you. Golf packages are available.

If golf is your game, there are two other resorts that offer good courses and accommodations: Half Moon Club and Wyndham Rose Hall. The Half Moon Club is as expensive as Round Hill or Tryall, so why not stay at Round Hill or Tryall, they're nicer. Wyndham Rose Hall is cheaper overall, but not anywhere near as elegant or luxurious as the above. But if you want to play more golf, here's a rundown of the courses as well as the resorts:

HALF MOON CLUB (809) 953-2211, fax (809) 953-2731
Stateside: (800) 626-0592
Rose Hall (P.O. Box 80), Montego Bay, Jamaica, W.I.

WYNDHAM ROSE HALL RESORT (809) 953-2650, fax (809) 952-2617
Stateside: (800) 822-4200; Canada: (800) 631-4200
Rose Hall (P.O. Box 999), Montego Bay, Jamaica, W.I.

About a half-hour away, adjacent to each other on the other side of Montego Bay, are Half Moon and Wyndham Rose Hall. While both are well maintained and par-72s, they are very different in

design. The Half Moon course, designed by Robert Trent Jones, has
a more traditional links layout and is a power hitter's dream. It is
long and narrow at 7,143 yards (Championship) and consists mainly
of straight fairways. There are four par-5 holes that will keep your
drivers very busy. In contrast, the course at Wyndham Rose Hall,
designed by Ian Smedley, is full of twists, hills, dips, and water
hazards. Starting at an attractive English-colonial–style clubhouse
containing the requisite dining room/bar and restaurant (and with
the added flourish of a cannon in the courtyard), this tough course
of 6,598 yards (Championship) starts you off with a par-5 hook left
that could wreck the rest of your game. The third hole, while short,
requires you to place the ball over a pond about as big as this
fairway that ends only feet from the green. The eighth hole is
considered the hardest; the left side is on the crashing surf and the
green is a blind hole left of the tee. The back nine are full of
obstacles and require real skill to finesse the ball to several blind
greens. The fourteenth and fifteenth holes are twin toughies. The
former features an uphill battle and a very tight right angle to the
green. The latter has water hazards both fore and aft of the green,
including a waterfall. (It was used in the 007 film *Live and Let Die*.)
Wyndham Rose Hall has a great driving range, which slopes gently
downhill and is set against the surf rolling in the distance.

The Half Moon Club is considered a deluxe resort on Jamaica.
While it's not top-drawer like Round Hill or Tryall, it is just as
expensive. It has a very good mile-long beach and 13 tennis courts
(7 lit at night) for serve-and-volley enthusiasts and 4 squash courts.
Of the several types of accommodations the best value is the "superior" rooms. The food is excellent—naturally, you have to pay
extra for it.

Rates for the Half Moon Club range from WICKED PRICEY for
singles all the way to OUTRAGEOUS for singles and doubles (EP).

The Wyndham Rose Hall Resort is best appreciated for its setting and golf course. The hotel caters to the convention crowd and
looks it. Its architecture is unattractive—big, pink (the company
hallmark), rectangular buildings that aren't exactly in harmony with
the natural setting. The parent company has another hotel in Kingston, which is much better suited to its surroundings and highly
recommended.

Rates are less than the other deluxe resorts mentioned: they're
still VERY PRICEY for singles and doubles (EP).

WHERE TO EAT

Besides eating at the above hotels, where the food is very good to excellent, here are a few places in town to try:

GEORGIAN HOUSE, 2 Orange Street, 952-0632

Probably the most elegant restaurant in Mo Bay, this is set in an old Georgian brick building in the heart of the old town. Beautiful mahogany floors and woodwork and big brass chandeliers create a very lovely, if somewhat formal, atmosphere. House specialties include tournedos Rossini, baked stuffed lobster, and pan-barbecued shrimp. Their dessert of baked bananas in coconut cream is heavenly. Reservations are required. $$$$$

PORK PIT, Gloucester Avenue, 952-1046

This is a real Mo Bay institution and a must stop for anyone in the area, especially if you're driving to Negril from the airport (or returning). Jerk pork or jerk chicken is the choice, with yummy side dishes like yams and sweet potatoes. Everything is open-air and informal—you sit at picnic tables and pig out. There are two jerk sauces, mild and hot (you can buy these to take home too). The mild will be spicy enough for most non-Jamaicans. $ *No credit cards.*

CASCADE ROOM, at the Pelican, Gloucester Avenue, 952-3171

With a man-made waterfall as one side of the restaurant, the Cascade Room specializes in seafood and has established itself as one of the best in town. This might be a good place to try ackee and codfish, the Jamaican national dish. Open for dinner only. $$$

DON'T MISS

THE PORK PIT—see the write-up above.

For nightlife and live music try SIR WINSTON'S on Gloucester Street (952-2084), THE SCARLET KEG on Barnett Street, PIER ONE, Howard Cooke Highway (952-2452) and THE CAVE DISCO at the Seawinds Resort (952-4070).

PORT ANTONIO

WHERE TO STAY

There aren't a helluva lot of choices in this pretty and lush part of Jamaica. This is the home of the Trident Villas and Hotel, one of Jamaica's oldest luxury destinations and by far the best in Port Antonio (there is no competition here). There are a few villa/efficiency choices and a guest house or two. Here we go:

TRIDENT VILLAS AND HOTEL (809) 993-2602, fax (809) 993-2590
Stateside and Canada: (800) 237-3237/(305) 666-3566; UK: (01) 730-7144
Route A4 (P.O. Box 119), Port Antonio, Jamaica, W.I.

Situated just a few miles east of Port Antonio on 14 rocky waterfront acres, Trident is an institution not only in Port Antonio but also in Jamaica, having been one of its top deluxe hotels for eons. Trident was badly damaged by Hurricane Gilbert, being very exposed on its rocky point. It has been rebuilt, although there are still traces of damage if you look closely.

The atmosphere at Trident is decidedly British—one of quiet and reserve; there are no pool aerobics here. Rather, afternoon tea is served at 4:30 P.M. with tea sandwiches and cakes. Croquet is set up on the lawn, and there are resident peacocks who will often fan their feathers and give you a real show. (They are also quite noisy and make the strangest sounds, especially in the middle of the night.) This resort is small, and staying here gives the impression of staying at someone's seaside estate while the owners are out of town. Actually, the owners are in town—they run the hotel. Owned by the Levy family of Kingston, daughter Suzanne is the manager and a friendly, cheerful and stylish presence at the property. Trident has had ample celebs as guests, many actors have stayed here while filming on location in the Port Antonio environs, including Tom Cruise and Whoopi Goldberg.

There are 27 guest accommodations ranging from superior and deluxe rooms to villa suites and the grand Imperial Suite. By far the best choice is one of the wonderfully designed villas, which have a spacious and airy living room, private patio (except for the security guards, who will walk in front of your villa at any time—hope you're not being naughty on your patio), and a huge bedroom with lots of closet space and a large bath. There is a breakfast gazebo where room service will set up your meal and where those peacocks will sometimes entertain you (P.S.—don't feed them). The sound of the surf crashing against the rocks is always present.

On the grounds is a free-form pool, a small beach in a protected lagoon, and two tennis courts. The hotel has a very tasteful parlor with piano and a separate publike bar. There is a very formal dining room where the waiters wear red coats and white gloves and you don't feel like speaking above a whisper. (The air conditioning and closed windows unfortunately keep out the breezes and sound of the sea.) Jackets are required. Dinner is prix-fixe at $50 U.S. per person (including tip but not drinks). The menu and food, however, were very disappointing on the night I ate there—all five courses. Included on the menu was salad called "House Wife Lambada" and a dessert of orange Jell-o. And they serve instant Sanka for decaf. If an establishment is going to charge these prices, the food should be good. It isn't, although breakfast was fine. Since there aren't many other dining options in the area, this could be a problem. The service, however, was excellent, as was their special drink, the Trident Rock.

Rates are WICKED PRICEY for singles in a superior or deluxe room, RIDICULOUS for singles in a villa (EP). For doubles, rates are RIDICULOUS for a superior or deluxe room and BEYOND BELIEF for a villa (EP).

THE JAMAICA PALACE HOTEL (809) 993-2021, fax (809) 993-3459
Stateside and Canada: (800) 423-4095
Williamsfield (P.O. Box 277), Port Antonio, Jamaica, W.I.

This is a rather unusual place. It looks very grand on approach, a stately and sprawling white Greek revival building set on a hill. Recently built by a German heiress, Siglinde von Stephani-Fahmi, I think the Palace is geared for the European and especially German market. Why, you ask? Well, it seemed like a place where Dieter of *Saturday Night Live*'s "Sprockets" would stay. Maybe it was the eerie portrait of a baroque woman in the lobby, or the painful-on-the-eyes black-and-white-checkerboard-painted concrete floors, or the black pool deck that would scorch your feet when you stepped out of the pool, or the rather odd décor in the rooms, or the dining room with its free-range, huge brown banquettes. A friend who was traveling with me said this place would give her nightmares. While I don't think it's that scary, there is definitely something a tad creepy about it, à la the Overlook Hotel in *The Shining*.

There are 80 rooms and suites. The rooms and suites are big, with high ceilings, spacious, marble baths, and the eclectic décor I mentioned. There is a 114-foot swimming pool shaped like the island of Jamaica and what seems like a football field of those dizzying checkerboards as a terrace (actually the roof of the building). With no shade or cover, the sun and the floor are blinding and very hot. But if the above is not a problem, or appealing, the rates here are very reasonable, which in itself is a reason to stay here.

Rates are PRICEY to VERY PRICEY for singles and doubles (EP). Add $55 U.S. per person per day for MAP.

GOBLIN HILL VILLAS AT SAN SAN (809) 993-3286, fax (809) 925-6248
San San (P.O. Box 26), Port Antonio, Jamaica, W.I.

The Goblin Hill Villas at San San resort sits high up on a hill on 12 beautifully landscaped acres. There are great views of San San Bay and the Caribbean from the grounds. It is peaceful and breezy up here, and would be well suited for families. There is a pool, 2 lighted tennis courts, a pleasant lounge area and the Tree Bar—a bar wrapped around the 12-foot trunk of a ficus tree.

The villas themselves are roomy and comfortable although they are rather seventies-looking in décor, which may be an irritant. All villas have fully equipped kitchens and come with a housekeeper and cook—a definite plus.

Rates are WICKED PRICEY for singles and doubles. However, they do include the services of the cook and housekeeper, a rental car, and airport transfers from Kingston. All in all, a good deal for Port Antonio.

DRAGON BAY VILLAS (809) 993-3281, fax (809) 993-3284
P.O. Box 176, Port Antonio, Jamaica, W.I.

If you're looking for a reasonably priced villa resort, Dragon Bay may be the one for you. Located on 50 acres along the water east of Port Antonio, this is where the movie *Cocktail* was filmed. There is a private beach with water sports, a beach bar and restaurant, and a swimming pool.

The resort has 88 one- to three-bedroom villas to choose from, all with fully equipped kitchen, air conditioning, and private bath. Personal cooks are also available. The accommodations are comfortable and pleasantly decorated.

Rates are NOT SO CHEAP to VERY PRICEY for singles and doubles (EP).

NAVY ISLAND RESORT & MARINA (809) 993-2667, fax (809) 993-2041
Navy Island (P.O. Box 188), Port Antonio, Jamaica, W.I.

Straddling the entrance to Port Antonio Harbour, Navy Island was once Errol Flynn's Jamaican hideaway. It is a large private island that can be reached only by boat (although people have been known to swim the distance between the island and Fort George). Under new management, the resort has several Jamaican-style cottages dispersed around the calm side of the island. All have lots of louvered windows and ceiling fans to keep the breeze going. Each also has a large veranda/lanai—great for cocktails and watching the lights of Port Antonio twinkle.

Since you have the entire island to roam, there are lots of paths on which to find some solitude, and two beaches, one of which is nudie (Trembly Knee Cove). The beaches are for the most part man-made, due to lots of shallow coral reefs. There is, however, a place to swim at the end of the pier on the non-nudie beach (and there's also a pool). Still, the beach is pleasant. Navy Island has a restaurant, bar, and marina. The ferry runs from early morning until 11 P.M., later if you make arrangements with the launchman.

Rates are PRICEY to WICKED PRICEY for singles and doubles (includes full breakfast).

BONNIE VIEW PLANTATION HOTEL (809) 993-2752, fax (809) 993-2862
P.O. Box 82, Port Antonio, Jamaica, W.I.

If you're on a budget, the Bonnie View offers decent rooms and fab views of Port Antonio. Perched at the top of a major hill (600 feet above sea level), the views are stunning as would be the walk down to town and back. There are 20 rooms, all fan-cooled, and a restaurant and pool on the 25-acre property.

Rates are CHEAP to NOT SO CHEAP for singles and doubles (EP).

DeMONTEVIN LODGE (809) 993-2604
P.O. Box 85, Port Antonio, Jamaica, W.I.

Skip it unless you are on an extremely tight budget or want to go to dine on some good Jamaican food at the restaurant.

Rates are DIRT CHEAP to NOT SO CHEAP for singles and doubles (EP).

WHERE TO EAT

The pickings here are slim. At the best hotel, Trident, the food is very pricey and disappointing. Your best bet is to hire a cook for the week—easily done if you have a villa. Here are a few other options:

BOSTON BAY JERK STANDS, Boston Bay

Located right by the entrance to the beach in Boston, there are several jerk stands that are renowned throughout Jamaica as serving the best jerk in the country. Jerk was originated in Boston. Careful, it is really hot, to the point of making you cry. You can buy jars of sauce to take home. Remember, it's five-alarm stuff. $

DeMONTEVIN LODGE RESTAURANT, 21 Fort George Street, 993-2604

While I haven't recommended staying here, this is probably the best Jamaican restaurant in town. Specialties include pepperpot and pumpkin soup, curried lobster or chicken, and flavorful desserts. Reservations are required. Very casual and cheap. $$

BONNIE VIEW PLANTATION, Richmond Hill, 993-2752

While the food is okay, with Jamaican specialties, the view is fab. $$

Don't Miss

FRENCHMAN'S BAY—Located east of Port Antonio, this is one of the most beautiful small beaches in Jamaica. It was once part of a very posh hotel that has since closed down. You can still hang out here for about $3 U.S. There is a cool, clean freshwater river with a sandy bottom that empties into the cove. There are lots of big shade trees like banyans to escape the sun. Actually, the foliage in the cove is really gorgeous. The cove itself gets some body-surfable waves and has a pretty, small sandy beach. There is a food concession for lunch. I really think this is a great place to spend the day so YOU MUST stop here.

BOSTON BAY—There is a pretty beach here with small fishing boats. You have to try the jerk at the beach stands.

BLUE LAGOON—Where they filmed the Brooke Shields movie of the same name, this calm, protected cove is called the Blue Lagoon because the water is so deep (188 feet) that it makes the water a cobalt blue. It's very scenic and fun to swim in too.

TEA AT THE TRIDENT—This is fun, relaxing, and well worth it. Tea is served between 4:30 and 5:30 P.M. After tea, have a Trident Rock, their special drink. Phone 993-2602.

KINGSTON

Where to Stay

If you are going to Kingston to see the Bob Marley Museum or the art scene, there are many accommodations options, as Kingston is a major city. I recommend staying at one of the big hotels, which are conveniently located, safe, and have pools in which to refresh yourself. With the first two properties listed below, be prepared to be asked for money by small but well-rehearsed barefoot children as soon as you step off the grounds. In addition, a number of street vendors will try to sell you many things, including recorded tapes and *ganja.*

JAMAICA PEGASUS HOTEL (809) 926-3690, fax (809) 926-5855

Stateside and Canada: (800) 225-5843
81 Knutsford Boulevard (P.O. Box 333), Kingston 5, Jamaica, W.I.

With 350 rooms, this high-rise hotel—Kingston's biggest—sits in the middle of New Kingston, the tony area of the capital, and offers all of the amenities of a large hotel, including 24-hour room service. Rooms are standard big-hotel fare, and each has a coffeemaker, cable TV, radio, air conditioning (of course), and a lanai. There is a large outdoor pool, tennis courts, a small health club, and jogging track, plus two restaurants on premises.

Rates are VERY PRICEY for singles and doubles (CP).

WYNDHAM NEW KINGSTON (809) 929-5430, fax (809) 929-7439

Stateside: (800) 822-4200
77 Knutsford Boulevard (P.O. Box 112), Kingston 10, Jamaica, W.I.

Located just north of the Jamaica Pegasus, this 300-room hotel is similar to the Pegasus, although I think a tad nicer. The rooms are pleasant and comfortable with cable TV, air conditioning, and a lanai. There is 24-hour room service, an olympic-sized pool and a pool bar, floodlit tennis courts, a small health club, 2 restaurants, and a nightclub on the property.

Rates are PRICEY to VERY PRICEY for singles and doubles (EP).

MAYFAIR HOTEL (809) 926-1610, fax (809) 926-7741

4 West King's House Close (P.O. Box 163), Kingston 10, Jamaica, W.I.

If you're on a budget, this is a good alternative. Situated next to the Governor General's residence, it has 32 air-conditioned rooms in eight houses. There is a restaurant and pool on the grounds.

Rates are CHEAP to NOT SO CHEAP for singles and doubles (EP).

MAYA LODGE & HIKING CENTER (809) 927-2097

P.O. Box 216, Kingston 7, Jamaica, W.I.

For naturalists and those who like being in the mountains in a rustic—i.e., just above camping—environment, the Maya Lodge is for you. Located about 15 minutes northeast of Kingston on 15 safe

hilltop acres (altitude 1,850 feet), Maya Lodge is the headquarters
of Sense Adventures (see below) and the base for lots of day hikes.
There is a cozy central lodge with three rooms, *rustic* cabins, camp-
sites, and communal washrooms. The rooms in the cabins are very
basic. There is also a hostel where you get a pillow, linens, and a
foam mat and bunk in with others. But the purpose here is to be
outside. There is a café serving Jamaican food and of course Blue
Mountain coffee.

Rates are DIRT CHEAP for singles and doubles (EP), for cabins,
hostel, and camping.

WHERE TO EAT

Kingston is a big city with lots of possibilities. However, I've se-
lected places that are either close to the recommended hotels, as it
is a big city and tourists should be alert here, or a drive or courtesy-
van trip away. Both the Pegasus and the Wyndham have two good
restaurants each, and you may be happy just to stay put. Otherwise,
consider the following:

SEAWITCH, 69 Knutsford Boulevard, 929-4386

This is a good and reasonably priced steakhouse and seafood restau-
rant within walking distance of the big hotels. $$$

GORDON'S RESTAURANT AND LOUNGE, 36 Trafalgar Road, 929-1390

If you're in the mood for cuisine from the Orient, Gordon's serves
Chinese, Japanese, and Korean dishes. $$

CHELSEA JERK CENTRE, 9 Chelsea Avenue, 926-6322

For a cheap and truly Jamaican meal, namely jerk pork or chicken,
within walking distance of the big hotels, here's the place. $ *No
credit cards.*

North of Kingston

THE RESTAURANT AT TEMPLE HALL, Constant Spring, 942-2340

Set up in the hills on a hundred-plus-acre former plantation, this is
one of Jamaica's premier restaurants. Its cuisine could be best de-

scribed as nouvelle Jamaican. Reservations are required and, upon request, they will pick you up at your hotel without charge. $$$

BLUE MOUNTAIN INN, Gordon Town Road, 927-1700

This is a Kingston institution, perched up in the mountains about a 20-minute drive north of Kingston. The cuisine is continental/Caribbean and the menus are changed periodically. Jackets are required for men (ties optional) but the cool night air in the mountains makes it bearable. Women should bring a wrap. This is a definite Caribbean dining experience and well worth the trip. Reservations are required. $$$$

Don't Miss

SENSE ADVENTURES, P.O. Box 216, Kingston 7, Jamaica, W.I. (809) 927-2097—Created by Peter Bentley, a Jamaican, Sense Adventures has pioneered adventure travel in Jamaica and they know more than anybody about the island and where to find nature's best. They are very environmentally conscious and their staff works with Jamaican nature experts to bring you exciting and different experiences. Sense Adventures has created over 25 different day and overnight trips to find the Jamaica that you'll never see on the standard tour bus. There are hiking trips throughout the Blue Mountains, a day-trip around Kingston, canoe trips, birding trips, camping trips, mixed adventure trips, day-trips to the deserted keys off Port Royal, reggae clubs in Kingston (the best way for a tourist to explore Kingston nightlife), cricket matches, and more. If you will be in Kingston for a few days, or for Sunsplash, definitely do one of their adventures. They also provide an excellent guide service. Prices are very reasonable.

PORT ROYAL—Located at the end of the airport peninsula, a ferry ride of 20 to 30 minutes will take you to this former "wickedest city on earth" that was mostly swallowed up by the sea in the 1692 earthquake.

MARGARITA ISLAND

Madonna sang of "La Isla Bonita" in her *True Blue* album. She may have had Margarita in mind when she wrote the song.

Margarita is not a particularly pretty island. Like the other islands in the Lesser Antilles, such as Bonaire and Aruba, it's very arid and scorched. Brown is much more prevalent here than green. The beaches are okay, but not great. The ocean is a greener hue here, not turquoise like the islands farther north. The main town of Porlamar is a dump—a haphazard mix of high-rise development, urban and commercial buildings, and suburban sprawl. There are billboards everywhere. And trash—it's not a clean island. (You'll see supposedly wealthy people in their brand-new Grand Cherokees toss beer cans and trash out the window; it boggles my mind how people can do that. The bottom line is, the picture I'm painting is not all that lovely.

So why do I like Margarita so much? It's the people. The Venezuelans are so much fun! They transcend the island's lack of beauty and cleanliness with their own beauty, spirit, and friendliness. (Remember, Venezuela has had more finalists and winners in the Miss Universe Pageant than any other country.) And they love to party and have fun (see "Going Out," which follows). The other reason is that it is so cheap here. The U.S. dollar has never been stronger. The top hotel on the island, the Hilton, is well under $200 a night and a good meal at a good restaurant will cost you around $15.

Most of the visitors to Margarita are from Caracas—called *Caraqueños*. There aren't a lot of foreigners here, although you will run into a few Americans on package tours at hotels and in town. They look at you in the elevator trying to figure out if you speak

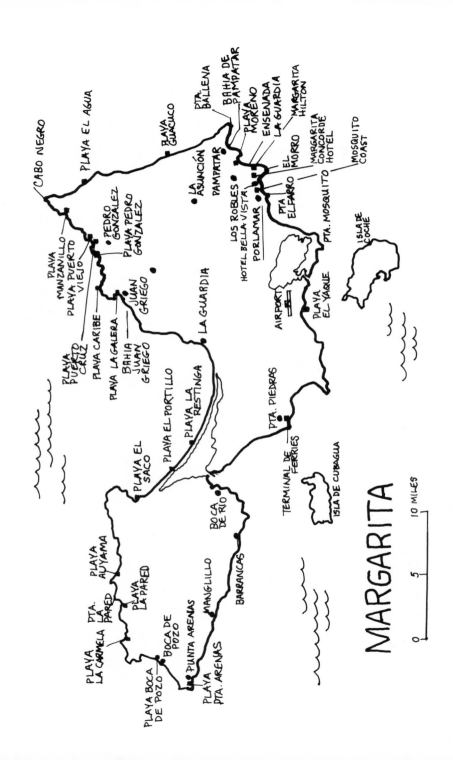

MARGARITA

English or not. I pretend I don't. "Lo siento, no hablo Ingles." It's cruel, I know, but it's so much fun. There are a smattering of other nationalities, including various Europeans. English is not widely spoken—as a matter of fact it is hardly spoken at all once you leave your hotel (some places, like the Mosquito Coast, require their employees to be bilingual).

The island basically divides into two distinct parts, east and west. Most people and activity are on the larger, eastern end. This is where Porlamar and the capital, La Asunción (Margarita is the biggest part of the state of Nueva Esparta), and the most popular beaches are located. The western end, called the Peninsula de Maca-ñao, is the most arid (read "desert"), but does have some pretty and deserted (no pun intended) beaches.

THE BRIEFEST HISTORY

Amerindians inhabited the island when Columbus landed across the bay on the Venezuelan mainland in 1498 and claimed the island (along with Venezuela) for Spain. Pearls were then discovered on Cubagua, one of two islets just off of the south of Venezuela (*Maragarita* is the Greek word for "pearl"). By the mid-1600s, however, the pearling industry was finito, as the oyster beds were depleted. The island was claimed by Spain and remained under its control, uncontested, until the War of Liberation by Simón Bolívar in the early 1800s. Actually, Margarita was a hotbed of discontent and struggles in the war. After the war, it remained a sleepy island until the early 1980's, when the devalued bolivar (the Venezuelan currency) and duty-free status made Margarita an attractive and affordable destination for mainland Venezuelans.

MARGARITA: KEY FACTS

LOCATION	11°N by 64°W
	18 miles north of Cumaná, Venezuela
	200 miles from Caracas
	2,100 miles southeast of New York
SIZE	414 square miles
HIGHEST POINT	Cerro El Copey (2,900 ft.)
POPULATION	200,000

LANGUAGE   *Spanish!*
TIME   Atlantic Standard Time (1 hour ahead of EST,
                  same as EDT)
AREA CODE   To call Margarita from the U.S. dial 011 (the
                  international dialing code), then 58 (the country
                  code for Venezuela), then 095 (the code for Mar-
                  garita), followed by the six-digit local number
ELECTRICITY   110 volts AC, 60 cycles
CURRENCY   The Venezuelan bolivar (Bs)
DRIVING   On the *right*; a valid U.S. or Canadian driver's
                  license is acceptable
DOCUMENTS   Passport (*Note:* You must keep it or a photocopy
                  of it with you at all times—keep the copy in your
                  wallet).
DEPARTURE TAX $15 U.S.
BEER TO DRINK   Polar
RUM TO DRINK   Pampero Aniversario
MUSIC TO HEAR   Salsa

GETTING THERE

Caracas is a major international destination, with flights coming in
from around the world. From the U.S., AMERICAN, VIASA,
AVENSA, and AEROPOSTAL all have nonstop and direct flights,
primarily from New York, Miami, and Orlando. AIR CANADA
and VIASA fly from Toronto. From the U.K., BRITISH AIR-
WAYS and VIASA fly from London.
     Once at the Simón Bolívar airport in Caracas, there are tons
of shuttle flights (at least 18) to Porlamar on AVENSA,
AEROPOSTAL, and AEROTUY. When booking your ticket, be
sure to have this connection included, as it will cost next to nothing.
You may want to allow for a stopover in Caracas (recommended),
to see what the cultural capital of Latin America is all about. If you
are already on the mainland, there is a car-ferry from Puerto La
Cruz to Margarita, which takes four to five hours.

GETTING AROUND

The roads are good and the gas is so incredibly cheap (about 25¢ a gallon—remember, Venezuela is the largest oil producer after Saudi Arabia), that it makes sense to rent a car. Besides, you'll need one to get from Porlamar to Playa el Agua (about a 25-minute drive). All the major rental companies are here, including AVIS ([800] 331-1084), BUDGET ([800] 527-0700), HERTZ ([800] 654-3001), and NATIONAL ([800] 227-3876). Check with your credit-card company before you leave to make sure that your policy covers for collision here. If you aren't covered, by all means accept the CDW insurance when renting a vehicle. Make sure you reserve in advance, you'll get a better deal.

Note that when driving at night, Venezuelans rarely stop for red lights—they just slow down—so be advised.

FOCUS ON MARGARITA: THE PLEASURE PRINCIPLE

There's no doubt in my mind that the Venezuelans like to have a good time. Not only do they like to have a good time, they go out of their way in search of it. And Margarita is one of the places they go to have it.

The Margarita pleasure pie is divided into six slices. The first slice is the beach, and *the* beach to be at is Playa el Agua. Located about a 25-minute drive from Porlamar (where you'll stay), this is about a 2-mile strand of white sand. Facing east, it is constantly cooled by the tradewinds. They also kick up a little surf, but nothing too rough. There are sit-down restaurants all along the beach, and almost all serve great seafood dishes from fish caught by local fishermen in Manzanillo (just down the road). Most of these restaurants have chaises and umbrellas for hire, as well as table service at your chaise. This can make people-watching even more pleasant. With a constant stream of folks parading by, it's very entertaining—especially when your cocktail glass is constantly being refilled. The northern end of the beach, where the restaurants stop, is where the young crowd hangs out. It's very easy to meet people here as they are so friendly. Speaking Spanish helps, but Venezuelans love Americans, so they'll help you communicate. You'll undoubtedly notice teams of T-shirted, attractive, and outgoing young people

who will invite you for free food and drinks at one of the restaurants on the beach. Don't panic, they're not Venezuela's version of
the Moonies; they're worse than that. They're selling time-shares—
which is really big business here (Venezuelans will have to learn the
hard way I guess). Even when you tell them you live in the States
and are only here on vacation, they still want you to come over.

The second slice is siesta. After the beach and a good late lunch,
you roll back into your hotel and hit the hay. A few hours' nap is
just what the Venezuelan doctor ordered.

Slice number three is dinner, of course. Eating is so pleasurable,
and with the plenitude of good and inexpensive restaurants available to you, it should be (see "Where to Dine," which follows).

The fourth slice is one of the most fun—nightlife. And there is
no better place to go out and spend hours than the Mosquito Coast
on the waterfront in Porlamar. Voted the Best Nightclub in the
Caribbean by the author of *Rum and Reggae*, this place is just a great
time. The music is a wild mix of favorites, from salsa, merengue,
and lambada to En Vogue and Rozalla to REM and Guns N' Roses.
When REM's "Losing My Religion" came pouring over the sound
system, everyone on the dance floor started screaming the words
and going crazy. You just don't expect that from a dancing horde
of *Caraqueños*. The temperature rises on the dance floor, as the
sparks from all that hip action generate lots of heat. To cool off, you
can head outside to the terrace, also a good place to mingle. Or you
can have a Bomba Bull. This is basically a Long Island Ice Tea
served in a small bucket. One of these will deck two Americans flat
out on the floor, yet Venezuelans will have two and still be walking!
The waitstaff is very friendly and bilingual, so you can order with
ease, and the bar is open usually till around 7 A.M., so you can go
home with a sleaze. Be sure to buy a T-shirt, they are only $7 U.S.
and are all cotton—they make great souvenirs. Also chat with Jake,
one of the owners and an ex-Californian by way of 19 years in
Southeast Asia. He's a very interesting and amiable guy, especially
to ladies.

Fifth slice on the pie is sex. After all, this *is* a Latin country. And
between Playa el Agua and Mosquito, you're bound to have met
someone.

Finally, the sixth slice is sleep. You'll need it after having the first
five. Most likely, noon will be the time to rise for the beginning of
the next Margarita Pleasure Pie.

WHERE TO STAY

Most of the accommodations on Margarita are in Porlamar. This is where you'll want to stay to be near the action and especially the Mosquito. Since they are not very expensive, I recommend staying at one of the three best hotels. They're big, they have great pools, and are all easy to get on a package deal—thus even cheaper.

MARGARITA HILTON INTERNATIONAL (011-58-095) 61-58-22, fax (011-58-095) 61-48-01
Stateside and Canada: (800) HILTONS
UK: (0800) 28-93-03
Urbanización Playa Moreño, Calle Los Uveros, Porlamar, Margarita, Estado Nueva Esparta, Venezuela

The Hilton is THE BEST PLACE TO STAY on Margarita. Located on the edge of Porlamar on its own private beach, it has everything you need: a friendly and attentive staff that speak English; a great pool/bar area for recovering from your hangover, a good beach with water sports in front, comfortable rooms with the Hilton standard of taste and cleanliness, a gym/health club to keep up the muscle tone, 2 lighted tennis courts, 2 restaurants, 4 bars, and 24-hour room service. There are 280 rooms in a 10-story building, each with its own lanai overlooking the ocean and with all the amenities. An "Executive Business Center" is open daily with full secretarial and telecommunications services if you have some business needs while you're away.

Rates are PRICEY to VERY PRICEY for singles and doubles (EP). Look for package deals.

BELLA VISTA HOTEL (011-58-095) 61-72-22
Avenida Santiago Mariño, Porlamar, Margarita, Estado Nueva Esparta, Venezuela

The most centrally located hotel in Porlamar, and virtually two steps away from the Mosquito Coast, this is a big hotel owned by VIASA. It has a great pool area and is on the beach, although the beach will be crowded. The rooms here are standard big-hotel fare.

Rates are NOT SO CHEAP to PRICEY for singles and doubles (EP). Look for packages.

MARGARITA CONCORDE (011-58-095) 61-33-33
Avenida Raul Leoni, Porlamar, Margarita, Estado Nueva Esparta,
  Venezuela

The best thing about the Concorde is its very pretty and spacious
pool area and grounds. This is another high-rise hotel located on
Punta El Diablo overlooking Porlamar. People seem to like it here,
although some guests I spoke with complained about the service.
All resort amenities are available, including tennis and water sports.
The beach here is not good, as the water is scummy—at least it was
when I visited.

Rates are NOT SO CHEAP to PRICEY for singles and doubles
(EP). Look for package deals.

WHERE TO EAT

There are tons of restaurants in Porlamar, enough to keep you
happy for a week. Among the best are BAHIA (seafood—$$$),
CHEERS (continental—$$), LE CHATEAUBRIAND (continen-
tal—$$$$), LA VECCHIA ROMA (Italian—$$$), (PARIS CROIS-
SANT (pizza, sandwiches, fun outdoor cafe, really cheap—$), LA
POSADA DE TITI (Italian—$$), MARTIN PESCADOR (seafood—$$$), and EL YATE (steaks—$$).

Be sure to have lunch at Playa el Agua and try LA DORADA
($$), AMARILLO ($), and CLOUD NINE ($). You may also want
to try lunch and/or dinner in the scenic little harbor of Juan Griego.
If you go, try TASCA-EL BUHO ($$), EL VIEJO MUELLE ($$),
and EL FORTIN ($$). All are on the water and have tables outside.
One block in from the water is the JUAN GRIEGO STEAK
HOUSE, offering a complete dinner, including wine, for $6 US.

GOING OUT

Porlamar hops at night. I've already raved about the MOSQUITO
COAST (see "Focus on Margarita"). Other options to try are the
VILLAGE CLUB, a cavelike disco on Avenida Santiago Mariño
(up a few blocks from Mosquito); LE GAVROCHE, a dressier,

French-owned club on Calle Tubores; and GIPSY GUITARRA, a dance and live music club with outdoor patio and a slightly older crowd (thirty and fortyish) located on Calle Fermín.

DON'T MISS

The Beaches:

- PLAYA EL AGUA—The place to hit the beach and have lunch.
- PLAYA MANZANILLO—A pretty fishing village and beach for a change of pace.
- PLAYA PUERTO CRUZ—This is the local favorite with a big sand dune/point at the southern end of the beach.
- PLAYA PIEL—Margarita's nude beach, located around the rocks on the western end of Playa Caribe.
- PLAYA EL YAQUE—This is the best windsurfing area on the island.

JUAN GRIEGO—This is a great place to watch sunset over a bottle of wine at one of several waterfront restaurants (see the "Where to Dine" section) or just to watch sunset from the fort La Galera.

PAMPATAR—This is a very scenic fishing village and harbor with some great old buildings. Located just north of Porlamar.

MACAÑAO PENINSULA—This is the desolate and dry western end of the island and worth the drive if you like deserts.

THE MOSQUITO COAST—The best nightclub in the Caribbean.

MIRA!—THE VENEZUELA TRAVELER—This free English-language newspaper is a must-read. Editor David Crocker has a witty and on the mark writing style and point of view. Available in most hotel lobbies.

LOS ROQUES—These beautiful, deserted islands to the east of Margarita are part of Venezuela's National Park system. AEROTUY offers great day and overnight trips from Margarita. If you have the time, it's well worth it.

CARACAS—If you have a couple of days, why not see the cultural capital of South America? It's very lively, cosmopolitan and interesting. Be sure to stay at the CARACAS HILTON, toll free (800) HILTONS, which is the best hotel in the city and at the center of business and cultural activities. It's across the street from the national theaters, performing arts center, and museums.

MARTINIQUE

TOURISTO SCALE ▣ ▣ ▣ ▣ ▣ ▣ ▣ 7

Mercedeses and BMWs whizzing by on the freeway, haute couture on the streets, high-rise residential areas in a cosmopolitan city, gourmet restaurants galore, huge shopping centers left and right—is this the Caribbean? You bet, because this is Martinique, the polished jewel in the French-Caribbean necklace.

Of all of the French islands (there are six main ones: Martinique, Guadeloupe, Les Saintes, Marie-Galante, St. Barts, and St. Martin), Martinique is the most French and the most sophisticated. It is *très français*, and the name of the capital says it all—Fort-de-France. Martinique is an extension of France and the only things that are different are the tropical setting and the color of the Martiniquaise's skin. The look and feel of this island—from the great highway and road system to the billboards advertising Gauloise cigarettes, to the gendarmes directing traffic in the capital—mandate that you *dîtes bonjour.*

Most English-speaking travelers to Martinique are Francophiles (see "Focus on Martinique") who want to indulge in the language and culture, eat great food, and get a tan while they're at it. Like Guadeloupe, most visitors here are from France, some on package tours, some on business, and some vacationing at their villas. Like an American in Paris, if you don't speak French you're going to encounter some of the classic French brusqueness here. But if you try to speak the language, the Martiniquaise warm right up and are very helpful.

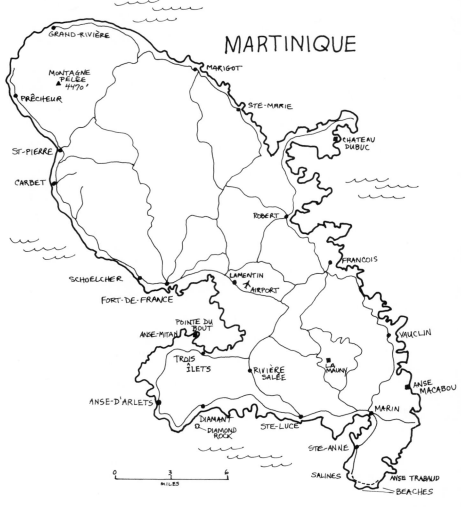

MARTINIQUE

GRAND-RIVIÈRE

MONTAGNE
PÉLÉE
4470'

MARIGOT

PRÊCHEUR

STE-MARIE

CHATEAU
DUBUC

ST-PIERRE

CARBET

ROBERT

FRANÇOIS

SCHOELCHER

LAMENTIN
AIRPORT

FORT-DE-FRANCE

POINTE DU
BOUT

ANSE-MITAN

VAUCLIN

TROIS
ÎLETS

RIVIÈRE
SALÉE

LA
MAUNY

ANSE
MACABOU

ANSE-D'ARLETS

MARIN

DIAMANT
DIAMOND
ROCK

STE-LUCE

STE-ANNE

SALINES

ANSE TRABAUD

BEACHES

0   3   6
MILES

CANAL DE STE-LUCIE

THE BRIEFEST HISTORY

Martinique was first settled by the Awawaks and then by the Caribs, who called the island *Madinina* (which means "Island of Flowers"). It was sighted by Columbus in 1493 but he did not come ashore until 1502. Martinique was first settled by the French in 1635. A year later, King Louis XIII authorized the introduction of slavery into the French West Indies to work the sugar plantations. That continued unabated until 1848, when it was outlawed by the Republic. In 1763, Marie-Josèphe Rose Tascher de la Pagerie was born in Martinique, the daughter of a plantation owner. She later became Napoleon's Empress Joséphine. Throughout the latter part of the 18th century, the island was periodically occupied by the British and it wasn't until 1814 that France regained permanent control of Martinique.

In 1902, Mount Pelée erupted and wiped out the capital, St-Pierre—at the time called "the Paris of the West Indies"—in three minutes with an inferno cloud of smoke, steam, and ash. More than 30,000 people were killed. The lone survivor was a man in a dank jail cell. The capital was then moved to Fort-de-France. Forty-four years later Martinique became a *département* of France, and in 1974 was made a *région*, along with Guadeloupe. The island is represented in the French Parliament by four M.P.s and two senators and locally by the *Conseil Régional.*

The main economy of Martinique is agriculture. Sugar, rum, bananas, pineapples, melons, avocados, limes, fruit juices and canned fruits are the major products. Tourism is a growth industry here, with about 250,000 visitors a year staying in almost 4,000 hotel rooms. It's big business.

MARTINIQUE: KEY FACTS

LOCATION	14°N by 61°W
	21 miles north of St. Lucia
	26 miles south of Dominica
	1,965 miles southeast of New York
SIZE	417 square miles
	50 miles long by 21 miles wide
HIGHEST POINT	Mount Pelée (4,586 ft.)
POPULATION	360,000 (Fort-de-France, 110,000)

LANGUAGE	*French!!!*
TIME	Atlantic Standard Time (1 hour ahead of EST, same as EDT)
AREA CODE	To call Martinique from the U.S. dial 011 (the international dialing code), then 596 (the country code), followed by the six-digit local number
ELECTRICITY	220 volts AC, 50 cycles
CURRENCY	French franc, F (5.2F = $1 U.S. at press time)
DRIVING	On the *right*; a valid driver's license from the U.S. or Canada is valid for up to 20 days; after that, an International Driver's License is required
DOCUMENTS	U.S. and Canadian citizens need proof of nationality (plus a photo ID) for up to 21 days; after that a passport is necessary; an ongoing or return ticket is always necessary
DEPARTURE TAX	None
BEER TO DRINK	Lorraine
RUM TO DRINK	La Mauny
MUSIC TO HEAR	Beguine

GETTING THERE

Martinique's Lamentin International Airport handles jumbo jets from all over. AMERICAN/AMERICAN EAGLE flies nonstop from San Juan, its Caribbean hub, where it connects with American flights from the mainland U.S. There is a Sunday nonstop from Miami on AIR FRANCE. NORTH AMERICAN AIRLINES has direct flights from New York–JFK and Miami every Saturday. The MARTINIQUE TOURIST OFFICE is offering direct service in conjunction with land packages from both New York–JFK and Miami every Saturday during the winter. AIR CANADA has a weekly flight from Montréal and Toronto. AIR MARTINIQUE flies from several neighbor islands, as does LIAT. You can also arrive by boat on the *Emeraude Express*, a high-speed catamaran from Guadeloupe and Dominica.

GETTING AROUND

With one of the best road systems in the Caribbean, replete with freeways and well-marked roads (and the European/French road signs, which are so good and easy to use) and driving on the right, it makes perfect sense to rent a car—especially if you want to hit the best beaches, which are in the southeast corner of the island. In addition to local companies, AVIS ([800] 331-1084/70-11-60), BUD-GET ([800] 527-0700/51-22-88), HERTZ ([800] 654-3001/51-28-22), THRIFTY ([800] 367-2277) and NATIONAL'S affiliate EUROP-CAR ([800] 227-3876), all have airport and island locations. Be sure to reserve in advance, or the cheapest and/or most desirable cars will not be available when you arrive (and by calling you'll also secure the best rates).

If you don't want to rent a car, you can hire a taxi (most are Mercedeses, popular but expensive), or use the public bus system, which is excellent and a great way to meet the locals.

FOCUS ON MARTINIQUE: PARLEZ-VOUS FRANÇAIS?

They are out there. A small but zealous group of Francophiles who can't get enough of Proust's mother tongue. Unfortunately for them, France is not the most inviting place to go in the winter. But there is a tempting option down here that combines the challenge of speaking French with a wonderfully warm climate.

Where is this stimulating, sophisticated tropical oasis? It's right here in Martinique. And the focal point of it all is the fashionable city of Fort-de-France. As its name implies, it is the most French city in appearance, style, and attitude in these latitudes. Everyone here is tuned into Paris, not Kingston. And this is a city that looks decidedly Mediterranean—many find it a smaller, more casual (and hotter) version of Nice. It features great restaurants, cafés, pâtisseries, lots of stores, and a central location. While the temperature is warm to hot in the daytime, the evenings are delightful.

The Martiniquaise may look like West Indians but they act like Frenchmen. You're more likely to see Paris fashions than the Rasta liberation colors, although the latter certainly have made an impact here since my first visit. However, Fort-de-France is definitely the most stylish and well-dressed city in the West Indies. Expect a little—maybe a lot—of that infamous French attitude.

The city of Fort-de-France (population 110,000) is located in the center of the island on the Baie des Flamands. It is surrounded by hills immediately to the north and east. Very large volcanic cones rise up in the distance to the north. Across the Baie is Anse-Mitan and Les Trois-Îlets, the main tourist areas, which are only a 20-minute ferry ride from the downtown area. The center point of this compact city itself is La Savane, a 12.5-acre park with a statue of Empress Joséphine (Martinique's Jackie O.) as its centerpiece. Most activities are within walking distance of it. On the southeast corner of the park at night are lots of food vendors, who set up little cafés by their trucks. You can get all kinds of superb cuisine from them at prices that won't burn a hole in your wallet. They're especially popular because the movie multiplex is right across the street. The city quiets down around 10 P.M., but there are cafés, salons de thé, and nightclubs that will take you into the night.

Author's Note: Since my last visit here six years ago, some things about Fort-de-France have obviously changed. The place has slipped a little, it's not quite as polished as I remembered it. The Savane needs some TLC and the statue of Empress Joséphine has lost her head (Is this telling us something?). Both McDonalds and Burger King have block-long outlets—not a good sign in the midst of le monde français. As in many other places, fast-food chains seem to be taking over. I once recommended staying right in town, but the places I recommended, like the Impératrice, look a little down at their heels now, so I've mostly chosen other places on the island (see "Where to Stay," below). However, the city is certainly worth a visit because there is so much to do.

WHERE TO STAY

There is no shortage of beds on Martinique, what with almost 4,000 hotel rooms of various persuasions. As with Guadeloupe, look for package deals to beat the currency inflation if you want to stay at a big resort. There are several resort areas, the primary one being Anse-Mitan/Pointe du Bout, which is right across the bay from Fort-de-France (and a 20-minute, regularly scheduled ferry ride away). The other majors areas (this means that there are good beaches in front or nearby) are Diamant, Ste-Luce, and Ste-Anne. Of course, there are exceptions scattered here and there. If you want to be near the beaches, the best area to stay is is Ste-Anne. If you want to be near lots to do, stay in Anse-Mitan/Pointe du Bout. Here we go:

FORT-DE-FRANCE

LE LAFAYETTE (011-596) 73-80-50, fax (011-596) 60-97-75
Stateside: (800) 223-9815/(212) 251-1800
5 rue de la Liberté, 97200 Fort-de-France, Martinique, F.W.I.

If you want to stay right in the center of town, across from La Savane, this is a good and relatively inexpensive hotel. This is a small (24 rooms), city hotel—that is, there's no pool. The rooms are fairly small and clean—try to get one with a terrace. Some of the upper-floor rooms have a great view of the harbor and Fort St-Louis. The entrance to the hotel is on rue Victor-Hugo. Le Lafayette's restaurant is one of the best on the island, serving French/Créole cuisine.

Rates are NOT SO CHEAP for singles and doubles (EP).

LA MALMAISON (011-596) 63-90-85, no fax
Rue de la Liberté, 97200 Fort-de-France, Martinique, F.W.I.

You have to look very carefully to find the entrance to this second-floor lobby hotel. The rooms have four-poster beds, armoires, and floor-to-ceiling French windows. The best rooms are on the top floors and have terraces. All have air conditioning, phones, and French TV. On the ground floor is a no-glitz café and pâtisserie that is a great spot to people-watch and count the number of languages you hear. While the hotel caters mainly to non-Martiniquaise, it is a favorite hangout for the crews of various Navy boats that call on Fort-de-France.

Rates are NOT SO CHEAP for singles and doubles (EP).

PLM AZUR SQUASH HOTEL (011-596) 63-00-01, fax (011-596) 63-00-74
Stateside: (800) 221-4542/(914) 472-0370
3 boulevard de la Marne, 97200 Fort-de-France, Martinique, F.W.I.

Located a stone's throw from the center of town, this is a great in-town accommodation for those who want to be in the center of the action yet have some amenities like a pool, sauna, Jacuzzi, squash courts, and an elementary health club. With a view of the bay, there are 100 air-conditioned rooms with phone, TV (it's French TV of course), and minibar.

Rates are NOT SO CHEAP to PRICEY for singles and doubles (EP).

HOTEL CASINO LA BATELIÈRE (011-596) 61-49-49, fax (011-596) 61-70-57
Stateside: (800) 223-6510
Route 32, 97233 Schoelcher, Martinique, F.W.I.

Located a little over a mile from downtown (2.1 kms), this modern, 195-room hotel bathed in white was *the* place to stay in Martinique before Bakoua stole the honors. But the rooms are large and there are all the big-resort amenities, such as room service (for champagne cocktails) and a beauty salon (for the hair and nails). It has its own beach with water sports and a large, comfy pool to lounge around in and see what everyone else is doing. For more exercise, there are six lighted tennis courts—the best on the island. Last but not least, there is a casino for those with loose change and bills to blow and a disco called Le Queen's.

Rates are WICKED PRICEY for singles and doubles (CP).

POINTE DU BOUT/ANSE-MITAN

HOTEL BAKOUA (011-596) 66-02-02, fax (011-596) 66-00-41
Stateside: (800) 221-4542/(914) 472-0370
Pointe du Bout, 97229 Trois-Îlets, Martinique, F.W.I.

This is the super-royal-deluxe resort to stay in on Martinique, thus, it is *the* place to stay for the see-and-want-to-be-seen crowd. It's situated on the point with its own small beach and with fab views of Fort-de-France and the volcanos behind. There are 136 chambres, decorated in a Créole/contempo style, and all are air-conditioned, of course, and have balconies or patios, phone, French TV/video, minibars, room safes, and radios (so you can sing "Sous le Ciel de Paris") in the good-sized baths. A scallop-shaped pool adjoins the beach, where there are the requisite water sports galore. There are two restaurants on the premises as well as two bars. Even better, when you step off the property there are loads more in Pointe du Bout—and lots of activity—an advantage if you suffer from resort/cabin fever. If you want to *jouer au tennis*, there are two lighted courts.

Rates are WICKED PRICEY for singles and doubles (EP).

LE MÉRIDIEN TROIS-ÎLETS (011-596) 66-00-00, fax (011-596) 66-00-74
Stateside: (800) 543-4300
Pointe du Bout (B.P. 894, 97245 Fort-de-France Cedex), Martinique, F.W.I.

If you want to stay at a big hotel and can get a package to match your budget, you might want to consider Air France's Méridien. This is a huge place and is second only to the Club Med in size on Martinique. There are 295 rooms in one large S-shaped building, which strides 3 man-made beach coves along the Baie des Flamands. The beach has little jetties that provide a cool and breezy spot for sunbathing. This is a full-service resort, so everything you need is on the premises, including a beauty salon, sauna, and dry cleaners. Rooms are standard big-hotel, but they all have balconies and air conditioning among the amenities. All water sports are available on the beach and there is a marina across the street. The resort also has two lighted tennis courts.

Rates are WICKED PRICEY to RIDICULOUS for singles and doubles (CP).

HOTEL CARAYOU (011-596) 66-04-04, fax (011-596) 66-00-57
Stateside: (800) 221-4542/(914) 472-0370
Pointe du Bout, 97229 Trois-Îlets, Martinique, F.W.I.

While it doesn't have the great views of Fort-de-France that its much more expensive neighbors (the Bakoua and Méridien) have, the views here are very pleasant, as are the breezes that cool off this rather large property (197 rooms). While the buildings themselves won't win *Architectural Digest* awards, the grounds are spacious and converge on a very nice man-made beach cove. All rooms have the standard resort amenities, including air conditioning, balconies, minibars, and phones. You'll find two restaurants and two bars on the property and all water sports are available at the beach. There are two tennis courts and Ping-Pong for the Glory Upson/Bunny Bixleys among you. You are also steps away from the marina (where the ferry will take you to Fort-de-France in 20 minutes) and all the hubbub of the Pointe du Bout/Anse-Mitan area.

Rates are PRICEY for singles and doubles (EP). Look for packages.

FRANTOUR TROIS-ÎLETS (011-596) 68-31-67, fax (011-596) 68-37-65
Stateside: (800) 223-9815/(212) 251-1800
Anse-à-l'Ane, 97229 Trois-Îlets, Martinique, F.W.I.

Located a few miles southwest of Anse-Mitan, this resort sits on a very pretty cove/beach that is much quieter and prettier than Anse-Mitan, yet there is still a ferry to take you to Fort-de-France in 25 minutes. It is an attractive, well-landscaped medium-sized hotel for those who want to be close to and yet removed from the hubbub. Renovated in 1990, there are 77 rooms, all equipped with air conditioning, lanais, phones, French TV/video, minibars, room safes, and dryers for your wet bathing suits.

Rates are VERY PRICEY for singles and WICKED PRICEY for doubles (CP). Rates drastically drop by over 50% in the summer.

DIAMANT

HOTEL DIAMANT LES BAINS (011-596) 76-40-14, fax (011-596) 76-27-00
97223 Le Diamant, Martinique, F.W.I.

For the money on Martinique, this cute little place offers great value. Situated at the edge of town on the water, Les Bains is a compact mini-resort with lots of character filling in where the luxury is lacking. It sits on the eastern end of the 2.5-mile-long Diamant Beach, with views of imposing Diamant Rock and St. Lucia in the distance, so you can stroll the beach till your heart's content. There are 24 rooms in cottages and the main building. All are air-conditioned, have private bath, fridge, and are clean and simple in décor. There is a pool and a restaurant/bar on the premises. Tennis and water sports are available within five minutes of the hotel, and restaurants and town activity are but steps away.

Rates are NOT SO CHEAP for singles and doubles (CP).

MARINE HOTEL-DIAMANT (011-596) 76-46-00, fax (011-596) 76-25-99
Stateside: (800) 221-4542/(914) 472-0451
Pointe de la Chéry, 97223 Le Diamant, Martinique, F.W.I.

This is a very pleasant new efficiency-hotel which slopes down to the sea just east of the town of Diamant. It's a full-service resort with most of the amenities of the bigger places and is good for families with small children, as there is a baby-sitting service and a laundry. There are 150 rooms, each with a double bed and a smaller "canapé-lît," and all have kitchenettes, air conditioning, room safes, phones, and lanais. All rooms have views of the sea. There are two restaurants, a large pool with a water-slide, two lighted tennis courts, and a good swimming beach. Water sports are available five minutes away at Club Blue Marine (open to hotel guests).

Rates are PRICEY for singles and doubles (EP).

SAINTE-LUCE

HOTEL LES AMANDIERS—PLM AZUR (011-596) 62-32-32, fax (011-596) 62-33-40
97228 Sainte-Luce, Martinique, F.W.I.

This is a new hotel located just west of the lovely little town of Sainte-Luce. Stretching from the road to the beach, the hotel has 117 rooms decorated in what could be called French contemporary/ Créole. Run by a very friendly and helpful staff, the hotel caters overwhelmingly to French and/or European tourists, so you'll definitely feel *une petite différence*. All rooms have air conditioning, good-sized lanais (although its a little to easy to see into your neighbor's room), French TV, and phones. There is a pool, a lighted tennis court, and beach facilities with water sports.

Rates are PRICEY for singles and doubles.

LE MARIN

THE LAST RESORT (011-596) 74-83-88, fax (011-596) 74-76-47
Rue Osman Duquesnay, 97290 Le Marin, Martinique, F.W.I.

If you're on a tight budget, well, you shouldn't really be on Martinique. But if you are, this place might be what you're looking for. It's a very simple but friendly B&B. Rooms are basic and there are no private baths. But the owners are very nice and they speak English (they once lived in Sausalito). They serve meals family-style, or guests may have kitchen privileges.

Rates are CHEAP for singles and doubles (CP).

SAINTE-ANNE

HOTEL ANSE CARITAN (011-596) 76-74-12, fax (011-596) 76-72-59
Stateside: (407) 777-2207
(B.P. 24), 97227 Sainte-Anne, Martinique, F.W.I.

Situated near the charming village of Sainte-Anne and the best beaches of Salines and Traubaud, this is a comfortable, unassuming efficiency-resort with a pool, beach, and water sports. There are 96 rooms, each with kitchenette, air conditioning, phone, room safe, and private bath. The hotel has a restaurant and a bar and is a short walk from others in town.

Rates are NOT SO CHEAP to PRICEY for singles and PRICEY to VERY PRICEY for doubles (CP).

CLUB MED—BUCCANEER'S CREEK (011-596) 76-72-72, fax (011-596) 76-72-02
Stateside: (800) 258-2633
Pointe du Marin, 97227 Sainte-Anne, Martinique, F.W.I.

It's one of the original Caribbean Club Meds, where a lot of those wild stories of the operation first started filtering back to the States after it opened. Built in 1969, the emphasis has changed at Club Med (more on families) since the crazy seventies, although this particular club still caters to a younger, singles and couples crowd. It's all-inclusive and offers the same deal as Club Meds everywhere. There are 300 rooms in a Créole-style "village," with all water sports activities and just about anything else, including seven tennis courts. The clientele here is very American (lots from New York and New Jersey), so staying here is an atypical experience for Martinique.

Rates are WICKED PRICEY for singles and doubles (AP). Most people come here on weekly packages.

THE NORTH

LEYRITZ PLANTATION (011-596) 78-53-92, fax (011-596) 78-92-44
Stateside: (800) 366-1510/(212) 477-1600
97218 Basse-Pointe, Martinique, F.W.I.

This is a refreshing alternative on an island of large resorts and hotels. Located on the fairly remote northeast corner of Martinique, the Leyritz is full of character and plantation charm. Originally an eighteenth-century sugar plantation, the manor house and the outbuildings are still intact and have been improved to provide 50 guest rooms. The oldest and most full of the "C" word (character) are in the manor house. Many rooms have four-poster beds, tile floors, and are comfortably furnished. There is an outdoor pool on the 16-acre grounds and the Plantation now also has spa facilities. Unfortunately, it's on the tour-bus–day-tripper route, so lunchtime is a good reason to go elsewhere. But the evenings are quiet, and the restaurant is quite good. *Note:* The nearest swimmable beach is a half-hour's drive away, but the hotel provides free transportation.
Rates are PRICEY for singles and doubles (CP).

HABITATION LAGRANGE (011-596) 53-60-60, fax (011-596) 53-50-58
Stateside: (800) 633-7411/(803) 785-7411
97225 Marigot, Martinique, F.W.I.

Located the tiny little town of Marigot, this is Martinique's new super-royal-deluxe hotel. Like the Leyritz, it's a former sugar plantation with an eighteenth-century manor house as focal point and additional guest accommodations in the surrounding cottages. There are 17 very tastefully appointed rooms and suites, with all the amenities you'd expect with this price tag. There are 7.5 acres of tropical gardens and lawns to stroll, and the Lagrange does have a pool and tennis for those who want more activity than reading a book or lifting a hand for another ti punch. There is no swimmable beach nearby, so guests here either don't care or shuttle about a half hour to the closest one.
Rates are WICKED PRICEY to RIDICULOUS for singles and doubles (full American breakfast buffet included).

VILLA/GÎTES RENTALS

Want a posh pad or a modest flat to call your own? Give the
following a holler and see what they can do for you:

Villa Rental Service
Centrale de Reservation
20 rue Ernest Deproge
(B.P. 823)
97208 Fort-de-France Cedex
(011-596) 71-56-11, fax (011-596) 63-11-64

Gîtes de France
(B.P. 1122)
97209 Fort-de-France Cedex
(011-596) 73-67-92, fax (011-596) 73-66-93

WHERE TO EAT

Like any French island, there are lots of restaurants, and most of
them would leave the majority of American, Canadian, and British
restaurants in the dust. Translation: It's pretty difficult to get a bad
meal here. Expensive, ah yes, but remember, this is France. But
you're on vacation, and the first *délicieuse* bite will soften the impact
of the dinner check *(l'addition, en français)*. Most restaurants feature what is termed *"cuisine gastronomique,"* which is French food
with Créole flair. Listed below are just some of what is good. For
a complete listing, stop by at the Tourist Board Office on the
Boulevard Alfassa (next to the Air France ticket office, phone 63-
79-60) and get a complete restaurant listing or pick up a free copy
of *Ti Gourmet*. Try to be adventurous and above all, *mange!*

FORT-DE-FRANCE

LE LAFAYETTE, in the Le Lafayette Hôtel, 5 rue de la Liberté,
   63-24-09

This is one of the best restaurants on the island, a very elegant
establishment serving refined French/Créole cuisine in a not-so-
elegant hotel. It gets accolades from everyone, so this is a must.
Reservations are required. $$$$$

LA BIGUINE, 11 route de la Folie, 71-47-75

About five minutes from downtown, the ground floor offers a pub-style grill room, while the upstairs room offers *cuisine gastronomique*. It's a popular place for non-Francophiles, as the menus are in both French and English. Not to be missed are the shark cooked in tomato sauce and the iced local clams. Reservations are suggested. Jacket required for men at dinner. $$$

LA GRAND' VOILE, boulevard Chevalier de Sainte-Marthe, Pointe Simon, 70-29-29

Located on the second floor of the Yacht Club with a very nice view of the ships on the Baie du Carenage, this is perhaps Fort-de-France's most famous restaurant. Its fame makes it a big tourist gathering place, much like Pier 4 in Boston, Tavern on the Green in New York, Alioto's in San Francisco, and so on. Reservations are required. $$$$$

LE SECOND SOUFFLÉ, 27 rue Blénac, 63-44-11

The true sign that you're not in the boonies is the presence of a strictly vegetarian restaurant. So Fort-de-France passes the test with the Second Soufflé. Situated one flight up, this one-room, earth-toned establishment features a variety of dishes with a French and Créole accent, including a veggie soufflé du jour. For single diners (for whom I have tremendous empathy), there is a table of reading materials, so you don't have to stare into space (or, in my case, write on my ever-present note pad). $$

LE LAUREAT, 30 rue du Capitaine Manuel, 70-63-29

An excellent choice for lunch, this simple Spanish-influenced restaurant offers a daily complete luncheon for 50F–60F. *Note:* Tuesday is paella day—not to be missed. You won't find many tourists here. Open only for breakfast and lunch. $$$

FOOD STANDS, southeast corner of La Savane

Great food, great prices, alfresco dining and a lively atmosphere— what more could you want? $

Are you just in the mood for a nice cold beer or a café au lait? If so, here are the best spots for refreshment and people-watching.

EL RACO, 23 rue Lazare-Carnot

This is a wine bar for all of my oeneophile readers.

LA CARAFE, rue Lamartine

A jazz club that's very local and *branché*—that is, hip—for the Martiniquaise.

TEA GARDEN, 41 rue Victor-Hugo

Open until 11 P.M. and serving great desserts and ice creams.

LE NAUTILUS, 69 rue Victor-Hugo

The balcony on the second floor overhangs the street and is a very romantic place.

MALMAISON—rue de la Liberté

For daytime fun and pizza, this is worth checking out. It's opposite the Savane and the post office, so lots of foreigners stream in, including the crews from docked ships.

L'EPI SOLEIL, 21 rue de la Liberté

There are several of these excellent pâtisseries and more throughout the island that are definitely worth a stop. Some are open late.

Located on just about every corner are other pâtisseries—stop and grab a bite.

POINTE DU BOUT/ANSE-MITAN

LE MATADOR, Anse-Mitan, 66-05-36

This is a very highly regarded restaurant throughout the island, despite its lousy view. Cuisine is *gastronomique*, with an emphasis on local specialties. $$$$

AU POISSON D'OR, Anse-Mitan, 66-01-80

Seafood is their specialty, especially stuffed conch, fried sea-eggs, or grilled lobster. $$$$

PIZZERIA NAPOLI, Anse-Mitan, 66-03-79

The place for pizza and pasta in the area, and English is spoken here. $$

LA LANGOUSTE, Anse-Mitan, 66-04-99

As it's name implies, spiny lobster is this restaurant's specialty. Eating here is a pleasure, as you are on the beach with great views of the bay and Fort-de-France. Reservations are suggested. $$$$

LE COROSSOL, Anse-Mitan, 66-02-07

For lunch and dinner, this is a casual crêperie and salad joint, just the ticket if you want lighter fare or don't want to spend a fortune for a meal. $$

TI CALEBASSE, Anse-à-l'Ane, 68-38-77

Ginette is the chef here, and she specializes in tasty Créole dishes. Taste her homemade black pudding. $$$$

LE DIAMANT

LE RÉLAIS CARAÏBES, La Cherry, 76-44-65

The best in Diamant, this restaurant—set amidst the eclectically decorated Le Rélais Caraïbes Hotel—serves up some very imaginative dishes, including ginger-pink shrimp bricks and coconut-rum anglerfish. Reservations are required. $$$$$

DIAMANT-LES-BAINS, Le Diamant, 76-40-14

Chef Hubert whips up a seafood storm at this fun little restaurant. He suggests his stuffed sweet peppers with sea-eggs. During the winter, there are lobster parties on Tuesday nights, complete with a band, and, you guessed it, limbo—fun for all. $$$$

LE DIAM'S, Place de l'Église, 76-23-28

This is a fun place, a sea of pink and green (no, not the preppie kind), flowers and objets d'art. The menu is quite diverse, from salads to a full-course Créole meal. But the price is right, which is why this place gets so busy. Reservations are suggested. $$$

SAINTE-ANNE

AUX FILETS BLEUS, Pointe Marin, 76-73-42

Set right on the beach and open for lunch and dinner, this charming little restaurant is the best in Sainte-Anne (and also the most expensive). Seafood is its thing. Reservations are a must. $$$$$

L'EPI SOLEIL, Sainte-Anne, no phone

If you just want something quick and cheap, this pâtisserie right in the heart of town is open all day and into the night and is very popular. Get your freshly baked baguettes here. $

AUX DÉLICES DE LA MER, Pointe des Salines, 76-97-36

This is the only restaurant at the beach and a good pit stop if you're hungry for a sit-down meal. The restaurant also operates a little tent/café with cheaper Créole fare. $$$

FOOD TRUCKS, Pointe des Salines

As at the Savane at night, all kinds of portable restaurants arrive at the beach, especially on weekends. The food is good and cheap, and you can eat in your bathing suit. They park themselves mostly in a spot past the entrance to the dirt road that goes along the beach in both directions. $

GOING OUT

Unlike most of the West Indies, where nightlife consists of the hotel disco and the occasional skeletal steel band, Fort-de-France has some great clubs which feature both current French and English/American hits. Note that like almost everything else on a French island, most clubs are closed on Sundays. Check ahead of time and ask your hotel concierge about which is the best place to go on a given night (he may even scoop you in on something new). Among the best:

LE NEW HIPPO, 24 boulevard Allegre, Fort-de-France, 60-20-22

This is a disco where you'll find a friendly mix of all types: Martiniquaise, French, black and white.

MONTE CARLO, 20 boulevard Allegre, Fort-de-France, 63-15-55

With live music on weekends, this is a popular place for French tourists.

LE BRUEL'S, 109 rue Ernest Deproges, Fort-de-France, 63-17-06

A large disco acclaimed locally for its design. Very local.

L'ELECTRA, Pointe Simon, Fort-de-France, 60-48-56

Martinique's version of the Hard Rock Café.

PAPAGAYO, Rond-Point du Vietnam Héroique, Fort-de-France, 72-62-62

Slightly out of the way, but very *branché*, with Latin music on weekends.

LE TERMINAL, 104 rue Ernest Deproges, Fort-de-France, 63-03-48

Just a few doors down from Le Bruel's, this is a video bar that prides itself on its selection of beer (beer lovers take note). A good place to stop before going to Le Bruel's.

LE NEPTUNE, route des Anse-d'Arlet, Diamant, 76-25-47

If you don't feel like driving into Fort-de-France, this is a fun disco attracting lots of tourists. It occasionally features live music, including "zouk," which mixes the Caribbean rhythm and an Occidental tempo with Créole words.

THE BEACHES

Tout le Martinique goes to the beach on the weekend, with families and major picnics in tow. They park their Mercedeses, set up the tarp and table, and voilà. Expect incredible traffic from Sainte-Anne to Le Marin returning from the beaches on weekends, as a stoplight at Le Marin backs up traffic for miles. I strongly suggest having dinner in Sainte-Anne to wait it out.

- *Anse-Traubaud*—Located on the southeastern corner of the island just past the beaches of Les Salines, it's actually part of the Baie des Anglais. This is Martinique's prettiest beach—a long stretch of sand bordered by groves of palm trees. To get there, drive past Aux Délices de la Mer and follow the dirt road until you can go no farther. Park, you are at Anse-Traubaud. If you cross over the footbridge and follow the path through the brush (there are cliffs to your right), you'll come to another series of beaches—a 25-minute walk. You can also access these beaches by car by heading north from Sainte-Anne. About one kilometer north of the entrance for Club Med, take the dirt road which forks to the right off the main road. Go about five kilometers and look for the parked cars (you'll have to pay an access fee of 50F to a farmer who owns the land where you park).

- *Les Salines*—The most famous of Martinique's beaches, it can get crowded and busy on weekends. This is where the food trucks set up, and if you keep driving to the right past the entrance, sometimes over a road you think your car cannot negotiate (it will), you come to some quieter beaches. If you go to the left after the entrance, you'll eventually hit Aux Délices de la Mer and then Anse-Traubaud. Feel free to park the car and set up wherever you want along the whole stretch.

- *Le Diamant*—If you don't feel like hassling with the drive and traffic of the Sainte-Anne beaches, Diamant is a long strand (2.5 miles) of salt-and-pepper sand with stunning views of Diamant Rock. A swim here can be included with a pleasant "ooh-cruise" around the southwestern tip of the island. After a day at the beach, visit Anse d'Arlet, a very scenic fishing village that inspired Gaugin and should inspire the photographer in you as well. The late-afternoon light is superb on the brightly painted fishing boats.

YACHT CHARTERS

Martinique is one of the major ports for those interested in cruising St. Lucia and the Grenadines. Among the major charter operators are ATM (97290 Le Marin, 74-98-17, fax 74-88-12); Soleil et Voile (97229 Trois-Îlets, 66-09-14), and Star Voyages (97229 Trois-Îlets, 66-00-72, fax 66-02-11).

BIKING

With the excellent road system on the island, Martinique is a favorite winter training ground for French racers. It's also a popular weekend activity for Martiniquaise. The Parc Naturel Régional de la Martinique (9 boulevard General de Gaulle, 97200 Fort-de-France, 73-19-30) has developed bike routes in conjunction with local bike clubs. For bike rentals, contact these outfits: Discount (Pointe du Bout, 66-54-37), Funny (Fort-de-France, 63-33-05), Centrale du Cycle (near the airport at Lamentin, 50-28-54), and Scootonnerre (Diamant, 76-41-12). If you want to go on mountain bike excursions, contact VT Tilt (Point du Bout, 66-01-01) and Basalt (Bellefontaine, 55-01-84).

TRIPS TO THE NORTH

• *St. Pierre*—This city, once acclaimed as the Paris of the West Indies, was wiped out by the eruption of Mont Pelée in 1902. The city never recovered its prominence, which was usurped by Fort-de-France. Of supreme interest to natural-disaster buffs is the Musée Vulcanologique (Volcanological Museum). Here you'll find photos, melted glass, warped musical instruments from the once-grand city theater, and other lurid paraphernalia. It's open daily from 9 A.M.–12:30 P.M. and 3–5 P.M. Admission is 10F for adults.

• *Rain Forest Coastal Walk*—Grand' Rivière Trail. For the fit, there is a six-hour, 15-mile walk through rain forest and volcanic topography that starts in Grand Rivière and ends in Prêcheur. Once there, you can haggle (in French) and hire a fishing boat to bring you back—or arrange to be picked up in Prêcheur. For more info, contact the Parc Naturel Régional de la Martinique (73-19-30), 9 Blvd. General-de-Gaulle, 97200 Fort-de-France.

ART GALLERIES

There are a number of art galleries in the city that are worth visiting. Of particular interest is the Galerie d'Art Pierre Subito at 51 rue Garnier Pages (72-68-88). There is some quality stuff here that isn't outrageously priced. Discuss Martiniquaise and Haitian art in French with Monsieur Subito; he is so impressed and pleased by Americans, Canadians, and Brits who can speak French that he may substantially drop the price. The gallery is open weekdays from 9 A.M. to 12:30 P.M. and 3 to 7 P.M.; Saturday, it's open from 9 A.M. to 1 P.M. Also try Galerie Singuliere in Pointe du Bout (68-14-23), featuring some excellent local pottery and sculpture.

THE SCHOELCHER LIBRARY (BIBLIOTHÈQUE SCHOELCHER)

Located on the rue de la Liberté across from the Savane in Fort-de-France, this is a marvelous piece of architecture. Don't miss it! The elaborate structure was first displayed at the 1889 Paris Exposition.

MONTSERRAT

TOURISTO SCALE   📷 📷 📷   3

Rebecca was in full throttle. Sipping a glass of white wine and perched on a bar stool at the Nest—a beach bar—she took another drag of her fifth Marlboro and with a delightful British lilt, said, "I gave the bailiff a good chase yesterday. I knew he was going to serve me an injunction so I hit the gas. He finally caught up to me at Cork's Hill." In other places, this action would be regarded as very serious, but here people just shrug it off with a laugh. Such is the life of the Montserratian, a wonderful combination of spunk, let's have fun, propriety, and friendliness.

The people here are wonderful. I noticed it as soon as I stepped off the plane. The immigration officer was actually welcoming, telling me to enjoy my stay. So was the Customs man. Yikes, I wondered, are *they* tripping or am *I*? Bracing for the usual cabbie rush as I walked through the doors, I found the cabbies very courteous. Incredible. It was then that the calm, which seems to be the raison d'être of this island, began to take hold of me.

Montserrat, like its people, is serene. It is also very verdant, living up to its nickname "The Emerald Isle of the Caribbean" in its lushness as well as its Irish heritage. As I drove past old sugar mills, past plunging cliffs of black rock, through mountain valleys, the richness of the foliage was intoxicatingly peaceful. This island is for those who want to be quiet, rest, and read. It is for those who want pleasant but not hot weather, or for those who really don't care about the beach, or for those penitent sun worshippers of years past who, because they now use Retin-A, avoid maximum exposure but still want a little color.

The island, at present, doesn't attract a younger crowd. Actually,

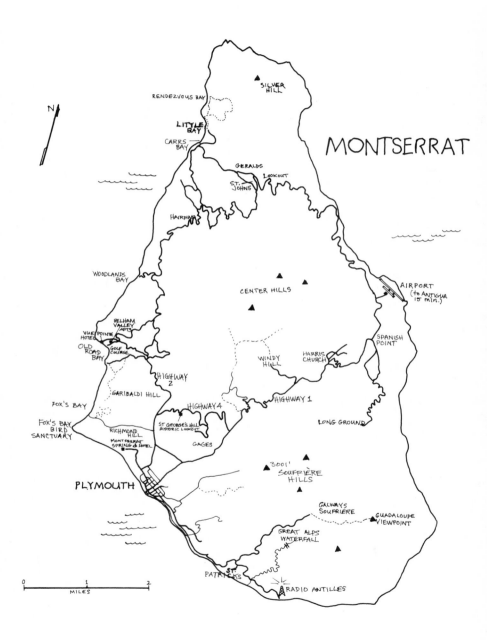

N

RENDEZVOUS BAY

SILVER HILL

LITTLE BAY

CARRS BAY

GERALDS

LOOKOUT

ST. JOHNS

HAIRPINS

MONTSERRAT

WOODLANDS BAY

CENTER HILLS

AIRPORT
(to ANTIGUA
15 min.)

BELHAM VALLEY APTS

VUE POINTE HOTEL

OLD ROAD BAY

GOLF COURSE

HIGHWAY 2

GARIBALDI HILL

WINDY HILL

HARRIS CHURCH

SPANISH POINT

FOX'S BAY

HIGHWAY 4

HIGHWAY 1

FOX'S BAY BIRD SANCTUARY

ST GEORGE'S HILL HISTORIC LOOKOUT

RICHMOND HILL

LONG GROUND

MONTSERRAT SPRINGS HOTEL

GAGES

3001'
SOUFRIÈRE HILLS

PLYMOUTH

GALWAYS SOUFRIÈRE

GUADALOUPE VIEWPOINT

GREAT ALPS WATERFALL

ST PATRICKS

RADIO ANTILLES

0   1   2
    MILES

it really doesn't attract any crowds. Who you do find are some honeymoon couples, young families, and a lot of well-to-do retirees who live in big villas scattered about the hillsides like itinerant cows. The nationalities tend to be American, British, Irish, and German. Music celebs once adorned the island when the famous recording studio, Air Studios, was in operation. Owned by former Beatles impresario George Martin, it used to bring in big names like little Stevie Wonder, the Stones, Elton John, and so on. However, Hurricane Hugo demolished it (along with most of the island) and currently there are no plans to rebuild it. Still, Mick Jagger was recently sighted here despite his fab villa on the fab Mustique (Montserrat thankfully lacks the fabness).

THE BRIEFEST HISTORY

Montserrat was "discovered" by Christopher Columbus on November 11, 1493, during his second voyage to the New World (although Carib Indians already had lived on the island for centuries). It is named after a Spanish abbey where Loyola received his inspiration for future fame. A few centuries after Columbus's find, the British settled it as a unique Irish-Catholic colony in the Caribbean (there are many Irish surnames here and St. Patty's Day is a big deal). The French wrestled with the Brits over ownership in the ensuing centuries until it was clearly established as a British colony in 1783 by the Treaty of Versailles. Today it is still a British colony and will probably remain so for a long time (Who in the Third World really wants to go it alone in these days of fiscal austerity?).

As with most of the islands, sugar has been replaced by tourism as the major economic turbine. The last sugar mill shut down in the sixties. However, everything on the tourism end was booming until 1989. Then Hurricane Hugo, which hit with incredible fury here before it pummeled South Carolina, devastated the island, leaving 95 percent of the man-made structures damaged or destroyed. Four years later, though, the first-time visitor would have a hard time identifying remnants of Hugo. The island has almost totally recovered, with a rebuilt cruise-ship dock/harbor completed in 1993 finishing off most of the rebuilding effort. The roads are in excellent shape, the foliage is lush again, and the sand on most of the beaches is back to normal. In the tropics, nature rejuvenates itself rather quickly.

MONTSERRAT: KEY FACTS

LOCATION	16°N by 60°W
	27 miles southwest of Antigua
	1,800 miles southeast of New York
SIZE	40 square miles
	11 miles long by 7 miles wide
HIGHEST POINT	Chance Mt. (3,002 ft.)
POPULATION	12,000
LANGUAGE	English
TIME	Atlantic Standard Time (1 hour ahead of EST, same as EDT).
AREA CODE	809
ELECTRICITY	220 volts AC, 60 cycles
CURRENCY	The Eastern Caribbean dollar, EC$ (EC$2.70 = $1 U.S.)
DRIVING	On the *left*; a temporary driving permit is necessary; you'll need to present a valid U.S. or Canadian license and pay EC$30 or $12 U.S.
DOCUMENTS	For U.S., Canadian and British citizens proof of nationality with a photo ID is acceptable; all others need a passport; everyone must have an ongoing or return ticket
DEPARTURE TAX	EC$15 or $6 U.S.
BEER TO DRINK	Red Stripe
RUM TO DRINK	Mt. Gay
MUSIC TO HEAR	Dancehall

FOCUS ON MONTSERRAT: BIKING, DIVING, AND READING

Montserrat is ideally suited for these three activities. You wouldn't go to Montserrat if you are a beach enthusiast, as the beaches are volcanic—meaning black, blackish, or dark-brown sand. There is one fine white-sand beach in Rendezvous Bay, but it takes a boat or a long hike to reach it. Only the black-sand variety will be a few steps away from your hotel.

BIKING

With 115 miles of well-paved roads, the hybrid mountain biker will find physical challenge in the major hills and inclines, yet greatly enjoy the warm temps and incredible scenery. Montserrat is small, only 11 miles by 7, but there are plenty of destinations and certainly plenty of hairpins, scenic stretches, steep ascents and descents to keep you entertained for a week and your legs begging for mercy perhaps longer. Assuming that you are staying at the Vue Pointe Hotel or in the vicinity of Old Road Bay, there are a number of day excursions to explore. My suggestions:

CARR'S BAY—This is a healthy ride over good roads, hairpins, with lots of scenery. You can really make it special by biking a bit farther on down a rough road to Little Bay, locking your bike, and hiking to the only white-sand beach, Rendezvous Bay (about a 45-minute easy walk each way along an inland path). If you take the coastal path at the north end of Little Bay, the hike is hot and tough.

PLYMOUTH—A short but interesting ride into the hub of Montserrat, where the name of the game is sampling the shopping and, more importantly, the rum punch (now, no drunk bikers, please!).

BLACKBURNE AIRPORT—Now an airport doesn't sound like a glamorous destination, but the ride to the airport is glorious—tough, yes (you climb the Central Highlands which are over 1,000 feet high, with many turns, curves, and hairpins), but beautiful. At St. George's Hill there is a historic lookout, and this is a good spot to down a Gatorade. From there you'll ride up and down a little bit until you begin a descent into Harris Church, another good place to stop. You'll continue downhill to the airport. If you still have energy, continue north for about two miles, as the road is spectacular and runs along the coastal cliffs and on to the Northern Highlands.

'ROUND THE ISLAND—If you're a Greg Lemond type, this is a strenuous bike trip not so much due to the distance as to the hills. Proceed to the airport as described above and continue north. You may encounter some construction and rough road for a stretch, but this is soon over and the road improves. You'll be stopping a lot due to the incredible views (and maybe to catch your breath, as there are many hairpins as you climb up the Northern Highlands). A good place to pause for refreshment is the scenic lookout. Soon after, you'll come to a fork in the road. If you go left toward St. John's, you'll encounter a narrow road with lots of hills and turns. If you go straight, you'll end up at Carr's Bay, where the road turns south to Plymouth.

GALWAYS SOUFRIÈRE—If you head south from Plymouth, the road will take you along the coast until you get to St. Patrick's. Turn northeast (follow the signs) for Galways Soufrière, a steady climb up a very scenic road. Just say no to the throngs saying you need a guide—you won't unless you want to do some serious hiking. Be sure to get a good trail map from the Tourist Office in Plymouth before heading up if you do want to go hiking. On the way you may want to stop at the Galways Plantation, a 1,300-acre former sugar plantation located at about 1,100 feet above sea level, where restoration and artifacts make it interesting. At the end of the road, there is a lookout and a trail leading down to the bubbling, boiling hot springs and vents, etc., if you are so inclined.

The above are just some suggestions. With a bike you can go just about anywhere. Now, what about a bike? Schlepping your own down to the islands will be a royal pain in the ass as well as costly. My recommendation is to rent one from Island Bikes, Harney Street (P.O. Box 266), Plymouth, Montserrat, W.I. ([809] 491-4696, fax [809] 491-5552). Reserve well in advance of your trip, so you'll be certain to get the bike you want.

DIVING

Diving as a business on Montserrat is rather new and undeveloped. There are some good dive sites around the island, although if you are a diving enthusiast there are other islands with better dives and operations such as Saba or Bonaire.

There are two dive operations on the island: Seawolf Diving School, George Street (P.O. Box 400), Plymouth, Montserrat, W.I. ([809] 491-6859) and Dive Montserrat, Vue Pointe Hotel (P.O. Box 223), Plymouth, Montserrat, W.I. ([809] 491-8812). Seawolf is run by a very friendly and accommodating German, whose name, of course, is Wolf. He doesn't have his own boat yet (at least at press time he didn't), so you may be going out with a local fisherman in his skiff, which promises to be a wet and wild experience in itself—especially getting back into the boat. Wolf is a seasoned Montserrat diver, and has a good knowledge of the underwater terrain. The other outfit is operated by Chris Mason, who was the first to pioneer the dive business on Montserrat.

The most talked about dive sights are: Pinnacle—a 65-plus-foot dive with lots of fish, big basket sponges, and brain corals; O'Garros—a multi-depth dive off the southern tip of the island—is a shelf which drops off quickly to the Guadeloupe trench (here you get lots of barracuda and sharks, good corals and occasional sightings of turtles and rays); Colby's—a good beginner dive site with elkhorn and pillar corals and a maximum depth of 45 feet, so bottom time is not a problem. There are dozens of other sites that your guide will know and many more as yet to be discovered. One site that wasn't very interesting was Antennas (the towers of Radio Antilles are in front on the shore), so avoid that one.

READING

A comfortable chair, a nice view, a gentle breeze, several good books (bring your own!); it's so easy.

GETTING THERE

Montserrat's Blackburne Airport can land only prop planes. Most flights connect via Antigua, which is 27 miles away, about 15 minutes' flying time. LIAT ([809] 491-2200) has four flights a day from Antigua, one from St. Kitts, and one from St. Maarten. MONTSERRAT AIRWAYS flies charters from Antigua and neighboring islands ([809] 491-5342, fax [809] 491-6205). Antigua is a major jet gateway served by AMERICAN, BRITISH AIRWAYS, BWIA, AIR CANADA, and LUFTHANSA.

GETTING AROUND

There are several rental companies on the island. The average daily rental costs about $40 U.S. per day, with discounts for a weekly rental. Before you can rent a car you will have to get a temporary Montserrat driver's license (EC$30 or $12 U.S.), which is only available at the airport and at the Treasury Building in downtown Plymouth—present your valid U.S. or Canadian license and pay the fee. Companies to rent from include BUDGET ([800] 527-0700/[809] 491-6065, fax [809] 491-6066) and AVIS ([800] 331-1084).

Cabs are available at the airport and it will cost about EC$45 to take you to the Vue Pointe, which is directly across the island. Your hotel can arrange for a taxi to pick you up and also provide an island tour, so check with them first.

WHERE TO STAY

In keeping with the "small is beautiful" theme of this low-key island, there aren't that many accommodation choices. There are no five-star hotels on Montserrat, but who cares? They wouldn't fit here anyway. The choices that remain, however, are just fine. Undoubtedly the best hotel to stay at is the Vue Pointe (Mick Jagger stays here). There are also many villa rental options for those who "vant to be alone" and self-contained, or for those with kids. Here are the options:

THE VUE POINTE HOTEL (809) 491-5210, (809) 491-4813
Stateside: (800) 235-0709
Old Towne (P.O. Box 65, Plymouth), Montserrat, B.W.I.

Located on the sunny western end of the island at Old Road Bay, this wonderful little "resort" sits on a sloping bluff overlooking the Caribbean to the south and west and the Soufrière Hills (they're really mountains) to the east. The breeze tumbles down from these mountains, completing the perfect Caribbean setting—fabulous sun, fabulous view and fabulous breeze—to sit on the lanai of your cottage with a rum punch and your favorite book. There are 28 rondavels/cottages comfortably spread out on the hill and 12 double rooms (twin beds) in three buildings by the bluff. The hexagonal cottages have a pleasant and tastefully furnished (tropical-style) seating area, twin or king-sized beds, a good-sized bath with tiled shower, lots of windows for ventilation (no air conditioning, but it's not necessary because of the natural breezes), and a phone, cable TV, and refrigerator. Room service is also available. There is a small swimming pool and bar which adjoins the spacious dining room. The staff is very friendly and the food is quite good. Owned by a lovely couple, Carol and Cedric Osborne (she's American from Massachusetts, he's Montserratian), the Vue Pointe has a homey feel to it without being too cutesy. Hurricane Hugo basically demo'd the place (they have pictures) and the Osbornes have worked very hard to bring it back; they have been successful. The clientele tends to be a little older here, so it is very quiet. However, there is a fun beach bar called the Nest, where they play reggae music, serve light fare and burgers, and attract an eclectic mix of people (including Rebecca). Next to the Nest are two lighted tennis courts and the beach. Golf is available nearby at the Montserrat Golf Club (11 holes—two sets of nine with different tees for each set). Conference facilities are available.

Rates are VERY PRICEY for singles and doubles for the cottages and PRICEY for the rooms (EP). Children under 12 stay free with two adults in a cottage. Add $35 U.S. per person for MAP.

MONTSERRAT SPRINGS HOTEL (809) 491-2481, fax (809) 491-4070
Stateside: (800) 223-9815 in New York, (800) 253-2134 elsewhere
P.O. Box 259, Plymouth, Montserrat, B.W.I.

Situated overlooking the Emerald Isle Beach and the capital, Plymouth, this is the largest hotel on Montserrat, with 46 "garden rooms" in 2-story buildings and 6 one- and two-bedroom efficiency suites (two double beds in each room, sitting area, kitchenette with fridge, washing machine, and balcony). All rooms have air conditioning, phones, cable TV, hair dryers, and lanais. They are attractively furnished in the tropical motif and have tiled floors. There is a 70-foot swimming pool by the hotel and two Jacuzzis by the beach, one with hot mineral water from the hot springs underground and the other with fresh water. At the bottom of the hill, there are two lighted tennis courts, a beach, the Jacuzzis, and the beach bar.

Rates are PRICEY for singles and PRICEY to VERY PRICEY for doubles in the garden rooms (EP). Suites are VERY PRICEY to WICKED PRICEY. Add $35 U.S. per person for MAP.

BELHAM VALLEY APARTMENTS (809) 491-5553
P.O. Box 409, Plymouth, Montserrat, B.W.I.

Located next to the best restaurant on the island, the Belham Valley Restaurant, and just down the road from the Vue Pointe there are three possibilities here: a studio apartment (the Jasmine), a studio cottage (the Frangipani), and a two-bedroom apartment (the Mignonette). All are air-conditioned and have kitchen facilities, cable TV, stereo, phone, laundry service, and access to tennis and golf. The beach is a five-minute walk away.

Rates are weekly at $375 U.S. for the Jasmine to $550 U.S. for the Mignonette. A good deal if you ask me ($53 U.S. to $79 U.S. per day—in the NOT SO CHEAP range).

FLORA FOUNTAIN HOTEL (809) 491-6092, fax (809) 491-2568
Lower Dagenham Road (P.O. Box 373), Plymouth, Montserrat,
B.W.I.

With a central location in town, this is a popular business traveler's
hotel and is clean and basic. There is no pool and not much of a
view, but the 18 rooms are air-conditioned and have balconies.
Rates are NOT SO CHEAP for singles and doubles (EP).

MARIE'S GUEST HOUSE (809) 491-2745, fax (809) 491-3599
P.O. Box 28, Plymouth, Montserrat, B.W.I.

Located about a half-mile from downtown Plymouth, this cute,
tidy, and quiet house has three rooms with private bath for rent and
the cheapest rates on the island. There is a lounge with cable TV and
a fully furnished kitchen and dining room.
Rates are DIRT CHEAP for singles and CHEAP for doubles.

VILLAS OF MONTSERRAT (809) 491-5513, fax (809) 491-7850
Isle Bay (P.O. Box 421, Plymouth), Montserrat, B.W.I.

If you really want to go the deluxe route, Villas of Montserrat has
for rent three houses that overlook Isle Bay, the Montserrat Golf
Course, and the Caribbean. Each house has three bedrooms, three
baths (one with a Jacuzzi), a living room with stereo and cable TV,
dining room, a fully equipped kitchen, a swimming pool, and is
furnished in island "décor." Included in the deal are a cold lobster
and champagne dinner on arrival, daily maid service, and island
tour, and private charter from Antigua (but oddly not for the return
trip except in the off-season).
Rates are weekly at $2,000 for a maximum of six adults and two
kids per villa.

There are several real estate companies that also rent villas. Among
them are:

NEVILLE BRADSHAW AGENCIES (809) 491-5270, fax (809)
491-5069
P.O. Box 270, Plymouth, Montserrat, B.W.I.

They represent 42 properties that rent from $500 to $2,500 U.S. per
week.

MONTSERRAT ENTERPRISES (809) 491-2506, fax (809) 491-4660

P.O. Box 58, Plymouth, Montserrat, B.W.I.

This company represents 21 properties, each with a private pool, with prices ranging from $600 to $2,000 U.S. per week.

WHERE TO EAT

As with accommodations, there aren't many choices for dining out, but the following ones are good:

BELHAM VALLEY RESTAURANT, Old Towne, 491-5553

This is the premier restaurant on the island. It occupies a former private home on a hillside in a lovely tropical setting. The cuisine is Caribbean/continental, with specialties including mountain chicken (frog), stuffed red snapper, lobster, pumpkin soup, and conch fritters. Reservations required, especially for dinner $$$$

VUE POINTE HOTEL, Old Towne, 491-5210

With wonderful views overlooking the Caribbean and Garibaldi Valley, the food and service are excellent. A must is the Wednesday-night barbecue—an island event with steel-band entertainment and all you can eat for about $25 US. Reservations are recommended if you're not a hotel guest. $$$$

THE IGUANA, Wapping, 491-2328

Located in Wapping just north of Plymouth and set in remnants of an old mill, the cuisine is primarily Créole with all kinds of international influences thrown in. $$$ No credit cards.

NIGHTLIFE

There's not much, but don't miss a HI-FI, which is a street party wherever someone sets up a thundering PA system playing reggae-dub. This is a very local event, so I highly recommend it. Check with your hotel staff to find out if one is happening (usually on weekends) and where.

Also, have a drink at the Green Flash, and try dancing at Club Africa and La Cave (Evergreen Drive), all in Plymouth.

MUSTIQUE

TOURISTO SCALE 🔲🔲🔲 3

You can't miss it. It sits like the House of Zeus atop Mount Olympus. It's the first thing you see approaching Mustique, the absurdly miscast Italianate mansion of Harding Lawrence—the founder of now-defunct Braniff—and advertising queen Mary Wells. Yours to love for a cool ten million. Down the road is HRH Margaret's "Les Jolies Eaux"—and David Bowie's villa, and Mick Jagger's, and on and on. Welcome to Mustique, vacationland of the rich, famous, and even more rich.

Owned by the Mustique Company, this is the Caribbean's Trump Tower or Costa Smerelda. Before being bought by the Company in 1970, it was owned by Lord Glenconner and home to a few fishermen. Now it is opulent. Many of the villas resemble separate miniresorts in the Victorian-gingerbread mold, elevated to the appropriate grandness. Besides the Cotton House, there are only about 75 houses on the island. A glance at the property titles would reveal a global representation of the fabulous and fortunate.

Don't know somebody with a villa? Well, you can easily rent one from the Mustique Company. There are over 45 available, at prices from $2,500 to $15,000 per week. Or, you can stay at the Cotton House on the northwest corner of the island. It's discreetly tasteful, the 24 rooms tucked into 2 plantation houses and 3 whitewashed, almost Swedish-looking cottages. All details are looked after, as is to be expected. The pool is small, but who swims anyway? The main activity here is to have a drink or maybe a bite to eat, sit by the pool, and see who shows up. Visually, the pool ensemble is stunning. Designer Oliver Messel framed it with the remnants of an old sugar-mill warehouse, its jagged edge outlined against the sky. The

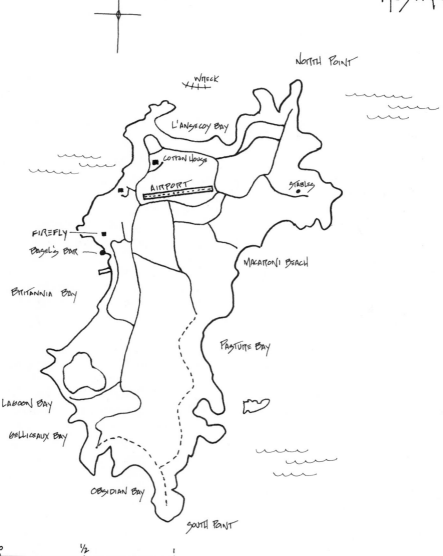

MUSTIQUE

NORTH POINT

WRECK

L'ANSECOY BAY

COTTON HOUSE

AIRPORT

STABLES

FIREFLY

BAGEL'S BAR

MACARONI BEACH

BRITANNIA BAY

PASTURE BAY

LAGOON BAY

GELLICEAUX BAY

OBSIDIAN BAY

SOUTH POINT

0   ½   1

MILES

pool itself conjures up memories of the Clampetts' pool in the TV show "The Beverly Hillbillies." Looking from the pool to the north, you can see the tennis courts and rooftops of a famous rock legend's compound giving him shelter. The beach in that direction, L'Ansecoy Bay, is very pretty and looks out on the wreck of the *Antilles*, a French cruise ship that ran a reef in 1971.

If Cotton House doesn't fit your style or budget, there is an alternative: the Firefly Guest House. Their motto is "You don't have to be rich and famous to enjoy Mustique." Now that's refreshing! You can actually stay on this island for under $100 a night. Mrs. Billy Mitchell runs this cute and simple villa overlooking Brittania Bay.

The hub of activity on this tiny island is most certainly Basil's Beach Bar. Located on Brittania Bay along with Basil's Market, Boutique, and Water Sports Center, it's a favorite with both the yachting set and occasional celebutantes. Basil himself is reputed to be Mustique's version of Mandingo. His thatched-roof-beach-bar-on-stilts also serves lunch or dinner (not surprisingly the prices aren't posted—don't be afraid to ask). On Wednesday nights there is usually a jump-up with pan bands from Bequia or St. Vincent. It's very possible you'll recognize someone—the tip-off is their body-guard(s). Basil's T-shirts are great collector's items and can be bought at Basil's Boutique.

MUSTIQUE: KEY FACTS

LOCATION	13°N by 61°W
	17 miles south of St. Vincent
	110 miles west of Barbados
	2,060 miles southeast of New York
SIZE	2 square miles
HIGHEST POINT	Fort Shandy (495 ft.)
POPULATION	732
LANGUAGE	English
TIME	Atlantic Standard Time (1 hour ahead of EST, same as EDT)
AREA CODE	809
ELECTRICITY	220 volts AC, 50 cycles
CURRENCY	The Eastern Caribbean dollar, EC$ (EC$2.70 = $1 U.S.)

DRIVING	On the *left*; U.S. and Canadian citizens need to present their valid driver's license and pay EC$20 ($7.40 U.S.) to obtain a temporary local driver's permit
DOCUMENTS	Canadian and U.S. citizens should have proof of citizenship with photo ID plus an ongoing or return ticket
DEPARTURE TAX	EC$20 ($7.40 U.S.)
BEER TO DRINK	Hairoun
RUM TO DRINK	Any Vincentian brand
MUSIC TO HEAR	Reggae/Dancehall

GETTING THERE

Somehow Mustique's developers squeezed a runway on the island that can only receive small planes—and only until dusk, since there are no landing lights. The easiest way to get here is to fly to Barbados (serviced by AMERICAN, AIR CANADA, and BWIA) and connect via charter service with MUSTIQUE AIRWAYS. There are also several scheduled flights a day from St. Vincent, St. Lucia, Grenada, and Martinique on LIAT or AIR MARTINIQUE. If you are on Bequia or another Grenadine, you can hire a boat to take you over for a day-trip. From Bequia, it will cost between $100 and $150 U.S.—depending on your negotiating skills—for the round-trip hire of boat and crew. It makes sense to fill the boat with a group (usually up to ten), since the cost is the same for one or ten. This is a great way to see the island if you are staying on Bequia.

FOCUS ON MUSTIQUE: EXPLORING THE ISLAND

The island is small, comprising only 1350 acres. It can be seen fairly easily by walking or hiring a scooter for $35 U.S. a day (inquire at Basil's Beach Bar). You can also hire a taxi at $35 U.S. for an hour—which should be enough time for a cursory tour of the island. Or you can walk. Starting from Basil's, go left up the hill and down until you can go no farther. Take a left and you'll pass a church/community center on your right, then the runway, and in the distance Cotton House. Proceed left up a dirt road and follow the road to the Cotton House, pick up a map at the office, and have a drink by the pool (notice the groovy ashtrays). After a few cocktails, ignore the boutique in the windmill (cute, but no Cotton House T-shirts) and walk down by the tennis courts, bearing right. This will take you past a bird sanctuary and to the horse stables. If you don't want to ride, take a left and a quick right at the eastern end of the runway. Turn left on the first road you come to, which will lead you to Macaroni Beach—the island's best—a curved beach of off-white sand, palm trees, and a few thatched huts to give you shelter. Time-out for a swim. When you're ready, head back the way you came: turn left at the end of the road and left again at the end of the next. This road will take you past Pasture Bay (too rough for swimming) and onto a dirt road that leads to South Point. This is where you'll find Les Jolies Eaux, winter retreat of HRH Princess Margaret. Heading north, you'll pass Obsidian Bay and Gelliceaux Bay. At Gelliceaux you'll find the island's best snorkeling at the bay's northern end. This is also a great spot for a swim, as by now you'll probably be quite hot. The road continues to Lagoon Bay with more good snorkeling reefs and finally back to Brittania Bay and Basil's.

WHERE TO STAY

If you really want to do Mustique with panache—and the best way to stay if you are a group or family—you can rent one of about 45 villas of various sizes, degrees of luxury and location. Prices range from about $2,500 to $15,000 U.S. per week. Princess Margaret's "Les Jolies Eaux" goes for about ten grand (references required, of course). Contact: The Mustique Company, P.O. Box 349, Mustique, St. Vincent, W.I. (809) 458-4621, fax (809) 456-4565.

Or you can stay at:

THE COTTON HOUSE (809) 456-4777, same for fax
Stateside: (800) 223-1108/(914) 763-5526
P.O. Box 349, Mustique, The Grenadines, St. Vincent, W.I.

The island's only true resort, the accommodations and pool are lovely as is L'Ansecoy Beach. The hotel offers minibus service (with box lunches) to Macaroni and other island beaches. There are also water sports (windsurfing, scuba, and snorkeling) as well as horse-back riding and tennis.

Rates are OUTRAGEOUS for singles and BEYOND BELIEF for doubles, FAP (fabulously affluent plan—accommodations, three meals a day, afternoon tea, room service, and all the hotel's facilities).

FIREFLY GUEST HOUSE (809) 456-3414
P.O. Box 349, Mustique, The Grenadines, St. Vincent, W.I.

The other down-to-earth option on Mustique, the Firefly has five simple but clean rooms here, all with private bath and balcony, refrigerator, and picnic equipment. Views from Mrs. Mitchell's villa are of Britannia Bay and the distant Grenadines. Breakfast is included. If you want air conditioning, it's an extra $5 per day. Long-term guests get discounts.

Rates are NOT SO CHEAP for singles and doubles (CP).

WHERE TO DINE

There are three choices. Your rented villa (have the cook whip up something light for you tonight), COTTON HOUSE (456-4777), or BASIL'S BAR AND RAFT (456-3350). P.S., Basil's is where it's happening, especially at the bar. Be sure to make reservations.

PUERTO RICO

There is a song from the musical *West Side Story* where the first lines
(sung in a languid voice) go:

> *Puerto Rico*
> *My heart's devotion*
> *Let it slip into the ocean.*
> *Always the hurricanes blowing*
> *And the population growing*
> *And the money owing.*

Well, Puerto Rico *is* my heart's devotion. I hope it doesn't slip into
the ocean. Despite the hurricanes blowing, and the population
growing (and we're all in the money owing), it's still a great place to
visit. Those famous lyrics (from the song "America") just don't
play by me.

Unfortunately, that musical was the beginning of a wave of bad
public relations for the island—mainly due to the mainland inner-
city barrios of poor and uneducated Puerto Ricans who built upon
the West Side Story gang image. Anyone who's lived in New York
City knows this. But the immigrants who came to these cities were,
for the most part, the bottom of society looking for a better life.
The Puerto Ricans who stayed in Puerto Rico, however, are a very
different lot. Gone is the hard edge of living in tough cities. In its
place is a very happy, warm people who seem to always be up and
wanting to have a good time. You'll notice this as soon as your
plane lands at Luis Muñoz Marín International Airport, when the

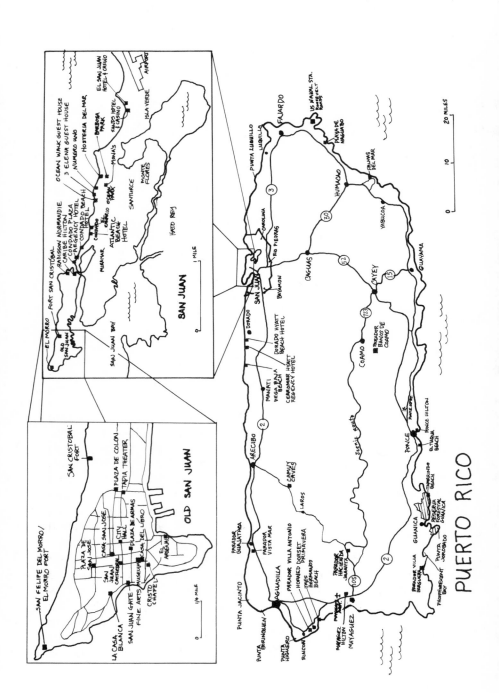

PUERTO RICO

OLD SAN JUAN

SAN CRISTOBAL FORT
PLAZA DE COLON
TAPIA THEATER
SAN FELIPE DEL MORRO / EL MORRO FORT
PLAZA DE SAN JOSE
SAN JOSE
CASA SAN JOSE
CITY HALL
PLAZA DE ARMAS
SAN JUAN CATHEDRAL
CASA DEL LIBRO
FINE ARTS MUSEUM
LA CASA BLANCA
SAN JUAN GATE
EL ARSENAL
CRISTO CHAPEL

0   1/4 MILE

SAN JUAN

EL MORRO
FORT SAN CRISTOBAL
RADISSON NORMANDIE
CARIBE HILTON
CONDADO PLAZA
REGENCY HOTEL
CONDADO BEACH HOTEL
MUÑARE
EL CANARIO
ATLANTIC BEACH HOTEL
MIÑA'S
NUMERO UNO
3 ELENA GUEST HOUSE
OCEAN WALK GUEST HOUSE
HOSTERIA DEL MAR
ENSENADA PARK
SANDS HOTEL & CASINO
EL SAN JUAN HOTEL & CASINO
ISLA VERDE
AIRPORT
MONTE FLORES
SANTURCE
HATO REY
OLD SAN JUAN
SAN JUAN BAY

0   1 MILE

AGUADILLA
PUNTA JACINTO
PUNTA BORINQUEN
PUNTA HIGUERO
RINCON
PARADOR VISTA MAR
PARADOR GUAJATACA
PARADOR VILLA ANTONIO
HORNED DORSET
TRES HERMANOS BEACH
PARADOR HACIENDA JUANITA
MARICAO
MAYAGUEZ HILTON
MAYAGUEZ
PARADOR VILLA PARGUERA
PARADOR OASIS
PHOSPHORESCENT BAY
PUNTA JOROBADO
GUANICA
RESERVA FORESTAL GUANICA
TAMARINDO BEACH
EL TUQUE BEACH
PONCE HILTON
PONCE
SCENIC ROUTE
COAMO
PARADOR BAÑOS DE COAMO
CAGUAS
BAYAMON
SAN JUAN
DORADO
DORADO HYATT BEACH HOTEL
CERROMAR HYATT REGENCY HOTEL
VEGA BAJA BEACH
MANATI
ARECIBO
CAMUY CAVES
LARES
PUNTA LUQUILLO
LUQUILLO
FAJARDO
US NAVAL STA. ROOSEVELT ROADS
PLAYA DE NAGUABO
PALMAS DEL MAR
HUMACAO
YABUCOA
GUAYAMA
CAYEY
RIO PIEDRAS
CAROLINA
3
22
52
15
723
105
2

0   10   20 MILES

Puerto Ricans on the plane burst into applause. And then there is also a very sophisticated and cultured element here as well as a thriving middle class.

Puerto Rico is a big island, roughly the size of Connecticut. There are 3.3 million people, a major metropolis, a diverse economy, mountains, rain forest, miles of beautiful beaches, and the hip-swaying beat of salsa and merengue. Being a Commonwealth of the United States, the American influence is very pervasive—from every conceivable fast-food and convenience chain (there are 50 Burger Kings on the island) to the huge pharmaceutical and high-tech companies. This is unfortunate but inevitable. Yet the culture is still Latino and the language is still Spanish, though most Puerto Ricans speak English or at least understand it to a degree. The new governor, Governor Rosello, has reinstated the policy that Puerto Rico officially has two languages—Spanish and English—to encourage bilingualism among the populace and inch the island toward statehood. More often than not, however, you'll hear and marvel at the hybrid, commonly known as "Spanglish."

Most visitors who come to Puerto Rico see only San Juan, a city of over one million people. This is where most of the big hotels and casinos are located. San Juan is also the second-largest cruise-ship port after Miami. The combination ensures lots of tourists, especially in places like Old San Juan and the Condado area. But San Juan is a big city, and with it comes the best nightlife (both straight and gay) in the Caribbean. If you want great restaurants, big and lively casinos without the Las Vegas tackiness, pulsating nightclubs, and want to mix with some of the hottest men and women you'll ever meet, look no farther for your next vacation spot. If you're single, you're crazy not to go here. But you must like Latinos and Latinas (you're even crazier if you don't). And Puerto Ricans are VERY Latin when it comes to romance. If you haven't had a Latin lover, I'll be the first to tell you—they invented the words heat and passion.

But there is much more to Puerto Rico than the throbbing beat of San Juan. There are beautiful mountains and lush valleys and small Puerto Rican seaside towns with lots of character like Boquerón and Guánica. There is Puerto Rico's second city, Ponce, which has undergone a restoration similar to Old San Juan. There are the twin resorts of Dorado Beach and Cerromar Beach with some of the best golf and tennis in the Caribbean. There are the extraordinary Camuy Caves—huge natural caverns several hundred feet in the earth. There is great windsurfing off Rincón on the west coast. There are the unspoiled out islands of Culebra and Vieques. There is the Caribbean National Forest, "El Yunque," which is an easily accessed rain forest. There are deserted beaches on all sides of the island. But you're never more than a two-hour drive from San Juan or far from a cash machine and a Big Gulp from 7-Eleven.

Puerto Rico gets all kinds of tourists and travelers. There are the convention and tour groups who come for a purpose as well as to play in the big casinos and on the beach. The cruise ships attract that unattractive element of middle America that always seems overweight and devoid of fashion sense. (Don't these people read the food labels for fat content or *Women's Wear Daily*?). There are lots of Europeans tourists, especially Germans, and South Americans up on shopping sprees. Of course, most of the visitors here are American. Then there are the independent travelers who dive into the culture and countryside in search of the real Puerto Rico and the long weekenders—down for a dose of sun and fun since San Juan is so easy (and cheap) to reach.

THE BRIEFEST HISTORY

Puerto Rico was first settled by Amerindians who ventured up the chain of West Indies from the Amazon and South America and had been on the island for thousands of years when Columbus landed here on his second voyage in 1493. He discovered about 60,000 Taíno Amerindians living off the land and sea who had named the island Boriquén. Spain claimed the island and Columbus called it San Juan, later renamed Puerto Rico. With Columbus was Juan Ponce de Léon, Mr. Fountain of Youth himself, who sensed gold in them-thar-hills and received permission to colonize the island. The first Spanish settlement began in 1508 at Caparra and Ponce de Léon became its governor. But that site proved disease-ridden, so in 1521, the settlement was moved to what is now Old San Juan. From the fortress it became, with El Morro fort at its entrance, Spain never lost control of Puerto Rico for more than 400 years, despite repeated attempts by the British, French, and Dutch to dislodge them. It wasn't until the Spanish-American War, in 1898, when Teddy Roosevelt led the charge up that hill in Havana, Cuba, shouting "Remember the *Maine*" and defeated the Spanish that control ceded to another power. That power was the United States. In 1917, Puerto Ricans became full-fledged U.S. citizens, and in 1952 Puerto Rico became a Commonwealth of the United States. It remains so today. There is a drive for statehood which is being spearheaded by the current governor. Under Commonwealth status, Puerto Ricans have a U.S. passport and can live anywhere in the U.S. They have local representation in a Commonwealth government and pay no federal income tax while residents of Puerto Rico. The drawback is that they have no voting representation in Congress (they can't vote for President either). However, there is a non-voting Interests Section in Congress. But no federal taxes—there's no sales tax either—what a deal, I'm moving to Puerto Rico!

Currently, the hot issue in Puerto Rico is the repeal of Federal Tax Code 936, which gives mainland companies huge tax breaks if they invest and establish companies on Puerto Rico (their profits are not taxed when repatriated). Taking advantage of Puerto Rico's cheap labor, all kinds of manufacturers, in particular the pharmaceutical companies, have set up shop and made a bundle. Now the Clinton Administration wants some of that money in its program to reduce the deficit. But the Puerto Ricans are very worried about the threats of companies to leave, if the code is repealed, and are raising a big brouhaha as of press time. As unemployment is hovering around 18 percent, I think they are justified. Stay tuned.

PUERTO RICO: KEY FACTS

LOCATION | 18°N by 65°W
70 miles east of Hispaniola (Dominican Republic)
1,040 miles southeast of Miami
1,662 miles southeast of New York
SIZE | 3,423 square miles
110 miles long by 35 miles wide
HIGHEST POINT | Cerro de Punta (4,398 ft.)
POPULATION | 3.6 million
LANGUAGE | *Spanish*, English
TIME | Atlantic Standard Time (1 hour ahead of EST, same as EDT)
AREA CODE | 809
ELECTRICITY | 110 volts AC, same as U.S. and Canada

CURRENCY	The U.S. dollar
DRIVING	On the *right*
DOCUMENTS	None for Americans and no Customs hassles either; Canadians need proof of nationality or a passport; Brits need a passport and visa
DEPARTURE TAX	None
BEER TO DRINK	Medalla
RUM TO DRINK	Don-Q or Bacardi
MUSIC TO HEAR	Salsa or merengue

GETTING THERE

Of all the Caribbean islands, Puerto Rico is the easiest to reach. San Juan has a huge international airport (Luis Muñoz Marín), is the hub of AMERICAN's Caribbean operation, and has over 30 airlines serving it. Most major East Coast cities have nonstop service to San Juan on AMERICAN, DELTA, TWA, UNITED, USAIR and CARNIVAL. From Canada, AMERICAN has connections via Chicago from Toronto and Montréal and CANADIAN INTERNATIONAL has nonstop service. From Europe, BRITISH AIRWAYS, LUFTHANSA, IBERIA, and AIR FRANCE all have nonstop service. From other Caribbean islands, AMERICAN EAGLE, LIAT, BWIA, DOMINICANA, AIR BVI, AERO VIRGIN ISLANDS, AIR CARIBE, AIR JAMAICA, and SUNAIRE EXPRESS all service San Juan. From Latin America, AEROPOSTAL VENEZOLANA, AVIANCA, VIASA, LACSA, and MEXICANA have service.

GETTING AROUND

With just about every major rental-car player here offering great weekly (and daily) rates, and with so much to see, it makes perfect sense to rent a car. AVIS ([800] 331-1084/[809] 791-2500), BUDGET ([800] 527-0700/[809] 791-3685), HERTZ ([800] 654-3001/[809] 791-0840), NATIONAL ([800] 227-3876), and THRIFTY ([800] 367-2277). Call your favorite for reservations. Check with your credit-card company to see what you are covered for by their policy before you rent.

There are plenty of cabs, some with meters (they may or may not turn them on). The best thing to do when taking a cab is to negotiate the price beforehand. A cab ride from the airport to the Condado area should cost about $10 to $12.

Within San Juan, there is a good bus system run by the Metropolitan Bus Authority (767-7979). The buses (called *guaguas*) pick up passengers at upright yellow post stops (called *paradas*) and the fare is 25¢.

Públicos (public cars) are cars or minivans that provide low-cost transportation to the main towns of Puerto Rico; their rates are set by the Public Service Commission.

Some words about driving in Puerto Rico. When driving on the freeways, particularly Route 52 from San Juan to Ponce, the left lane is much smoother, as trucks don't drive on it. Actually, the left lane is the de facto travel lane. If you want to pass, you pass on the right. Remember, Puerto Rican drivers are pretty crazy behind the wheel, so be alert. In addition, don't be confused when you see highway mileage signs in kilometers and speed signs in mph. You're never really sure about what is what. Finally, Puerto Rico is the land of many, many cars—too many cars for the current infrastructure. It often seems that everyone who lives here and owns a car is on the road at the same time, especially in the cities. Due to the effects of traffic lights on multilane roads, beware of traffic on Route 2 through most of the northern part of the island, and particularly around Manatí (when Route 22, a toll Autopiste, is completed, this won't be a problem). East of San Juan, on Route 3, traffic can be heavy all the way to Fajardo. Traffic on roads around Ponce (Routes 1 and 2) can also jam up. If you want to go to Rincón or Mayagüez from San Juan, it's faster to take the southern route even though it's longer, but once Route 22 is completed, the northern route should be faster. Of course, all major roads in and around San Juan will be very busy during rush hours, so plan accordingly. Be sure to ask your rental-car company for road sign translations (most are in Spanish) or bring your Spanish-English dictionary.

FOCUS ON PUERTO RICO: SAN JUAN—THE NEW HOT SPOT

What's the hot and trendy place in the sun? South Beach, in Miami? Forget it, the Beach reached its peak already and the groove-setters are on to something different. And with the fall of Castro still up

in the air, Havana won't be it for a while. Where, then, you ask?
Well, the answer is easy. There aren't many other choices where the
weather is guaranteed and the destination is easy to reach for weekends. Now the wise are heading for San Juan.

What used to be a glittering tourist destination—the Condado
area—has become a little seedy, which, of course, provides the
seeds for a great rejuvenation. All of the indicators signaling a
renaissance are here—slightly rundown, a high crime rate, a faded
image—the area is a prime target for New Yorkers and other urban-
ites with their insatiable appetite for something new, different,
dangerous, and, above all, hip.

The Condado resembles a cross between Waikiki and Miami
Beach. There are some art-deco buildings and there are lots of
high-rise buildings. There is a nice beach here; the water is clean;
there is surf, so it's fun; and then there is the nightlife. Best of all,
it is just a short hop away from many of the major metropolises of
the East Coast.

San Juan is reasonably inexpensive, although South Beach is still
cheaper. But while you can go to Miami and taste its nightlife, its
restaurants and the beach, here you are IN the tropics. You have the
same weather all year round and the summer in San Juan is actually
much cooler due to the tradewinds. Another bonus is that you can
drive an hour out of San Juan and be in the mountains, or two
hours and be in a beautiful Caribbean beach town. In Miami, where
do you go for diversion—Ocala?

Finally, Puerto Rico is Latin, not part-Latin like Miami.

So what's the game plan for a weekend in the new hot spot? Here
are all the essentials for your new getaway place:

ITINERARY

FRIDAY NIGHT:
• Arrive at 9 P.M. from New York (dinner flight)

• Check into the Caribe Hilton or Hostería del Mar, depending on
  your budget

• Out the door for a last-minute workout at the Muscle Factory in
  the Condado

• Back to hotel to dress for the evening

• Head to Peggy Sue (straight) or Krash (gay). One is around the
  corner from the other, and both are just south of the Condado.

If you're at the Hilton, stop to listen to hopping salsa band at the Terrace Bar

- Stagger in around 5 A.M.

SATURDAY:
- Rise and shine at noon

- Head for brunch at Hostería del Mar, Ocean Park

- Beach it at Ocean Park

- Work out at Nacional Gym, Santurce

- Happy hour at Mona's (straight—in Ocean Park) or the Atlantic Beach/Barefoot Bar (gay—in the Condado)

- Club nap

- Dinner at Ajili Mojili, Condado

- Hit the Condado Plaza casino and plan to lose some money

- Head out to Lazers (straight—Old San Juan) or Krash (gay)

- Stagger in at 5 A.M.

SUNDAY:
- Rise and shine at noon, breakfast at hotel

- Head for the hotel pool or the beach at Ocean Park

- Fry and drink

- Happy hour at the Ocean View Terrace (straight—Isla Verde) or Atlantic Beach (gay—Condado)

- Back to hotel to collect bags and change clothes (they'll hold your bags and provide a place to change)

- Flight back to New York at 7 P.M.

- Arrive home at 10 P.M. (you gain an hour in winter), exhausted, sunburned but refreshed—the perfect weekend!
  Tienes feliz!

WHERE TO STAY

Yikes, there are so many hotels, inns, resorts, guest houses, and paradores on Puerto Rico that the choices are staggering. However, with some weeding and sifting, which is my job, here are some suggestions. Most of the accommodations are in San Juan, but there are certainly great alternatives like Dorado Beach, the Horned Dorset Primavera in Rincón, and Boquerón.

The Puerto Rico Tourism Company also operates what they call *paradores de Puerto Rico*, small hotels and inns scattered about the island, often in great locations. Don't expect cute little Vermont–style B&Bs or inns. The paradores are simple, motelish–Hotel-6ish accommodations, which are well under $100 a night and clean. Some are in the mountains, some are on or near a beach. But they provide an inexpensive and comfy place to hang your hat while you explore the island. All have basic amenities, like air conditioning, TV and phones, and many have pools. There are currently 15 of them all around the island. For a complete listing, call (800) 443-0266 from the mainland U.S., or from Puerto Rico call (800) 462-7575 (outside San Juan), 721-2400 (in San Juan).

SAN JUAN

There are four different parts of the city where you can stay. The primary area is the *Condado*. This is where most of the big hotels are located. Next is *Isla Verde*, which is a newer big-hotel strip near the airport. I would caveat staying in Isla Verde if the roar of jets landing and taking off will bother you. Between the Condado and Isla Verde is *Ocean Park*. This is a personal favorite of mine as its a residential neighborhood of charming, two-story homes and some big old stucco houses on the beach. The beach itself is the best in the city (and a pretty beach in its own right). Accommodations here are guest houses, which are casual, relaxed, beachy, and cheap. Perfect. The last area is *Old San Juan*, which is full of colonial architecture and character, although it is inconvenient to nightlife and the beach (everything is a cab ride away) and during the day the cruise-ship/tour-bus circuit swarms the area. Still, it's unique, and the one place I'd recommend there, Casa San José, is superb.

With all that in mind, here are my favorites:

CONDADO

CARIBE HILTON AND CASINO (809) 721-0303, fax (809) 725-8849

Stateside: (800) HILTONS
Canada: (800) 268-9275
UK: (0800) 28-93-03
Calle San Jerónimo (P.O. Box 1872), San Juan, PR 00902-1872

If you want to stay at a full-service hotel and resort in San Juan, this is by far the best. Opened in 1949, the Caribe Hilton is an institution on the island and is a focal point of activity in the city. Business, government, and cultural meetings and events are always happening here. You can just sit in the breezy lobby of the hotel and see people from all walks of life and from everywhere—it is a hubbub of activity. The resort is a huge property for being in the midst of a city. Nestled on 17 acres on the other end of the Condado Bridge in an area called Puerto de Tierra, there are 2 multistory buildings and a tower, all of which house 619 rooms and 49 suites (it's a big hotel). There are gardens with fish ponds, a huge pool (there are actually two) centering the airy Terrace Bar (where the piña colada was invented in 1957), and the beach, which is manmade but still attractive and protected by a lagoon. On the grounds are six lighted tennis courts, lighted and air-conditioned squash and racquetball courts, and a health club and spa. Water sports can be arranged by the hotel. The hotel recently underwent a $40-million renovation and the refurbished rooms look fabulous. The décor has hints of deco but is still contemporary and very attractive. All rooms have a lanai and all the amenities you would expect from a Hilton International (not to be confused with the American Hiltons—they're a different company and not at all in the same league). There are five restaurants, four bars and a new 12,000-square-foot casino. The hotel often has great Latin bands/orchestras at the Terrace Bar, which is well attended by dressed-up locals. There is also an Executive Business Center, which is free for use by hotel guests, but there are fees for some services. You can get secretarial and translation services, fax and photocopy service, and the use of PCs.

Rates are WICKED PRICEY to RIDICULOUS for singles and WICKED PRICEY to OUTRAGEOUS for doubles (EP). Suites are BEYOND BELIEF. Look for package deals.

CONDADO PLAZA HOTEL & CASINO (809) 721-1000, fax (809) 722-7955
Stateside: (800) 624-0420
999 Ashford Avenue, San Juan, PR 00907

The Condado Plaza is another large hotel (580 rooms and suites) and is on the other side of the bridge from the Caribe Hilton. While not having an impressive lobby, it does have a fairly airy, manageable casino with windows, so you know when the sun is coming up and it's time for bed. The best thing about the hotel is the pool area (there are three—one is saltwater) and it shares a small, calm public beach which anchors one end of the bridge that spans the lagoon. The rooms are attractive and comfortably furnished and have all the standard amenities. Isadora's, a dressy nightclub popular with the locals, is on the property, as are five very different restaurants.

Rates are WICKED PRICEY to RIDICULOUS for singles and doubles (EP). Look for package deals.

THE CONDADO BEACH HOTEL (809) 721-6090, fax (809) 722-5062
Stateside: (800) 468-2775
1071 Ashford Avenue, Condado, San Juan, PR 00907

Built by the Vanderbilts in 1919 as the place to stay in San Juan, this hotel looks like a classy old hotel in the tropics should—the Condado's version of the Royal Hawaiian. Inside, its glamour fades a bit—the remodelings over the years have made it lose its edge, although the lobby is still graceful. There is no beach in front, just rocky coast, so if you want to use the beach you'll have to traverse to the side and use the beach at La Concha—its sister hotel. There is a good-sized pool for swimming laps, although the pool deck is carpeted—an unfortunate occurrence. The 245 rooms are nicely done in a décor consistent with the style of the hotel, and have all of the standard amenities.

Rates are VERY PRICEY to WICKED PRICEY for singles and doubles (EP). Look for packages.

THE REGENCY HOTEL (809) 721-0505, fax (809) 722-2909
Stateside: (800) 468-2823/7927
1005 Ashford Avenue, Condado, San Juan, PR 00907

It doesn't look like much from the street, and it's *not* a Hyatt, but this 12-story hotel offers good value. It was recently renovated and features comfortable rooms and suites. Best of all, guests have privileges at the Condado Plaza next door (including those great pools—although there is a pool here too). All rooms have air conditioning, lanai, refrigerator, and cable TV. Be sure to request an oceanfront room on a high floor.

Rates are PRICEY to VERY PRICEY for singles and doubles (CP).

RADISSON NORMANDIE HOTEL (809) 729-2929, fax (809) 729-3083
Stateside: (800) 333-3333
Corner of Avenida Muñoz and Avenida Rosales, Puerta Tierra (Box 50059), San Juan, PR 00902

Located next to the Caribe Hilton complex and on a slice of beach, this is San Juan's only real art deco hotel. It looks like it's right out of South Miami Beach. Architecturally, it's a very interesting hotel inside and out. However, the recent restoration left it very stark and one gets the feeling of it being very cold—(besides the fact that the air conditioning is cranked to sub-zero). The lobby does not exude warmth—in contrast to the rest of Puerto Rico. There is a large atrium inside with the usual glass elevator and a restaurant and bar. But the place just screams for a decorator and some foliage. Warm this place up—puh-lease. The rooms are a bit warmer feeling, with tones of pink and pink and pink. The pool is small, and again is missing landscaping (you must walk from the hotel across the asphalt driveway to reach it—a missed opportunity). There is a small beach, but, folks, if you want art deco, go to South Beach.

Rates are WICKED PRICEY for singles and doubles (EP).

EL CANARIO BY THE SEA (809) 722-8640, fax (809) 725-4921
Stateside: (800) 742-4276
4 Condado Avenue, San Juan, PR 00907

A 25-room hotel located in a quieter part of the Condado but still centrally located, this is a very popular hotel with budget-conscious travelers and businessmen. The rooms are standard fare—clean, simple, air-conditioned, and comfortable (all have phones, cable TV, and baths). A small courtyard is the setting for continental breakfast in the morning. The tiny lobby bar has two great bartend-ers, Melissa and Jimbo, who are very popular with guests. The hotel is steps away from the beach.

Rates are NOT SO CHEAP for singles and doubles (CP).

EL CANARIO INN (809) 722-3861, fax (809) 722-0391
1317 Ashford Avenue, San Juan, PR 00907

El Canario is another affordable accommodation (25 rooms) in the heart of the Condado. It is bordered on the left by the now-closed Dupont Plaza (it was shut down after business plummeted in the aftermath of a fire that killed 88 people; the Dupont Plaza has apparently been sold to the Marriott people and it will reopen with renovations, etc., in the next few years). The other side borders apartment buildings. There is a small but pleasant courtyard with the ambient sound of air conditioners. You can also hear the noise of the street. All rooms have private baths, air conditioning, phone, and cable TV. But it's a pretty little place, and if you want to be right in the thick of it, this is an option.

Rates are NOT SO CHEAP for singles and doubles (CP).

BEST WESTERN HOTEL PIERRE (809) 721-1200, fax (809) 721-3118
Stateside: (800) 528-1234
105 De Diego, San Juan, PR 00914

While it's not anywhere close to the beach (although it's only a ten-minute walk), the Hotel Pierre is a great value for a full-service hotel in the Condado. It's very popular with the business set, which is always a good sign. There are 184 standard big-hotel rooms that are pleasant and quiet. All rooms have air conditioning, phone, and cable TV. There are three restaurants, a bar, and pool on the grounds.

Rates are NOT SO CHEAP to PRICEY for singles and doubles (EP).

ATLANTIC BEACH HOTEL (809) 721-6900, fax (809) 721-6917
Calle Vendig 1, Condado, San Juan, PR 00907

This is the Condado's gay hotel and site of the daily afternoon happy hour (4–6 P.M.) that is popular with both tourists and locals.

If you want to stay in the heart of the scene, this is the place. There are other gay accommodations farther east (see the Ocean Park write-ups). Rooms here are standard motel fare. Some rooms have shared baths (they're cheaper), so be sure to clarify what you want when making a reservation. There is a restaurant adjoining the bar. Given the hotel's orientation, the beach in front of the hotel is the Condado's gay beach (the hotel provides chaises).

Rates are NOT SO CHEAP to PRICEY for singles and doubles.

ISLA VERDE

Isla Verde is a strip of large condos and hotels on the ocean side and every conceivable fast-food joint known to man on the other side. There is a great little health-food store and café called Happiness adjacent to a good seafood restaurant and shop called Pescadería y Marisquería Atlántica. Both are worth a stop.

EL SAN JUAN HOTEL AND CASINO (809) 791-1000, fax (809) 791-0390
Stateside: (800) 468-2818
187 Isla Verde Road (P.O. Box 2872), San Juan, PR 00902

The El San Juan is the second deluxe hotel-resort-casino in San Juan (the Caribe Hilton is the first). And it's also a big place (it sprawls over 15 acres). You enter through a dim and dark-carved-wood lobby with a massive crystal chandelier hovering over a bar like the cloud shadow in the Magritte painting. The floors are dark marble. Off to the right is the best-looking casino in San Juan and it's very spacious. To the left is the reception area and beyond it are the pools. They get the award for the best hotel pool setup in San Juan. First there is a nice-sized lap pool—swimmers take note. Then there is the requisite resort pool with waterfalls, islands, etc. Around it are a Jacuzzi and some very comfortable chaises with cushions (which are hard to find these days). Pool bars seem everywhere, and overall it is a very attractive setting. There are beachfront villas (casitas) which can be rented that border the best big-hotel beach in San Juan. Three lighted tennis courts and water sports round out the outdoor activities. The El San Juan has 392 rooms, including the casitas, in a full range of luxury accommodations. Rooms are decorated in pastels (pink is popular here) and are fully loaded, including such items as VCR, stereo, a tiny TV in the bath, an iron and ironing board, a hair dryer, and three phones. Downstairs, there are five restaurants, two snack bars, eight cocktail lounges, the Club Tropicoro supper club with shows, and the Amadeus disco (a dressy club where locals take their dates to impress them).

Rates are RIDICULOUS to OUTRAGEOUS for singles and doubles (EP). Suites are BEYOND BELIEF. Look for packages.

SANDS HOTEL AND CASINO (809) 791-6100, fax (809) 791-8525
Stateside and Canada: (800) 223-0888
187 Isla Verde Road, Isla Verde, PR 00913; mailing address: P.O. Box 6676, Loíza Station, Santurce, PR 00914

The Sands Hotel has a very fabulous early-sixties look—what Lincoln Center in New York would look like if it were a hotel in the tropics. Entering the lobby, you walk into shades of white, white, and more white from the white-tiled floors, white walls, and all the mirrors and chrome furnishings reflecting this left and right. There is a good-sized casino where, when I was there, someone was gambling away thousands of dollars at the craps table (and enjoying every minute, strangely enough). Outside, there is a large pool with the standard-tropical-resort-feature of an island in the middle with bridges. There is a spacious beach in front with chaises. When I visited, the crowd was very Middle America and rather unhip. That fact alone would steer me away from this place. The rooms all have little lanais with sliders and pink and green standard hotel furnishings. There are also several well-frequented restaurants on the premises. This hotel was not one of my favorites, however.

Rates are VERY PRICEY to WICKED PRICEY for singles and doubles (EP). Look for packages.

OCEAN PARK

This is a wonderful residential neighborhood without high-rise hotels and with the best beach in San Juan. There are several guest houses, four of which I recommend. All are gay and straight mixed, with the Ocean Walk tending to be the most gay. But everyone of any persuasion is welcomed at all four.

HOSTERÍA DEL MAR (809) 727-3302, fax (809) 268-0772
Calle Tapía 1, Ocean Park, Santurce, PR 00911

This is the prettiest and most deluxe of the guest houses in Ocean Park. Situated right on the beach, there is a very tranquil air here, which you notice as you enter through a gate, pass a goldfish pool and step into a breezy lounge attractively decorated in light woods, rattans, and tropical plants. To your left is one of my favorite places to have lunch in San Juan (see the write-up in the "Where to Eat" section). The setting is so extraordinary, especially since it's in a city. You definitely wouldn't know you were in San Juan sitting inside—the sound of the surf is omnipresent. The rooms are simply but nicely decorated, with wood floors, rattan furnishings, air conditioning, cable TV, and phones. Many have lanais and ocean views and some have kitchenettes. The beach out front is never crowded.

Rates are NOT SO CHEAP to PRICEY for singles and doubles (EP).

OCEAN WALK GUEST HOUSE (809) 728-0855, fax (809) 728-6434
Atlantic Place 1, Ocean Park, Santurce, PR 00911

A rambling Spanish-stucco guest house on the beach, this is an inexpensive, clean, kinda-funky, and very friendly accommodation. The clientele here is mixed, although the guests tend to be mostly gay Americans and Europeans (both straight and gay). There are 40 rooms, almost all with private bath. While the rooms are on the smallish side (and the baths can be tiny), some of the rooms have windows on the ocean, where the sound of the waves is almost deafening (room 108 is one such). But the space works, the beds are comfortable, and remember you're not paying big bucks for an oceanfront room on the best beach in San Juan. While the trades really do keep the place cool, there are ceiling fans to help. Rooms also have huge TVs hung on the wall à la hospital rooms. There are no room phones, so if you need to make and receive a lot of calls, that may be a problem. Activity centers around a courtyard/patio with a small pool, snack bar, and bar. The beach in front is crowded on weekends with local college kids who seem to coexist quite peacefully with the guests. If you want more space, walk five minutes down the beach to your right and the crowd thins out dramatically. The Ocean Walk provides beach chaises for its guests for a couple of bucks.

The Condado section is a 15-minute walk away.
Rates are NOT SO CHEAP for singles and doubles (CP).

NUMERO UNO GUEST HOUSE (809) 726-5010, same for fax
Calle Santa Ana 1, Ocean Park, Santurce, PR 00911

Located on the beach about halfway between Hostería del Mar and
the Ocean Walk, this three-story guest house is another very pleasant, friendly, and comfortable accommodation in Ocean Park. Like
all other guest houses in Ocean Park, the clientele here is mixed
straight and gay, American and European. New owners and ex-New
Yorkers Esther and Chris Laube have embarked on an ambitious
refurbishing program of the property, which should be completed
by press time. There are eight rooms, six with air conditioning and
the others with ceiling fans. All rooms have double or king-size bed,
private bath, and are comfortable and clean. The downstairs patio
has a pool and lots of shady places to sit and sip a cocktail from the
bar while you read a juicy and trashy novel. The beach in front is
never crowded and is sort of the gay section of the beach. Numero
Uno provides chaises and beach towels for its guests.
Rates are NOT SO CHEAP for singles and doubles (CP).

THREE ELENA GUEST HOUSE (809) 728-7418
Calle Elena 3, Ocean Park, Santurce, PR 00911

This charming ten-room guest house, just one house in from the
beach on a very quiet street, caters to a mostly gay clientele. All
rooms have private bath and ceiling fans (air conditioning is available in certain rooms at an additional cost); they are clean and simply
and comfortably furnished. The best of the bunch is room 6, which
has a great ocean view (four rooms have views). Keep in mind that
the rooms don't have phones. There are three sundecks, a TV
lounge and bar, and a garden, which is a pleasant place to read.
Beach towels and chairs are provided for guests.
Rates are NOT SO CHEAP for singles and doubles (CP).

OLD SAN JUAN

CASA SAN JOSÉ (809) 723-1212, fax (809) 723-7620
Calle San José 159, San Juan, PR 00901

Casa San José, tucked away in the heart of Old San Juan, is a
delightful small and deliciously decorated hotel. Once a colonial
mansion that has been beautifully restored, the décor here is the

most tasteful of any hotel in Puerto Rico—down to the last throw pillow. The central lobby has a fountain that quietly reverberates the sound of water throughout the marble floors, white walls, columns, arches, and potted plants. There is no pool, sundeck, casino, or beach. This hotel is strictly for those who need none of the above but want comfort and elegance in Old San Juan. There are four double rooms, four one-bedroom suites, and one two-bedroom suite. All are beautifully furnished, sumptuously comfortable and loaded with amenities. There is a very stately lounge, called the Sala Grande, complete with grand piano, spacious sofas, and terrace. The kitchen is open to all guests if they wish to make a cup of coffee or tea in the middle of the night. Continental breakfast and a light lunch is served in the charming little dining room next to the Sala Grande.

Rates are VERY PRICEY to WICKED PRICEY for singles and doubles (CP).

WHERE TO DINE

Restaurants galore! There are tons in San Juan and your choices are almost unlimited, from the very expensive, chichi bistros to the little snack bar on the street. In the following section, I've tried to pare them down to give you a good cross-section of the San Juan dining scene. Keep in mind that all the large hotels and resorts will have one or more restaurants. If there is only one, it will serve generally continental cuisine. If there are two, the second will be a more casual and inexpensive version. More than three, then there will be ethnic cuisines such as Italian or Japanese. And so it goes. While the food at many of these hotels is good, the one thing that they will all have in common is that they are *very expensive and overpriced.* Now, if you're at a Dorado Beach, for example, you may bite the bullet and eat at the resort because of the convenience of it. However, if you're staying right in San Juan, *why sit home? Get thee out and about!*

Here are my suggestions:

AJILI-MOJILI, Calle Joffre, Hotel Condado Lagoon, Condado, 725-9195

This is the best place in San Juan to sample authentic Puerto Rican cuisine. The restaurant is very attractive and full of locals, so you know it's good. Great service too. Open for lunch and dinner (on Saturdays for dinner only). Reservations are suggested. $$$

HOSTERÍA DEL MAR, Calle Tapía 1, Ocean Park, 727-3302

The best spot for lunch in San Juan—you dine in a wooden pavilion with windows open to the beach and the tradewinds. The menu is diverse, from macrobiotic and vegetarian to criollo and chicken/ fish dishes. They also serve delicious sandwiches. It's also wonderful for dinner ($$$) and breakfast ($) too. $$

CAFE BERLIN, Calle San Francisco 407, Old San Juan, 722-5205

If you're looking for lighter and healthier fare, this is a fine and rather hip place for lunch and dinner in Old San Juan. It's not at all expensive, and there are great breads, salads, and desserts. If you just want coffee or herbal tea, this is it. $$

LA CHAUMIÈRE, Calle Tetuán 367, Old San Juan, 722-3330

If you want French/Provençale cuisine, this is San Juan's best. It's also one of San Juan's most elegant and most expensive restaurants. Closed Sunday. Reservations are advised. $$$$$

AMADEUS, Calle San Sebastían 106, Old San Juan, 722-8635

Serving all kinds of Puerto Rican and Caribbean cuisine, this very attractive restaurant in the heart of Old San Juan is a must stop for lunch or dinner. Open till 2 A.M., except Monday. Reservations are suggested. $$$

RAMIRO'S, Avenida Magdalena 1106, Condado, 721-9049

Serving delicious international cuisine with Spanish/Castilian flourishes (dubbed "New Créole") Chef Jesús Ramiro creates food that is as pretty to look at as it is good to eat. Closed for lunch on Saturday. Reservations are suggested. $$$$$

LA MALLORQUINA, Calle San Justo 207, Old San Juan, 722-3261

This is a fine old-style restaurant that serves Puerto Rican and Spanish specialties (try the asopao—a Puerto Rican rice dish). Set in an old building with murals and ceiling fans, this is a very pleasant place for lunch. San Juan's oldest restaurant, La Mallorquina, has been owned and operated by the same family since 1848. Popular at lunch. Closed Sunday. $$$

MARISQUERÍA ATLÁNTICA, Loíza 81, Isla Verde, 728-5444

If you want really fresh seafood, this is a great choice. (The restaurant also has a seafood shop next door.) Popular with locals at lunch and dinner; don't expect a fancy restaurant, just fresh fish. $$$

GOURMET RESTAURANTE VEGETARIANO, 1125 Ashford
    Avenue, Condado, 722-4072

Wedged between a Subway's and a Wendy's, this is a very simple restaurant that serves very good vegetarian dishes and protein shakes and smoothies. Be sure to notice their collection of Soviet naval hats. Open for lunch and early dinner (it closes by 8:30 or 9 P.M., depending on how busy it is). $

VIA APPIA, 1350 Ashford Avenue, Condado, 725-8711

If you want Southern Italian cuisine (lasagna, baked ziti, spaghetti, eggplant parmesan, etc.) and pizza, this is a pleasant place to sit and eat under the awning in front. While the service can be slow and at times indifferent, the food is hearty and the price is right. $$

AURORITA, Calle De Diego 303, Puerto Nuevo, 783-2899

Good Mexican food, live Mariachi music (Thursday through Sunday), and an out-of-the-way location (take a cab) make this a fun excursion. $$

MONA'S, Calle María Moczó 57, Ocean Park, 728-0140

Great margaritas, loud music, a young crowd (American and Puerto Rican), and good Mexican food make for a lively atmosphere. If you want to have fun while you eat and perhaps meet someone at the same time, try Mona's. Open daily from 11:30 A.M. till midnight; bar open till 2 A.M. $$$

BOUNTY STEAK HOUSE, Avenida de Castro 200B, Santurce, 268-5855

This is a well-kept secret on the corner of Castro (the expressway) and Las Flores. Great steaks and reasonable prices. $$

KASALTA BAKERY, Calle McLeary 1966, Ocean Park, 727-7340

This is very popular local bakery and cafeteria/eatery for breakfast, lunch, and dinner (open daily from 6 A.M. till 10 P.M.). The prices are really cheap here! Lunch and dinner specials include Puerto Rican dishes (*caldo gallego*, for instance) that you absolutely have no idea what they'll taste like. Also popular are the Cuban sandwiches—a meal in themselves. A definite must stop! $

BONANZA CONDADO, Ashford Avenue and De Diego, Condado, 268-2207

If you're on a budget, this chain restaurant offers good food cheap and its salad bar is legendary. $$

LA BOMBONERA, Calle San Francisco 259, Old San Juan, 722-0658

An institution in Old San Juan, this is a great place for cheap Puerto Rican food when in the historic district. It's packed at lunchtime. Reputed to have the best Puerto Rican coffee in town. Open daily from 7:30 A.M. till 8:30 P.M. $$

GOING OUT

Cha-cha-cha. With the best and most variety in the Caribbean, this is why you stay in San Juan. There are lots of bars and clubs of all persuasions and there is no set time that they must close. Most do close when the last person spins off the dance floor and stumbles into the street. As in any city, weekend nights will be the busiest and most crowded in the clubs. Also, all clubs will usually have a cover charge of between $5 and $15 (especially on weekends), which usually includes at least one free drink. And if you like to gamble, all the big hotels in the Condado and Isla Verde have *casinos* (the most glittering is the one at the El San Juan in Isla Verde). So take your disco nap, strap on those high heels or Doc Marten's, and off you go into the night.

BARS AND DISCOS

The two hottest straight clubs in San Juan at the moment are Peggy Sue and Lazers. But I've listed some other choices if you get tired of them and want a change of pace. Note that when going to the straight clubs here, people tend to get dressed up—that means no shorts, T-shirts, athletic shoes, or sandals for men (*jeans are iffy*; best to wear dressier pants); for women, dresses are preferred (the tighter and more leg showing, the better—remember, this is Latin America).

PEGGY SUE, Avenida Roberto H. Todd 1, Condado, 725-4664

Currently the *hot club* in San Juan, this is a sort-of dressier version of a Hard Rock Café. It's located just south of the Condado and the expressway, across the street from the fast-food plaza. The clientele here are mostly the Puerto Rican version of yuppies, who are much more exciting and interesting than their American counterparts. There is a dance floor featuring current and past hits. Singles, this is the place.

LAZER VIDEOTEQUE, Calle Cruz 251, Old San Juan, 725-7581

This is San Juan's *premier disco*, located in the heart of Old San Juan. Here you'll hear all the current dance hits with all the high-tech accoutrements you expect in a hot club. It's stylish, it's fun, and it gets packed.

BABALOOS, Calle Tanca 203, Old San Juan, 722-7582

In Old San Juan, this is a good alternative if Lazers gets too crowded and unbearable.

ISADORA'S, Condado Plaza Hotel, 999 Ashford Avenue, Condado, 721-1000

Located in the Condado Plaza, this is where locals take their dates to impress them.

AMADEUS DISCO, El San Juan Hotel, Route 187, Isla Verde, 791-1000

This is another dressy disco for good date impressions (like Isadora's). This gets the Euro-trashy element as well as local flashy types. Closed Monday.

LEVELS, Avenida Ponce de León 1600, Santurce, 725-1085

A multilevel disco with a strong local clientele; you won't find many tourists here.

MONA'S, Calle María Moczó 57, Ocean Park, 728-0140

It may be a restaurant, but the bar hops with loud music and great margaritas. This may be a good warm-up place before heading out for dancing. Casual.

DUNBAR'S, Calle McLeary 1954, Ocean Park, 728-2920

This is a casual, popular bar next to Mona's in Ocean Park and another alternative should you not want to venture into the dressier Condado.

GAY BARS AND CLUBS

San Juan has the best, and pretty much only, gay nightlife in the Caribbean. While there is a little nightlife scene in Santo Domingo, Dominican Republic, and one small club in Guadeloupe, San Juan is it until you get as far south as Caracas, Venezuela. For those of you who may be in the Cabo Rojo/Boquerón area on the other side of the island, there is a club in San Germán called THE WORLD UPSIDE DOWN (busy on weekends—local road 360 at the intersection of Route 2); one in Aguadilla called CARL'S BY THE SEA (Calle Comercio); and one in Ponce called STUDIO 143 (calle Villa 198—in front of Salgado Auto Parts). For those staying in San Juan, try to get a Puerto Rican to take you to VILLA CAIMITO for its very local Sunday afternoon/ evening tea dance (they play salsa and merengue). It's located in the hills outside of Caguas and impossible to find unless the driver has been there before. Finally, be sure to pick up a copy of Caribbean Heat for local listings and events.

KRASH, Avenida Ponce de León 1257, Santurce, 722-1390

This is the *hot gay club* in San Juan, located next to the Metro Theater and just around the corner from Peggy Sue. The DJ spins all the latest hits and there are often shows starting around 1 A.M. Closed Tuesday.

LIME, Avenida Condado 112, Condado, 721-8291

Located behind Peggy Sue (it has often been witnessed that late in the evening, guys will come out the back door of Peggy Sue and go into Lime), this is the other popular choice for dancing. Tuesdays are big here, as Krash is closed.

ATLANTIC BEACH/BAREFOOT, Calle Vendig 1 and 2, Condado; Atlantic Beach—721-6900; Barefoot—724-7230

Situated across the street from each other on the beach, these two places work in tandem for the popular happy-hour circuit. From 4 to 6 P.M., it's the Atlantic Beach. At 6 P.M., everyone crosses the street and goes to the Barefoot (happy hour there is from 5 to 7 P.M. Both places have wonderful settings for drinks and conversation, as the waves roll in out front.

BOCACCIO, Avenida Miguel Rivera, Hato Rey, no phone

The place for salsa and merengue Thursday through Sunday. Very local.

LESBIAN BARS AND CLUBS

There aren't as many choices for lesbians as for gay men, but there are a few spots. Be sure to ask around for the up-to-the-minute info. Among the best:

CUPS AT THE BARN, 1708 Calle San Mateo, Santurce, no phone

Very popular on Wednesday and Friday.

CIGNEL, Avenida Ponce de León 1203 (in rear of bldg.), no phone

Wednesday night is Women's Night with DJ Anne of Villa Caimito and bartendress María from Backwards Café and Stop 22.

PICASSO, 77 Avenue Isla Verde Avenue, Isla Verde, no phone
Dancing in Isla Verde.

THE REST OF PUERTO RICO—WHERE TO STAY, DINE, ETC.

DORADO

HYATT REGENCY DORADO BEACH (809) 796-1234, fax (809) 796-4647
HYATT REGENCY CERROMAR BEACH (809) 796-1234, fax (809) 796-2022
Stateside: (800) 233-1234
Dorado, PR 00646

These sister resorts, built by the Rockefellers' RockResorts company in 1958 (Dorado Beach) and 1972 (Cerromar Beach) and purchased by Hyatt in 1985, share a 1,000-acre former grapefruit and coconut plantation just west of the town of Dorado and 22 miles west of San Juan. With over 2 miles of beaches and coastline, four 18-hole Championship golf courses (the best in the Caribbean—if you are a golfer, this is it), 21 tennis courts, a windsurfing and water-sports center, the River Pool, 3 other pools, 10 restaurants, cafés and snack bars, 2 casinos, and over 800 guest rooms, this is Puerto Rico's premier resort and one of the Caribbean's best and grandest. The grounds are beautifully planted and well maintained as you would expect the Rockefellers would have wanted it. Su Casa (Dorado Beach), a seasonal restaurant that serves Spanish and Puerto Rican cuisine, is the original plantation house.

The two resorts share the same huge property but are distinctly different in character. Dorado Beach, the older of the two, is a classic RockResort—low-key, two-story buildings, breezy and tastefully designed lobbies and common areas with subtly stated elegance in the décor and furnishings. The total concept is to provide quiet luxury while fully integrating the natural setting with the design. A first-time visitor would have no idea how big the resort is by driving up to the main building. Everything is spread out and landscaped to make you feel like your staying at a small country club. And the clientele who stay here prefer it that way. On the other hand, Cerromar impresses you as a big, splashy resort where lots is happening all the time. The design is totally different from

Dorado Beach. This is a seven-story hotel with several wings and pavilions. With all the activity, Cerromar is preferred by families or those who need lots going on. Guests of both resorts have reciprocal privileges, so Cerromar guests can golf, dine, or beach at Dorado and Dorado guests can hang out at Cerromar at will—a nice feature.

DORADO BEACH: Pulling up to the entrance of the hotel past a fleet of golf carts parked by guests, you walk into a very elegant and comfortable lobby with tile floors, objets d'art, and an advantageously angled location for generous ocean views and tradewind breezes. There are beaches on both sides of the main building—a man-made reef keeps the lagoon water fairly calm from the turbulent Atlantic and makes it great for swimming.

There are two restaurants here, the rather formal Surf Room (jackets required) and the screened-in Ocean Terrace (to keep out the birds who like to help guests eat their meals), and a small casino that is only open in the winter (guests use Cerromar's in the off-season). A third restaurant, the intimate and exclusive Su Casa, is located down the beach in an old plantation house.

The guest rooms fan out in both directions from the main building. The best, of course, are the beachfront units. They come in two versions—upstairs and downstairs. The downstairs ones have two double beds (better for families or non-intimate roommates), whereas the upstairs units have one king-size bed. The floors of both are tiled with terra-cotta and the furnishings are comfortable and tropical. Given that this place was built in the fifties, it still holds its own quite well. The casitas, slightly larger and much more expensive, are exemplary in the spacious and naturally lit bathrooms (the shower roof is a greenhouse). A patio in front leads right down to the beach. For the money, however, you're better off at the beachfront units (and the terraces are more private).

CERROMAR BEACH: Cerromar Beach is a multiwinged seven-story building with over 500 guest rooms with a big resort feel to it (the lobby looks much like an airline terminal). But Cerromar has very comfortable, attractively furnished rooms with marble baths and the standard amenities you would expect from a Hyatt. This resort is very popular with conventions because the facilities are bigger and geared to handle them. Families also love it with its huge pool complex, a bigger and wider beach than Dorado, and activities geared for kids and adults of all ages. Where Dorado is very quiet, Cerromar is bustling with activity—especially the casino in the evening. One of Cerromar's unique features is the "River Pool"— at 1,776 feet long, it's the longest current-propelled pool in the world. It moves water at 22,600 gallons per minute, has 14 water-falls and 4 water slides. The slide at its conclusion is three stories high and requires stairs to climb, but it is a blast. Be prepared to get a noseful of water from the splashdown. While the whole River Pool idea is contrived (it was added in the eighties to attract families and vacationers who like the mega-resorts), it is different, fun, and both adults and kids will enjoy it (there is a bar with barstools in the water about halfway down, for a quick piña colada). Another great program for kids and teens (and for their parents because it gets the kids out of their hair) is Camp Hyatt and Rock Hyatt. Camp Hyatt is for ages 3–15 and provides supervised activities from 9 A.M. to 4 P.M. and again from 6 to 10 P.M. (now that's a vacation). The cost is $25 per day per child and well worth it (you receive a 50 percent discount on the second room rental if the kids are enrolled). Rock Hyatt is for teenagers and is a program to provide fun activities for them as they choose. There is no fee for this one. There are five restaurants (including Swan Café and Medici's), four bars, and a casino on the property.

Golf: These two resorts are a golfer's paradise. There are four 18-hole, Robert Trent Jones II Championship courses (called North, South, East, and West) on flat and rolling terrain that will challenge all golfers. They have been the site of numerous golf tournaments. All feature Mr. Jones's signature trademarks: huge greens, lots of bunkers and water hazards, and long fairways. Proba-bly the toughest links are the East and West courses. The East, at 7,005 yards, has the super-tough 13th hole, a double-dogleg, 540-yard, two-pond nightmare. The West, at 6,913 yards, has the tough-est par-threes at the resort, spiting you with sloping greens and mucho bunkers. The North course is a 6,841-yard links-style course, and the South, at 7,047 yards, is a challenge of winds and mega–water hazards. Greens fees are $49 for guests and $75 to $100 for nonguests. Carts are mandatory ($34). Golf packages are availa-ble.

Rates for Dorado Beach are RIDICULOUS to BEYOND BE-LIEF for single and doubles (EP).

Rates for Cerromar Beach are RIDICULOUS for single doubles (EP).
Look for packages at both resorts.

RINCÓN

THE HORNED DORSET PRIMAVERA (809) 823-4030, fax (809) 823-5580
Route 429, Km 3 (P.O. Box 1132), Rincón, PR 00677

The Horned Dorset Primavera is a small and lovely property tucked away on the coast south of Rincón (it's so tucked away you can easily drive past it). A symphony of taste, the owners have gone to great pains to make the property a tranquil and comfortable hideaway. They proudly claim that this is a place without activities—no pool aerobics, radios, or TVs. It's well-appointed, nicely decorated, and features a fantastic library. Readers will be thrilled. You can sink into a big comfy chair, order a drink, check out the spectacular western view of the water, and occasionally look up to see who might be passing through the lobby—a piece of heaven to some, including me. There are 22 suites with four-poster mahogany beds and antiques for comfortable accommodation. Check out the brass-footed tubs in the marble bathrooms. The well-manicured grounds contain a medium-sized pool and a small beach for sunning and swimming. But I'd say the main reason to come here is to read, be quiet, enjoy great food (the restaurant is on the second floor with fantastic service and food), and maybe have that secret tryst with that certain someone.

Rates are WICKED PRICEY for singles and RIDICULOUS for doubles (EP). The hotel does not have facilities for children and none under 12 will be accepted as guests.

PARADOR VILLA ANTONIO (809) 823-2645, fax (809) 823-2285
Stateside: (800) 443-0266
Route 115, Km 12.3 (P.O. Box 68) Rincón, PR 00743

This is one of the paradores de Puerto Rico discussed earlier in the chapter. This one sits right on the beach. There are 53 clean and simple rooms, all with kitchenettes. The beach, a pool, and two tennis courts round out the facilities. It's also near Playa Los Almendros, a very pleasant little beach with a snack bar.

Rates are NOT SO CHEAP for singles and doubles (EP).

BOQUERÓN

Boquerón is a charming little village in the southwest corner of the island, between Mayagüez and Ponce. It's a boat town—lots of cruising boats stop here bringing with them the weathered and alcoholic "boat rats." They hang out at the bar, get smashed, and by a miracle of gravitation and balance, somehow manage not to fall off their bar stools. They're always in bed early because they get so trashed.

The center of activity is the main intersection in town, by the bay, where there are two bars on opposite corners. The one with the action and a very competitive pool table is called Schamar. You know it's a yachty favorite from all the tattered burgees and ensigns donated to the bar by boaters from yacht clubs and countries from around the world.

There are several small restaurants in town, including Robert's and Galloway's, which are nothing fancy. Actually they are very simple, but they promise fresh seafood which, in keeping with the atmosphere here, is all you need anyway. In the morning there are several little breakfast spots next to the happening bars, which are cheap and simple.

The beach in Boquerón is very pretty and very calm, considered one of the island's best bathing beaches. It sits on a very scenic bay, with mountains at the southern end. Actually, the entire area is quite wonderful. It's very rural, with pastures and fields rolling up to green hills and mountains.

PARADOR BOQUEMAR (809) 851-2158, fax (809) 851-7600
Stateside: (800) 443-0266
Route 307 (P.O. Box 133), Boquerón, Cabo Rojo, PR 00622

This is the parador in Boquerón that is clean, efficient, and cheap. It has 64 rooms (all with baths), a swimming pool, restaurant (Las Cascadas), and bar. The town junction, where all the activity happens, and the beach, are just around the corner and down the street. Be sure to make reservations well in advance, as Boquerón is very popular with folks from San Juan, especially on weekends, and this is the best place to stay in town.

Rates are NOT SO CHEAP for singles and doubles (EP).

GUÁNICA

Located on the southern coast of the island west of Ponce and near three great natural sites—the Reserva Forestal Guánica, Phosphorescent Bay, and Gilligan's Island—Guánica is an example of the "real" Puerto Rico. There are no fast-food chains, 7-Elevens, or Blockbuster Videos, just lots of bodegas and panaderías. There's a cool-looking waterfront too (cameras please). Just outside of town, the Reserva Forestal Guánica has some gorgeous and deserted beaches. Just follow Route 333 until you can go no farther. You'll see places to stop along the way. West of town, Phosphorescent Bay (La Parguera) is great after sunset, as all the phosphorescent plankton (dinoflagellates, to be precise) create "sparks" in the water when it gets dark and you move through and disturb their nesting. The bay is due west of Guánica on Route 324 (watch for signs). Gilligan's Island is a small uninhabited, mile-offshore key with a secluded beach and excellent snorkeling. The folks at Copamarina (821-0505) will arrange for you to go there for a fee if you like.

COPAMARINA BEACH RESORT (809) 821-0505, fax (809) 821-0070
Toll free in Puerto Rico: (800) 462-4676
Stateside: (800) 468-4676
Route 333, Km 6.5 (P.O. Box 0805), Cana Gorda, Guánica, PR 00653-0805

Copamarina is a very reasonably priced mini-resort in a quiet part of Guánica. This resort is a great place to go if you want to be somewhere tranquil and near a park where you can take long walks or bike rides. Copamarina is very popular with weekenders from San Juan who want a secluded getaway. The grounds and beach are pretty. The seas are calm as there is a sheltered bay here. Recently refurbished, the rooms are attractive—with neutral-toned carpeting, bamboo and wood furnishings, air conditioning, cable TV, and phones—and they sport little lanais. The main lobby has a very pleasant veranda on which to sit and read. The only thing I don't like about the resort is the chain-link fence between the beach and the grounds. You'll also find a restaurant, bar, pool, some water sports, and two tennis courts.

Rates are PRICEY for singles and doubles (EP).

PONCE

Ponce is a wonderful mélange of Spanish and Caribbean architecture, with other styles thrown in for the hell of it. In downtown Ponce, the Spanish colonial influence is very pronounced and most of the center district (around the Cathedral of Our Lady of Guadalupe and the very colorful Parque de Bombas, the old municipal fire station) is now being restored and is definitely worth seeing. Other must stops while in Ponce are the Museum of Puerto Rican Music, La Perla Theater, and the Ponce Museum of Art. Note that once you leave the center, there are very few street signs, so be sure to have a good map and a sense of humor.

Just south of town is the new PONCE HILTON—call toll-free (800) HILTONS for reservations—or you can stay right in town at the venerable and inexpensive Hotel Meliá

HOTEL MELIÁ (809) 842-0260, fax (809) 841-3602
Calle Cristina 2 (P.O. Box 1431), Ponce, PR 00733

Located adjacent to the Parque de Bombas, this family-owned and -operated hotel is convenient to all the historic sites of Ponce by foot. There are 80 clean, simply but comfortably furnished rooms, all with air conditioning, private bath, phone, and cable TV. While there is no pool, there is a very pleasant garden terrace and a wonderful rooftop terrace where breakfast is served—it is also a great place for evening cocktails. There is a restaurant and bar at the hotel, and you are steps away from countless others.

Rates are NOT SO CHEAP for singles and doubles (EP).

Don't Miss

EL YUNQUE—You can't visit Puerto Rico without a visit to El Yunque (the Caribbean National Forest). This is a great example of rain forest for those of you who have never seen one before. It's only about an hour's drive east of San Juan and you can almost drive up to the summit (that was possible before Hurricane Hugo). The drive up takes you past towering banks of green ferns and canopies of trees and vines. The Forest itself consists of 28,000 acres, and is the largest and wettest in the U.S. National Forest System (240 inches per year or 100 billion gallons of water fall on the forest every year). Note that there are no poisonous snakes on Puerto Rico. Be sure to stop at the Sierra Palma, an interpretive center located at Km 11.6 on Route 91, just before the parking area for the hiking trails; it's open daily from 9:30 A.M. to 5 P.M.

If you decide to hike (you should), the first section of the trail to the summit of El Yunque is a cement path and is well worn. While a steady climb, it is fairly easy but it's humid. Remember that this is the rain forest. The second section turns into a path which, while a little muddy, still is rather easy to walk. If you walk at a steady pace, you can make it to the summit in one hour (we did). For the length of the trail, you will be walking through forest: For some people the concept may be over in 15 minutes. The few vista points you come to, including the towers, are more often than not shrouded in clouds—so don't expect spectacular vistas; expect the forest and its hundreds of varieties of foliage and birds (which you hear more often than see). In this age of video bites and short attention spans, if you don't like the forest you may be bored fairly quickly. Once you get near the top, there is a choice—you'll reach a fork in the road. I recommend going to the tower, which is a scant .3 kilometers away. The temptation is to go to the peak of El Yunque, because it *is* the summit. However, when you get to the peak, there are at least seven huge microwave transmission towers to thoroughly irradiate you. And since the clouds usually block the view, these lovely structures will be what you see. The only advantage to going to the peak is that you can take the road (open to official vehicles) down—which is faster and a different way down.

SCENIC DRIVES—There are several on this very scenic island. The two I would recommend are a half-day and a full day's journey, respectively.

• Trip 1 takes you east on Route 3 to Luquillo (there's a great public beach) and south past Fajardo and the very scenic Playa de Naguabo. It continues on Route 3 through industrial Humacao and into sugarcane territory. When you get to Yabucoa, you start to climb through some very scenic mountains with great vistas of valley and the sea (watch out for the cane trucks—don't worry, you'll hear their horns). The road descends to Maunabo and eventually follows the sea along the Caribbean. When you get to Guayama, take Route 15 north to Cayey. This is *incredibly* scenic—

lots of mountain vistas and lush foliage and vegetation. At Cayey, hook
on to the highway (Route 52) and head north back to San Juan.

• Trip 2 takes you through the Cordillera Central, the mountain spine of
  Puerto Rico. This is a *long, twist-and-turn drive*, so leave early in the
  morning so you can take your time. You may want to arrange to stay in
  Cabo Rojo or Rincón at the other end of the road. Take Route 52 south
  from San Juan and get off in Cayey and take Route 14 to Coamo (hot
  springs—Baños de Coamo—if you want to take a dip). At Coamo, take
  Route 155 north to Route 143. Turn left and go east on Route 143. This
  stretch is *very scenic* and will take you past the biggest mountains in
  Puerto Rico. At the junction of Route 10, head north until you get to
  Route 135. If you've had enough and you want to head back to San Juan,
  continue on Route 10 until you reach the junction of Route 22, then go
  east on 22. If you want to continue, take Route 135 to Route 105. Follow
  this all the way to Mayagüez. Once in Mayagüez, the best route back is
  the southern one (Route 2 to Route 52).

RÍO CAMUY CAVE PARK—Everyone raves about these, "oh you've
got to see them," etc. Personally, the last thing I want to do in the tropics
is go subterranean. However, if it interests you (kids will love it), make
plans to come here. Located near Lares, tours are conducted Wednesday
through Sunday from 8 A.M. to 4 P.M. You must call ahead to reserve a
space on the tour (898-3100).

WINDSURFING AND SURFING IN RINCÓN—If you're a windsurfer
or surfer, this is one of the best places to do both in the Caribbean. Many
championships in both sports are held at Surfer and Wilderness Beaches,
and there is a small, California-style surfer community.

BOQUERÓN AND GUÁNICA—Two wonderful and scenic towns for
those in search of the real the Puerto Rico (see previous writings).

GIMNASIO NACIONAL AND THE MUSCLE FACTORY—If you
need a gym to keep those pecs and bis in shape for the beach and going out,
these two gyms near and in the Condado offer reasonable day and weekly
passes. Call the Nacional at 723-5951 (Avenida Ponce de León 1208, corner
of R. H. Todd, 3rd floor) and the Muscle Factory at 721-0717 (Ashford
Avenue).

LUNCH AT HOSTERÍA DEL MAR—The best spot for lunch in San
Juan is here in Ocean Park (see the "Where to Dine" writeup in San Juan
section above).

DRINKS AT WINDOWS ON THE CARIBBEAN—Located in the Clarion Hotel in Miramar, the views of the city from the tallest building in the Caribbean are fab.

¿QUÉ PASA?—Published by the Puerto Rico Tourism Company, this is an excellent publication to peruse for events and the latest info. It also has a complete listing of hotels and restaurants in Puerto Rico.

CULEBRA AND VIEQUES—These two small islands off the east coast of Puerto Rico offer a fun day-trip or overnight excursion (see pages 131–37).

MUSEO DE LA MÚSICA PUERTORRIQUEÑA—Located in central Ponce down the street from the Parque de Bombas at Calle Cristina 70, this museum presents a a very interesting exploration into the different kinds of Puerto Rican music both past and present. This is a must stop when in Ponce. Open Wednesday to Sunday from 9 A.M.–noon and 1–5:30 P.M. Call 844-9722 for information.

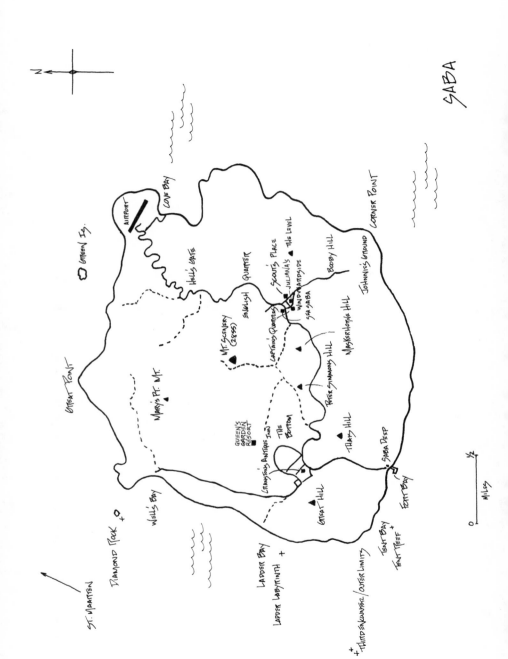

SABA

N

ST. MAARTEN

DIAMOND ROCK

UTTERN POINT

GREEN Iy.

COVE BAY

AIRPORT

HELL'S GATE

SNGLISH QUARTER

MT. SCENERY
(2855)

MARY'S PT. MT.

QUEEN'S GARDEN RESORT

JOHNSON'S ANTIQUE INN

THE BOTTOM

GREAT HILL

WELL'S BAY

LADDER BAY

LADDER LABYRINTH

THIRDSKWOMPER / OUTER LIMITS

TENT BAY
TENT REEF

CAPTAIN'S QUARTERS

SCOUT'S PLACE
JULIANA'S
WINDWARDSIDE
SPA SABA

THE LEVEL

BOOBY HILL

JOHNNY'S GROUND

CORNER POINT

PETER SIMMONS HILL

MAKERHORNE HILL

TROY HILL

SABA DEEP

FORT BAY

0   ½
MILES

SABA

Saba is probably best known for its airport (Juancho Yrausquin Airport), which not only has one of the shortest runways in the world (1,312 feet) but a landing strip clearly defined at both ends by precipitous cliffs, plunging over 100 feet into the crashing surf below. Be sure to have a few cocktails (or Valium) in St. Maarten before making the 15-minute flight. Watching the landing approach from the DeHavilland Twin Otter aircraft will remind you of an old movie filmed in Cinerama—only *you're* in the plane heading directly for the rocky cliff, when at the last possible moment the aircraft banks to avert disaster. Fortunately, you are on the ground before you can get out a scream. The plane seems to land on a dime.

Saba is certainly different from other islands in the West Indies. There are no permanent beaches, only a wandering one of black sand that exists, if at all, for a few winter months at Wells Bay. The island is basically one big mountain with roads and villages clinging to its sides. Mount Scenery is the highest point, about 3,000 feet above sea level and usually in the clouds. There are four villages—Hell's Gate, Windwardside, St. John's, and Bottom—that are home to Saba's 1,000 residents. The road that connects the villages has only been in existence for about forty-five years. When Dutch engineers declared the steep and mountainous terrain unfit for construction, a local man designed and built the roads with knowledge culled from a correspondence course.

It sounds pretty bleak, but the island is surprisingly lush and beautiful. The climate is ideal—the elevation of the villages keeps it comfortably cool and breezy in the evening, just right for sleeping. The days are warm but not hot, and the temperature of both air and water is around 80 degrees all year round. The vegetation is tropical and verdant—this is not a dry island. And the villages have the charm and appeal of small towns in coastal Maine. By tradition, most of the tidy houses are white with green trim and red roofs. It's very picturesque. It's also probably the cleanest island in the Caribbean. If it had a beach and a decent harbor it would quickly become the next St. Barts. Thank God it doesn't!

There are three reasons to come to Saba. The first is for solitude and quiet: the deadline for your latest novel or screenplay is swiftly approaching and you need a place with few distractions and no one to call. The second is that you hate beaches, are scared of the sun, or just want a pleasant climate without boatloads of tourists and the hassle of Third World politics. The last is by far the best reason to come here—the diving. It is one of the last "virgin" dive sites and has probably some of the finest diving you'll find in the Lesser Antilles (that is, Puerto Rico all the way down to Trinidad).

THE BRIEFEST HISTORY

Saba was uninhabited when Columbus sighted this rock in the sea on his second voyage in 1493. Since the island had no harbor and is basically all mountain, it wasn't settled until the 1640s, when some Dutch colonists built the towns of Tent Bay and The Bottom. The island then changed hands 12 times among the Dutch, British, French, and Spanish. In 1816, a treaty gave the island permanently to the Netherlands. It remains today a part of the Netherland Antilles.

SABA: KEY FACTS

LOCATION	17°N by 63°W
	28 miles south of St. Maarten
	150 miles east of Puerto Rico
	1,680 miles southeast of New York
SIZE	5 square miles
HIGHEST POINT	Mount Scenery (2,855 ft.)
POPULATION	1,000
LANGUAGE	English, although the official one is Dutch
TIME	Atlantic Standard Time (1 hour ahead of EST, same as EDT)

AREA CODE	To call Saba from the U.S., dial 011 (the international access code), then 599 (the country code), and finally 4 (the area code for Saba) plus the five-digit local number
ELECTRICITY	110 volts AC, 60 cycles—same as the U.S.
CURRENCY	The Netherlands Antilles guilder (NAf), also called the florin (1.77 NAf = $1 U.S.), but U.S. dollars accepted everywhere
DRIVING	On the *right*; a valid driver's license from your own country is acceptable
DOCUMENTS	U.S. and Canadian citizens must show proof of citizenship and have a return or ongoing ticket
DEPARTURE TAX	$2 U.S.
BEER TO DRINK	Heineken
RUM TO DRINK	Mt. Gay
MUSIC TO HEAR	Dancehall

GETTING THERE

WINAIR (Windward Islands Airways) makes the flight three times a day from Juliana Airport on St. Maarten. Juliana is a major gateway to the Caribbean, with nonstops from New York on AMERICAN, CONTINENTAL, BWIA, and ALM. AMERICAN EAGLE flies to St. Maarten from San Juan and LIAT flies from neighbor islands.

GETTING AROUND

Given the hair-raising nature of the mountain-clinging road that Hassle built, take a taxi. (There really aren't that many places you can drive to anyway.) This way, you can enjoy the view rather than worry about plunging off the cliff.

FOCUS ON SABA: DIVING

Saba is becoming known for its diving. It has been kept fairly quiet largely because of the island's uniqueness and its inability to accom-

modate big numbers of divers. But as more divers see what it has
to offer—and as dive magazines keep heralding it—Saba will soon
lose its innocence. Fortunately, the government has recently declared the entire island to 200 feet below the highwater mark the
Saba Marine Park—to prevent the looting and souvenir hunting
that have ravaged the more popular dive sites elsewhere in the
Caribbean.

There are two major dive operations on Saba: Saba Deep and Sea
Saba. Saba Deep Dive Center (011-599-4) 63347, fax (011-599-4),
63397 owned by Mike Meyers (and not to be confused with the
Wayne's World Mike Meyers), is conveniently located in Fort Bay
(address P.O. Box 22, Saba, N.A.), the center of all boating activity
on the island. Unfortunately, the "harbor," rebuilt after Hurricane
Hugo, is just plain ugly. There is no village here, just a rock and
cement pier that also serves as a breakwater. An upwind gravel
crusher (which grinds rocks into sand for other islands' beaches and
cement) sends clouds of grayish-white powder into the air, coating
everything in sight with layers of dust. That aside, there is a new café
called In Too Deep that is a fun place to hang out with a Heineken
and play dominoes or study dive tables. The shop has two decent-
sized boats (18 feet and 20 feet), a compressor, and will rent out all
necessary gear, including an underwater video camera to record
your dive experience. A two-tank dive (the norm) costs $80 U.S.
Mike also offers resort courses ($50 U.S.) and with advance notice
will conduct a PADI certification course ($375 U.S.). Located next
to Saba Deep is the island's new decompression chamber. This
makes the sport safer for all on Saba.

Sea Saba Dive Center (011-599-4) 62246, fax (011-599-4) 62362 is
the best dive operation in town. Joan and Lou Bourque have gone
all out to become *the* dive center of Saba, with a modern, attractive
shop, new and well-maintained equipment, and a complete package
worked out with the Captain's Quarters and Juliana's. This includes
dives, equipment, taxis (which can cost a lot when negotiated sepa-
rately), all meals, accommodations, taxes, and service. The
Bourques throw a rum punch party for their group and sponsor
such things as slide shows, marine biology seminars, and lessons in
underwater photography. Prices range from $745 U.S. to $910 U.S.
per person (airfare extra), depending on accommodations and time
of year. They also will assist in other recreational activities like
hiking and fishing expeditions. If the above is not enough to lure
you to Lou and Joan's operation, they offer a free package—with

groups of more than six the seventh person goes free. So if you can pull a group of six friends together, you've got it made.

Sea Saba has 2 covered dive boats (40 and 38 feet). A 2-tank dive costs $85 not including mask, fins, regulator, and BC. A resort course is $75 U.S. and certification $350; both prices include all gear.

There are twenty-six known dive sites that rim the Saba coastline and probably just as many yet to be discovered. Diving as a sport is relatively new to the island, so there is still territory to be explored. Also, the current spots are so good that the incentive to find more is low. Of particular interest are the deep dives, where you really feel like you've entered another realm. The ones named Diamond Rock, Shark Shoals, Third Encounter, and Outer Limits are the most spectacular. The shallow dives, while not quite as profound, are exceptional and longer. On my first shallow dive I saw a shark swimming right at me. Staying calm and thinking, "Oh, it's a shark," I turned to Ed Arnold (my diving instructor), who wrote on his tablet, "Nurse shark—not dangerous." Somehow I already knew that, especially when he swam right by without showing the slightest interest. (We later were able to swim within three feet of him while he was resting on the bottom, until he decided we were too close and swam away.)

There are so many great dives on Saba that it's hard to pick a favorite. But if I must, it would have to be Third Encounter. This dive takes you down 110 feet to a plateau about the size of a football field. Because of the depth, you can only stay down twenty minutes before needing decompression. The time passes much too quickly. As you descend, it doesn't seem like you've gone very far until a check of your depth gauge tells you otherwise. Once there, you feel that perhaps you've found Nirvana. Big groupers and bar jacks swim close—out of curiosity (and possibly hoping for a handout). A sea turtle swoops by giant sponges, oblivious to the bubbling intruders. Then the guide motions you to swim off the plateau into the blue water, to the surprise of all. As you follow him you think, "Maybe he's got nitrogen narcosis"—"rapture of the deep" (caused by breathing compressed air, which is mostly nitrogen, at very high atmospheric-pressure levels). Then you see the reason. It seems like an apparition at first, a fuzzy spire of darkness against a light blue background. Images of Devil's Tower in Wyoming come to mind. (If you haven't seen it in person then you probably know it as "the shape" in the movie *Close Encounters of the Third Kind*.) Close up, you can see the pinnacle is covered with brilliantly colored coral. Keeping a watchful eye on the depth (if you go deeper than 110 feet it will alter your available bottom time), it's fun to explore this wonder of nature. Unfortunately, the beeps you suddenly hear are the signal from the guide's watch indicating twenty minutes are up and it's time to surface. But the memory of this experience will stay with you forever.

Other favorite sites include Diamond Rock, another pinnacle that juts out of the water about 100 feet. From a distance, the rock seems translucent, a grayish mass that lives up to its name. The illusion is shattered when you arrive to see that what you thought was beautiful is really just a rock covered with bird droppings. However, you won't be disappointed with what's 80 feet below the surface. Circumnavigating this large structure reveals schools of all kinds of fish; here I encountered the biggest barracuda (about six feet) I've ever seen.

Two other superb shallow dives are Tent Reef and Ladder Labyrinth. Tent Reef is a long overhang of coral that harbors all kinds of marine life, including spotted moray eel. This is also a preferred spot for night dives as it's close to port and in the dark has a dreamlike quality. Ladder Labyrinth has the look of a Tolkien or Lewis Carroll fantasy. Coral heads resemble giant mushrooms and the barrel sponges would be a perfect home for the White Rabbit. There is actually a mazelike network of sandy-floored passages, between the "Middle Earth"-looking piles of coral.

In between dives, the island of Saba offers a quiet calm that is very soothing. You can hike up Mount Scenery (1,064 steps that just won't quit!) from the village of Windwardside. Queen Beatrix of the Netherlands did it in forty-five minutes—a very steady clip indeed. Some guidebooks claim you can go up and down in an hour. Hah! *Running* up and down with a five-minute break at the top took me an hour and five minutes. Down on the coastline, the Ladder is another series of steps that at one time was how goods— even pianos—were hand-carried up to Bottom (it took 12 hours to carry a Steinway).

Nightlife, as on any small island, consists of the local bars. Here it's the Captain's Quarters (pretty but not at all lively). Otherwise, ask if something special is happening the time you are here.

WHERE TO STAY

There are two options available for lodging on Saba. You can stay at one of the three inns on the island or rent an efficiency apartment from Juliana's or one of several listings for homes and cottages managed by Glenn Holm at the Tourist Bureau ([011-599-4] 62231; fax 62350). If electing the former, it's a good idea to include meals on a MAP plan, as the best places to eat are the hotel restaurants. I prefer staying in Windwardside—it's prettier, cooler, and livelier (if liveliness is possible on Saba). A new resort, the Queen's Gardens Resort, is presently under construction on the hillside above The Bottom. Plans for a resort/condo complex east of the harbor are on the drawing board and hopefully will stay there.

CAPTAIN'S QUARTERS (011-599-4) 62201, fax (011-599-4) 62377
Stateside: (800) 328-5285/(800) 328-2288
Windwardside, Saba, Netherland Antilles

This is the best, most "upscale" hotel on the island. It also has one of Saba's only public swimming pools (for hotel guests and bar patrons). The accommodations are in several restored buildings at the bottom of the hill in Windwardside. The view from the pool is fabulous: blue water framed by the green mountains and valley below. The bar is compact but pleasant and comfortable. The dining pavilion is outdoors. Unfortunately, they replaced the old wooden furniture with white plastic, a big mistake. The food is probably the best on the island, however, so try to ignore the somewhat tacky décor. There are ten rooms with private bath and balcony; many of them have four-poster beds.

Rates are PRICEY for singles and doubles (CP). Available as part of the Sea Saba package for less.

SCOUT'S PLACE (011-599-4) 62205
Windwardside, Saba, Netherland Antilles

Scout's motto is "Bed and Board, Cheap and Cheerful," which is an accurate description. It's a funky place, no doubt about that. The rooms are not squeaky clean but they're comfortable and adequate. There is a living room with VCR and an enclosed dining terrace that make the furnishings of the Captain's Quarters look like those of Louis XIV. But it's the cheapest alternative on the island.

Rates are NOT SO CHEAP for singles and for doubles (MAP). Available with the Sea Saba dive package.

CRANSTON'S ANTIQUE INN (011-599-4) 63202
The Bottom, Saba, Netherland Antilles

A quaint two-story, shuttered house in the heart of Bottom. The building was once a Dutch guest house, and includes on its guest list Queen Juliana. Built about sixty years ago, there is a pleasant terrace in the front and a restaurant that specializes in West Indian fare.

Rates are NOT SO CHEAP for singles and doubles (MAP).

JULIANA'S APARTMENTS (011-599-4) 62269, fax (011-599-4) 62389
Stateside: (800) 344-4606/(800) 223-9815
Windwardside, Saba, Netherland Antilles

These are very nice and comfortable efficiency apartments that are just up the hill from the Captain's Quarters. Each unit has a private bath, balcony, and use of the facilities at the Quarters. Saba's other public pool is here, along with the Tropics Café.

Rates are NOT SO CHEAP to PRICEY for singles and doubles (EP).

ST. BARTHÉLEMY
(ST. BARTS)

TOURISTO SCALE ▢ ▢ ▢ ▢ ▢ ▢ 6

Years ago, before St. Barthélemy (St. Barts, also called "St. Barths" by old-time visitors) became the ultraexpensive retreat it is today, the only bar in town was Le Select—a one-room affair jammed with memorabilia and the crews of visiting yachts. Jimmy Buffet's "Cheeseburger in Paradise" lyric got its inspiration from the hamburger stand that shares the outdoor patio with Le Select. Remarkably, the Select and Cheese are still intact today, a pocket of sanity on this isle of vanity. Step outside, and you're in the Caribbean's version of the Hamptons-times-ten.

There's no doubt that St. Barts is the most pricey public island down here. There are some resorts that are more expensive and more exclusive, but you can't pay more for what you get than here, especially when the dollar is down. Going out to eat on St. Barts— the major evening pastime—almost requires an armored truck. What was once a sleepy hideaway for the Rockefellers, Rothschilds, and Biddles has become the glitz capital of the New York and L.A. creative elite.

St. Barts is also the most un-Caribbean of Caribbean islands. It's almost as though the 15-minute flight from St. Martin traveled at Warp One and landed in Cap d'Antibes in the Med (St. Barts is part of the French *région* of Guadeloupe). Most shocking, particularly after spending time on the other islands, is the population, which is almost totally white. And there is no poverty—no one-room houses with water from a public tap. Perhaps this is why it's so popular with rich Americans—over 90 percent of the visitors are from the U.S. There's no unsightliness or destitution to make them feel guilty about enjoying their wealth. The French themselves find

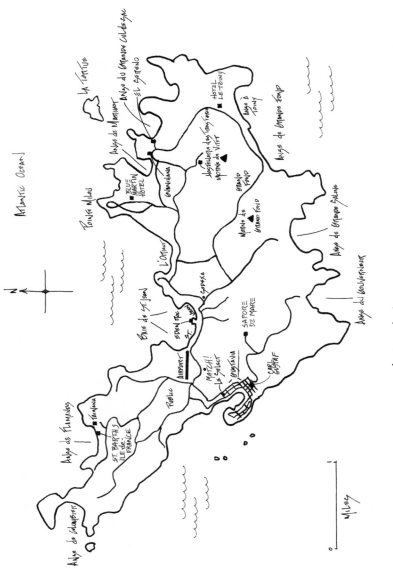

ST. BARTS

Atlantic Ocean

CARIBBEAN SEA

Anse de Colombier

Anse de Flamands

St. Barth's Ile de France

Fanvana

Public

Anse du Grande Cul-de-sac

La Tortue

Anse de Marigot

El Sereno

Pointe Milou

Blue Martin Hotel

Colonihana

Hotel Le Toiny

Hostellerie des Trois Forces
Morne de Vitet

Anse à Toiny

Anse de Grande Fond

Grand Fond

Morne de Grand Fond

L'Orient

Baie de St. Jean

Eden Roc
St.

Saporxa

Anse de Grande Saline

Airport

Match! Le Select
Gustavia

Sapore de Mare

Anse du Gouverneur

Carl Gustaf

Anse de Grande Fond

N

Miles

0   1

St. Barts too expensive, although when the rates go down around Easter, there's an influx of Parisians.

This hilly island is tiny—not even ten square miles. Most of the terrain is fairly dry and developed. This is not a place for enthusiasts of the wild kingdom. Most activity centers on the water, the stomach, and the right side of the brain. There are twenty-two beaches—six are quite good, one is nude. There are over 50 restaurants, most specializing in *cuisine gastronomique*, which is basically French food with Créole flourishes. And there are several bars and cafés, places to see and be seen, and a tiny disco called Le Petit Club. (The old disco, Autour du Rocher, burnt down and was not rebuilt. Lightning in the tropics?)

People say they come to St. Barts to get away from it all. Hah! One of the main attractions of the island is running into other people you know from the States. A prime example is Christmas here, the hottest ticket you can find in the Caribbean. Everyone who is anyone is on the island, at someone's house—never at a hotel. Life consists of house-hopping and dinner parties. Celebrity name-dropping is the name of the game. By day, many hang out at their pools while the more adventurous may go to a beach.

When I came here six years ago, I was really put off by all of this attitude and sheer fabulousness which was St. Barts. It was just too much. Now, on my return, I like the island a whole lot better. Maybe it's changed (it doesn't seem quite so ultrachic, attitudinal, and fabulous as it used to be), maybe I've changed (I'm older), but whatever happened, it's actually a great island to visit—if you can afford it. St. Barts still takes a Swiss bank account to stay here. That has not changed.

THE BRIEFEST HISTORY

St. Barts was first settled by the Ciboney about 1000 B.C., then the Arawaks around A.D. 200. The Caribs invaded and conquered in the tenth century, and called the island *Ouanalao*, which roughly means "Bird Sanctuary." Columbus sighted the island on his second voyage in 1493, and named it after his brother, Bartolomé. But the island wasn't settled by Europeans until 1648, when French colonists from St. Kitts set up shop, hence St. Barthélemy (pronounced San Bar-te-le-*mee*). They were wiped out by the Caribs five years later. The second attempt to colonize, in 1678, took hold, when some French men and women arrived from Normandy and Brittany. Their influence is still present on St. Barts today. Many of these settlers were pirates preying on Spanish galleons, the most infamous of whom was Monbars the Exterminator. The island remained in French hands except for a period in 1758, when the British briefly took control. Then the ill-fated Louis XVI, to get trading rights in Gothenburg, Sweden, sold the island to Sweden in 1784. Again the British occupied in 1801–2 (it's the same old story) and, finally, after the abolition of slavery in 1848 (the virtual universal defeat of slavery throughout most of the Caribbean), St. Barts was returned by plebiscite to France in 1878 and the rest, as they say, is history. Today St. Barts is a dependency of Guadeloupe, which in turn is an overseas *région* of France.

St. Barts: Key Facts

LOCATION	17°N by 62°W
	15 miles southeast of St. Maarten
	1,693 miles southeast of New York
SIZE	9.6 square miles
HIGHEST POINT	Montagne de Vitet (922 ft.)
POPULATION	5,043
LANGUAGE	French, but English is widely spoken.
TIME	Atlantic Standard Time (1 hour ahead of EST, same as EDT)
AREA CODE	To call St. Barts from the U.S., dial 011 (the international access code), then 590 (the country code), and finally the six-digit local number
ELECTRICITY	220 volts AC, 50 cycles
CURRENCY	French franc (F), but most hotels, restaurants and stores prefer payment in U.S. dollars and will grant a discount for their use
DRIVING	On the *right*; a valid U.S. or Canadian driver's license is acceptable
DOCUMENTS	A passport or proof of nationality for U.S. and Canadian citizens is all that you'll need, plus an ongoing or return ticket
DEPARTURE TAX	15F
BEER TO DRINK	Heineken

RUM TO DRINK   Rhum Bologne
MUSIC TO HEAR   Any version of "La Vie en Rose"

GETTING THERE

Landing at the aptly named St. Barts Aerodrome la Tourmente is one of the most thrilling aerial experences in the Caribbean, topped only by the cliff approach of Saba. The nineteen-seater STOL aircraft (usually a DeHavilland Twin Otter) flies stomach-wrenchingly low over a notch in the mountains, then dips down fast to the runway. With trees and cars rushing past your window, the plane seems to bounce on the runway as the pilot hits the brakes so hard that you lurch forward in your seat.

There are several airlines that do this regularly. From St. Maarten's Juliana Airport, one of the Caribbean's primary gateways, WINAIR has at least four flights daily. AIR ST. BARTHÉLÉMY has the latest flight from Juliana at 5 P.M. From St. Thomas and San Juan, VIRGIN AIR flies daily, and AIR ST. BARTHÉLÉMY does on certain days (check schedules). AIR GUADELOUPE has daily flights from Pointe-à-Pitre, Guadeloupe.

GETTING AROUND

Of all the islands in the Caribbean, this is the best place to rent a minimoke. This is a simple vehicle without doors or windows and a soft top that can or cannot be removed, depending on the condition and age of the vehicle. Of course, there are other cars and jeeps for rent, but this is such a small island and the roads are good *(Vive la France!)*, so why not have some fun. Theft here is not a major occurrence, so having a trunk, etc., is really not an issue. You must be able to drive a stick shift, however. There are several international rental-car branches, including HERTZ ([800] 654-3001), AVIS ([800] 331-1084), BUDGET ([800] 527-0700) and EUROPCAR—NATIONAL ([011-590] 27-73-33) as well as smaller, local companies. Be sure to call ahead to ensure availability and to get the best possible rates.

If you just can't deal with driving, there are taxis available but they can get expensive if you plan to move around a lot. Note that

fares are 50 percent higher from 8 P.M. to 6 A.M. and on Sundays
and holidays.

If you're squeamish about small planes and hairy landings, just
have a few stiff drinks and close your eyes. Or, you can take the
St. Barth Express ([011-590] 27-77-24, fax [011-590] 27-77-23), a high-
speed catamaran (hope you don't get seasick!). The trip takes about
an hour and leaves from Philipsburg on the Dutch side of St.
Maarten (why bother with this, just fly!). If your flight to St.
Maarten gets in late, after the St. Barts airport closes at sundown,
you can arrange to be met at the Juliana Airport on St. Maarten and
be taken by the White Octopus ([011-599] 52-31-70) to Gustavia,
where your hotel will send a driver to pick you up; this costs about
$75 U.S. per person.

FOCUS ON ST. BARTS: EXPLORING ITS FABULOUSNESS

St. Barts is very small (only a third the size of St. Thomas) and is
split into two sections by the airport. On the smaller western section, there are two nice beaches—the Anse des Flamands and Anse
de Colombier. Flamands is really a beautiful beach despite its steep
rake and the presence of several hotels. Columbier, also known as
Rockefeller's beach, is more remote—about a half-mile walk from
Le Petit Anse. This is one of the island's best and a favorite of
visiting yachts. Besides these beaches, there's not a lot to see on this
side, except lots of hills, vistas, and valleys.

East of the airport is where you'll find most of the action. St.
Jean, with its beach, is the focal point of the island (even more so
than Gustavia, the capital). Everyone goes through St. Jean at some
time during the day. The beach features several hotels and restaurants as well as water-sports centers, and the area itself has the
highest concentration of hotels, restaurants, and stores on the island. If you're staying in a house (recommended), the beach here is
good only for meeting people. You'll find them to the west of Eden
Rock (the big promontory in the middle)—especially by the St.
Barth Wind School and the Filao Beach hotel pool. Off the beach,
the major people-spot is the shopping center at the east end. Plan
on having a café au lait at the ice-cream shop up the street just past
La Louisiane (skip the ice cream—that's one dish the French have
yet to master).

Heading east out of St. Jean is a very pleasant drive that takes you around a loop that winds through the hills and around the windward side. There's a very pretty, small beach on the right end of Anse de Marigot. It used to be fairly deserted until someone built a hotel next to it. The stretch of road that hugs the Anse à Toiny is very scenic, with hilly pastures rising up on the opposite side. Here you may spot some expert windsurfers at the "Washing Machine" break. Once you pass through Grand Fond, take a left at the sign for Salines. Go all the way to the end of the road (a salt pond will be on your right—and dunes in front of you) and park where you can. Follow the path and you'll quickly arrive at St. Barts de facto nude beach. Almost everyone here is either topless or naked, so you may feel uncomfortable if you don't remove something—even if it's just to swim. Otherwise your neighbors will think you came to gawk at them. It's not hard to strip down, just remember when you used to do it in the seventies. Around the point to the west is the other great beach, Gouverneur, a smaller version of Salines (and not nude). To reach it, however, involves driving all the way back to Gustavia and up the hill past Castelets for almost two miles.

Gustavia (on the other side from St. Jean and the airport) is the capital, where the four banks are located as well as Le Select. It's very pretty and very clean for a Caribbean capital. The harbor is U-shaped with most of the shops and restaurants located on the north side. Be sure to head up the hill and have a sunset cocktail at the Carl Gustaf, then stroll around, browse, then go in to Le Select and have a Heineken. Welcome to the real St. Barts.

WHERE TO STAY

For those in the know, which is what everyone who comes to St. Barts thinks they are, the thing to do is to rent a house or bungalow from SIBARTH REALTY, rue Général-de-Gaulle (B.P. 55), Gustavia 97098, St. Barthélemy, F.W.I. (011-590) 27-62-38, fax (011-590) 27-60-52. Renting a house will also save you a considerable amount of money on food, as you won't have to go out to eat all the time.

The woman to speak to here is Brook Lacour—the power broker of rental (and sales) properties on the island. She handles over 80 percent of the available accommodations, or over 150 houses. She and her husband Roger maintain a stateside office as well. Call WIMCO at (800) 932-3222 or in Rhode Island (401) 849-8012, fax (401) 847-6290. The mailing is address is: P.O. Box 1461, Newport, RI 02840.

Book as early as possible, especially for the Christmas season. The toniest section seems to be Pointe Milou—a breezy headland with some very *Arch. Digest*-type homes. Rentals for a week in high season generally run between $2,000 and $5,000 U.S., although there are some places to be had for more or less. Kudos for those who can get one with a pool. Many of the homes can sleep up to eight, so with a group the cost becomes less prohibitive. If you're not fortunate enough to wangle an invitation or a house and still want to come here, there are a number of hotels that are quite good and expensive. Even the low end will run you over $100 a night during high season. Since the last edition six years ago, there have been a rash of new hotels built on St. Barts. While you would think that the increased competition (and the worldwide recession) would drive the prices down, they haven't. Remember, this is St. Barts, where the motto really is "Why pay less?" Some of the hotels will cost you as much as a villa rental, so you should check out both options. There are some good values, however, which won't break the bank, including the Blue Marlin, Hostellerie des Trois Force, and La Normandie. Keep in mind that many hotels close in September and/or October.

BLUE MARLIN HOTEL (011-590) 27-76-50, fax (011-590) 27-82-72
Stateside: (800) 366-1510/(212) 477-1600
97133 Pointe Milou, F.W.I.

The Blue Marlin is a delightful and friendly cottage-hotel run by a very nice couple, Patrick and Patricia Quenet. Located up in the hills of Pointe Milou, the views sweep down to the bay from your lanai and the breeze sweeps up from the bay—a great tradeoff. There are 11 rooms, mostly 2 to a cottage, with high ceilings, pastel décor, louvered doors, white tile floors, air conditioning, TV, phone, minibar, and a good-sized bath. Best of all, each room has a boombox, a rarity in any hotel, so you can play your tapes or listen to Radio St. Barts. There is a very good restaurant, Comme en Provence, on the property as well as a pool and Jacuzzi.

Rates are VERY PRICEY for singles and doubles (EP).

HOSTELLERIE DES TROIS FORCES (011-590) 27-61-25, fax (011-590) 27-81-38
Vitet, 97133 St. Barthélemy, F.W.I.

Now this is a wonderful place, a New Age accommodation designed to take care of body, mind and spirit. Set high up in the windward mountains with views of the water to the east, it is St. Barts' cosmic alternative. Owner Hubert Delamotte, an astrologer in a big way, has designed rooms to match each sign of the zodiac. Each room is in a separate or shared bungalow with nice detail and gingerbread trim as well as special features to complement the personality traits of each sign. The Aquarius Room, for example, is water-focused with little color (because Aquarians don't need color—especially in the bathroom). Most of the rooms have four-posters and double hammocks on the porches. Currently there are rooms for eight signs; the remaining four may come in the future.

There is a pool and an excellent restaurant (with organic veggies) on the premises. The bar is very comfortable and the whole place is just well done and *not at all pretentious*, like so many other establishments on this island. Mr. Delamotte is also into yoga and meditation, and welcomes all lifestyles to his holistic retreat. He encourages all kinds of spiritual and self-help groups to stay at his place.

Rates are PRICEY for singles and VERY PRICEY for doubles (EP).

TAIWANA (011-590) 27-65-01, fax (011-590) 27-63-82
97133 St. Barthélemy, F.W.I.

Talk about accommodations with attitude, this place takes the cake! In all my travels, this is the only hotel that wouldn't even let me walk around the premises, let alone look at a room, even though I explained that I was a travel writer. There is no brochure or rate sheet for Taiwana, just a small white card with its name and address. And this is the only place I saw with mirrored windows on the nine guest cottages.

Located at the right end of the pretty beach of Anse des Flamands, the complex is small and insular, with a small pool, red tennis court on top of the new parking garage, and a color scheme of bright pastels. The interiors are probably very tasteful, but I could only see my own reflection when I tried to look in.

Rates are OUTRAGEOUS for singles and doubles.

SAPORE DI MARE (011-590) 27-61-73, fax (011-590) 27-85-27
Morne (B.P. 60), 97133 St. Barthélemy, F.W.I.
Stateside: (212) 319-7488
c/o Jane Martin, 717 Fifth Ave., 13th floor, New York, NY 10022

Perched way up the mountain from Gustavia on Morne Lurin,
Sapore di Mare (né Castelets) is worth mentioning only because its
former self was an institution. The restaurant is still one of the best
and among the most expensive on the island—it's close to Anse
Gouverneur and it's possible to stay here for around $100 per night.
While the rooms are very tasteful, there are better places to stay
that are much more convenient to the water and action. And the
triangular pool is about the size of a blow-up model from the
five-and-dime.

Rates are PRICEY for singles and doubles in the club accommodations and PRICEY to OUTRAGEOUS for singles and doubles
in the better villas (CP).

GUANAHANI (011-590) 27-66-60, fax (011-590) 27-70-70
Stateside: (800) 223-6800/(212) 838-3110
Anse de Grand Cul-de-Sac (B.P. 109), 97133 St. Barthélemy, F.W.I.

This too expensive resort opened in December 1986 on the end of
the west peninsula of Anse du Grande Cul-de-Sac. It's big by St.
Barts' standards and similar to the Manipany on the western end of
the island. Since its opening, the resort has expanded—making the
property seem a tad cramped. Everything is painted in bright Caribbean colors. There are two overpriced restaurants located on the
premises.

The best units are the oceanfront cottages on the bluff to the
right. Each has a tiled terrace with a fridge and hotplate set up
outside—vaulted ceilings with fans, air conditioning, queen-size
beds, wood and canvas furnishings, and terrific double-sinked/
bideted bathrooms. You can also get units with their own pools.
There is a beautiful pool/Jacuzzi/bar-cabana similar to the Messel
design of Cotton House on Mustique. A reef keeps the water calm
for swimming and snorkeling. The water-sports center (sailing,
waterskiing, scuba, and fishing) is located on the beach. The beach
itself is adequate—a short walk around the point to Marigot will
reveal the best beach in the area. Two hard-surface, lighted tennis
courts round out the recreational facilities.

Rates are OUTRAGEOUS for singles and BEYOND BELIEF for doubles (CP).

LA NORMANDIE (011-590) 27-61-66, fax (011-590) 27-68-64
L'Orient, 97133 St. Barthélemy, F.W.I.

One of the rarest of birds on St. Barts—the cheap hotel—this is the best choice for those on a budget who can't spend over $100 a night for accommodations. It's simple, clean, and run by a French family—a true *auberge antillaise*. Set in lush foliage, there are eight rooms—all with private bath and ceiling fans (a few of the rooms have air conditioning). There is a restaurant/bar on the premises and a pool with sundeck. Orient Beach is about 150 yards away.

Rates are NOT SO CHEAP for single and doubles (EP). *No credit cards.*

HOTEL MANAPANY COTTAGES (011-590) 27-75-26, fax (011-590) 27-75-28
Stateside: (800) 847-4249/(212) 719-5750
Anse des Cayes (B.P. 114), 97133 St. Barthélemy, F.W.I.

One of the original resorts on St. Barts, it sweeps up a hill from the beach at Anse des Cayes. For a long while, it was one of the only luxury resorts on the island; now there are eight. The maturity of the Hotel Manapany shows in its landscaping and gardens—it looks established. There are 32 cottages perched on the hill, and while the ones at the top have the best views, for those views you will have to climb up a fairly steep hill and stairs if you forgot something (there are golf carts available). If you don't want to climb, four of the cottages are on the beach. The rooms and suites themselves are not extraordinary but they are attractive, spacious, and very pleasant. All have the amenities one would expect from a luxury resort with a stiff price tag. However, one of the Manapany's strongest points is its service, which is friendly, very helpful, and efficient. There are also two excellent restaurants, the Ouanalao (Italian) and the Ballahou (*cuisine gastronomique* with Oriental flourishes). Facilities include a pool, Jacuzzi, lighted tennis court, and a small private beach.

Rates are WICKED PRICEY for singles and RIDICULOUS to BEYOND BELIEF for doubles (includes full breakfast).

HOTEL YUANA (011-590) 27-80-84, fax (011-590) 27-78-45
Stateside: (800) 366-1510/(212) 477-1600
Anse des Cayes, 97133 St. Barthélemy, F.W.I.

Just a few minutes up the hills from the Manapany is the three-year-old Yuana. A small (12-room) hotel nestled in the cleft of a hill with views of the bay, this is an efficiency hotel. All rooms come with fully equipped kitchenettes, which include microwave ovens. Rooms are spacious with lanais, white tiled floors, bright turquoise wicker furniture, and Mexican-tiled baths. There is a small pool with some very large iguanas that keep an eye on you. About 95 percent of the clientele here is American.

Rates are WICKED PRICEY for singles and doubles (EP).

HOTEL LE TOINY (011-590) 27-88-88, fax (011-590) 27-89-30
Stateside: (800) 932-3222/(401) 849-8012
Anse de Toiny, 97133 St. Barthélemy, F.W.I.

Le Toiny is very tony and is tied with the Carl Gustaf as the toniest place to stay (hotel-wise) on St. Barts. While it bills itself as a hotel, it actually looks more like a private club, with 12 villas—each with its own pool—emanating from the main building. Everything is sparkling new, as it opened in October 1992, and the whole place looks like a photo shoot for *Architectual Digest*. The villas are totally loaded and furnished in mahogany period furniture, including four-poster beds. It's as expensive as the Taiwana and one guest told me that after years of going there, he'll never go back there now that there is Le Toiny. There is an excellent restaurant, Le Gaiac, and a bar on the premises, and the most attractive staff I've seen in some time. The only flaw is a rather ugly brown pond at the bottom of the hill before the bay, which takes the view down a few pegs.

Rates are BEYOND BELIEF for singles and doubles (CP).

HOTEL CARL GUSTAF (011-590) 27-82-83, fax (011-590) 27-82-37
Stateside: (800) 932-3222/(401) 849-8012
Rue des Normands (B.P. 700) Gustavia, 97133 St. Barthélemy, F.W.I.

Now this place is truly fab, real super-royal-deluxe (after all, the hotel is named after a Swedish king). With a commanding view of

Gustavia's harbor—one of the most scenic in the Caribbean—this is truly an outrageously expensive place to stay not only for St. Barts but for the entire Caribbean (about $850 U.S. per day). Why pay less? The rooms are really gorgeous, with their own plunge pools and open-air parlors with oh-so-tasteful *and* comfortable furniture and, of course, totally loaded (including a fully equipped kitchen, two phone lines—one for your fax, which is provided—stereos and TV in both the living room and bedroom). Beautiful lanais with dramatically columned removable canopies frame your view. Needless to say (but I'll say it anyway), the sunset views here are awesome. There is a bar/restaurant and a small fitness center. Got the money and you want to be in a hotel? Go for it.

Rates are BEYOND BELIEF for singles and doubles (CP).

HOTEL ST. BARTH ISLE DE FRANCE (011-590) 27-61-81, fax (011-590) 27-86-83
Stateside: (800) 628-8929/(201) 265-5151
Baie des Flamands (B.P. 612), 97098 St. Barthélemy, F.W.I.

Located on the Baie des Flamands next to the ultra-insular Taiwana, this is one of St. Barts' new luxury resorts. Besides being very attractive inside and out, the big plus about this hotel is that it is on Flamands Beach, which is the nicest hotel beach on the island. Like the other super-royal-deluxe places, rooms here are ridiculously expensive, starting at around $300 U.S. per night (for the rooms across the road which don't have water views). Its primary competition are the Manapany and Guanahani, and the nice thing about the latter two is that most rooms have views, whereas here that's not the case. But then you have the best beach here. So it's up to you (you're going to have to pay outrageous amounts of money regardless of where you stay if you go the deluxe route). The building and rooms are very tasteful, as you would expect, and all the amenities are here. There is a pretty pool at beachside and tennis, squash, and a small but fully-equipped gym and fitness center. Water sports and horseback riding can be arranged through the hotel. The restaurant serves traditional French cuisine.

Rates are RIDICULOUS to BEYOND BELIEF for singles and doubles (CP).

FRANÇOIS PLANTATION (011-590) 27-78-82, fax (011-590) 27-61-26
Stateside: (800) 932-3222/(401) 849-8012
Colombier, 97133 St. Barthélemy, F.W.I.

Perched on a peak in Colombier, this is an expensive but low-key place to stay with great views and beautiful gardens and landscaping. There are 12 bungalows, which are tastefully done and have everything you need. Perhaps the best thing about the François is its feeling of informality. The public rooms are comfortable and quiet—a good place to read a book or have a conversation. This is not a pretentious or slick establishment. And the restaurant here is excellent. There is a small pool with a dizzying view at the top of a steep hill (you'll climb a lot at the François).

Rates are WICKED PRICEY to RIDICULOUS for singles and doubles (includes full breakfast).

WHERE TO EAT

With over 50 restaurants to choose from on this tiny island, you'll never go wanting for more, particularly because the food here is so good—and very expensive (remember all the food has to be imported from faraway places). Most of the luxury hotels have excellent restaurants, and I'd recommend any of the following establishments for dining: Hostellerie des Trois Forces, the Carl Gustaf, Le Toiny (La Gaiac), Hotel Manapany (Ballahou/Ouanalao), François Plantation, the Blue Marlin (Comme en Provence) and Sapore di Mare (see above write-ups for phone numbers). They are all in the $$$$$ price range, as are most restaurants on this island. Other recommendations are:

EDDY'S GHETTO, rue du Général-de-Gaulle, Gustavia, 27-87-00

Located behind La Galerie art gallery on the corner of Général-de-Gaulle and Guadeloupe in Gustavia, this is a gem of a restaurant, one of those that is excellent, but not expensive or pretentious. For this reason, it's one of St. Barts' most popular eateries. Serving Créole cuisine in an old, kind of funky-looking house, Eddy's serves dinner only, is closed on Sunday, and does not take reservations, so get there early. A MUST STOP! $$$ No credit cards.

MAYA'S, on the waterfront in Public, 27-73-61

With gorgeous views of the harbor and sunsets, this Créole restaurant directly west of Gustavia has great food, atmosphere, and service. Another MUST STOP. Serves dinner only, Monday through Saturday from 6 to 11 P.M. Closed from June to October. $$$$$

MARIGOT BAY CLUB, Marigot, 27-75-45

Set in an old Antillean house overlooking the water, this is an excellent seafood/Créole/French restaurant with daily fresh fish and lobster catches. Closed Sunday all day and Monday lunch. Make reservations. $$$$

LE SAPOTILLIER, rue de Centenaire, Gustavia, 27-60-28

Serving dinner only from 6:30 till 11 P.M., this is another excellent in-town restaurant serving classic French cuisine in a très romantique outdoor garden setting. Closed Sunday in the off-season. Reservations are required. $$$$$

L'ESCALE, rue Jeanne d'Arc, Gustavia, 27-81-06

Located on the waterfront on the south side of the harbor, this is St. Barts' best place for pizza. It also has a bar à la Hard Rock Café, replete with the Caddy convertible out front. They also serve pastas and other dishes, all at very reasonable prices. Closed for a month in the off-season. $$

LE LAFAYETTE CLUB, Grand Cul-de-Sac, 27-62-51

This is *the* lunch institution of St. Barts. The prices here are unbelievably expensive, try $60 U.S. for lobster at lunch, or $20 U.S. for a salad. But the clientele dining amidst the green and white tables here doesn't seem to mind. In fact, they seem to relish the prices. Again, why pay less? The food is excellent classic French, however, so if you feel like a splurge, go for it. It's only open for lunch. Besides the beach, there is a pool where you can cool off after getting the check. Reservations are a must. Closed during the off-season. $$$$$!

LE RIVAGE, Grand Cul-de-Sac, 27-82-42

Just down the street from the Lafayette, this is another great lunch *and* dinner spot with a very reasonably priced menu. This place has a nice, relaxed atmosphere and an excellent French/Créole menu. $$

LE TAMARIN, route des Salines, 27-72-12

On the road to Anse des Salines, this is a great place to take a break from the sun, surf, and sand for a little sit-down. Good French/ Créole cuisine in a garden setting. Le Tamarin is open for lunch daily from 12:30 until 4 P.M., and for dinner on Friday and Saturday. Don't miss their full-moon parties if you happen to be on the island at such a time. $$$

DON'T MISS

ANSE DES SALINES AND ANSE DU GOUVERNEUR—These are the best beaches on the island, the former is nude.

DIVING—For certified divers, the diving off St. Barts, while not terribly deep (about 80 feet max), offers bountiful marine life. Call the St. Barts Diving Center/Marine Service, quai de Yacht Club (PADI certified), (27-70-34), or Scuba Club La Bulle (27-68-93).

ST. BARTHS CUP AND THE ST. BARTH REGATTA—The first is a serious three-day yachting event held by the St. Barths Yacht Club at the end of January. The latter is four days of local fun on the water held in mid-February.

WINDSURFING—There are some excellent places to boardsail on the island for all levels. Call the St. Barth Wind School, St. Jean (27-71-22) or Wind Wave Power, St. Barth's Beach Hotel (27-62-73).

ST. BARTHS GYM—Need a well-equipped free-weight gym to keep those pecs pulsating? Try this place located at the St. Barths Beach Hotel. Like everything else on this island, it's expensive (100F for a day's pass, 400F for 5 days, 700F for 10 days). Closed on Sundays.

MATCH!—The best supermarket on the island, located across the street from the airport terminal.

LE PETIT CLUB—Located in a corner of the Côte et Jardin restaurant behind L'Ananas in Gustavia, this is unquestionably the smallest disco you will have ever seen. But still it has a disco ball, and owners Veronique Botte and Marc de Bono keep this place open nightly (weekends are best). It gets going late.

RADIO ST. BARTHS—At 98 MHz on your FM dial, this station plays great music. Call (27-74-74) for requests.

LE SELECT—Of course; at rue de la France. The bar across the street, Au Bar de l'Oubli, is also a fun hangout.

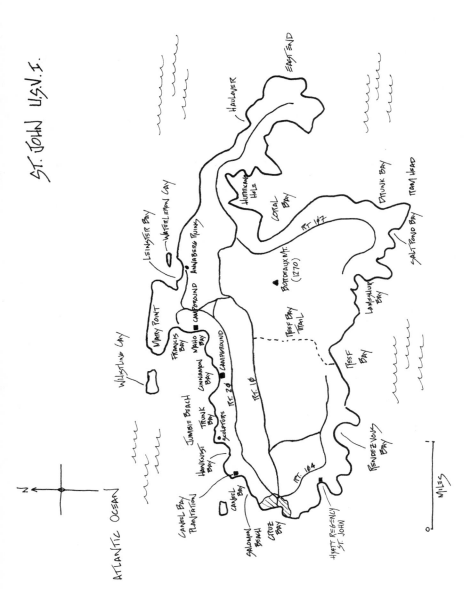

ST. JOHN

TOURISTO SCALE ◙◙◙◙◙◙ 6

At some point the Rockefellers probably owned a chunk of all this country's most beautiful property, including the land that became Yellowstone National Park in Wyoming and Acadia National Park in Maine. Can you imagine being that wealthy? Fortunately, they gave the land to the government for everyone's enjoyment (and I imagine a sizable tax writeoff).

In another instance of philanthropy, Laurance Rockefeller bought 5,000 acres of land on St. John in the U.S. Virgin Islands in 1954 and donated it to the National Park Service. The following year President Eisenhower signed the bill creating the Virgin Islands National Park. Today, it's nearly twice as large—having grown to 9,500 acres or about two-thirds of the island—preserving some of the most beautiful beaches and last stretches of undeveloped sand, hills, and vistas in the Caribbean for us—the above-average public. While I don't recommend either St. Thomas or St. Croix, St. John is definitely a must-see.

St. John is far and away the nicest U.S. territory in the Caribbean. Because of the national park, it is also one of the most unspoiled and handsome islands in the West Indies. There are some incredible snorkeling and swimming areas within an easy swim of shore, and trails to hike, ruins of the old Annaberg sugar plantation to explore, and a variety of programs conducted by the Park and outside vendors to experience.

St. John is also the St. Barts of the Virgin Islands. It's pretty, it's expensive, it has cachet, it's more exclusive and it's harder to reach. It is not, however and thankfully, St. Barts. People come here not to be français pretenders, to eat French cuisine or to see and be seen, but to swim, to snorkel, and enjoy the park. It has some of the most beautiful beaches anywhere as well as some of the last un-developed stretches of sand in the Caribbean. There are also terrific reefs for snorkeling within an easy swim of the shore. As with any beautiful and scenic public property, there will also be many peo-ple. While the more renowned beaches (such as Hawksnest, Trunk Bay, and Cinnamon Bay) are gorgeous, they can be crowded—at least crowded enough to ruin your idea of a deserted Caribbean beach. But there are smaller and little-known beaches where you still might fulfill your fantasy. These include Jumby Bay, Salomon, and Honeymoon Beach on the north coast, and Salt Pond Beach on the south coast. Finding these beaches may take a little patience and determination (see map), but they're worth the effort. The reefs are easily accessed and not hard to find (you can see them in the water from the beach). There is a marked underwater trail at Trunk Bay, but this is exciting only for beginners. Fantastic snorkeling can be found off Hawksnest Beach, Cinnamon Bay, and Waterlemon Cay in Leinster Bay.

About two-thirds of St. John is national park. The remainder is primarily composed of the towns of Cruz Bay and Coral Bay, on the western and eastern ends of the island respectively. To explore the whole island, it's a good idea to rent a jeep: some of the less-traveled roads are very rough. If you don't want to deal with driving, espe-cially on the left, most of your shopping, dining, and bar needs can be met in Cruz Bay—the biggest town on the island.

Just north of town is the Caneel Bay resort, one of three Rock-Resorts in the Virgin Islands. The veranda bar is a very pleasant spot for a cocktail. The beach at Caneel is not very large or private and is restricted to use by hotel guests (although the latter rule never stopped me before). But do stop by for a drink.

Besides the locals (who are much friendlier here than on the other U.S. Virgins), there are four types of visitors to St. John: the villa owner/renter—the elite who come for weeks or months; the resort/ honeymooner type, who stay at either Caneel (establishment) or the Hyatt (arrivistes); the camper or guest-houser—the naturalist or the budget-minded; and the cruise-ship or St. Thomas day-tripper— the touristo hordes. Fortunately, the latter leave on the late-after-noon boat, as the attraction for the day-tripper are primarily three beaches—Hawksnest, Trunk, and Cinnamon. Although they are beautiful, especially Trunk, they become fairly crowded with the types of people you and I are trying to escape.

THE BRIEFEST HISTORY

St. John was first settled around A.D. 700 by Amerindians (Arawaks) migrating north from South America. The Caribs soon followed and replaced the Arawaks. On Columbus's second voyage in 1493, he landed on St. Croix and laid claim to the islands for Spain. Nothing much happened until 1694, when the Danish West India Company claimed St. John from nearby St. Thomas. In 1717, Danish settlers (and their slaves) arrived and built over 100 sugar plantations and cleared 90 percent of the land. Slaves revolted in 1733 due to bad living conditions, only to be squelched, but the sugar industry continued to prosper until 1848, when the slaves were freed by Danish decree. With the lack of a labor force and the low cost of sugar beets on the mainland, sugar production dropped dramatically and most of the island went fallow. In 1917, the U.S. purchased St. John, St. Thomas, and St. Croix for $25 million. As mentioned before, following the donation of 5,000 acres on St. John by Laurance S. Rockefeller, President Eisenhower authorized the creation of the Virgin Islands National Park in 1956.

St. John: Key Facts

LOCATION	18°N by 64°W
	3 miles east of St. Thomas
	1,600 miles southeast of New York
SIZE	20 square miles
	7 miles long by 3 miles wide
HIGHEST POINT	Bordeaux Mt. (1,270 ft.)
POPULATION	3,000
LANGUAGE	English
TIME	Atlantic Standard Time all year (one hour ahead of EST, same as EDT)
ELECTRICITY	110 AC, 60 cycles—same as U.S.
CURRENCY	U.S. dollar
DRIVING	On the *left*; your valid U.S. or Canadian driver's license is acceptable
DOCUMENTS	None for U.S. citizens; proof of nationality for Canadians; passport and visa for U.K. visitors
DEPARTURE TAX	None
BEER TO DRINK	Corona

RUM TO DRINK   Cruzan Gold
MUSIC TO HEAR   Dancehall

GETTING THERE

Since there is no airport on St. John, you'll have to fly in to St. Thomas and take a ferry. AMERICAN flies nonstop to St. Thomas from New York, Miami, and Raleigh/Durham, and direct from Boston and Dallas; AMERICAN EAGLE flies from San Juan and St. Croix. CONTINENTAL flies nonstop to St. Thomas from Newark, N.J.

There are two ferries, one from Charlotte Amalie and one from Red Hook. The most convenient to the airport is the one from Charlotte Amalie, which leaves every two hours from the downtown waterfront from 9 A.M. to 7 P.M. The trip takes 45 minutes. The Red Hook ferry leaves every hour on the hour starting from 6 A.M. to midnight. The ferry dock on St. John is right in the middle of Cruz Bay. For more details, call Inter-Island Boat Services at (809) 776-6597.

GETTING AROUND

With plenty of taxis to take you from town to the North Shore beaches, you won't need a car if you're staying in town and just want to go to these beaches. However, if you are renting a villa or want to see the whole island, you will need a car. Most people rent Jeeps here, and they can be had at O'CONNOR'S JEEP RENTAL ([809] 776-6343), ST. JOHN CAR RENTAL ([809] 776-6103), SPENCER'S JEEP RENTAL ([809] 776-6628), and COOL BREEZE JEEP RENTAL ([809] 776-6588).

FOCUS ON ST. JOHN: CAMPING OUT

Camping on St. John is not your typical camping experience. First of all, the weather is about as perfect as can be—no cold, rainy days to put a damper on your fun. Next, there is the warm, clear water and palm trees right at your doorstep. Finally, you don't have to rough it; you can choose accommodations that allow you to be outdoors without the usual aggravations. Remember, mosquitoes go hand in hand with St. John. Here are your choices:

CINNAMON BAY CAMPGROUND (809) 776-6330, fax (809) 776-6458
P.O. Box 720, Cruz Bay, St. John, USVI 00830
Stateside: (800) 223-7637 or (800) 442-8198/(212) 586-4459
RockResorts Reservations, 30 Rockefeller Plaza, Room 5400, New York, NY 10112

Now you can say you stayed at a RockResort without spending a fortune. Located on the north coast of the island and on one of St. John's "big three" beaches, this well-managed campground is affiliated with the National Park Service. There are villas, tents, and bare sites available, all within a few hundred feet of the water. My recommendation is to stay in one of the forty villas on the grounds (by all means avoid tent clusters A, B, and C—there is no privacy). The villas are clustered in blocks of four, with the best (that is, closest to the water and offering a view) situated in the "nine" and "ten" blocks. The villa is really just a 15-foot-by-15-foot room, with two of the walls consisting only of screens with adjustable shades for privacy (the walls that separate your "cottage" from the one next door are made of concrete, as is the floor). Though very basic (remember, you are camping), it is actually quite pleasant for two people. The furnishings, while sparse, are comfortable. There are twin trundle beds (with linens), a table, and four canvas captain's chairs under spot lighting. Cooking is done on a propane stove or charcoal grill outside, and there is a cooler, water container, and utensils. Outside, there is a backyard patio and picnic table. The bathrooms are communal with cold water. It's rustic but functional and very rewarding, especially when you fall asleep to the jungle sounds you hear through the screen walls.

The campground has a commissary and a very attractive outdoor dining pavilion called The Rain Tree, where meals are available three times a day. There is a water-sports center on the beach, with windsurfing, sailing, scuba and snorkel gear available. The campground also offers a weekly dive package.

The park rangers conduct a weekly program of slide presentations, hikes, and snorkeling trips. Of particular interest is the Reef Bay Trail hike that takes five hours and leads you past old sugar mill ruins, ancient petroglyphs, and culminates in a boat ride back to town. You'll need reservations for this: 776-6201.

Rates for two people are NOT SO CHEAP for cottages and tents

(there is only a $6 U.S. difference between the costs) and DIRT
CHEAP for bare sites. Reservations should be made months in
advance and you are limited to a two-week stay. Sometimes there
are cancellations, so it's worth a shot to call at the last minute.

MAHO BAY CAMPS (809) 776-6240, fax (809) 776-6504
P.O. Box 310, Cruz Bay, St. John, USVI 00830
Stateside: (800) 392-9004/(212) 472-9453

Of the two campgrounds, Maho Bay is smaller, more intimate, and
more deluxe. It's also the place I would stay if I had a choice
between the two. Situated about eight miles out of Cruz Bay and a
few miles past Cinnamon Bay, it consists of tented cottages connected by a series of wooden walkways à la Fire Island. Each unit
has a view of the bay (the best views are on the Skyline Trail—but
they're a hike from the beach) or the dense vegetation, which provides privacy. There are double beds (or twins) with linens, electricity, reading lights, a convertible couch, table and chairs, a cooler,
utensils, a porch with deck chairs, and Coleman stove. Like Cinnamon Bay, the bathrooms are communal (cold-water showers, remember you're camping).

The friendly management here is very ecology-minded, hence the
boardwalks so as to not disturb the ground growth, the organic
toilets to save water, and the help-yourself herb garden. The clientele is very nature-oriented, New Agey, or escapist. Male employees
wear bandannas on their heads, female employees wear Indian-print
dresses. The campground is surrounded by national park, so there's
lots of room and ample opportunity to commune with nature.
There is an open-air dining pavilion and breakfast and dinner are
available daily. A small, expensive commissary is on the grounds
for that quart of milk you forgot to buy at the supermarket in Cruz
Bay. Maho Bay has its own beach and a fully equipped water-sports
and activities center. Self-help groups often hold retreats here.

Rates are NOT SO CHEAP for two people (EP). Reservations
should be made months in advance.

WHERE TO STAY

Besides the campgrounds, there are a lot of options for accommodations on St. John. The rapid development of the southwestern

part of the island over the last ten years has added lots of private villas and condos for rent and the Hyatt Regency–Virgin Grand Estates development. There are three relatively inexpensive guest houses in Cruz Bay and, of course, there is Caneel Bay. But the best way to go here is to rent a villa.

VILLA RENTALS

PRIVATE HOMES FOR PRIVATE VACATIONS (809) 776-6876
Mamey Peak, St. John, USVI 00831

Mary Phyllis Nogueira has a great selection of homes and villas, some with pools and/or stunning views. Jeeps too. Ask for Sago Palms—it has incredible views.

CATERED TO (809) 776-6641
P.O. Box 704, St. John, USVI 00831

Eileen Sundra rents homes and villas for two to ten people, at all levels of luxury, including pools.

ST. JOHN PROPERTIES INC. (809) 776-7223, fax (809) 776-6192
P.O. Box 1299, Cruz Bay, St. John, USVI 00831

A full-service real estate office with short- and long-term rentals.

CARIBBEAN VILLAS & RESORTS (809) 776-6152
Stateside: (800) 338-0987
P.O. Box 458, Cruz Bay, St. John, USVI 00831

Homes, villas, and condos for rent—some are very sought after, so reserve early.

THE RESORTS

CANEEL BAY (809) 776-6111, fax (809) 776-2030
Stateside and Canada: (800) 223-7637
Virgin Islands National Park (P.O. Box 720, Cruz Bay), St. John, USVI 00831-0720

The original RockResort, developed by Laurance Rockefeller in the fifties, this is one of the grandes dames of luxury resorts in the Caribbean. The ambience here is low-key and the clientele sophisticated and tony. Ensconced on a 170-acre peninsula of the primest of St. John real estate, the 171-guest-room resort is spaciously and subtly laid out on the property. There are seven beaches on the property, three of which are just for hotel guests. Rooms are in two-story buildings, where two walls are just screened louvres—to allow the tradewinds to blow through (this is one of the few luxury resorts without air conditioning). The rooms do have ceiling fans as well as tiled floors and attractive décor in shades of khaki and brightly colored upholstery. There are 3 restaurants, 11 tennis courts, a pool, and several bars.

Rates are RIDICULOUS to BEYOND BELIEF for singles and doubles (EP). There are several packages available.

HYATT REGENCY ST. JOHN (809) 776-7171, fax (809) 775-3858
Stateside: (800) 233-1234
Great Cruz Bay (P.O. Box 8310, Cruz Bay), St. John, USVI 00831

The former Virgin Grand, Hyatt took over management of the property in 1990 and has made it a strikingly different (sort of the difference between old money and nouveau riche—it's the mauve leather sofas in the lobby) but very pleasant alternative to Caneel Bay (people who need air conditioning will want to stay here). There are 285 guest rooms, making this the largest resort by far on St. John. The resort is nestled on a hillside and beach of Great Cruz Bay. There are lots of boats in the harbor and the beach itself is okay (Caneel's location and beaches are much prettier). The rooms are nicely appointed, with all the standard Hyatt amenities. There are four restaurants, room service, and two bars. Kids have the "Camp Hyatt" program, which gets them out of their parents' hair—a definite plus.

Rates are RIDICULOUS to OUTRAGEOUS for singles and doubles (EP).

GALLOWS POINT (809) 776-6582, no fax
Stateside: (800) 732-6747/(216) 237-7158
Suite St. John, Gallows Point, Cruz Bay, St. John, USVI 00831

If you want to rent a condo on the water with a sunset view, this place has 60 units for rent. There are fab views from the lanai of sunsets and St. Thomas, with the loft units being the best and most spacious. Units come with VCRs, a bartender—stainless-steel blender (the best for making piña coladas), quarry tile floors, and are attractively decorated—a hard thing to find in a condo. There is a small but sunny pool and no beach—but there is great snorkeling in front.

Rates are WICKED PRICEY to RIDICULOUS for singles and doubles (EP).

THE GUEST HOUSES

THE CRUZ INN (809) 776-7688, no fax
Stateside: (800) 666-7688
P.O. Box 566, Cruz Bay, St. John, USVI 00831

This is a cute little guest house with simple, clean rooms and a bar and patio for hanging out. Rooms have ceiling fans (it does get hot in Cruz Bay) and share a bath, while the housekeeping units have private baths. Its location is within walking distance of town and the Paradise Gym. The friendly manageress is very helpful.

Rates are NOT SO CHEAP for singles and doubles (CP).

THE INN AT TAMARIND COURT (809) 776-6378, no fax
Stateside: (800) 221-1637
P.O. Box 350, Cruz Bay, St. John, USVI 00831

This is a funky but all right guest house on a busy street—so it can get noisy. There are 20 clean, simple rooms. The best are on the second floor, as they have high ceilings and are more airy and spacious, but the rooms on the ground floor have air conditioning, so you decide. There is a courtyard bar and excellent Créole restaurant called Etta's. A steel band plays here on Mondays and Saturdays.

Rates are NOT SO CHEAP for single and doubles (CP).

THE RAINTREE INN (809) 776-7449, same for fax
Stateside: (800) 666-7449
P.O. Box 566, Cruz Bay, St. John, USVI 00831

Located right in town a few blocks from the water and in a relatively quiet spot, this place reminds me of a ski lodge. The rooms, all with private bath, are very woody (wood walls, floors, etc.) and there are both rooms and efficiencies available. The best rooms are on the top floor. The efficiencies are spacious (with high ceilings) and comfortable. All units are air-conditioned, which is necessary because the mountains block the tradewinds and it does get hot in town. There is an excellent restaurant on the premises, the Fish Trap (it's closed in August, however).

The Raintree is a non-smoking inn.

Rates are NOT SO CHEAP for single and doubles (CP).

WHERE TO EAT

The last few years have brought some very good restaurants to the island. In addition to the resort restaurants, which are good but overpriced, here are my suggestions:

MORGAN'S MANGO, North Shore Road, Cruz Bay, 693-8141

This is excellent Créole/continental cuisine with very reasonable prices. For that reason, it's always packed, and fun. Reservations are suggested. $$

BARRACUDA BISTRO, Wharfside Village, Cruz Bay, 779-4944

The best place for breakfast on the island also serves hearty lunches and dinners in an informal, café style. AND it wins the *Rum and Reggae's* "BEST T-SHIRT IN THE CARIBBEAN" Award, so stop in, eat, and buy one. $

LIME INN, Lemon Tree Mall, Cruz Bay, 776-6425

Wednesday night is "Shrimp Feast," all the shrimp you can eat for $15.95. $$

ETTA'S, Inn at Tamarind Court, Cruz Bay, 693-8246

This is the best West Indian cuisine on the island at great prices. Live music on Monday, Friday, and Saturday. $$

PARADISO, Mongoose Junction, Cruz Bay, 776-8806

Set on the second floor with tables on a wraparound veranda, this is the best Northern Italian food on the island. Thursday from 4 to 6 P.M. is 2-for-1 Cuervo margaritas time. Reservations for dinner are suggested. Closed Monday. $$$$

THE FISH TRAP, Raintree Inn, Cruz Bay, 776-9817

With more than 40 seafood entrees and fresh fish daily, this funky restaurant is the best place for seafood on the island. Reservations are suggested. Closed Monday. $$$$

CAFE ROMA, Vesta Gade, Cruz Bay, 776-6524

Southern Italian cuisine and pizzas make this second-story eatery popular. Dinner only, daily from 5 to 10 P.M. $$

GOING OUT

Called "limin' " by locals, there aren't a lot of choices, but what does happen goes on in Cruz Bay. MORGAN'S MANGO (693-8141) is a popular bar to hang out at—try a Hurricane Hugo. FRED'S (776-6363) has bands on Wednesday and Friday. The BACKYARD (776-8553) has sports on cable TV, games and is a lively place to down a few brews. The ROCK BAR (no phone) has live music and dancing on Wednesday, Friday, and Saturday. SHIP-WRECK LANDING (776-8460), in Coral Bay, has a jazz band on Sunday evenings.

DON'T MISS

THE BEACHES—The best and least crowded beaches are Salomon (nude), Honeymoon, Little Hawksnest, Francis, Salt Pond, Lameshur, and Waterlemon Cay. The most scenic and crowded are Trunk Bay and Cinnamon Bay.

HIKING—The national park has 22 trails marked for hiking. The most popular is the Reef Bay Trail, a 2.2-mile hike (one way) to the south side of the island. Guided hikes by park rangers are available. The Ram Head Trail hike affords some dramatic ocean views (1 mile each way). Be sure to stop at Park Headquarters for info and a trail map.

DIVING—Both Low Key Watersports, Wharfside Village ([809] 776-7048), and Cruz Bay Watersports, Cruz Bay ([809] 776-6234), offer full-service dive facilities and all kinds of scuba instruction, from resort (intro) dives and night dives to advanced certification programs. Don't miss diving in the Virgins.

SNORKELING—There are some great snorkeling spots here. The best is around Waterlemon Cay (easily reached from the shore).

SUNSET DRINKS AT ELLINGTON'S—The best perch for a cocktail while the sun sets over St. Thomas, Ellington's is at Gallows Point, overlooking Cruz Bay (776-7166).

PARADISE FITNESS CLUB—Located on Route 104 just out of Cruz Bay, the club has decent free-weights and Universal machines. Call 776-8060 for hours.

MARINA MARKET/NATURE'S NOOK—The former is a clean, well-stocked and reasonably priced market. The latter is a stand near the waterfront that offers a good selection of produce.

A BARRACUDA BISTRO T-SHIRT—The Best T-Shirt in the Caribbean (see write-up above).

ST. KITTS AND NEVIS

TOURISTO SCALE ▣ ▣ ▣ ▣ ▣ 5

Driving around St. Kitts with my taxi driver, James Brown (no, the Godfather of Soul has not taken to driving cabs in the Caribbean—they just share the same name), I couldn't help but be surprised at how much sugarcane was still being cultivated. There were just miles and miles and miles of it. I commented to Mr. Brown about it, and after saying, "ah-huh" (he said this a lot, with emphasis on the second syllable), he said that on St. Kitts, you are always in sight of "the cane." That, and the towering mountains, which the cane surround like a green set of ex–First Lady Barbara Bush choker pearls. Nevis, not the cane producer it used to be, is like a baby version of St. Kitts without the cane. Both are beautiful if you love mountains, sweeps of green fields, and plantation ruins down to the azure sea.

This plantation bucolia also gives St. Kitts (né St. Christopher) and Nevis an appealing sense of peace and quiet. With only a few large resorts on St. Kitts, which are all concentrated in one area near the best beaches, and only one on Nevis—the super-royal-deluxe Four Seasons—there is no tourist-on-the-loose frenzy here (which can be so unpleasant). Hence the pace is *slow*, especially on Nevis and the northern two-thirds of St. Kitts.

These dual lures of plantation settings and peace and quiet attract a well-heeled and sophisticated crowd. It's perfect for those frazzled corporate managers who want a week to be "out to lunch and cannot be reached." With a plethora of restored and re-created plantation inns (see below), you can stay sequestered here on your plantation—stroll the grounds, loll in the pool, sip rum punches to oblivion, catch up on all your Anne Rice and John Grisham novels,

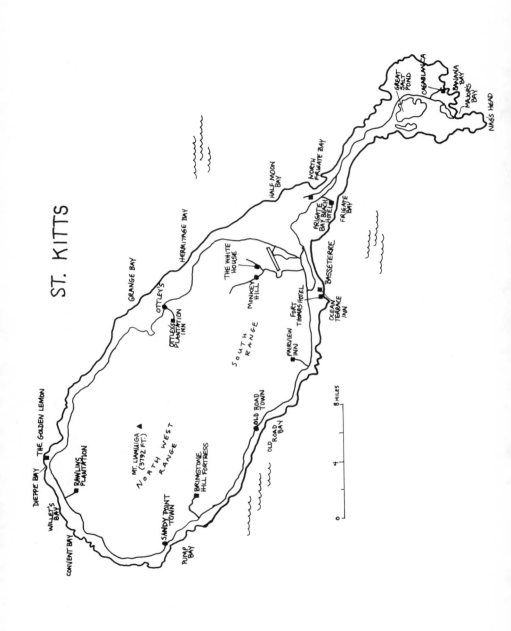

ST. KITTS

and muse about how much longer you can maintain the staff (what with the price of sugar these days). You may even feel strong enough to hit the beach or try a round of golf at the new Four Seasons' Robert Trent Jones II course.

Both islands are volcanic, and each have 3,000-foot-plus dormant volcanos which usually have a halo of clouds. Nicknamed "The Sisters of the Caribbean," they are separated by a two-mile-wide channel. Each has beautiful golden-sand beaches which are concentrated in one area. On St. Kitts, they are at the southern tip of the island. On Nevis, they are on the northeast side of the island. Each also has monkeys, the green vervet monkey to be exact, which is a rarity in the West Indies. The monkeys were introduced by a Frenchman and have proliferated to the point at which its easy to see them. St. Kitts is the big sister, about twice the size of Nevis and with about four times as many people. About half of the population on St. Kitts resides in the capital, Basseterre. North of the capital, the island is wonderfully scenic as three mountain ranges soar into the clouds. Their steep slopes gradually fade into fields of sugarcane as they get close to the sea. Baby sister Nevis is just a much smaller version. Sugarcane farming is not prevalent here anymore, but the miles of fields remain. Of the two, Nevis is the more mellow, but has become more "discovered" with the advent of the Four Seasons and the vacationing of Princess Di and her kids (they stayed at the Montpelier Plantation Inn).

A BRIEF HISTORY

St. Kitts and Nevis were first settled by the Arawaks and then the Caribs. Columbus sighted the islands on his second voyage in 1493, and named St. Kitts after his patron saint and the patron saint of travelers, St. Christopher (you've seen him—or used to see him—on the dashboards of many cars). Nevis (pronounced *Nee*-vis) was named *Nuestro Senora del las Nieves* or "Our Lady of the Snows," because the clouds around the volcano reminded him of snow. Snow! In the tropics! Chris, you were on that boat too long. The Caribs, fierce fighters that they were, held off the Europeans until 1623, when England established its first colony in the West Indies on St. Kitts. The French came a year later, and you can imagine that there were problems between the two. Nevis was settled five years

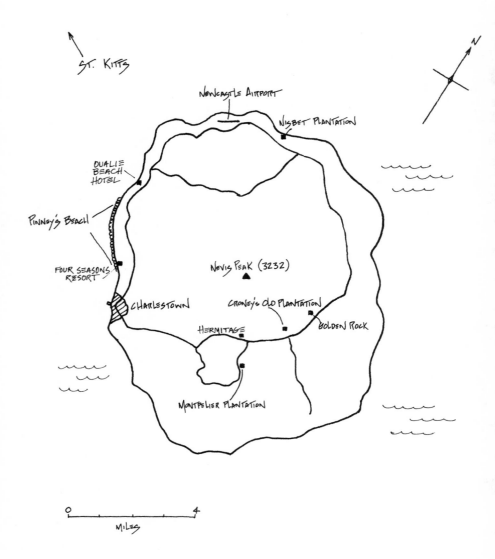

ST. KITTS

N

NEWCASTLE AIRPORT

NISBET PLANTATION

DUALIE BEACH HOTEL

PINNEY'S BEACH

NEVIS PEAK (3232)

FOUR SEASONS RESORT

CHARLESTOWN

CRONEY'S OLD PLANTATION

GOLDEN ROCK

HERMITAGE

MONTPELIER PLANTATION

0 ———————— 4
MILES

NEVIS

later, in 1628. Sugar production became big business, as did the slave trade. After a century and a half of battling and squabbling, the Treaty of Versailles finally deeded all rights to Britain in 1783. In 1967, St. Kitts and Nevis (together with Anguilla) achieved self-government as an Associated State of Great Britain. Anguilla soon broke away. In 1983, St. Kitts and Nevis became a fully independent nation. Under the constitution, Nevis is allowed to secede, and there have been rumblings about independence, but nothing definite was afoot at press time. Finally, Hurricane Hugo hit hard in 1989, especially on Nevis, where it demolished one plantation property, Zetlands, which still remains closed today.

ST. KITTS AND NEVIS: KEY FACTS

LOCATION	17°N by 62°W
	1,750 miles southeast of New York
SIZE	St. Kitts—68 square miles
	Nevis—36 square miles
HIGHEST POINT	St. Kitts—Mount Liamuiga (3,792 ft.)
	Nevis—Nevis Peak (3,232 ft.)
POPULATION	St. Kitts—36,000
	Nevis—10,000
LANGUAGE	English
TIME	Atlantic Standard Time (1 hour ahead of EST, same as EDT)
AREA CODE	809 for both
ELECTRICITY	230 volts AC, 60 cycles, so you'll need an adapter and transformer for U.S.-made appliances; some big resorts have 110 volts
CURRENCY	The Eastern Caribbean dollar, EC$ (EC$2.70 = $1 U.S.)
DRIVING	On the *left*; you'll need a local permit to drive (EC$30); present your valid U.S. or Canadian driver's license and pay the fee
DOCUMENTS	U.S. and Canadian citizens can enter with proof of citizenship and a photo ID; other nationalities need a passport; all need an ongoing or return ticket
DEPARTURE TAX	EC$20 ($8 U.S.)—no fee to go from St. Kitts to Nevis, or vice versa

BEER TO DRINK   Carib
RUM TO DRINK   Cane Spirit Rothschild
MUSIC TO HEAR   Dancehall

GETTING THERE

St. Kitts has Golden Rock Airport, which can handle jumbo jets. Nevis' Newcastle Airport can handle only smaller-sized prop planes, such as the 19-seat DeHavilland Twin Otter. To reach St. Kitts, AMERICAN/AMERICAN EAGLE flies via San Juan; BWIA flies direct from New York, Toronto, Miami, and London; AIR CANADA flies via Antigua; LIAT flies nonstop from Anguilla, Antigua, Nevis, and St. Maarten, and one-stop from St. Thomas and St. Croix (from most other islands you connect through Antigua). WINAIR and AIR BVI also make connections from the Virgins. To get to Nevis, you will have to connect through St. Kitts or Antigua on LIAT or WINAIR. AIR ST. KITTS-NEVIS runs charters from many islands, including Puerto Rico.

There are also two ferries that run from Basseterre, St. Kitts, to Charlestown, Nevis, in a 45-minute trip—the M.V. *Caribe Queen* and the *Spirit of Mount Nevis.*

GETTING AROUND

There are ample taxi drivers to take you around either island. You can negotiate for an island tour at a reasonable price, depending on the time involved. Rates to and from hotels are posted at the airports. Always negotiate, you should be able to get an agreeable fare.

Rental cars are in ample supply and will run you about $30 to $50 U.S. per day. AVIS ([800] 331-1084) has an outpost in St. Kitts (the only big multinational in this country) and there are many local outfits. On Nevis, I had good luck with T.D.C. RENTALS, Charlestown (469-5690). Be sure to reserve in advance, as most of the rental agencies are not located at the airport. This way they will pick you up (and you may also secure a better rate). Roads are in good shape here so driving is not complicated or difficult.

FOCUS ON ST. KITTS AND NEVIS: PEACE AND QUIET ON THE PLANTATION

Once upon a time, before Nutrasweet, no-fat diets, and Diet Coke, sugar was king. A glimpse into the life of the Caribbean sugar plantation during the last century makes this point very clear: big manor houses, a sprawling sugar-mill complex, fields and fields of cane, and presumably overworked, underpaid or slave labor scurrying around. Indeed, vestiges of the once-opulent plantations remain today. Windmill towers, mill foundations, and ruins of warehouses that once housed a fortune still stand on practically every island. Fortunately, the manor houses have fared much better, kept intact by the remnants of the plantation wealth that once was.

Recent interest in the glory days of the distant past has created a wave of acquisitions and restorations of these places. Many of the interested are refugees from the north, pouring money into the Taras of yesteryear and turning them into gilded resorts for the unlanded aristocracy of the urban nineties. And nowhere is this trend more prevalent than in the two-island nation of St. Kitts and Nevis.

WHERE TO STAY

There are no fewer than ten "plantation-style" accommodations on these islands, five on each. While they all vary in degrees on luxury, amenities and cost, almost all will give you the feeling of space, old-world charm, and relaxation. If its a luxury resort that you want, the Four Seasons on Nevis is the only AAA five-diamond resort in the Caribbean. Of course, there are a few other options for those on a budget. *Note:* I would avoid the Jack Tar Village on St. Kitts; it's all-inclusive, and I found it hideous and rundown.

ST. KITTS

THE BEST CHOICES

OTTLEY'S PLANTATION INN (809) 465-7234, fax (809) 465-4760
Stateside: (800) 772-3039 or (800) 742-4276
Ottley's (P.O. Box 345, Basseterre), St. Kitts, W.I.

This is the best place to stay on St. Kitts, one of my favorites in the Caribbean, and certainly one of the most romantic. It has one of the most stunning settings for this type of accommodation I've ever seen. Located on 35 acres at the foot of Mt. Liamuiga, where the rain forest spills down the slopes to the fields, the beautifully maintained grounds provide sweeping views down to the sea. The restoration of the white eighteenth-century Great House is excellent, retaining its charm but providing modern amenities, like great bathrooms. Down the slope, set in the ruins of a mill, they have put in a 65-foot spring-fed pool alongside a patio and restaurant. It's very pretty and tasteful, especially when it's lit up at night.

There are 15 guest rooms in the two-story Great House and a wraparound veranda on each floor. Each room is beautifully and simply decorated and has louvered doors and windows that open to the trades (there is also air conditioning for those who need it). All rooms have private bath. You can also get a room or a two-room suite in the two very private Stone and English Cottages or the two-bedroom Gatekeeper's Cottage (which has a fully equipped kitchen). There is a very comfortable sitting area in the Great House and a library and video room for those who want to watch CNN or a movie. The inn has one of the best restaurants on the island too, the Royal Palm, serving a nouvelle Caribbean continental cuisine. Their Sunday brunch is becoming island-famous. The inn also offers a daily shuttle to the beaches on the southern tip of the island.

Rates are VERY PRICEY to WICKED PRICEY for singles and doubles (EP). Add $50 U.S. per person for MAP. The inn also has five- and seven-day packages with meals—a good deal.

RAWLINS PLANTATION (809) 465-6221, fax (809) 465-4954
Stateside: (800) 346-5358; UK: (071) 730-7144
P.O. Box 340, Mount Pleasant, St. Kitts, W.I.

The original plantation inn on St. Kitts, the Rawlins also occupies a stunning setting on the north coast of the island. Situated about 350 feet above sea level in the canefields at the foot of rain-forested mountains, the views to Statia and the sea are magnificent. Its perch also guarantees a steady breeze from the trades. Like Ottley's, the grounds here are wonderfully maintained, with ample room to stroll and muse. There is a comfortable veranda from which to watch the sunset while sipping the omnipresent rum punch. There is a small spring-fed pool, a croquet lawn, and a grass tennis court for those inclined to get out of their chair on the veranda and leave the punch behind.

There are ten tastefully furnished guest rooms, many with antiques. One of the rooms is in an old windmill, and there are several more private stone cottages with rooms too. The Rawlins restaurant is one of the best on St. Kitts and was cited by *Connoisseur* magazine as having the best food in the Caribbean. Meals are served on the veranda, and there is a comfortable library/lounge where you can catch up on your reading. The nice beaches are far away, so if beaches are key, you may want to consider something closer to the south, like Ottley's, or Nevis.

Rates are WICKED PRICEY for singles and RIDICULOUS for doubles (MAP only). Rates include afternoon tea and laundry service.

THE GOLDEN LEMON INN & VILLAS (809) 465-7260, fax (809) 465-4019
Stateside: (800) 633-7411
Dieppe Bay, St. Kitts, W.I.

Another institution on St. Kitts, and a formidable one at that, is the Golden Lemon. It's been around for over 25 years, providing world-class service and luxury to its guests under the close scrutiny of Arthur Leaman, its owner *and* manager. A former decorating editor at *House & Garden*, you can imagine that the Golden Lemon is decorated tastefully, to within an inch of its life. Unlike the plantation inns on St. Kitts, the Golden Lemon is on the water. It has a black-sand beach, which is just okay as far as beaches go (the best are on the southern tip of the island). What is nice about the location is the sound of the waves breaking over the coral reef and the steady tradewinds. The grounds are rather small, so strolling the lower-40 is limited here. But the villas more than make up for any deficiency in space, especially the ones with their own pools.

The Great House has tons of character, and a big veranda on each floor. The spacious and differently sized rooms are very comfortable, furnished with antiques, and decorated, as I said earlier, to a tee. Beds are four-posters or wrought-iron bedsteads, there are antique armoires and the décor tends to be more on the traditional side. Room 1 is highly recommended if you want to stay in the

Great House (the rooms are also cheaper here). On the other hand, the one- and two-bedroom villas are more contemporary looking, but still very wonderfully decorated (there is real art on the walls). Furnishings are comfortable, tasteful, and eclectic—an African floor vase may sit next to a chintz-upholstered wicker armchair. Many of the villas have plunge pools and all are walled in for maximum privacy. If you want the best, the Lemon Grove villa 7 is spacious, has a great pool, sits behind a wall on the beach, and has a wonderful veranda with table for alfresco dining. All the villas have fully equipped kitchens, complete with microwave and dishwasher. Nice touches like fresh flowers daily add to Arthur's statement.

Besides the beach and the private plunge pools of the villas, there is a tennis court and a 40-foot pool for guests set amongst a walled courtyard with lots of tropical foliage. Adjacent is the very pleasant Brimstone Bar, and another of the island's best restaurants, the Golden Lemon Restaurant, where you can dine on the veranda or in the ornate dining room.

Rates are WICKED PRICEY for singles and RIDICULOUS for doubles in the Great House. For the villas, rates are RIDICULOUS for singles (with pool) and RIDICULOUS to BEYOND BELIEF for the rest. Rates are MAP.

OTHER OPTIONS

THE WHITE HOUSE (809) 465-8162, fax (809) 465-8275
P.O. Box 436, St. Peter's, St. Kitts, W.I.

Sitting high up on a hill overlooking the capital, Basseterre, and Nevis in the distance, this restored 250-year-old guest house is a very quiet place. It has ten tastefully decorated rooms with four-poster beds and Laura Ashley fabrics. There is a grass tennis court, a croquet lawn, and a swimming pool. Meals are served in the inn's dining room, which serves good continental/West Indian cuisine. The White House runs a beach shuttle service for guests. For the price, I'd rather stay at one of the three inns listed above.

Rates are WICKED PRICEY for singles and RIDICULOUS for doubles (MAP).

FAIRVIEW INN (809) 465-2472, fax (809) 465-1056
Box 212, Basseterre, St. Kitts, W.I.

The Fairview Inn is also considered a "plantation-style" accommodation, although it seems more like a motel to me and hardly stands up to the other choices on the island. I was very disappointed—I wouldn't stay here myself. It is, however, at least $60 U.S. cheaper per night for a standard room. There is a great house, but it lacks any sense of décor, as do the cottages; the furnishings are functional. The grounds also don't have that manicured look about them. But if you're watching your dollars, the Fairview's prices are quite reasonable and you will see great sunsets, as the accommodations face west. There are 30 rooms, all with private bath; some have air conditioning, others fans. A pool and restaurant/bar is on the premises. The beach is a 15-minute drive away.

Rates are PRICEY for singles and doubles (EP). Add $30 U.S. per person for MAP.

OCEAN TERRACE INN (809) 465-2754, fax (809) 465-1057
P.O. Box 65, Fortlands, Basseterre, St. Kitts, W.I.

A better and cheaper choice than the Fairview is the OTI, located in Basseterre on the water. In the nicest neighborhood, the OTI sits on a terraced hill and affords good views of the harbor and Nevis. There are two pools, a Jacuzzi, two bars, and a restaurant that is famed island-wide—the Fisherman's Wharf. All rooms are comfortably furnished and have air conditioning, private bath, and terrace. OTI has its own Beach at Turtle Bay, a short ride away.

Rates are NOT SO CHEAP to VERY PRICEY for singles and PRICEY to WICKED PRICEY for doubles (EP). Available packages make it cheaper.

FORT THOMAS HOTEL (809) 465-2695, fax (809) 465-7518
P.O. Box 407, Fortlands, Basseterre, St. Kitts, W.I.

Although it looks like a Days Inn, the Fort Thomas sits high up on a hill and enjoys great views of Nevis. This is a businessperson's hotel, so it does have a heavy West Indian clientele, which makes it interesting. It also is the cheapest place to stay that I'd recommend on St. Kitts.

There are 64 standard hotel rooms, each with private bath, air conditioning, phone, cable TV, and private balcony. There is an Olympic-sized freshwater pool, terrace bar/restaurant, and the hotel offers free transportation to the beach.

Rates are NOT SO CHEAP for singles and doubles.

NEVIS

THE FOUR SEASONS RESORT (809) 469-1111, fax (809) 469-1112
Stateside: (800) 332-3442; Canada: (800) 268-6282; UK: (081) 941-7941
Pinney's Beach (P.O. Box 565, Charlestown), Nevis, W.I.

It all came clear to me in an instant. I was calling Trinidad and had dialed the wrong number, which, in the Caribbean, is at least five bucks. So, I called the Four Seasons hotel operator to get credit, as anyone would (even people with lots of money do this). She laughed at me, she laughed! In that laugh was the definite insinuation, "You're paying over $500 a night for a room and you want a refund for a call. What a schmuck!" I was briefly humiliated. Then that age-old credo dawned on me, "If you have to ask, you don't belong." Welcome to the Four Seasons, where you'll happily pay through the nose for everything, or else even some peon like the hotel operator will make you feel insignificant.

The Four Seasons is one of the most luxurious resorts in the Caribbean and the only one with a five-diamond rating from AAA (they don't just tow your car anymore or make up those TripTiks—now they're international). This is *the* option on St. Kitts and Nevis for those who want a full-fledged resort (a beautiful beach where the attendants bring you cool spritz bottles and iced towels to beat the heat), 24-hour room service, golf, tennis, health club, two superb restaurants, water sports, and *great* service (aside from the hotel operator). On the last attribute (not the hotel operator), I applaud the Four Seasons. The Caribbean is not known as the capital of hotel service, but somehow the Four Seasons has managed to attain five-star service on a very mellow island like Nevis, and in only two short years! With that one exception, the service was strictly professional. All of this luxury comes with a whopping price tag, and just a touch of attitude, especially from many of the guests who stay here. The Four Seasons is not an old-money place, if you get my drift.

The resort is relatively new, having opened in 1989. Built on a stunning stretch of the finest strand on Nevis, Pinney's Beach, the resort is 350 acres big. There are just under 200 rooms and suites spread out among two-story, architecturally tame buildings (the resort reminds me of a nineties version of Dorado Beach). The rooms are truly fab and show off the resort's attention to detail. Let's begin with the huge marble baths, all with double sinks, separate shower and bath, separate head, and tons of big fluffy towels. The rooms are large and tastefully furnished, including mahogany-carved headboards and armoires to house the cable TV and VCR. There is a wet bar with an icemaker—a big plus—and an attractive rattan-and-chintz seating area and cushioned armchairs with hassocks on your screened-in veranda or terrace. Of course all the rooms have air conditioning and ceiling fans. Finally, there is a complimentary washer/dryer in every building—a very thoughtful touch—especially for a traveling man like me who encounters a laundry crisis every seven days.

Moving around the resort, the 18-hole Robert Trent Jones II course is maturing well and provides lots of challenges on its 6,766 yards (see the "Don't Miss" write-up later in the chapter). There are ten tennis courts, both all-weather and red clay, with a tennis program run by Peter Burwash. All water sports are available, and there is a pool and Jacuzzi as well. There are two restaurants, the more informal Grill Room and the fancier Dining Room. Dress codes in the main Great House are in effect in the evening; jackets and ties aren't required, but, ladies, no culottes please. To accommodate arriving passengers in St. Kitts, the resort runs a launch service from a very comfortable clubhouse in Basseterre for $40 U.S. per person. It's a nice way to arrive, as you check in at the clubhouse in St. Kitts and then the waiters pump you with rum punch. (I had so many I could have landed in China and I wouldn't have known it.)

Rates are OUTRAGEOUS to BEYOND BELIEF (EP) Golf, tennis, and romance packages are available.

MONTPELIER PLANTATION INN (809) 469-3462, fax (809) 469-2932
Stateside: (800) 243-9420/(804) 460-2343
St. Johns, Fig Tree Parish (P.O. Box 474), Nevis, W.I.

One of my favorites, Montpelier provides a wonderful sense of privacy and intimacy. If I were a famous movie star traveling incognito, I might stay here. There are lots of rooms, gardens, and secluded spots to lose oneself and snooping paparazzi. (Princess Di stayed here with the kids after her separation was announced by

Buckingham Palace.) And British owners and managers James and Celia Galway are always there to attend to their guests' (mostly British) needs.

An air of grandeur still permeates the Montpelier. The great house is a magnificent structure of stone with white-and-black trim. Inside, there are twin mahogany bars and four chintz-covered sumptuous seating areas. Handsome antique furniture dominates the interior and vintage paintings adorn the stone-and-wood walls, which are capped by a high, vaulted ceiling. Off to one side, there is a library and card room, and a terrace ideal for viewing sunsets through tall coconut trees as well as for candlelight dining. Through the doors to the left of the great hall is an arched stone loggia leading to a covered terrace where breakfast and lunch are served. Adjacent to the terrace is a lap-sized swimming pool distinguished by its wall murals. There are comfortable chaise longues and a great pool cabana/bar. I was very surprised to learn that the entire complex is only thirty years old, built on the ruins of the old estate. It looks authentic even to an old hack like myself. They did use the original stones from the ruins, so it's sort of real. And, of course, there is the requisite windmill tastefully landscaped with hibiscus and bougainvillea.

The sixteen newly redone guest rooms are well-appointed, with king-size beds, large padded swivel chairs (and individual reading lights—very thoughtful), fresh flowers daily, and the biggest bathrooms I've ever seen in these parts. The rooms themselves are not huge but comfortable enough and there is a veranda with lounge chairs and views of the ocean. A small family suite can also be rented for larger groups. Combined with the rest of the package, you will be very happy here for a week.

There are 60 acres on rising ground to meander around. For exercise, there is a tennis court near the great house and a new beach club on the northernmost and prettiest end of Pinney's Beach. A shuttle will take you there and pick you up. The inn also has a Boston Whaler with twin 40's on it for waterskiing and excursions.

Rates are VERY PRICEY to WICKED PRICEY for singles and WICKED PRICEY for doubles (full breakfast included). Prices are cut in half during the off-season (April 16–December 14)

NISBET PLANTATION BEACH CLUB (809) 469-9325, fax (809) 469-9864
Stateside: (800) 344-2049/(410) 321-1231
Newcastle, St. James' Parish, Nevis, W.I.

The overwhelming impression you get when seeing the Nisbet Plantation Beach Club for the first time is that of a fairway on the sea. The grounds are so spacious and well manicured that you almost expect a golf ball to land at your feet at any time. Very tall coconut trees form an airy canopy for the eclectic mix of cottages comfortably spaced across the lawn. And a very dramatic planting of palm trees creates a Champs Elysées effect from the great house to the sea. Very grand indeed.

The plantation house itself is very attractive and charming. Wide stone steps lead to a screened-in, sunny veranda with very comfortable seating areas, where you can stretch out with a book and spend hours undisturbed. And the bar is within finger-snapping distance for that occasional libation. There is an excellent library if you forgot your Jane Austen vacation reading. The dining veranda commands that majestic Champs Elysées vista I mentioned earlier, lending a regal air to the dramatic setting.

On the grounds are thirteen cottages of various styles, some octagonal, some in the Victorian/gingerbread mold, scattered about the premises. Each has two units, with veranda, twin or king-sized beds, vaulted ceiling with fan, vanity, bookcase, rattan furnishings, and modern bath. Some of the older units have four-poster double beds and like décor for those seeking "character." The new Premier units are very sumptuous with huge baths.

The Nisbet's big advantage is that it has its own beach. It's not the nicest beach on the island, but it is sand and salt water and you don't have to hop in a van to get there. An outlying reef keeps the water fairly calm for swimming. There is a new beach bar (drinks are pricey) and pool at the beach and an outdoor restaurant for lunch. Horseback riding is available nearby and there is a tennis and croquet court with racquets, mallets, and balls provided.

Rates are VERY PRICEY for singles and WICKED PRICEY for doubles (MAP only) but are reduced by almost half after April 15.

THE HERMITAGE (809) 469-3477, fax (809) 469-2481
Stateside: (800) 223-9815
Hermitage Village
St. John's Parish, Nevis, W.I.

Sitting high up on hill overlooking Montpelier and the Caribbean beyond, this delightful property of shingled gingerbread cottages is a very relaxed and casual place and a must if you're into horses. The

Hermitage maintains thoroughbred stables for those who want to ride among the palm trees and bougainvillea. The focal point of the Hermitage is a very comfortable and charming 1740 great house. In it there is a very good library, a comfy sitting room and bar, and a restaurant terrace serving good food. Around and up from the great house are 13 cottages in three levels of style, comfort, and price: hillside, deluxe, and luxury. For those who want to cook their own meals, the luxury cottages have full kitchens. Three great choices are "Pasture House" (hillside), "Twin Gables" (deluxe), and the "White House" (luxury). There is also a two-bedroom villa with its own ceramic-tiled pool called "Mahogany Manor," which sits at the crest of the property and is very private. All units are nicely and tastefully furnished and feature verandas with hammocks, four-poster canopy beds, and ceiling fans.

On the grounds, there are the aforementioned stables, a pool, and a tennis court. Because of the stables, this is a great place for families and kids. There is no beach or beach club, but transportation to the beach can be arranged.

Rates are WICKED PRICEY to RIDICULOUS for singles and doubles (MAP only). Rates for the Manor House are BEYOND BELIEF (MAP).

GOLDEN ROCK HOTEL (809) 469-3346, fax (809) 469-2113
Stateside and Canada: (800) 223-9815/(212) 545-8469; UK: (01) 730-
    7144 or (01) 602-7181
P.O. Box 493, Gingerland, Nevis, W.I.

The drive up to the Golden Rock is quite stunning—past stone walls and bougainvillea that set a stage for a truly magnificent great house to loom up in front of the car at any moment. So it's a letdown when you arrive and see only several rather plain-looking buildings and an occasional windmill. But what it lacks in grandiosity is made up for in the warmth and wealth of knowledge of its manager, Pam Barry. She's a great person and a direct descendant of the original owner.

Not to say the place isn't special—in its own low-key sort of disheveled way it's actually quite exquisite. The grounds, on 150 acres, are lush and verdant, with fantastic views of the windward side from over 1,000 feet above sea level. The low stone buildings are attractive and overgrown with vegetation, particularly the bougainvillea-covered, 180-year-old Estate Long House—where a courtyard serves as the alfresco daytime dining area and is the place for afternoon tea. The interior of the Long House contains a neat bar and games room with nets and ivy on the ceiling. The old stone walls of the dining room once housed the plantation's kitchens.

There are 15 decent rooms for guests in a cluster of cottages with verandas, king-size (or twin) four-poster handmade beds made of bamboo, dressing rooms, and baths. There is also a duplex suite available in the old windmill that the management promotes as the "honeymoon suite." It consists of an upstairs "playpen" with the centerpiece a king-size four-poster bed ("Oh sweet mystery of life, at last I've found you"). A circular staircase follows the stone walls around to the lower level, where two more double four-posters can accommodate whoever else wants to join the party.

There is a tilted tennis court and spring-fed rather industrial-looking swimming pool on the grounds. The hotel maintains facilities at Pinney's Beach (with restaurant and water-sports facilities) and at their own beach down on the rough-and-tumble windward side—watch the undertow. The Pinney's Beach location is not nearly as prime as Montpelier's, being located farther south nearer the crowds that come up from Charlestown.

Rates are VERY PRICEY for singles and WICKED PRICEY for doubles (MAP).

CRONEY'S OLD MANOR ESTATE (809) 469-3445, fax (809) 469-3388
Stateside: (800) 223-9815/(212) 840-6636; Canada: (800) 468-0023
P.O. Box 70, Gingerland, Nevis, W.I.

Run by a mother-son duo since 1981, this compact plantation east of Charlestown and north of Gingerland will have tremendous appeal for character-seekers. There are restored buildings next to the soon-to-be-restored dilapidated original ones—the combination of which is marvelous. Renovations first began in the mid-sixties, when, according to the current owners, the place looked like London in 1945.

There are 15 units built into the restored original structures, like the blacksmith's shop and carriage house, so each is unique in shape and style. There are rooms with touches of excellent wood craftsmanship, marble terrazzo floors, vaulted ceilings with fans, wide-board floors with carpeting, stone walls, and Jacuzzis in their own gardens. The honeymoon suite (it seems every place has to have one) has a 35-foot ceiling, a sleeping loft with king-size four-poster bed, a gallery above the living room for romantic strolls and a reenactment of the balcony scene in *Romeo and Juliet*. There is also a kitchen, wet bar, and dining room so you never have to leave or get dressed.

The pool is also unique, built out of volcanic stone that was originally the water-collection cistern for the mill boiler and steamer. It's 44 feet wide and 7 feet deep at the center (5 feet at the side). There is a cabana with a hammock and a view of Mt. Nevis.

There is a patio grill and bar where on Friday nights a steak and lobster buffet is spread out to the tunes of pan (steel band) music. The bar and grill room is actually the old plantation kitchen—the ovens are still intact. The card and piano room was originally the birthing room for the slaves. The dining room is in the old cooperage room, the library was the old disco (just kidding), and so on.

Rates are VERY PRICEY for singles and WICKED PRICEY for doubles (MAP).

Other Options

OUALIE BEACH HOTEL (809) 469-9735, fax (809) 469-9176
Stateside: (800) OUALIE-1
Oualie Beach, Nevis, W.I.

This is a great find on Nevis. The Oualie Beach is a small, unpretentious place on a nice little beach that won't cost you an arm and a leg. It's very casual and down-to-earth with a friendly staff (although we'll miss former manager Nigel Cosans—he's gone to greener pastures in Belize). The informal atmosphere attracts a local following, who mingle at the bar.

There are 12 rooms situated in gingerbread cottages along the beach, with your choice of studio rooms (double bed with bath and kitchen and optional connecting doors to form two- and three-bedroom suites); honeymoon rooms with four-poster mahogany canopy beds and baths; and standard rooms with two double beds and a bath. All have screened-in lanais facing west (and sunsets), mini-fridges, phones, and ceiling fans; cable TV is available. The furnishing are simple and tasteful.

There is a West Indian restaurant on the premises featuring some of the best dining deals on the island, and the bar serves a killer rum punch.

Rates are PRICEY for singles and doubles (EP). Children under 12 stay free in parents' room. Dive packages are available.

SEA SPAWN GUEST HOUSE (809) 469-5239, fax (809) 469-5706 Old Hospital Road, Charlestown, Nevis, W.I.

Located right in Charlestown across the street from the water, this is a simple, clean, and cheap alternative for those looking for a true West Indian accommodation or for those on a tight budget. There are 18 rooms, most with private bath, and a dining room and lounge area. Kitchen facilities are also available. Pinney's Beach is a two-minute walk away (Sea Spawn has a cabaña there), and downtown Charlestown is a seven-minute stride. I recommend the upstairs rooms (they're quieter and cooler).

Rates are CHEAP for singles and doubles (EP).

WHERE TO EAT

On both St. Kitts and Nevis, there are a number of options for where to dine. Among the best (and most expensive) are the plantation inns, including Ottley's, the Golden Lemon, Rawlins, and the White House on St. Kitts, and Montpelier, the Nisbet, the Golden Rock, Croney's Old Manor Estate, and the Hermitage on Nevis. Many of you who elect to stay at one of the above will have an MAP plan anyway, although a few allow you to dine elsewhere for a few meals. Let's also not forget the Four Seasons. In any event, the above inns' cuisine should keep you happy for a week.

Other choices—well here goes:

ST. KITTS

GEORGIAN HOUSE, S. Independence Square, Basseterre, 465-4049

Located right in town in a restored Georgian manor house, this is Basseterre's fanciest and best restaurant for continental Mediterra-

nean cuisine with a West Indian flair. Open for lunch and dinner
Tuesday through Saturday and for dinner only on Sunday. Reservations are required. $$$$

ARLECCHINO, Amory Mall, Basseterre, 465-9927

If you want pizza, a surprising array of pastas, and cappuccino, this
is the place. $$

BALLYHOO, The Circus, Basseterre, 465-4197

Good West Indian/Caribbean food in the middle of town at reason-
able prices. Closed Sunday. $$

NEVIS

MISS JUNE'S, Stoney Grove Plantation, 469-5330

Miss June, originally from Trinidad, has been living here for over
40 years and has a Trinidadian's sense of cuisine, combining Indian,
Chinese, Arabic, French, Spanish, and Créole cooking styles into
her own blend. For $50 U.S., you get an evening of food and drink,
from cocktails in the bar lounge and sit-down dinner to brandy and
crystallized grapefruit on the front porch. She seats only 24, so
reservations are a must. This should be a definite stop when on
Nevis. $$$$$

CLA-CLA-DEL, Shaw's Road, Newcastle, 469-9640

The best West Indian food on Nevis, including fresh seafood; Cla-
cla-del is also open late for the fashionably late dinner set. $

EDDIE'S RESTAURANT, Main Street, Charlestown, 469-5958

A casual restaurant for lunch during the week and dinner on weekends, Eddie's features primarily West Indian cuisine with American
twists. $$

OUALIE BEACH HOTEL, Oualie Beach, Charlestown Harbour,
  469-9735

Don't miss the fresh lobster dinners here for $15 U.S., or the
Sunday brunch reggae parties. The Caribbean pizza here is a knock-
out. $$

Don't Miss

ST. KITTS

BRIMSTONE HILL—Now a historic park, this is a massive fortress built by the British that earned the title "Gibraltar of the West Indies." It sits on a steep hilltop 800 feet above sea level on 40 acres, 9 miles west of Basseterre; it was built entirely by slave labor.

MAJOR'S, SAND BANK, AND COCKLESHELL BAYS—Located on the southern tip of the island, these are the best and least crowded beaches. Unfortunately, the Casablanca resort chain is developing Major's Bay.

NEVIS

GOLF AT THE FOUR SEASONS—This is by far the best golf option in the country (there is another course on St. Kitts). Designed by Robert Trent Jones II, the 6,766-yard Championship course undulates over the slopes between the resort and Nevis Peak. It's a par-72, with lots of water hazards and hilly terrain to maneuver. While it's a new course, it is being well-tended and is maturing nicely. The tough holes include: the 4th, a 394-yard par-4 with a long water hazard running parallel to the fairway; the 8th, a tough, 511-yard uphill dogleg par-4—this is the course's hardest; the 10th, another uphill dogleg par-5; the 13th, a par-4 with a hidden flag; and the 15th, a long 663-yard downhill dogleg, with the tee at the highest point on the course (and great views too). The golf-cart access to the 15th tee is as exciting as any hole, with hairpin turns and a steep grade through a ravine. Greens fees aren't cheap, but the pro shop does have some great hats and visors for sale that won't break the bank.

DIVING ON ST. KITTS AND NEVIS—There are several dive shops that may make a dive or two a worthwhile endeavor here. Try Pro-Divers at the Ocean Terrace Inn, Wigley Avenue on St. Kitts (465-3223), and Scuba Safaris on Oualie Beach (469-9518) on Nevis.

HORSEBACK RIDING AT THE HERMITAGE—This is a great place to go riding if you want to hop in the saddle (469-3477).

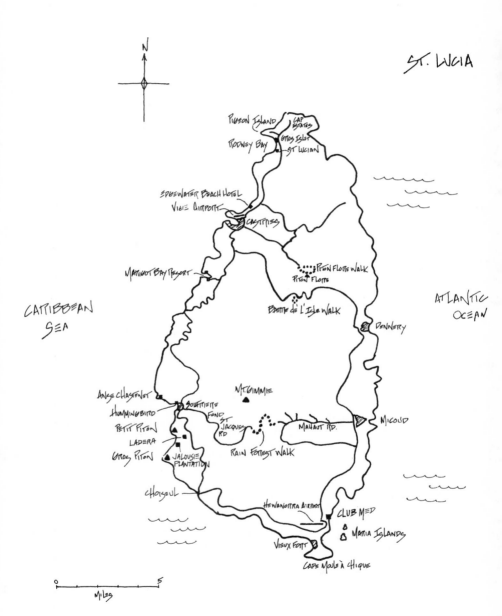

ST. LUCIA

N

PIGEON ISLAND
CAP ESTATES
RODNEY BAY
GROS ISLET
ST LUCIAN

EDGEWATER BEACH HOTEL
VIGIE AIRPORT
CASTRIES

PITON FLORE WALK
PITON FLORE

MARIGOT BAY RESORT

BARRE DE L' ISLE WALK

CARIBBEAN
SEA

ATLANTIC
OCEAN

DENNERY

MT GIMMIE

ANSE CHASTENET
HUMMINGBIRD
SOUFRIERE
FOND
ST
JACQUES
RD
MAHAUT RD.
MICOUD

PETIT PITON
LADERA
GROS PITON
JALOUSIE
PLANTATION
RAIN FOREST WALK

CHOISEUL

HEWANORRA AIRPORT
CLUB MED
MARIA ISLANDS

VIEUX FORT
CAPE MOULE À CHIQUE

0   5
MILES

ST. LUCIA

The Pitons are two massive volcanic cones which soar up next to the sea on the southwest coast of St. Lucia. The sight of them is truly breathtaking. They inspire. Well, at least enough to make you get your camera out and figure out a way to somehow squeeze them into the frame. There is nothing else quite like them in the Caribbean and they are just part of the beauty of this very scenic island.

St. Lucia (pronounced *Loo*-sha) is a very interesting place and it seems to be going in two different directions at once. On the one hand, its scenery makes it seem so serene and peaceful—like nothing eventful or worrisome would ever happen here. But on the other hand, there's a growing restiveness amongst the population for better conditions. This can be seen in the increased animosity of the island's political parties toward each other and in the increased hostility of some residents toward tourists. The latter may be due to the increase in tourism and the resultant bitterness about the economic conditions of the St. Lucian populace. Tourism is a big industry here, especially from Europe. Compounding this is the high unemployment rate in certain areas (over 35 percent), especially in Soufrière, where the Pitons are located. In all my travels throughout the Caribbean, this is the only island besides St. Thomas where I experienced outright unprovoked rage against me. This left an impression that has been hard for me to forget. The incident happened in the town of Soufrière, as someone started chasing our Jeep when we refused to use him as a guide. He screamed some very nasty things at us. This occurred on my first trip to St. Lucia in 1987. On my recent second trip, I didn't have any negative experiences. But the point is that I've heard of similar things happening to others in Soufrière, so enjoy the view, be polite, *ask if you want to take a St. Lucian's picture*, and be prepared to move along quickly. This shouldn't prevent you from coming, but you should know what you might encounter.

That said, St. Lucia is a wonderful place to visit. There are lots of options here in both activities and accommodations. There is plenty to see and explore in a week, as well as a fun yachty scene, good hiking, and some diving as well. With this depth, St. Lucia attracts a diverse crowd—a mix of Brits, Germans, Scandinavians, and Americans. There are large tour groups, adventurers who do things like climb the Pitons or sail the Grenadines, and the sophis-ticated, content-to-read-a-book traveler. The island has something for everyone, although don't expect it to be undiscovered. As I said before, tourism is a highly developed industry here.

THE BRIEFEST HISTORY

The Arawaks were the first people to settle St. Lucia. They pros-pered until about A.D. 800, when the Caribs invaded and killed them off. The latter tribe called the island "Hiwanarau." Columbus first sighted the island on his fourth journey in 1502 (though this is disputed), but it wasn't settled until 1605 when English settlers from St. Kitts arrived. But the Caribs drove them off soon after and again after a second attempt in 1639. The French came twelve years later and claimed the island. Of course, the British did not agree and the island changed hands fourteen times, with many battles and burnings. During one of the French occupations, the French managed to set up shop successfully in Soufrière in 1746. Sugarcane production was also started by them, along with slavery. Finally, after Napoleon's defeat, the island went to Britain for keeps in 1814. With all the squabbling, the sugar industry did not grow enough to compete with the other islands. By the time peace was established, slavery was soon abolished in 1838. Without free labor, it wasn't going to happen. Coaling steamships sustained the economy in the latter part of the nineteenth century and also led to the importation of indentured Indian labor (their influence can be seen here today). But that failed for several reasons in the early 1900s, and the island fell into a sustained slump until the advent of tourism and bananas in the fifties and sixties. In 1979, St. Lucia became an independent state within the Commonwealth of Nations.

ST. LUCIA: KEY FACTS

LOCATION	14°N by 61°W
	21 miles south of Martinique
	26 miles north of St. Vincent
	2,020 miles southeast of New York
SIZE	238 square miles
	27 miles long by 14 miles wide
HIGHEST POINT	Mt. Gimmie (3,117 ft.)
POPULATION	140,000
LANGUAGE	English
TIME	Atlantic Standard Time year round (1 hour ahead of EST)
AREA CODE	809
ELECTRICITY	220 to 230 volts AC, 50 cycles—you'll need an adapter and transformer
CURRENCY	The Eastern Caribbean dollar, EC$ (EC$2.70 = $1 U.S.)
DRIVING	On the *left*; you'll need a local permit; present your valid driver's license and pay a fee of $12 U.S.
DOCUMENTS	Proof of nationality and ongoing ticket
DEPARTURE TAX	EC$27 ($10 U.S.), except departures on LIAT, which cost EC$37 ($14 U.S.)
BEER TO DRINK	Piton
RUM TO DRINK	Lucian Rhum
MUSIC TO HEAR	Dancehall

GETTING THERE

There are two airports on St. Lucia. The most convenient is Vigie Field, which is very close to downtown Castries and close to most hotels on the island (between $10 and $12 U.S. in a taxi). Only small planes fly here: LIAT, AIR MARTINIQUE, HELENAIR, AMERI-CAN EAGLE, and other interisland airlines. The international flights and jets land at the newer Hewanorra International Airport, about an hour from Castries by car or taxi ($45 to $55 U.S.). WINLINK flies a shuttle to Vigie from Hewanorra and it doesn't cost much more than a cab. BWIA, AMERICAN, BRITISH AIR-WAYS, and AIR CANADA fly direct into Hewanorra.

GETTING AROUND

This is a big island and in order to really see it you should rent a car. The roads here can go from very good to horrendous, depending on how bad the rainy season has been and what side of the island you are on. Presently, the eastern side has the best roads, but they are working on the twist-and-turn western side. (A huge section of it was closed when I was there.) By all means, be sure to ask when you're renting your car where the bad spots are. The closure of the western road meant that you couldn't drive a loop around the island and had to backtrack. This added another two hours to the trip. Hopefully, by the time this is published, the road will be open.

There are several of the major car-rental players here, including AVIS ([800] 331-1084), NATIONAL ([800] 227-3876), BUDGET ([800] 527-0700), HERTZ ([800] 654-3001), and DOLLAR ([800] 800-4000/[809] 452-0994). As noted above, you'll have to purchase a temporary local driver's license and driving is on the *left*.

If you don't want to drive, there are taxis galore (they're expensive). Make sure you determine if a driver is quoting a rate in U.S. dollars or EC$.

There are also very efficient and very cheap minivans with colorful names that ply the major roads and blast dancehall. It's a great way to meet the locals.

FOCUS ON ST. LUCIA: THE DINGHY CRAWL/WALKING AND HIKING

THE DINGHY CRAWL

The joint was jumpin'. Already our table had been tossed out the window and a couple's unsuccessful attempt to execute a flip had smashed the stand-up menu in half. And it wasn't even ten o'clock. We hadn't even hit the other pubs—this one was just too interesting to leave.

It was just another Saturday night on the Dinghy Crawl—the wildest yachting nightlife scene in the Caribbean next to Antigua Race Week. But unlike Race Week it happens every weekend. It's called the Crawl because the festivities are accessed by boat on a rather small bay—just about every bar has a dock. You need not have a boat, however, to join in the fun.

The action takes place at Rodney Bay on the northwestern corner of St. Lucia, where the marina and Stevens Yachts have spawned a number of services, including no fewer than eight bars and clubs. Lining the perimeter of the bay are the A-Pub, Pat's Pub, Capone's, the Chart House, the Lime Inn, the Mortar & Pestle, the Eagle's Nest, and Splash (a disco in the St. Lucian Hotel). And then there's Gros Islet.

Gros Islet is a small town that borders Rodney Bay on the north. This is where the Dinghy Crawl weekend blow-out begins. Every Friday night, the town hosts what amounts to a minicarnival on the main street. You can't miss it, just head for the music.

An impressive PA system is set up in the middle of the town's major intersection, playing calypso mixed with reggae and disco. The street is lined with food and beer vendors. Smoke swirls around the crowd, making the scene look rather tribal. For EC$5 (about $2 U.S.) you can buy barbecue chicken with pepper sauce or lambi (conch) on a skewer. Heineken, brewed on St. Lucia, is sold in buckets for EC$3 by children barely old enough to read. There are roadside carts selling rum punch and the western end of the street is an easy place to find *ganja* for EC$5 a stick.

There are three other notable fun bars. My favorite is Scott's Café, recognized by the Cockspur sign hanging in front. The two-story building has the look and air of a western saloon. The upstairs has a porch that provides a great vantage point to watch the action. Across the street is the Golden Apple and down the road near the beach is The Wall. It has its own calypso and jump space as well as a garden with tables to rest for a spell.

The best action, though, is on the street. The crowd is primarily black St. Lucians, who are friendly, though the young males will try to hustle your money for almost any reason (except sex). There are some tourists—the bulk of whom are boat people. The town heats up around 10:30 P.M. and the action goes on until the wee hours.

Plan to sleep in on Saturday or catch some rays on pretty Reduit Beach (on the ocean side of Rodney Bay)—you'll need lots of strength for the second phase of the Crawl. The commotion begins at sundown, when the boat people have finished their chores and are ready to party. They begin with a few stiff cocktails, then hop in their inflatables and roar off to the dock with the most dinghies tethered to it. Watching them dock is quite amusing. The name of the game is rubber-baby-bumper-boats, as the objective is to drive your dinghy as close to the dock as possible—splitting the flotilla up the middle to the sound of vinyl squeaks and rope groans. Give your engine gas and let 'er rip. I've actually seen a boat plow through what appeared to be an impenetrable dinghy-lock and arrive at the dock without major damage. Getting back out is another ball game.

The current hot spot could be any of the bars on the bay. But at the moment it seems to be the A-Pub, where the owner's laissez-faire attitude is very popular among the charter crews who frequent or turn around at Rodney Bay. Here they can act out their fantasies, whether it be Fred and Ginger gliding across the crowded dance floor, or Hulk Hogan and André the Giant in Wrestlemania V. It was at the A-Pub (in a former incarnation at a different location—the A-Frame) that our table flew out the window (followed by my beer mug) and twirling couples wiped out several tables. The music is very eclectic, from the Andrews Sisters and Johann Strauss to Springsteen and calypso. The floor bounced so much you had to cover your glass with a coaster, *while* holding it, to keep it from spilling. Good humor prevails, and the staff seems to get a big kick out of the patrons' antics. On Sunday morning, there's a run on aspirin and bromides at the marina drugstore, so make sure you've brought an adequate supply.

If you're staying south of Rodney Bay, you can reach the Dinghy Crawl by taxi or bus, which is real cheap and a lot more fun. The buses are actually minivans with names painted on the front (Xterminator, etc.). They leave for Gros Islet (be sure to ask) from Jeremy Street near the market in Castries and will stop for anyone who flags them down. It's remarkable how many people they can hold. Calypso or reggae resounds from the formidable stereo, creating a convivial atmosphere. All types ride the bus, from Rastas to old ladies with baskets on their heads. The bus I was on had a flat that was fixed within five minutes—uncharacteristic efficiency for the islands. The buses run until very late on weekends and leave from the eastern end of the main street in Gros Islet.

WALKING AND HIKING

For those who love the outdoors but think camping is slumming it with nature, there is St. Lucia. This island, wonderfully diversified in vegetation, climate, and geography, has excellent and accessible trails that are both beautiful and invigorating. Yet it also has all the creature comforts necessary for a nineties' lifestyle.

These amenities are concentrated in St. Lucia's northwest corner.

Here you'll find the rather unattractive city of Castries, which does have most services you might want. A majority of the island's hotels are located north of the city, on a calm and attractive, though certainly not pristine, stretch of beach. There are also accommodations and resorts around the island's two other major towns, Soufrière and Vieux Fort. These have much more West Indian character and ambience than Castries as well as far more dramatic natural settings.

But the beauty of St. Lucia lies in the countryside, the villages, and its rugged coast and interior. Here the feeling is reminiscent of a more tranquil, unhurried era—a marked contrast to the bustle of Castries. Yet it's all easily accessible by car. And the visuals are truly phenomenal. The lush green expanse of the banana plantations, a cricket game on the east coast, the incredible Pitons, and the center's tropical wilds can all be experienced in one day.

While you can see a lot of St. Lucia by car, it doesn't allow you to get very close. Fortunately, there is a well-developed system of walks and hikes that enable you to do so. These access the entire island and can be reached by rental car, tours, and in a few instances by public minibus.

THE SHORT WALKS

For those who desire minimal exertion, there are three short walks cooled by breezes or the shade of the forest. Any one is within an hour's drive from wherever you are on St. Lucia, making the entire expedition a half-day affair.

In the north, above Gros Islet, there is Pigeon Island, connected to the mainland by a causeway. This is a very short walk with several marked trails around the point. There is a small entrance fee for the National Trust, which maintains the park. The "island" will appeal to history buffs. It was first used as a pirate's ambush point, then weathered hundreds of years of English/French squabbles, and also served as a whaling station and the retreat of an obscure English actress, Josset Agnes Huchinson. The visitor's center will have all the gory details. Pigeon Island will also appeal to bird watchers who, if they happen to be around after a heavy storm, may see a large number of exotic sea birds blown in from all over the Caribbean.

The second walk is right on the main west-to-east coast highway, between Castries and Dennery. It is a *very* short loop called Barre de l'Isle (about a quarter-mile long), and not very interesting. Another trail branches off by the picnic table gazebo to Mt. LaCombe.

It's a pleasant 2.5-mile round-trip walk that takes you along a ridge with some nice north/south views. This trail is also noteworthy because it is by far the easiest forest walk to access. Crime has been a problem on this walk, so be sure to get an update from your hotel before embarking.

The third walk is an excursion to the Maria Islands off the southeast corner of St. Lucia. This is the only place in the world where the Maria Islands ground lizard and the Couresse snake can be found. Tours can be arranged through the National Trust (452-5005) or the Maria Islands Interpretive Centre on the highway near the Hewanorra Airport. While you're in that area, there is a very short walk offering fantastic views of the southern end of the island on Cape Moule à Chique. To get there, drive through Vieux Fort up to the lighthouse and walk behind it until you reach a cliff and the vista point.

THE LONG WALKS

Muddy shoes are the vogue here. These walks are for those who really enjoy getting into more remote areas. Each walk will average between three and four hours, exclusive of travel time. Plan to carry some refreshment, wear cool clothes you can sweat in, and bring your camera.

In the north, there is a good walk around the northern tip of St. Lucia from Cap Estates. There is a path and Le Sport (450-8551) occasionally organizes tours for anyone interested. The headlands to the east can also be interesting, but in almost all cases you'll need a four-wheel-drive vehicle to get close enough. If you do try this, don't leave any valuables in your jeep and don't carry any—practically all hikes are in uninhabited areas.

Moving farther south to the north-central part of the island, there is an excellent walk at Forestière called Piton Flore. As it is located within the Forest Reserve, you *must* get permission from the Forestry Department before embarking (452-3231). This trail, actually a loop in and out of Forestière, used to be highly traveled but Hurricane Allan changed that, toppling trees to make passage much more difficult. Begin by parking your car at the Forestière school (just after the town—you can't miss it). The vehicle is safer there. Directly in front on your left will be a Caribbean pine plantation. Keep going down the road and you'll pass several houses on the right. Eventually you'll come to a flatter area where you will see a house on the left that is actually a Forestry Department rest house.

There may or may not be someone living there (an employee in the field). Next to the house you'll see and hear a pumping station. If you take the steps down to the pumping station, you'll find yourself on a trail that will lead you around a loop and bring you back to the top of the stairs. It will take about two hours to walk the loop, which provides some superb glimpses into the rain-forest habitat. An alternative to walking the entire loop is to keep walking straight past the pumping station (do not go down the steps). This will put you on the lower part of the loop. Follow this path for about a half-hour until you come upon an old concrete block house on the right. Behind this, there are steps that lead up to Piton Flore and a TV tower. The walk up, about a half-hour, is quite strenuous. The top, though, offers some terrific views of the east and northern coasts. From the top of Piton Flore back to your car, the walk will take you a little over an hour.

The main rain-forest walk is down in the south-central part of the island. It links the Fond St. Jacques road, west of Soufrière, with the Mahaut road, which is east of Micoud. The trail actually traverses the entire island and originally was the major trading route for the Arawak and Carib Indians. It is clear all the way across and makes for a very interesting walk, about three and a half hours from end to end. By law you must go with a guide from the Forestry Department, although exceptions can be made if you work it out in advance.

The trail, called the Rain Forest Walk, can be accessed on either end. The most enjoyable way to get to the Walk is from the west, as the drive down from Castries takes you through Anse La Raye, Canaries, and Soufrière and is wonderfully scenic. From the road you can see the Pitons, which have become the symbol of St. Lucia—two twin volcanic cones that rise almost 3,000 feet out of the water. When you get to Soufrière, don't be surprised if lots of young men insist on guiding you to the volcano. Just be firm. Your best bet is to ask an older man or woman how to get to the Still restaurant. On the way to the Still, you'll pass the cathedral on your left. Follow the road until you arrive at the restaurant, which features local cuisine and is a great spot for lunch. You'll also pass the sulphur springs—actually part of a dormant volcano whose waters were cherished by Louis XVI. Today it's billed as the world's only drive-in volcano. You can tell you're near it when you start smelling rotten eggs. If you've seen a sulphur spring at a national park out West, don't bother with this one. If you do choose to go, be

prepared to be surrounded by Rastas selling trinkets or their services as trail guides for the springs (which is a rip-off—you don't
need one). Don't let their official trail-guide T-shirts fool you, and
don't leave anything valuable in the car.

Continue inland on the road past the Still restaurant—on the
entire stretch there are only two turnoffs. At the first fork, after
about two miles, bear right (or down) and keep driving for approxi-
mately another two miles where the road forks again. Bear left (or
uphill)—this will bring you to the village of Fond St. Jacques. You'll
know you're there when you see an enormous church. Keep on
going—the road will get progressively worse—but you can make it
with the average rental car. Soon you'll come upon some fabulous
views, on the left-hand side, of Mt. Gimmie—St. Lucia's highest
peak. And the scenery gets better and better with each mile. Eventually you come to a lily farm that grows a very exotic, pinkish-red
flower called anthurium. Ahead the road becomes a track but you
can still drive it. Go straight down until you come across a clearing
with a sign that reads DESIGNATED A NATURE RESERVE. There will
also be a small hut on the right. This is the forest reserve house and
may or may not be occupied. Park the car in the clearing ahead of
you. The track continues, but it's not motorable: it now becomes
a trail and is the beginning of the Rain Forest Walk. If you walk this
trail for about three and a half hours you'll eventually come to the
road on the other side (there is another clearing and "designated"
sign). That's the end of the walk. It's probably a good idea to walk
to the halfway point and then turn back, as the entire end-to-end
round-trip takes seven hours—and you still have the long drive
back. (You'll know you're halfway when you come across the Quilesse Forest Reserve, a clearing with rest houses.) The exception is
if you've arranged for someone to meet you on the other side, or
if you switch car keys with another party midway to rendezvous
back at the hotel—great if you can do it.

If you aren't up for the very scenic but tedious drive down the
west coast, the hike can be accessed much faster via the east coast
highway. Just before you get to Micoud there is a turnoff for
Mahaut. Keep driving straight inland on what looks like the main
road. Pay no attention to several turnoffs along the way. Keep on
driving until you can drive no farther and happen upon the "designated" sign.

On this hike you will see both natural and planted forestation.
The planted part, consisting mostly of blue mahoe (a tree hibiscus

from Jamaica) and Honduras mahogany (from Belize), is basically a thin strip about 100 feet on either side of the trail. You can tell it's planted because there is usually only one species per grouping. Beyond that is indigenous vegetation. There are scattered strips of natural forestation along the trail, recognized by the denser and varied species. Benches are provided so you can rest and enjoy the flora. The Forestry Department strongly urges that you not leave the trail as you can get very lost very easily.

Quilesse, especially at dawn or dusk, is a birdwatcher's heaven. If you're quiet and patient you may see from thirty to forty species of birds. With luck you may see the rare green St. Lucian parrot— recognized by its loud squawking. There are only about 200 left in the world. Fortunately, they are on the rebound, having doubled their population in the last ten years—thanks to the diligence and dedication of the Forestry Department. There are also three varieties of hummingbirds: the very small Antillean crested hummingbird (the male has a gold crest), the green-throated Carib and the purple-throated Carib. You'll also see the broad-winged hawk—a smaller predator—and various species of doves. And if you're really lucky, you may see the St. Lucia oriole, readily distinguishable by its black-and-orange markings. The small bird with a bright reddish tail that flits out to snag moths and flying insects is the stolid flycatcher. Other species flying about include Adelaid's warbler, the Antillean peewee, and the mangrove cuckoo. And there are more that your guide or a good birding book will point out. You might, if you're fortunate, see a boa constrictor. You needn't worry about the deadly pit viper—that's found in the island's drier scrub areas and is nocturnal.

There are two tour companies that will take you down the east coast route for this walk, each on different days of the week. You can book one at any hotel through St. Lucia Representative Services, also known as St. Lucia Reps, Brazil Street in Castries (452-3762) and Barnard Travel, Bridge Street, Castries (452-2214). It will cost about EC$100 (about $38 U.S.), which includes everything and spares you the hassle of driving and parking. Depending on road conditions, some may drop you off in Mahaut and drive around to meet you at Fond St. Jacques. You'll have to check with the tour operators when you book.

Much has been written advising tourists not to swim in the fresh water on St. Lucia due to a microscopic parasite called the blood fluke that burrows into your skin and does horrific things to your body. This should be clarified. Researchers from the Rockefeller Institute came to the island in the seventies and virtually wiped out the problem. You *can* swim in the fast-moving mountain streams, if you can find water deep enough, because the snails, which host the parasite through several stages of its development, cannot exist there. It's only in the slow-flowing flat coastal rivers, which you really wouldn't think of getting near anyway, where the possibility of exposure may exist.

THE HIKES

The last two vigorous walks—I'll call them hikes—are exhilarating climbs that on completion will give you a real sense of accomplishment. The first is the grueling hike up Mt. Gimmie, the tallest mountain on the island at 3,117 feet. It can be arranged through the Forestry Department if several days' notice is given. This is a very long and hard hike—it will take you four hours just to reach the base, and the summit is an hour after that. It should only be attempted in the dry season (the summit is surrounded by clouds otherwise).

The other hike, not under the jurisdiction of the Forestry Department, is up Petit Piton—the smaller of the two dramatic volcanic cones (2,438 vertical feet) on the west coast. This is a very strenuous yet rewarding hike, about two and a half hours up and one and a half hours down. You won't need rope, but don't try it if you suffer from any degree of acrophobia. It is exactly like climbing stairs for two and a half hours. There are two particularly difficult stretches where you must use hand-holds and walk across a rock ledge. It's not dangerous, just scary. Get up there before it gets hot (before noon) and carry water. Bring very little else except maybe your camera, and wear *good* walking shoes. To find the trail, go to the police station in Soufrière and ask them to help you find a guide who will take you up. It will cost you about EC$100 (about $38 U.S.) whether you are one or ten. It's a hard climb for the guide as well, so the charge is reasonable. Negotiate before you start, and tell him that the negotiated fee is for the group, not per person—repeat it at least two or three times.

It should be stressed that all hikes into the Forest Reserve must be sanctioned by the Forestry Department for several reasons. The first is that the Department lacks the manpower and facilities for large-scale manhunts and it's very easy to get lost in the dense vegetation. Second, there is illicit marijuana farming going on and woe to the hiker or tourist who stumbles upon that. The Forestry Department, by the way, is not too keen on camping—you'll have to clear that with them well in advance. To reach the Forestry Department, call (809) 452-3231, or write: Forestry Department, St. Lucia, W.I. Allow two weeks for the letter to reach its destination.

WHERE TO STAY

St. Lucia is a big island with a wide range of accommodations. As with Jamaica, there are a lot of all-inclusive resorts here—which I usually don't recommend (I hate buffets). There are two here, however, that are worth looking into—Jalousie and Le Sport. Most of the hotels and resorts are in the northwest quarter of the island, especially around Rodney Bay. The other significant destination is Soufrière, where the most deluxe resorts are located. When you find a place that appeals to you, look for package deals, which will bring the cost down substantially over the daily rack rate. Here are my recommendations:

THE NORTHWEST QUARTER

This is a strip of beach that starts at Vigie, just north of Castries, and goes virtually all the way to the northernmost point.

THE ROYAL ST. LUCIAN (809) 452-9999, fax (809) 452-9639
Stateside: (800) 255-5859/(305) 471-6170
Reduit Beach, P.O. Box 977, Castries, St. Lucia, W.I.

A relatively new hotel, this is the most deluxe property in this part of St. Lucia. Situated on pretty Reduit Beach and only steps away from the action of Rodney Bay, this attractive West Indian–style resort has a modern, spacious, and airy feel to it. You enter through a stucco, white marble, and bleached wood lobby with a fountain. Stepping outside, 4 three-story buildings surround a huge treeless courtyard where there's a curvy pool complex called La Mirage (wasn't that the name of Fallon's place on *Dynasty?*) replete with islands and a pool bar with seats in the water. There is little shade out here except for the pool umbrellas. Inside, all of the accommodations are suites, with a separate bedroom and sitting room. The off-white rooms are attractive and decorated in tropical pastels and rattan. Baths are ample and feature lots of marble. The deluxe amenities you'd expect are here too. There are two restaurants in the resort and guests are welcome to use the tennis and water-sports facilities next door at the St. Lucian (they're owned by the same company).

Rates are WICKED PRICEY to OUTRAGEOUS for singles and doubles (EP).

THE ST. LUCIAN (809) 452-8351, fax (809) 452-8331
Stateside: (800) 255-5859/(305) 471-6170
Reduit Beach, P.O. Box 512, Castries, St. Lucia, W.I.

If you want the amenities of a big hotel at fairly reasonable prices, the St. Lucian will work for you. A former Holiday Inn, the 222 accommodations are standard in décor and size. All are air-conditioned and have baths, phones, and radios. The beach is very good and the free water sports add variety and value. There are lighted tennis courts, two restaurants, and Splash, the premier disco on the island.

Rates are PRICEY to VERY PRICEY for singles and doubles (EP).

CANDYO INN (809) 452-0712, fax (809) 452-0774
Rodney Bay, P.O. Box 386, St. Lucia, W.I.

This place is a find for those who want to be in Rodney Bay but don't want to spend over $100 U.S. a day on a room. The Candyo has both rooms and apartments with kitchens at very good prices. The rooms are clean, bright, and comfortably furnished. All have air conditioning, phone, and TV. There is a pool on the property and both Reduit Beach and the fun of Rodney Bay are but steps away.

Rates are NOT SO CHEAP for singles and doubles (EP).

LE SPORT (809) 450-8551, fax 450-0368
Stateside: (800) 544-2883; UK: 0(800) 59-07-94
P.O. Box 437, St. Lucia, W.I.

The former Cariblue Resort, this is now an all-inclusive resort, which I normally don't recommend. However, Le Sport has something called the Oasis. This is a wonderful, Moorish-style spa that features all kinds of delicious things to do with your body—including massage, reflexology foot massage, hydro-massage, salt-loofah rubs, algae baths, eucalyptus inhalations, seaweed nutrient wraps, facials and hair treatments. The resort also offers a daily program of aerobics, stretching, yoga and stress management; there's even a relaxation temple. Guests at the hotel get a daily package of pampering included in their all-inclusive rate. (Nonguests can join the Oasis for $30 per month and choose from a menu of treatments paid for on an à la carte basis.) The cuisine at Le Sport is meant to be lighter and health-aware—all of this is part of their theme to "free your mind and body." Just about every conceivable sport is available to you here too, including tennis, biking, scuba, fencing, archery, golf, and of course a gym. The 128 rooms and suites are a tad fluffy and frilly but are quite comfortable. The beach is not St. Lucia's prettiest but it's pleasant enough.

Rates are WICKED PRICEY for singles and doubles (all-inclusive).

EDGEWATER BEACH CLUB (809) 452-4872, fax (809) 452-3125
P.O. Box 962, Castries, St. Lucia, W.I.

This place was the best value on St. Lucia in this book's last edition and continues to be so now. While prices have gone up a tad, the place has received a much-needed face-lift, including a new dining room, called D's Restaurant and Bar. This small hotel sits right on Choc Beach, only minutes from Vigie Airport and Castries. There are three beach cottages and six one-bedroom units. All are simply furnished, clean, and have fully equipped kitchens and air conditioning. You won't find a better deal on St. Lucia.

Rates are CHEAP to NOT SO CHEAP for singles and doubles (EP).

TOP O' THE MORNE ESTATES, LTD. (809) 452-3603, fax (809) 452-2531
P.O. Box 376, Castries, St. Lucia, W.I.

If you desire a fully furnished apartment with sweeping views of the capital, Castries, and the sea, this establishment offers 11 one- and two-bedroom apartments (and one studio) at good prices. Once the old British Military Administration Building, Top o' the Morne sits at 820 feet above sea level on Morne Fortune, with views, on a clear day, of Martinique. Each unit is individually owned so the décor can vary, but all the apartments are really large. They also have huge lanais for lounging and dining. There is a small pool on the property.

Rates are PRICEY for singles and doubles (EP).

THE WEST COAST

MARIGOT BAY RESORT (809) 453-4357, fax (809) 451-4353
Stateside: (800) 334-2435
P.O. Box 101, Castries, St. Lucia, W.I.

Acclaimed as one of the most beautiful harbors in the Caribbean, Marigot Bay probably was before all the development and boats. While the accommodations are pleasant—cottages are tastefully appointed and spacious—I would feel claustrophobic staying here for a week. The exception is for those participating in the diving program, which will get you out and about. This is also the headquarters of the Moorings yacht charters to the Grenadines. Staying here for a night or two is usually part of the charter package. There is no decent beach—a major drawback. The resort includes the Hurricane Hole Hotel—the best value—and the Marigot Bay Inn and Hillside Villas (complete with an escalator-type tram). A water taxi (free of charge to all) connects the two complexes on either side of the tiny bay.

Rates are PRICEY for singles and VERY PRICEY for doubles at the Hurricane Hole and the Inn, VERY PRICEY for singles and doubles at the Hillside Villas.

ANSE CHASTANET (809) 459-7000, fax (809) 459-7700
Stateside: (800) 223-1108/(914) 763-5526
Anse Chastanet Beach (P.O. Box 7000, Soufrière), St. Lucia, W.I.

With great views of the Pitons, this is St. Lucia's premier beach resort. Tucked away in dense foliage on a hilly point 18 miles north of Hewanorra Airport, Anse Chastanet is reached by one of the most horrendous roads on the island. Once there, however, the 48-room resort offers a superb retreat from wherever you've been. There are 500 acres; 2 gray-sand beaches, including one that's totally deserted; and all water sports, including the best scuba diving on the island. There are all types of accommodations, from Deluxe Beachside rooms to eleven Premium Hillside suites at the top of the crest. The latter are large, from 900 to 1,600 square feet, and offer great things like gigantic cathedral ceilings, spacious lanais, and open-air showers with views of the Pitons (ask for 7B). Unit 14B of the Deluxe Hillside suites has a full-grown tree in your open-air shower. All the units are unique, however, and are furnished with local woods, fabrics, rugs and crafts. Amenities include privacy, fridges, coffeemakers, and ceiling fans. These rooms are the kind that you could stay in all day and not want to leave, especially if you have someone to romp with in tow. There is no pool, but that wouldn't be the style of this place—the beach and nature is. Despite the access road, Anse Chastanet is well located for the Piton/Mt. Gimmie hikes and the rain-forest walk. The hotel will help you arrange these too. Note that this resort is located on a steep hill, with about 100 steps from the beach to the main building (more climbing up a road if you're in a hillside unit), so you'll have a workout every time you leave your room. Don't forget anything or you'll be exhausted by the time you return.

There is a very good restaurant and beach bar on the property.

Rates are VERY PRICEY to RIDICULOUS for singles and WICKED PRICEY to OUTRAGEOUS for doubles (MAP). Packages, including one for scuba, are available.

LADERA RESORT (809) 459-7323, same for fax
Stateside and Canada: (800) 841-4145/(607) 273-9484
P.O. Box 225, Soufrière, St. Lucia, W.I.

Ladera has the best view of any resort or hotel in the Caribbean. From a perch 1,000 feet above sea level and right in the middle of the two Pitons, you just cannot beat the scenery. Even better, the 16 villas and suites (formerly called Dasheene) feature a completely open western wall, so there is nothing obstructing your view. The effect is spectacular. If there was ever a place where you wanted to go and live outdoors yet in total luxury (with your own plunge pool, if you'd like), this is it. The happiest guests here are the ones who want to romp and read, all with the magnificence and power of the Pitons right there before their eyes. The villas and rooms are wonderfully and comfortably furnished in local woods and fabrics. I would be very happy here for a week with a companion. There is an excellent restaurant, Dasheene, on the premises and a common, spring-fed pool with views of life. Why Ladera wants to call itself a resort, I have no idea. It's just a fantastic small hotel—the ultimate room with a view. There is no beach, no tennis, no water sports, etc. (although they can be arranged), just a great space and heavenly vistas.

Rates are WICKED PRICEY to OUTRAGEOUS for singles and doubles (CP).

JALOUSIE PLANTATION (809) 459-7666, fax (809) 459-7667
Stateside: (800) 877-3643/(305) 856-5405
Soufrière, St. Lucia, W.I.

This former plantation of Lord Glenconner is set on the hillside and gray-sand beach *between* the Pitons, and you couldn't ask for a more stunning setting. This is a new resort, owned by the same company that brings us Casa de Campo in the Dominican Republic. The second of the all-inclusive resorts on St. Lucia that I would recommend, there are 115 suites and cottages scattered about the hillside and connected to the Great House, Spa, and beach/pool by a shuttle. All are loaded with amenities and the cottages feature their own plunge pools. There are four restaurants, room service, tennis, squash, all water sports, a spa with gym, aerobics, massage, and saunas. A hydroponic garden provides fresh veggies for the resort's restaurants. If you want to pay only one price and want it all, soup-to-nuts plus the view of life, this is for you.

Rates are RIDICULOUS to OUTRAGEOUS for singles and WICKED PRICEY to OUTRAGEOUS for doubles (all-inclusive). It pays to come here with someone else.

WHERE TO EAT

There are lots of restaurants to choose from on St. Lucia and certainly enough good ones to keep you happy for a week. Many of the hotels and resorts have superb restaurants, which charge appropriately superb prices. If you're not staying at an all-inclusive resort, try one of these local character-laden places:

NORTHWEST QUARTER

GREEN PARROT, Red Tape Lane, Morne Fortune, 452-3399

Overlooking Castries Harbor, this is a St. Lucian institution with
Chef Harry at the helm. The menu features West Indian dishes
served with a Créole flair—try the Stuffed Pussy (in season); no
joke, it's on the menu. There are floorshows on Wednesday (Princess Tina bellydances) and Saturdays (Chef Harry entertains with
limbo). On Mondays, ladies dine free when they wear a flower in
their hair and their dates wear a jacket and tie. (What about two
women wearing flowers?)

Be sure to visit Jane Tipson at the Curio Shop when at the Green
Parrot—she has a wealth of information about St. Lucia and is a
great person as well.

Reservations are a must. Jackets are suggested at dinner. Open
daily. $$$$$

SAN ANTOINE, Morne Fortune, 452-4660

People go to this very elegant restaurant higher up on Morne Fortune as much for the ambience as for the food. Built on the ruins
of an old hotel destroyed by fire in 1970, it has been beautifully
restored. It was originally constructed in the nineteenth century as
a great house. The views of Castries are spectacular. Reservations
are a must. Lunch is served weekdays and dinner every day except
Sunday. Jackets suggested. $$$$$

LA CAPRICE, Royal St. Lucian Hotel, Reduit Beach, 452-9999

Pink marble, crystal chandeliers, and a beachside view are the setting for Royal St. Lucian's premier restaurant. The cuisine is continental and there is a daily prix-fixe dinner. Reservations are
suggested. $$$$$

KEY LARGO, Rodney Bay Marina, 452-0282

This is a fun and lively place featuring California-style brick-oven
pizzas and great salads. This is also where you come for your
cappuccinos and espressos on St. Lucia. $$

FLAMINGO, St. Lucian Hotel, Reduit Beach, 452-8351

Located in the St. Lucian Hotel, the cuisine in this too-pink place
is French/Créole and is very highly regarded. It can get noisy next

to the adjacent night stage, so ask for a table as far away from it as possible. Reservations are suggested. $$$$$

THE LIME, Rodney Bay, 452-0761

A Rodney Bay staple, the Lime serves good West Indian food and is especially popular at lunch. The bar is one of the mainstays of Rodney Bay nightlife. Closed Tuesday; also one month in summer. $$

GOLDEN APPLE, Gros Islet, 452-0634

The is the place to eat when you head to the jump-up on Friday. The food is local-style, good and cheap. Barbecue nights are Wednesday, Friday, and Saturday. $$

CHARTHOUSE, Rodney Bay, 452-8115

Need a steak? It's a Charthouse, like all the rest. They also serve lobster in season. Open for dinner only. Closed Sunday and the month of September. Make reservations. $$$$

A-PUB, Rodney Bay, 452-8725

Chris and Jenny's off-spring of the fabled A-Frame (the building was sold and they had to move—now's it's the Marina Steak House), this place serves good pub-style food and some of the best steaks on the island (Jenny picks them out herself). $$

CAPONE'S, Rodney Bay, 452-0284

A kind of hokey setup (all the waitstaff are dressed like thirties Chicago gangsters), but still the food is good and you can get cheap pizzas at the restaurant's fast-food–style pizzeria at the entrance. $$

PAUL'S PLACE, Bridge Street, Castries, 453-1588

Consistency is one of this restaurant's foibles. But when Paul is around and in command, this is a terrific restaurant, featuring Créole, European, and Southeast Asian cuisine. $$$$$

RAIN, Columbus Square, Castries, 452-3022

Set in an old, wooden Victorian gingerbread building overlooking the square, this restaurant strives for the Somerset Maugham décor and atmosphere. The cuisine is a mix of Créole and American, but the nightly "Champagne Banquet of 1885"—a seven-course, four-wine extravaganza (EC$95)—is lots of fun. Closed Sunday and holidays. $$$$

NATURAL CAFE, Chaussee Road, Castries, 452-6421

This is your veggie-and-soy option for meals on St. Lucia. $$

THE WEST AND SOUTH COASTS

DASHEENE, Ladera Resort, Soufrière, 459-7850

This is the best place for lunch on St. Lucia. The food and views are fabulous (see the write-up in the "Where to Stay" section above). It's also open for dinner. Lunch $$$; dinner $$$$$

HUMMINGBIRD, Anse Chastanet Road, Soufrière, 459-7232

Another great restaurant in Soufrière, Hummingbird features West Indian cuisine and a dining terrace overlooking the Pitons. If you're lucky, they may have some freshwater mountain crayfish, which are delicious. Open for lunch and dinner daily. Reservations are recommended. $$$$

PITON RESTAURANT, Anse Chastanet, 459-7000

If you can survive the road to Anse Chastanet (your car will make it), the reward is this delightful restaurant with terrific views of the Pitons and sunsets as well as a friendly staff. The cuisine is Créole and continental. $$$$

THE STILL, La Perle Estate, Soufrière, 459-7224

Located on a 250-acre working plantation owned by the DuBoulay family for five generations, this lunch-only establishment serves excellent Créole food. Virtually all the food served here is from the Estate. Reservations are suggested. Ask about possible buffet-only dinners, which are sometimes offered. $$$

CHAK CHAK, downtown Vieux Fort, 454-6260

This is a popular and local favorite in the heart of Vieux Fort. Local seafood catches are the specialty, along with West Indian/Créole cuisine. Open until midnight. $$

IL PIRATA, Vieux Fort, 454-6610

Situated on the highway from Vieux Fort to Soufrière and right on the beach, this is a fun place to stop and have some pasta. $$$

Don't Miss

THE PITONS—It would be a crime if you didn't see them.

A DRIVE AROUND THE ISLAND—A must-do as you won't grasp the beauty of this island any other way, and you'll see the Pitons.

THE OASIS AT LE SPORT—Treat your body to a day of indulgence (see the write-up above in "Where to Stay").

LUNCH AT DASHEENE—With a breathtaking view of the Pitons and great food, this is a must (see the write-up above).

THE A-PUB AND THE DINGHY CRAWL—Tie one on here; Chris and Jenny will love you more for it as they adore it when the joint is jumpin'.

GROS ISLET ON FRIDAY—A must-do street "jump-up" on Friday (see the "Focus on St. Lucia" feature above).

SCUBA AT ANSE CHASTANET—If you're a diver, the diving and dive shop here (a five-star PADI facility) are excellent. Call Scuba St. Lucia at 459-7000.

THE MOORINGS AT MARIGOT BAY RESORT—Check out one of the home ports for bareboat charters in the Grenadines. Maybe next time this could be you.

THE WALKS AND HIKES—See the beauty that Mom Nature has given the island. Check out the "Focus on St. Lucia" section above

CHOISEL SCENIC DRIVE—A beautiful drive through the lovely seaside village of Choisel and continuing along the coast to La Pointe Beach on the island's southwest corner. Also in the area is the "St. Lucian Stonehenge," man-made stone formations that have been tentatively carbon-dated at 2500 B.C. Contact the Tourist Board (452-4094) for more info. The locally published book *Historic Sights* is available at most bookshops and tourist stands. It sells for $10 U.S. and provides history buffs with more detailed information.

AVOID

THE DRIVE-THROUGH VOLCANO—It's not worth the hassle of the guide wannabees.

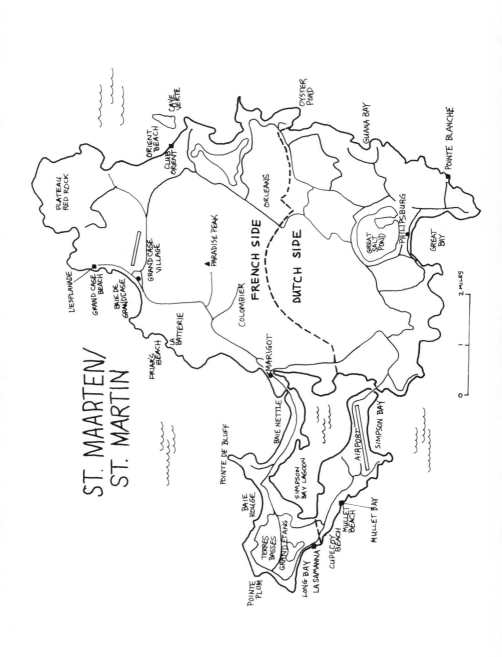

ST. MAARTEN/
ST. MARTIN

PLATEAU
RED ROCK

L'ESPLANADE

GRAND CASE
BEACH

BAIE DE
GRANDCASE

GRAND CASE
VILLAGE

FRIAR'S
BEACH

LA
BATTERIE

PARADISE PEAK

COLOMBIER

POINTE DE BLUFF

BAIE NETTLE

MARIGOT

BAIE
ROUGE

POINTE
PLUM

LONG BAY
LA SAMANNA

TERRES
BASSES

GRAND ETANG

SIMPSON
BAY LAGOON

CUPECOY
BEACH

MULLET
BEACH

MULLET BAY

AIRPORT

SIMPSON BAY

ORIENT
BEACH

CAYE
VERTE

CLUB
ORIENT

ORLEANS

FRENCH SIDE

DUTCH SIDE

OYSTER
POND

GUANA BAY

POINTE BLANCHE

GREAT
SALT
POND

PHILIPSBURG

GREAT
BAY

0   1   2 MILES

ST. MARTIN

One of the most vivid images of my entire Caribbean whirlwind happened here on St. Martin. I had just left the overcrowded and too-developed Dutch side of the island—St. Maarten (the island is split in half and co-governed by France and the Netherlands). I was driving along in what was suddenly a very pastoral setting, with fields on either side of me, when I looked in my rear-view mirror. There, about four feet from my taillights, was a beautiful woman dressed in a Gaultier bustier riding a three-wheeler dune bike. Her long brunette hair whipped behind her Armani sunglasses. She was the last thing I expected to see in the mirror. It was riveting. Realizing that I had to look at the road again to make sure I didn't drive off it, I looked straight ahead quickly and glanced back in the mirror. She was gone. A hallucination, perhaps? No, there she was zooming ahead of me on that bike going 80 miles an hour, her hair flowing behind her like a black swan flapping its wings. Welcome to (French) St. Martin, I thought, another French brushstroke in the West Indies.

St. Maarten/St. Martin is schizophrenic. The Dutch side is a madhouse and much too developed. The French side is quieter, more stylish, and much less developed, although it too is becoming more built up. (There are no immigration or Customs posts between the two sides, just road markers indicating the boundaries.) The island has seen tremendous expansion in the last fifteen years. Developers have essentially ruined the Dutch side and only one beach there, Cupecoy, still remains somewhat in its natural state. The French side is much nicer and still retains a sense of what used to be, especially in the north at Grand Case. The huge Juliana

International Airport has not only made the island a major destination for package tours but also a gateway for the smaller, satellite islands around it, like St. Barts, Saba, and Anguilla. This has increased the touristo flow. Add to that the cruise ships, which make Philipsburg, on the Dutch side, a routine stop. (That town has become very similar to Charlotte Amalie on St. Thomas and should be avoided with one exception—a record store that sells excellent prerecorded tapes of all kinds of Caribbean music.) Both sides are duty-free ports, so shopping frenzies are a daily event—a great place to get that Rolex or Tag Heuer you always wanted. Finally, the Dutch side has several casinos. The result of all of this, of course, is lots of tourists, lots of traffic, and a growing animosity toward tourists by the locals (although the latter is not anywhere as bad as in the U.S. Virgin Islands). If you decide to come here, by all means stay on the French side.

Why go to St. Martin when there are other, better choices? Probably the best reason to come here is to get a taste of France. For a French island, St. Martin is the most affordable, there are good restaurants, and English is spoken everywhere. The latter is not the case on Martinique or Guadeloupe. And while English is widely spoken on neighboring St. Barts, the island is so expensive that it's unaffordable or intimidating to some. On St. Martin, you can easily get air/land packages that are very reasonable. The other reason to come here is that it's easy to get to—no connections on small planes, which eat up precious time, are necessary. The French side does get French tourists looking for something different from the other French islands, and, of course, there are North Americans galore. So the mix is actually quite interesting.

THE BRIEFEST HISTORY

All right, how the hell did this small island get split in half politically in the first place? Patience, readers, I will enlighten. But first, as with most of the islands in the region, let me note that the island was settled by the Ciboney around 1000 B.C., then the Arawaks around A.D. 300, and finally the Caribs about 600 years later. Columbus sighted the island on his second voyage in 1493 on the feast day of St. Martin of Tours, hence St. Martin. The Dutch were the first to battle the Caribs and set up shop on the salt ponds (salt was the major industry before sugarcane). Then came the Spanish and French. The Spanish lost interest in the island in the mid-seventeenth century, and a group of French and Dutch settlers established separate communities. Of course, the two groups fought like cats and dogs, until a treaty was signed in 1648 on the summit of Mt. Concordia, establishing boundaries between France and Holland. The French got the bigger slice of the pie because their navy was a bigger force in the region. The Dutch got the best port, Philipsburg. With the advent of sugar and tobacco plantations, and with it slavery, the British became interested. The island became a battleground again and changed hands 16 times between 1648 and 1816, when a final settlement was reached. Relations between the two countries settled into a groove and have remained stable to the present day. However, the demise of slavery (in 1848 on the French side and in 1863 on the Dutch—can you imagine how the Dutch slaves must have felt?) brought the economy to a standstill. Things didn't start looking up until 1939, when the island was made a duty-free port. That brought in all kinds of business and commerce. Juliana Airport, built in the fifties, started the tourist boom, which is in full force today.

St. Martin/St. Maarten: Key Facts

LOCATION	18°N by 63°W
	150 miles east of San Juan
	1,680 miles southeast of New York
SIZE	37 square miles
	St. Martin—21 square miles
	St. Maarten—16 square miles
HIGHEST POINT	Paradise Point (1,500 ft.)
POPULATION	60,000 (32,000—St. Maarten; 28,000—St. Martin)
LANGUAGE	English, although you will hear some Dutch and French
TIME	Atlantic Standard Time (1 hour ahead of EST, same as EDT)
AREA CODE	To call St. Martin from the U.S., dial 011 (the international access code), then 590 (the country code), then the six-digit local number; to call St.

Maarten, dial 011, then 5995, then the five- or six-digit local number.

ELECTRICITY   St. Martin—220 volts AC, 50 cycles—adapters and transformers probably necessary
St. Maarten—110 volts AC, 60 cycles
Bad planning by both sides!

CURRENCY   St. Martin—French franc, F (5.2F = U.S. $1); check at departure time
St. Maarten—Netherlands Antilles guilder, NAf (1.77 NAf = $1 U.S.)
U.S. dollars accepted just about everywhere at current exchange rates

DRIVING   On the *right*; a valid U.S. or Canadian driver's license is acceptable

DOCUMENTS   U.S. and Canadian citizens should have a passport, voter's registration card or proof of nationality with a photo ID; all need an ongoing or return ticket

DEPARTURE TAX $10 U.S.

BEER TO DRINK   Heineken

RUM TO DRINK   Wild Sint Maarten Guavaberry

MUSIC TO HEAR   Dancehall

GETTING THERE

St. Maarten (the Dutch side) has the Queen Juliana International Airport, which can handle jumbo jets from all over. AMERICAN, CONTINENTAL, and BWIA fly nonstop or direct from the States. BWIA also flies direct from Toronto. AMERICAN EAGLE flies from San Juan. LIAT flies from most neighbor islands and San Juan. From the French islands, AIR MARTINIQUE and AIR GUADELOUPE have daily flights. WINAIR also has many daily flights from neighbor islands and AIR ST. BARTH'S from St. Barts.

GETTING AROUND

As taxis are expensive and the roads are good on the island, there is no reason not to rent a car. There are many rental-car agencies, including AVIS ([800] 331-1084), HERTZ ([800] 654-3001), BUD-GET ([800] 527-0700), DOLLAR ([800] 800-4000), and NA-TIONAL ([800] 227-3876), so prices are reasonable. Be sure to call ahead to ensure a reservation and the best rate. Driving is on the *right*.

FOCUS ON ST. MARTIN/ST. MAARTEN: DUTY-FREE SHOPPING

If you ever wanted to buy a good Swiss watch or any kind of jewelry, the prices here are great. With electronics and cameras, there are some deals to be had, but you're better off shopping for sales on the mainland or ordering from the discount houses in New York (47th St., Executive, etc.) Both Philipsburg and Marigot have major duty-free stores. Of the two, Marigot is much more civilized, and you can go out for a wonderful lunch too. The prices are very similar, as all the stores on both sides are owned by Indians. All accept major credit cards. You can and should negotiate; the price will come down a tad. If you pay cash, you will get a small discount on top. Bon shopping!

WHERE TO STAY

There are thousands of hotel rooms on this island. I strongly sug-gest staying on the French side, as it's much more agreeable and away from that noisy airport. Look for package deals here—you'll save a lot of money and there are many from which to choose.

HOTEL L'ESPLANADE CARAÏBES (011-590) 87-06-55, fax (011-590) 87-29-15
B.P. 5007, Grand Case, 97150, St. Martin, F.W.I.

A new hotel set on the hillside overlooking Grand Case and the bay, this is a truly great find for spacious living at a reasonable price. Designed by an Argentine, the décor uses lots of dark woods from the Caribbean. The managers, Mark and Sandy Tramoni, are a wonderful couple (he's French, she's American), who used to live in Santa Monica and are practitioners of holistic/alternative (read "Oriental/Eastern") medicine. While at the moment they are just managing the hotel and adapting to life in the tropics, there are plans to make this hotel a center for alternative healing. I'm sure this would be a big hit. Stay tuned to the next edition of *Rum and Reggae*. But I digress. There are 24 units, the best being the lofts, which are huge and would be a wonderful space to *live* in, let alone stay in for a few days. Each space has a large lanai with a view of the town and the sea, a fully equipped kitchen, phone, TV, air conditioning, etc. There is a pool and bar on the property and the beach is a five-minute walk away. Both Mark and Sandy are very helpful and will arrange for any other activities that you desire.

Rates are PRICEY to WICKED PRICEY for singles and doubles (EP).

LA SAMANNA (011-590) 87-86-51, same for fax
Stateside: (800) 854-2252/(212) 319-5191
Baie Longue (B.P. 576, Marigot), 97150, St. Martin, F.W.I.

When I first came to St. Martin in 1977 on spring break, La Samanna was one of *the* places to stay in the Caribbean. It sort of lost its shine in the eighties, but was recently bought by Rosewood Hotels (which owns the Bel-Air in L.A., among others). This promises to bring it back to its former glory. There are 85 rooms and apartments. Some are in the main building, which commands a stunning view of the whole Baie Longue beach and the sea beyond. Sunset cocktails by the pool here are a must-do, even if you don't stay here. The rest of the rooms are in units at the beach—each with a spacious and private patio. The décor throughout has a stucco/Moorish accent, and you'll find all the amenities of a luxury hotel here. There is an outdoor swimming pool, an incredible beach that is never even remotely crowded, three tennis courts, a spa and small fitness center, and water sports can be arranged.

Rates are OUTRAGEOUS to BEYOND BELIEF for singles and doubles (full breakfast included).

CLUB ORIENT (011-590) 87-33-85, fax (011-590) 87-33-76
Stateside: (800) 742-4276
Baie Orientale, 97150, St. Martin, F.W.I.

There is a song by the B-52's called "Theme for a Nude Beach," which immediately popped into my head as I strolled into the Club's beach bar/restaurant and took a seat at the bar next to two buck naked patrons. This is the original "naturalist" (nudist, but they prefer naturalist) colony in the Caribbean. Actually, it's listed as a "clothing-optional" resort, but really everyone except the employees were naked. Located on the southern end of Orient Beach, there are 77 red-pine chalets imported from Finland, which are scattered about the property. All are furnished in simple yet comfortable, summer-cabin-retreat décor (the interior looks like a sauna with furniture) and all units have fully equipped kitchens, lanais and ceiling fans (Orient is on the northeast corner of the island and thus faces the tradewinds). There are two tennis courts (nudie tennis, anyone?) and all water sports, including a nude cruise (open to the public for $75 U.S. per person) to Tintamarre Island (across the bay). While the resort welcomes singles, most guests are couples or families.

Rates are VERY PRICEY to WICKED PRICEY for singles and doubles (EP).

MARINE HOTEL SIMPSON BEACH (011-590) 87-54-54, fax (011-590) 87-92-11
Stateside: (800) 221-4542/(914) 472-0370
Baie Nettle (B.P. 172, Marigot), 97150, St. Martin, F.W.I.

There are now lots of hotels on the nice stretch of strand west of Marigot, basically one right after the other. Of all of them, this is the best value and is a stylish and reasonably priced resort. There are 128 rooms, all with air conditioning, cable TV, radios, room safes, patios, and kitchenettes. The décor is pleasant, with tiled floors and pastels throughout. There is a restaurant and a beach bar, plus a pool, Ping-Pong, volleyball, tennis, and all water sports. The beach here is very calm as it is on the lagoon, so this place would be great for small children.

Rates are PRICEY to WICKED PRICEY for singles and doubles (full breakfast included).

WHERE TO EAT

Being a French island, the food here is superb. Like the other French islands, it's hard to find a bad meal anywhere. But here are some suggestions:

L'ESCAPADE, Grand Case, 87-75-04

This is an established, family-run restaurant with good French/Créole food and fair prices. $$$

CANNE A SUCRE, Grand Case, 87-28-79

The best restaurant in Grand Case, this cute little place has patio dining and delicious *cuisine Créole et Français*. Try their *Escalope de merou avec sauce enragée* or the *Huîtres chaudes au Champagne et jus de truffe*. Reservations are suggested. $$$$

CHA-CHA-CHA, Grand Case, 87-53-63

The place for *tapas* in St. Martin. It's very busy, has reasonable prices, good food, and a fun backyard bar. $$$

TALK OF THE TOWN, Grand Case, no phone

One of the most popular eateries on St. Martin, this is a "lo-lo"—basically a food stand with barbecue and bar. There are tables and table service under a canopy, and the whole place is wonderfully beach-shack-casual (because it basically is a beach shack). You can get grilled lobster, chicken, and ribs for next to nothing. Well, the lobster is not cheap, but it's affordable (around $15 U.S.). A must-stop on your hit list, it's always packed. $$

CALIFORNIE, Grand Case, 87-55-57

A new restaurant situated on the beach, this is a fun and very affordable pizza/pasta place featuring wood-fired pizza ovens. The menu isn't extensive, but the fair prices make the restaurant popular. $$$

BAR DE LA MER, Marigot, 37-81-79
LA FIESTA, Marigot, 98-99-11

Both of these restaurants are café/bistros and have tables outside for dining alfresco. They are about 50 yards apart and are also fun places to hang out, people-watch, and schmooze, particularly Bar de la Mer. La Fiesta turns into a fun club with live music later in the evening. $$

LA VIE EN ROSE, boulevard France, Marigot, 87-54-42

An institution on St. Martin, the classic French cuisine here is renowned and ridiculously expensive. But if you're up for a splurge, go for it. There are tables on a second-floor balcony overlooking the town or harbor (and the parking lot). If you don't want to break the bank, the prix-fixe lunch is excellent and a great deal (under $20 U.S.). Reservations are required. $$$$$

GOING OUT

Leaving the casinos to the Dutch side, there are some fun places to go out and kick it up on the French side. In Marigot, try BAR DE LA MER (37-81-79) and COCO LOCO (next door) and LA FIESTA (98-99-11) down the waterfront. They are fun to sit and hang out at, and all have live music at different times of the week, particularly La Fiesta—which can be a blast. For discos, there's ATMOSPHERE at the Port Royale Marina (87-50-24)—it's all mirrors and glass, and STUDIO SEVEN ([599] 154-2115) at Mullet Bay (on the Dutch side). In Grand Case, CHA-CHA-CHA (87-53-63) has a fun backyard bar and LE JUNGLE/LA MADRAGUE kicks up later.

DON'T MISS

ORIENT BEACH—This is the island's official nude beach, and while not the best beach on the island, it's certainly interesting. Of particular note are the concessions located next to Club Orient. They sell crafts, T-shirts, and food (including crêpes). The funny thing is that there are people who are totally naked browsing next to people who are totally clothed. The same as the Club's restaurant and bar next door (which is open to the public).

CUPECOY BEACH—Still the nicest beach on the island, although development and overuse have taken their toll. However, the rose-colored bluffs are still there, as are the nooks and caves carved out by the sea. This is also the island's gay beach.

FUTURE FITNESS CENTER—Located in Marigot (87-90-27), this is actually a good free-weight gym with decent equipment and machines. There is an aerobics room upstairs.

LO-LO'S—On the beach in Grand Case, these offer cheap fast-food Caribbean-style.

TRINIDAD AND TOBAGO

TOURISTO SCALE ◙◙◙◙ 4

Like night and day and Jeckyl and Hyde, Trinidad and Tobago couldn't be more different. Trinidad is a major industrial and petroleum force in the Caribbean basin with a dynamic energy level and fast pace. Tobago is the poor, sleepy cousin and much more typical of a West Indian island than its sister. Somehow they got stuck together in a political marriage. But both benefit from each other. Tobago gets the much richer Trinidad to fund government services and build roads, schools, and bridges. Trinidadians get to go to beautiful Tobago for weekends and holidays. The relationship seems to work.

The islands are 21 miles apart and located just off the coast of Venezuela. (Only seven miles separate Trinidad from Venezuela.) Yet they are very West Indian in orientation. Trinidadian influences can be seen all over the Caribbean, both economically and culturally. For the traveler, Trinidad is interesting only for Carnival—the biggest in the Caribbean and the third largest after Rio and New Orleans. It will appeal to the adventurous party-type who loves mass celebrations, calypso and pan music, and rubbing sweaty elbows with the local populace. Tobago is a year-round destination that will appeal to the lover of quiet, very friendly, and rather-undeveloped islands where few Americans roam.

THE BRIEFEST HISTORY

Being virtually part of the South American continent, Trinidad was first settled by Amerindians thousands of years ago. When Colum-

bus landed on the island on his third voyage in 1498, he found
several tribes living on the island, including the familiar Arawaks
and Caribs. The latter, who lived in the north, warded off coloniza-
tion attempts until the late 1500s. Spain ruled Trinidad until 1797,
when the British seized control. It was formally deeded to England
in 1802. After the emancipation of the slaves in 1834, when labor
opportunities developed, massive immigration from Europe and
even the U.S. occurred. Then, there still being a need for cheap
labor, waves of indentured servants from India and China arrived.
These immigration waves account for the unique racial and cultural
makeup of Trinidad. Indeed, Trinidadians are among the most
beautiful people I have ever seen.

Tobago was also sighted in 1498 by Columbus, who found Caribs
inhabiting the island. They were observed growing tobacco, hence
the name. No settlements were attempted until the mid-seventeenth
century. The island was contested for the next 100 years by the
British, French, and Dutch. The British were deeded control in the
Treaty of Paris in 1763.

Both islands were united under one government in 1888 as a
Crown Colony of Britain. In 1962, both islands gained their independence within the British Commonwealth, finally becoming a
republic in 1976.

There was a coup attempt in 1990 by Muslim fundamentalists,
which was quickly squelched by government forces. However, the
experience created a tense atmosphere in Trinidad that is now just
beginning to dissipate.

TRINIDAD: KEY FACTS

LOCATION	10°N by 61°W
	8 miles east of Venezuela
	2,250 miles southeast of New York
SIZE	1,864 square miles
	50 miles long by 37 miles wide
HIGHEST POINT	Cerro del Aripo (3,087 feet)
POPULATION	1.2 million
LANGUAGE	English, with many different accents
TIME	Atlantic Standard Time year round (1 hour ahead
	of EST, same as EDT)
AREA CODE	809

ELECTRICITY	110 or 220 volts AC, 60 cycles—but always ask at your hotel
CURRENCY	The Trinidad and Tobago dollar, TT ($4.25 TT = $1 U.S.)
DRIVING	On the *left*; valid driver's license okay
DOCUMENTS	A valid passport or proof of citizenship, plus an ongoing or return ticket
DEPARTURE TAX	$50 TT
BEER TO DRINK	Carib
RUM TO DRINK	Vat 19
MUSIC TO HEAR	Calypso/Pan

GETTING THERE

Trinidad's Piarco International Airport is a major international gateway. UNITED and BWIA (which is based in Trinidad) fly nonstop from New York. BWIA also flies nonstop from Miami and Toronto. AMERICAN EAGLE connects with American flights in San Juan and flies nonstop from San Juan. AIR CANADA has nonstops from Toronto. LIAT and BWIA fly in from other Caribbean islands. BWIA and BRITISH AIRWAYS fly nonstop from London. AEROPOSTAL flies from Caracas and Margarita Island.

GETTING AROUND

The only reason to come to Trinidad is for Carnival, so take a cab. Port-of-Spain is a 45-minute taxi ride away from the airport and will cost you about $85 TT ($20 U.S.). You'll be in the city and walking everywhere, so there's no need for a car.

FOCUS ON TRINIDAD: BOOM BOOM TIME— CARNIVAL IN PORT-OF-SPAIN

Wine de boom boom. It's the motto of Carnival. The "wine" is a wonderfully lewd grind of gyrating hips that would shame Elvis. It's usually—but not always—done in duos with both participants

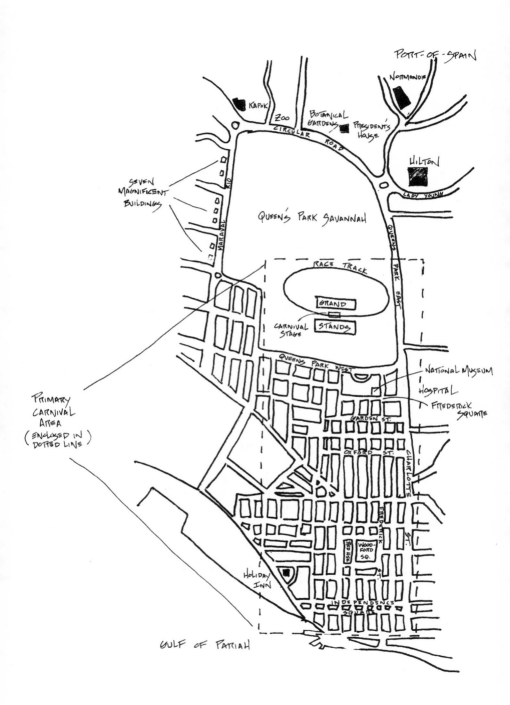

PORT-OF-SPAIN

NORMANDIE

KAPOK

ZOO

BOTANICAL GARDENS

PRESIDENT'S HOUSE

CIRCULAR ROAD

HILTON

SEVEN MAGNIFICENT BUILDINGS

MARAVAL RD.

QUEEN'S PARK SAVANNAH

LADY YOUNG

QUEENS PARK EAST

RACE TRACK

GRAND STANDS

CARNIVAL STAGE

QUEENS PARK WEST

NATIONAL MUSEUM

HOSPITAL

FREDERICK SQUARE

PRIMARY CARNIVAL AREA (ENCLOSED IN DOTTED LINE)

GARDEN ST.

OXFORD ST.

CHARLOTTE ST.

FREDERICK ST.

HIGH ST.

WOODFORD SQ.

HOLIDAY INN

INDEPENDENCE SQUARE

GULF OF PARIAH

pressed together in any number of lascivious ways. The slower and more exaggerated the better. *Boom boom* is local slang for one's rear end. And Carnival, in the words of a calypso hit, is boom-boom time. There are more pelvises pushed, shoved, and slammed in the last forty-eight hours of Carnival than in a million reruns of *Deep Throat*. Sex is in the air—you can feel it everywhere. This is hedonism at its finest.

Where does this bacchanalia happen? How soon can you get reservations? Carnival takes place in Port-of-Spain, Trinidad, a relatively large metro area wedged between the Gulf of Pariah and the hills of the Maraval Valley. The focal point of the celebration is the Queen's Park Savannah—an open expanse right in the middle of the city with most recommended hotels within easy walking distance. Carnival always falls in the dry season, although Port-of-Spain is still rather humid and very hot (you're only 10° above the equator). This is wilt weather. The Savannah is appropriately named—it looks like Africa, especially when the wind blows and huge dust clouds swirl (bring an array of bandannas to cover your nose and mouth—most locals do).

But Carnival is really a street scene. That's where most of the jumping takes place. "Jump-up" is the West Indian term for a party or good time and often you *are* literally jumping up and down. Most of the downtown area south of the Savannah is packed, particularly on Frederick Street and Independence Square. Music blares from the largest collection of PA systems in the Caribbean. Each road march has about fifty life-size speakers precariously balanced on a tractor-trailer and every corner seems to have a system suitable for a concert in New York's Central Park. These provide the amperage for the calypso. Perhaps it is the decibel level that makes one learn the songs so quickly.

Now Carnival is not for everyone. It's not Mardi Gras in New Orleans or Carnaval in Rio. The former is a real drunk and the latter more of a spectator event. Trinidad's Carnival is truly a people celebration. To enjoy it, you must participate, get down, lose your inhibitions, and join the boom-boom spirit. Those that don't participate stand out, looking like misplaced tourists who took the wrong exit for Disney World. They stay on the fringes, avoiding the hot and steamy downtown streets—where the action is.

What does it mean to participate? It means throwing yourself into the sweaty crowd, giving in to the calypso beat, and having a good sense of humor. Above all Carnival is meant to be fun. In fourteenth-century France, the celebration was a public orgy. While I never saw anybody doing it in the street, it's likely that any female companions—particularly if they are sexy and white (a novelty on the streets)—will get wined a lot. So women, be forewarned that you will be treated as sex objects. Of course, you can turn the tables and surprise the winers. But please don't take offense—it's really harmless play and you won't be "molested." Undoubtedly you'll hear lots of "pssssts" and lip-smacking. These are meant as compliments and the appropriate response is a good-natured one. Like it or not, that's the way it is.

The people of T & T make Carnival the celebration that it is. There are no brawls or drunken fights—people don't get "ugly" drunk, just silly and happy. You won't see this in Times Square on New Year's Eve. Why is everyone so up?

It is the music. Calypso has a contagious rhythm that makes the body move almost involuntarily. The lyrics are pretty much incomprehensible to the inhabitants of middle latitudes. But the constant repetition will make at least the refrains familiar. By the last three days, you should have a repertoire of about ten songs you just can't live without. Several of the smaller record shops sell mix tapes of your favorite calypsos—for about $20 TT (or about $5 U.S.). Just ask at the counter. It also helps to buy one of the lyric books sold at record stores or from vendors on the Savannah.

Sharing the music scene is steel-band music—or "pan," as it is called in the West Indies. Both calypso and pan were born in Trinidad and both have avid fans. Pan in particular has become a high art form. Purists can tell if just one of almost a hundred drums is out of sync. What's really amazing is that most pan musicians can't read music; they learn each song in pattern segments. For the Panorama competition (the main pan event of Carnival), new songs are often rehearsed on paper patterns so that no other band will hear the practice sessions and lift the tune. Even the band members won't have heard the song until it is played in the competition. It's a tough business.

Carnival actually begins right after New Year's although preparations start immediately after the previous Carnival. It's a local joke that if Trinidadians put as much effort into work as they do into preparing for Carnival, they'd be a major power. The fact is that Carnival is big business, employing tens of thousands in such cottage industries as costume making. And, of course, there are thousands more in calypso and pan entourages. While the last three days are the climax, there are scores of "fêtes" from New Year's on. Each road march or "mas" camp (for masquerade) has several and the rounds of eliminations for "Calypso Monarch" and "Pan King" take weeks throughout Port-of-Spain and Trinidad.

If you only have a week, the best way to do Carnival is to fly in on Friday night or Saturday before Ash Wednesday, stay in Port-of-Spain until Wednesday, and then take the BWIA Airbridge to Tobago to recuperate for a few days and fly out the following Saturday or Sunday. This allows you to see the best of both islands. While the week before Dimanche Gras (the start of the major festivities on Sunday night) is packed with activities, its primary attraction is the music eliminations. Otherwise, unless you are in one of the mas camps, you won't be plugged into all the fêtes going on about town. Thus, arriving on Saturday will place you right in peak Carnival time. You'll be able to see the Panorama finals, join some of the big fêtes around the Savannah (you'll hear them, everyone is welcome, some have small covers if they're inside a tent), and sleep in on Sunday—a major requirement for survival during the next three days.

So put on your dancing shoes, it's time to j-u-m-p.

DIMANCHE GRAS

This is the big windup. Eat a good dinner. It will probably be the last relaxed, balanced meal you will have until Wednesday. Then head toward the Savannah to catch the finalists for the Calypso Monarch. This event can look like a set for a Cecil B. DeMille epic. People are *literally* hanging from the rafters. There is a continuous roar from the crowd and the ever-present dust cloud shimmering in the spotlights casts a surreal edge to the whole scene. Don't miss it. It is an unforgettable experience to be wedged among thousands chanting "burn he" or "burn she" when the name of some Third World oppressor is mentioned in a song. Once the Monarch is crowned, it's best to head down to Frederick Street for the beginning of a twenty-four-hour nonstop jump. Around three A.M. you may want to return to your hotel to freshen up. Then listen for the nearest road march—its distance detected by the volume of the calypso—and join in the band. J'ouvert has begun.

J'OUVERT (PRONOUNCED JOO-VAY)

Meaning daybreak or sunrise *en français*, J'ouvert (Jour Ouvert) is my favorite part—and the most free-spirited and silly day—of Carnival. It begins with the road march bands assembling at bars and other locations throughout Port-of-Spain. At four A.M., they begin a slow procession through the neighborhoods and toward the Savannah. Bands can number anywhere from 100 to 5,000 people. For J'ouvert they usually have a theme, often different from the next day's, which can be outrageous. One that comes to mind is the Zulu Warriors. Members of this troop cast spells on spectators' private parts. One of the female warriors even had a retractable penis—and boy, was she having fun with that!

Once you hear the march, grab a Carib—the beer of choice—and start "chipping" with them. Chipping can best be described as a pouty walk where you slide the balls of your feet ahead in small steps to the beat of the music. Dawn will break with a twist. Usually you would be heading home after a night of partying. Here, the fun is just beginning.

After chipping with the march for a while, step out and head for downtown. As the road marches approach the central streets, it becomes more fun to party-hop, or party-jump. Allow yourself to wander and explore the streets to see what might turn up. With a crowd on virtually every corner, there is no shortage of possibilities. Pickup trucks piled high with fresh coconuts provide refreshment as well as a man wielding a huge and intimidating machete. He'll adroitly split one open for you. The milk is warm but very tasty and nourishing. A piece of the shell is used to scoop out the meat. There are also vendors selling peeled oranges if you don't want coconut juice dripping down your chin. And, of course, you can always have another beer, rum punch, or soft drink that are on sale about every hundred feet.

As you wander, you'll notice lots of bodies smeared with mud or pitch (a Trinidadian natural resource). Beware of a group of Brits called the Muddies who look and act like extras from a Monty Python epic. Slogging along with a bathtub of mud on wheels, they scout out white T-shirts (as they did mine), surround you, and begin smearing. At that point there's not much you can do. The mud does keep you cool and it *is* a look. Just don't wear your favorite clothes. The stains still haven't come out of mine—my personal souvenir.

Around noon you'll begin to fade. The combination of heat, jumping, and a walking hangover will have taken its toll. Time to take refuge in your hotel pool. The swim will feel marvelous and lunch may quell your throbbing temples. You might want to sneak in a quick nap but plan to be back on the streets by three P.M. as many road marches will now be in partial costume. Jump until about seven P.M. and retire for a simple repast. Chances are you'll crash around ten. But for those with more energy to burn, the party goes on all night.

CARNIVAL TUESDAY

Rise and shine at around eight A.M. as the grand finale is ahead and you shouldn't miss any of it. Eat a good breakfast and once more head downtown. The road marches are in full regalia and seemingly there's one on every street. Bring your camera for today everyone who's not a tourist is in costume. I would strongly suggest a camcorder as the music is so much a part of what you are seeing. The mas camps will be winding their way swiftly through the streets to get in good position to cross the stage for the final judging (judges are posted throughout the city). The grandstand, for which you will need tickets, is a good place to watch Tuesday's parade—especially if it's your first time. It's a long show in hot, dusty conditions. Sitting down in the shade will help you stand the heat. Keep an eye out for the mas camps of Peter Minshall, Stephen Le Heung, and Edmond Hart—they are the best. Mr. Minshall, the enfant terrible of Carnival bandleaders, is the most creative and visionary (he helped design and choreograph the festivities at the 1992 Barcelona Olympics). His mas camps are tight, well conceived, and well organized. The full impact from watching Minshall's road march comes not from the sight of a single costume but from seeing all 5,000 en masse. Note: If you want to join a Minshall Mas Camp for the next Carnival, write to Peter Minshall, Mas Camp Pub, French St., Woodbrook, Trinidad, W.I.

If you take a break and peer down the Savannah, you'll see an endless sea of bands. The show goes on for hours. If you get itchy, take a walk past the bands, still jumping, chipping, and having fun.

By six P.M., you'll most likely be "mas'd out." Head back to the hotel, have a swim, grab a bite to eat (maybe some pelau), and be back out on the streets by nine P.M. for "Las Lap"—the final hours of partying before the ax falls at midnight on Ash Wednesday. There's a sort of sentimental air about Las Lap. It's almost like graduation—everyone is trying to make the most of their last few hours together. In reality, Lent doesn't stop Trinidadians from partying as it used to. There are several big parties the following weekend (they say it's for the tourists but we're no fools). Lent *does* mark Carnival's symbolic end, which is what makes Carnival so much fun and so intense.

The music will be going strong and then suddenly it will stop at twelve A.M. sharp—right in the middle of a song. The dancing and jumping will cease and people will momentarily mill around, then gradually disperse. You'll walk home incredulous, planning Carnival for next year, not wanting the fun to end. Now is a good time to sit by the pool, mellow out with some cold Caribs (stored in a cooler in your room), and recap this truly wonderful experience.

WHERE TO STAY

Here are a few hotels that work well with Carnival. Nothing quaint or cozy—these are city accommodations. Keep in mind that the rates increase dramatically during Carnival (up to 50 percent in some cases). The hotels listed are all within walking distance of the Savannah and downtown.

HILTON INTERNATIONAL TRINIDAD (809) 624-3211, same for fax
Stateside: (800) HILTONS
Lady Young Road, Port-of-Spain, Trinidad, W.I.

Yes, it *is* a Hilton International, so you know it is the best hotel in Port-of-Spain. Even better, it's close to the action and has essential services and a great pool. You know what to expect, and after a few days of jump-up, the Hilton seems like an oasis. All 412 rooms have balconies and face the Savannah—a plus when you want to join a road march on J'ouvert. Two disadvantages: no room service during Carnival and a hill that feels like Everest when you're tired.

Rates are WICKED PRICEY for single and double rooms during Carnival (EP).

HOTEL NORMANDIE (809) 624-1181, same for fax
10 Nook Avenue, St. Ann's (P.O. Box 851), Port-of-Spain, Trinidad, W.I.

A smaller, more stylish alternative to the Hilton and just as close. It looks like it belongs in Santa Fe. An artsy pool and courtyard are the focal points of the hotel. There is also a terrific nouvelle West Indian restaurant (everything goes nouvelle eventually) called La Fantasie, but don't go there during the three major Carnival days—service will take forever. Four galleries featuring local artists round out the complex. And it's half the price of the Hilton.

Rates are VERY PRICEY for singles and doubles during Carnival (EP).

KAPOK HOTEL (809) 622-6441, fax (809) 622-9677
16–18 Cotton Hill, St. Clair, Port-of-Spain, Trinidad, W.I.

Near the Savannah in a nice residential area. It has 71 rooms with views, a pool, and an excellent restaurant called Café Savannah.

Rates are PRICEY for singles and doubles during Carnival (EP).

HOLIDAY INN (809) 625-3361, fax (809) 625-4166
Wrightston Road, Port-of-Spain, Trinidad

It's near the party and has 221 rooms and a pool. You also know what to expect here.

Rates are PRICEY to VERY PRICEY for singles and doubles during Carnival (EP).

WHERE TO EAT

Going out to eat at a restaurant during Carnival is a bad idea because no one wants to work. Thus, the restaurants will be under-staffed with service by the next century. So why bother? Your best bet is to eat on the street. Don't be scared—it's good stuff and it's cheap. Here are some of the most popular selections:

PELAU: CHICKEN OR BEEF

This is a national dish of T & T, composed mainly of rice with pigeon peas or black beans. There are chicken or beef chunks mixed in, too. It's tasty, nutritious, and not too spicy for tender tummies.

RÔTI: CHICKEN OR BEEF

This is the Caribbean version of a burrito minus the rice and beans. Instead, you get curried potatoes and chunks of meat. If you get chicken, make sure you ask for boneless or you'll be biting into the more esoteric parts like the neck or pope's nose. A safer bet is beef.

BUSS UP SHOT

The mock-pasta dish of T & T. It tastes like shredded flour tortillas with meat, curry, and spices. The name alone is compelling enough.

DON'T MISS

MARACAS BEACH—Where everyone goes. It's a short drive over a very scenic North Coast Road and good for a swim and general oooh-cruise. Las Cuevas, about eight kilometers to the west, is a less crowded alternative.

TOBAGO—The best place I can think of to be on Ash Wednesday (see "Tobago," which follows.)

TOBAGO

LOCATION	11°N by 60°W
	22 miles northeast of Trinidad
	2,300 miles southeast of New York
SIZE	116 square miles
	21 miles long by 7 miles wide
HIGHEST POINT	Pigeon Peak (1,890 feet)
POPULATION	49,300
LANGUAGE	English, with many different accents
TIME	Atlantic Standard Time year round (1 hour ahead of EST, same as EDT)
AREA CODE	809
ELECTRICITY	110 or 220 volts AC, 60 cycles—always ask before you plug in
CURRENCY	The Trinidad and Tobago dollar, TT ($4.25 TT = $1 U.S.)
DRIVING	On the *left*; valid driver's license okay
DOCUMENTS	A valid passport or proof of citizenship, plus an ongoing or return ticket
DEPARTURE TAX	$50 TT
BEER TO DRINK	Carib
RUM TO DRINK	Vat 19
MUSIC TO HEAR	Calypso/Pan

GETTING THERE

While you can get a direct flight to Tobago from Miami, the fastest way is to fly UNITED or BWIA nonstop to Piarco International

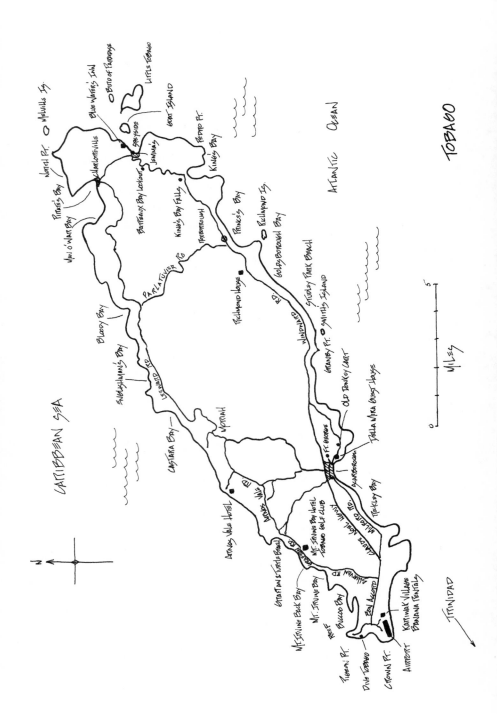

TOBAGO

Airport in Trinidad and connect with BWIA's Airbridge DC-9 service to Tobago.

If you're not in a rush and you happen to be in Port-of-Spain, you can sail on the Port Authority ferry, which is a 5½- to 6-hour journey. Call for times and prices (626-4906 in Port-of-Spain; 639-2181 in Scarborough).

FOCUS: EXPLORING TOBAGO

They don't make 'em like this anymore. Deserted beaches, cheap hotels, great snorkeling and scuba, lots of unspoiled places to explore, and the most friendly, smiling people (it sounds like a cliché but it's true) I've ever met anywhere. You have to pinch yourself to believe it—could a place like this really exist or am I having a flashback from the sixties?

Tobago has yet to be "discovered" by the package-tour pariahs who eventually make Miami Beaches out of popular Caribbean destinations. There is little tourist hype here—most visitors are weekenders from sister island Trinidad. The possibility of running into someone you know is fairly remote, so you don't have to hide in an exclusive or expensive resort for privacy. Indeed, some of the smaller guest houses in the more remote locations on Tobago are probably more private than the larger hotels concentrated on the western end of the island. This is also a place that goes to bed early. There is virtually no nightlife, which makes it a wonderful spot to recuperate from the fast lane of Carnival (see my write-up earlier in this chapter).

The slow pace and mellow atmosphere don't mean that there is nothing to do. Au contraire. The best way to spend time on Tobago is to explore. While the island's western end at times resembles standard tourist fare found elsewhere in the Caribbean, the center and eastern end are magical.

There are several excursions that will take you all over the island. Each is detailed in the following pages. They are best done early in your visit so that the places you really adore can be revisited. Also, there are other activities, such as scuba and snorkeling, that should find a way into your schedule. And of course there are the Tobago beaches, among the finest and least crowded in the Caribbean—even at the height of winter—that will command your body and soul.

EXCURSION 1—THE WINDWARD ROAD (all day)

Starting from Crown Point, head east on the Claude Noel Highway to Milford Road. Turn right and follow the road to Scarborough—the island capital. You'll pass a long beach at Rockley Bay with several spots to turn in and stop. When you reach Scarborough, check out Acadia Records on Castries Street, where you can buy premixed calypso tapes of your favorite hits (they do a brisk business right after Carnival). Then go up the hill to Fort George. Here you'll find beautifully landscaped grounds and some old buildings that are just screaming to be photographed. When you're ready, proceed on the Windward Road—there is little else to see in Scarborough.

Windward Road will be your course for the remainder of the day. There are many points along the way that are worth stopping for. Note that there is a gas station in Roxborough in case you need to fill up. Here are the possibilities:

• GRANBY POINT, Mt. St. George—A high-up vista view of Hillsborough Bay and Smith's Island.

• STUDLEY PARK BEACH, Studley Park—A very pretty, palm-lined, brown sand beach. Just beyond the new bridge.

• RICHMOND HOUSE, Belle Garden—Definitely worth checking out.

• KING'S BAY WATERFALL, Rosenwald Estate, Delaford—A good place for a fresh-water swim. Turn into the cocoa plantation at the 20-mile post and proceed to a car park.

• BATTEAUX BAY LOOKOUT, above Speyside—After a twisting and turning ascent through a landslide area and gorge, there is a lookout at the top of the road on your left. Extraordinary views of Little Tobago Island and the blue Atlantic beyond.

• SPEYSIDE, Speyside—Have a lunch at Jemma's Sea View Kitchen and check out the Blue Waters Inn.

• CHARLOTTEVILLE, Charlotteville—The end of the road belongs to this very interesting fishing village. There are good beaches on both Pirate's and Man O' War bays.

The best way back is the way you came. It will give you a chance to stop and linger at favorite places.

EXCURSION 2—THE LEEWARD SIDE

This outing will be slower, more laid-back and beach-oriented. There will be many occasions when you will pass a road or path that leads to a beach not even mentioned here. By all means investigate. It may be just the secluded cove for an unscheduled tryst.

Beginning at Crown Point again, follow the signs for:

- PIGEON POINT—Acclaimed as the nicest beach on the island—forget it! It's crowded and small, but it *is* a good place to people-watch. There is a $5 TT (about $1.10 U.S.) admission fee. Dive Tobago (639-0202) is located at the entrance and will take you on snorkel trips to Buccoo Bay, Tobago's famous reef. For $25 TT (about $6 U.S.) you get gear, instruction if you need it, and a ride in a vessel about as stable as a canoe.

  If you skip Pigeon Point, head east on the Claude Noel Highway and turn left (the only major left) at the Milford-Shirvan Road. Follow Shirvan Road to Grafton Road to Arnos Vale Road. It sounds complicated but keep in mind that all you are doing is following the north coast road. Once you reach Bloody Bay you will probably want to turn around. The road beyond to Charlotteville is in bad shape. On the way to Bloody Bay, there are lots of points of interest and many deserted or secluded beaches. Half the fun is discovering your own. Here are a few suggestions:

- MT. IRVINE GOLF COURSE, Grafton Road—This is reputedly one of the fifty best courses in the world (639-8871). You can't miss it as you drive by several fairways and greens before you get to the clubhouse. The pro shop sells Tobago Golf Club T-shirts.

- MT. IRVINE BEACH, Grafton Road—With public facilities set up by the Tourist Board, this beach is noteworthy as Tobago's only surfing beach. On some days the surf can break quite nicely. The best waves (especially in July and August) are found on the reef just to the right of the beach.

- MT. IRVINE BACK BAY, Grafton Road—After you pass Mt. Irvine Beach heading east, you'll notice Gleneagles Drive on your right. On your left will be a track through a field. Follow this to the end, park the scooter, and take the footpath down to one of the best beaches on Tobago.

- GRAFTON BEACH, Grafton Road—When you pass Gleneagles Drive, follow the first road (not track) on the left. This will take you to Grafton Beach.

- TURTLE BEACH, Grafton Road—Before you get to the Turtle Beach resort, you'll notice a small dirt road with white-and-black-striped posts. Follow this road to this lovely beach. You'll be the only ones there.

- ARNOS VALE HOTEL, Arnos Vale Road—From Grafton Road, turn onto Arnos Vale Road and follow it to the Arnos Vale Hotel for a rum punch at the beach bar (639-2881; description follows).

- ENGLISHMAN'S BAY, Arnos Vale Road—After you pass Castra Bay, you'll see grazing cows in a pasture and will cross two bridges. Look for a large tree with a black barrel on your left. Park the bike and walk to Englishman's Bay for real seclusion.

WHERE TO STAY

There are numerous accommodations on Tobago but only six that I'll bother mentioning. Two are guest houses, two are a little fancier, and the last are resorts. In no particular order:

KARIWAK VILLAGE (809) 639-8442, fax (809) 639-8441
Crown Point (P.O. Box 27, Scarborough), Tobago, W.I.

Its location next to the airport is suspect at first, but you will soon understand why so many people want to stay here. It's a very comfortable and casual place, with fourteen air-conditioned duplex cottages around an attractive pool and a thatched-roof loggia/hut arrangement housing the bar and restaurant. What makes Kariwak so popular is the food and service—all at a reasonable price. Owners Cynthia and Allan Clovis are very helpful and keep the Village running smoothly. It is also the in-vogue weekend retreat for Trinidadians. Breakfast here is the best on the island. The beach and airport are a five-minute walk away.

Rates are NOT SO CHEAP to PRICEY for singles and doubles (MAP).

BLUE WATERS INN (809) 660-4341, fax (809) 660-4077
Batteaux Bay, Speyside, Tobago, W.I.

This is an ideal place for a romantic tryst. The inn's location seems to be at the end of the world. Indeed, it's far—a 2-hour (24-mile) drive from the airport along the Windward Road and then a semihairy climb and descent on a dirt road to the inn. The accommodations are simple, villa-style buildings with standard double rooms. What makes them special is that all 29 rooms face the bay and are only a few steps away from the beach. When the wind blows (almost steadily), the sound of the waves will lull you to sleep. The food is commendable and features fresh seafood. There is no printed menu and the fare changes daily. The dining room and bar remind me of a ski lodge on a beach—lots of padded chairs and a conversation pit. The inn has a tennis court, and birdwatchers and other naturalists can take a short boat trip from the beach in front of the inn to Little Tobago Island.

Rates are NOT SO CHEAP to PRICEY for singles and doubles (EP).

RICHMOND GREAT HOUSE (809) 660-4467, no fax
Belle Garden, Tobago, W.I.

Smack dab in the middle of nowhere sits the Richmond Great House. Located in Belle Garden on the Windward Road, it is a restored eighteenth-century plantation house perched on top of a windy hill on a 1,500-acre cocoa- and coconut-growing estate. From the outside it looks ho-hum, but the interior is surprisingly stately with dark mahogany and high white ceilings. The furnishings are a funky reddish velvet and the rooms are *huge*—especially Room 4. The parlor is invitingly relaxing and beckons you to curl up with a good book. There is a bar and meals can and should be arranged as the closest good restaurant is an hour away. There is a beach nearby that, while pretty, can get rough. But you come here not for the beach but to emulate the long-lost life of the Tobago planter.

Rates are NOT SO CHEAP to PRICEY for singles and doubles. (CP).

DELLA MIRA GUEST HOUSE (809) 639-2531, no fax
Windward Road (P.O. Box 203, Scarborough), Tobago, W.I.

Now *this* is a funky place. The water will stop flowing through the showerhead just as you've worked your hair into a lather. Then the hot-water knob (if you can call the water hot) will fall off, missing your big toe, but letting the water gush forth like something out of a Three Stooges rerun. Forget the pool furniture—it looks like it washed up during the last hurricane. And yet, the Della Mira has

definite style—run-down, yes, but style nonetheless. It's very simple. I think my college dorm room was more sumptuous. However,
it *is* cheap and beggars unfortunately can't be choosers. It's run and
owned by Neville Miranda—a spunky older gentleman who holds
the place together (barely)—and his wife, Angela. The staff is very
friendly and will even do your laundry. Mrs. Miranda is a barber,
should you need one. There is a pool I wouldn't swim in and an
overpriced restaurant that isn't worth it. When requesting a room,
pay a little more to face the bay as the rooms are much bigger.

Rates are CHEAP for singles and NOT SO CHEAP for doubles
(CP).

THE MT. IRVINE BAY HOTEL (809) 639-8871, fax (809) 639-8800
Stateside: (800) 44-UTELL
Mount Irvine (P.O. Box 222, Scarborough), Tobago, W.I.

You've seen this resort many times before, most likely at a convention or business meeting. Every island or state has at least one and
this one came right out of the cookie cutter. But what makes this
expensive hotel noteworthy is its Championship golf course (see the
"Don't Miss," which follows), widely renowned as one of the best
in the Caribbean. The hotel is big, especially for Tobago, with 110
rooms, 2 lighted tennis courts, and the standard amenities. But it
lacks character, which is not surprising, and it only overlooks the
water—no beachfront villas here.

Rates are VERY PRICEY for singles and WICKED PRICEY for
doubles (EP).

ARNOS VALE HOTEL (809) 639-2881, fax (809) 639-4629
P.O. Box 208, Scarborough, Tobago, W.I.

Once an old plantation estate, the Arnos Vale Hotel is a much
smaller (30 rooms) and tasteful version of what the Mt. Irvine
should be. On a hill are a main house and cottages cooled by ceiling
fans. The bulk of the accommodations are in more modern suites
near the beach, and are more expensive. There is a pool and a tennis
court as well as lovely landscaped grounds. The reef at the beach
offers excellent snorkeling.

Rates are VERY PRICEY for singles and doubles (MAP).

WHERE TO EAT

There are four places I'd recommend for your dining pleasure:

KARIWAK VILLAGE, Crown Point, 639-8442

Cynthia cooks and supervises a menu that concentrates on West Indian cuisine. Their callaloo soup and dolphin in spiced coconut sauce are excellent. $$$

THE OLD DONKEY CART HOUSE, Bacolet Street, Scarborough, 639-3551

The Old Donkey Cart House is owned and operated by a local woman named Gloria Jones Schoen, who used to model in Germany. This explains the fine collection of somewhat overpriced German wines. The food is quite good and will particularly appeal to garlic addicts. Don't miss the garlic bread. Most of the dining is alfresco and the staff is friendly and efficient. Reservations are advised. Check on days of operation—is usually closed Sunday and Monday. $$$

JEMMA'S SEA VIEW KITCHEN, Speyside, 660-4066

Tucked away in a tiny shop on the beach at Speyside, Jemma's is a special place. The dining room has several lace-covered wooden tables of the old schoolhouse variety (matching chairs of course) with a window overlooking the sea. Outside there is a big tree that leans out over the beach with a built-in loveseat. The food is mostly simple seafood but the taste of Jemma's fish-and-chips is forever etched in my memory. It was just great—a kingfish steak dipped in batter and served with a sweet and spicy sauce. Jemma was a little startled at how fast I ate it up. $$

CORAL BEACH FOOD SHACKS, no phone

If you really want good local food fast and cheap, this is where you'll find it. Probably the most celebrated is Miss Esmay's (no one, including Miss E., is sure of the spelling). The dish to get is crab and dumplings, although the crab looked like a very large tarantula to me. She uses land crabs, which are big and hairy. Still, everyone loves 'em. Moving down the road a bit, there's a green shack that sells Buss Up Shot (T & T's idea of pasta) with curried beef and chana (chick peas). To drink there's mauby—a spiced drink that's made from tree bark, looks like swamp water, and is definitely an acquired taste. You can also try sea moss—a seaweed milkshake that's supposed to put lead in your pencil, and tamarind nectar—a very tart juice made from the coating of the tamarind seed. Other favorites are rôti (the Caribbean burrito), pelau (a seasoned rice dish), and fresh coconut. The latter is macheteed open for you as you cringe, terrified that the man will chop off his hand as well. The coconut milk is very tasty and the meat is scooped out with a piece of the shell.

Don't Miss

GOLF ON TOBAGO—You wouldn't think that one of the best courses in the Caribbean (and some say the world) would be tucked away on the relatively remote island of Tobago, but it is. The Tobago Golf Club, (809) 639-8871, part of the Mt. Irvine Bay Hotel, is a Caribbean links-style course that is 6,793 yards long (Championship) and a par-72. It's a tough course all around, despite the lulling landscape of gentle rolling hills and turquoise Caribbean. Especially infamous on these coconut-tree–studded fairways is the ninth hole, with a hook right past a water hazard, and a green that seems the size of a postage stamp. There's no relief until the "nineteenth" hole, as number eighteen will torment you with a sharp hook left, a water hazard, and a humiliating finish by the golf club.

JEMMA'S—A wonderful little seafood place along the main road in Speyside (660-4066).

ARCADIA RECORDS—Great tapes of the latest Carnival hits on Castries Street in Scarborough.

CARNIVAL IN TRINIDAD—Don't miss it! See the write-up earlier in this chapter.

Appendix

TOURIST BOARD ADDRESSES

ANGUILLA

U.S. & CANADA:
Anguilla Tourist Information
c/o Medhurst & Associates,
Inc.
271 Main St.
Northport, NY 11768
(516) 261-1234, fax
(516) 261-9606

U.K.:
Anguilla Tourist Office
WINDOTEL
3 Epirus Rd.
London SW 67UJ, England
071-937-7725, fax
071-938-4793

ANTIGUA

U.S.:
Antigua & Barbuda
 Department of Tourism
610 Fifth Ave., Suite 311
New York, NY 10020
(212) 541-4117, fax
(212) 757-1607

CANADA:
Antigua & Barbuda
 Department of Tourism
60 St. Clair Ave. E., Suite
205
Toronto, Ont. M4T 1N5,
Canada
(416) 961-3085

U.K.:
Antigua & Barbuda
 Department of Tourism
and Trade
Antigua House
15 Thayer St.
London W1M 5DL, England
071-486-7073

ARUBA

U.S.:
Aruba Tourism Authority
1000 Harbor Blvd.
Weehawken, NJ 07087
(201) 330-0800, toll free
 (800) TO-ARUBA,
fax (201) 330-8757

CANADA:
Aruba Tourism Authority
86 Bloor St. West, Suite 204
Toronto, Ont. M5S 1M5,
Canada
(416) 975-1950, fax
(416) 975-1947

U.K./EUROPE:
Aruba Tourism Authority
Amaliastraat 16
2414 JC The Hague,
Netherlands
070-356-6220, fax
070-369-4877

BARBADOS

U.S.:
Barbados Board of Tourism
800 Second Ave.
New York, NY 10017
(212) 986-6516, toll free (800)
221-9831,
fax (212) 573-9850

CANADA:
Barbados Board of Tourism
5160 Yonge St., Suite 1800
North York, Ont. M2N
GL19, Canada
(416) 512-6569, toll free (800)
268-9122,
fax (416) 512-6581

U.K.:
Barbados Board of Tourism
263 Tottenham Court Rd.
London W1P 9AA, England
071-636-9448, fax
071-637-1496

BONAIRE

U.S.:
Tourist Corporation of
Bonaire
Bonaire Government Tourist
Office
444 Madison Ave., Suite
2403
New York, NY 10016
(212) 688-1166, fax (212)
838-3407

CANADA:
Tourist Corporation of
Bonaire
Bonaire Government Tourist
Office
815-A Queen St. East
Toronto, Ont. M4M 1H8,
Canada
(416) 465-2958

BRITISH VIRGIN ISLANDS

U.S.:
British Virgin Islands Tourist
Board
370 Lexington Ave., Suite 416
New York, NY 10017
(212) 696-0400, toll free (800)
835-8530,
fax (212) 949-8254

U.K.:
British Virgin Islands Tourist
Board
110 St. Martin's Lane
London WC2N 4DY,
England
071-240-4259, fax
071-240-4270

DOMINICA

U.S.:
Dominica Consulate
820 Second Ave., 9th Floor
New York, NY 10017
(212) 599-8478, fax (212)
  808-4975

U.K.:
Dominica Tourist Board
1 Collingham Gardens
London SW5, England
071-835-1937, fax
  071-373-8743

DOMINCAN REPUBLIC

U.S.:
Dominican Republic Tourist
  Office
2355 Salzedo St., Suite 307
Coral Gables, FL 33134
(305) 444-4592, toll free (800)
  358-9495, fax (305) 444-4845

CANADA:
Dominican Republic Tourist
  Information Centers
1650 de Maisonneuve Ouest,
  Suite 302
Montréal, Québec, Canada
  H3H 2P3
(514) 933-9008, fax (514)
  933-2070

FRENCH WEST
INDIES—GUADELOUPE, ST.
BARTS, ST. MARTIN,
MARTINIQUE

U.S.:
French Government Tourist
  Office

610 Fifth Ave., 5th floor
New York, NY 10020
(212) 757-1125, fax (212)
  247-6468

CANADA:
French Government Tourist
  Office
1981 Ave. McGill College
  (490)
Montréal, Québec, Canada
  H3A 2W9
(514) 288-4264

GRENADA

U.S.:
Grenada Tourist Board
820 Second Ave., #900D
New York, NY 10017
(212) 687-9554, toll free (800)
  927-9554,
fax (212) 573-9731

CANADA:
Grenada Tourism Office
439 University Ave., Suite
  820
Toronto, Ont., Canada M5G
  1Y8
(416) 595-1339, fax (416)
  595-8278

U.K.:
Grenada Tourism Office
1 Collingham Gardens
Earls Court
London SW5 OHW,
  England
071-370-5164, fax
  071-370-7040

JAMAICA

U.S.:
Jamaica Tourist Board
801 Second Ave., 20th floor
New York, NY 10017
(212) 688-7650, fax (212)
856-9730

CANADA:
Jamaica Tourist Board
1 Eglinton Ave., Suite 616
Toronto, Ont., Canada M4P
3A1
(416) 482-7850, fax (416)
482-1730

U.K.:
Jamaica Tourist Board
1-2 Prince Consort Rd.
London, SW7 4BZ, England
071-224-0505, fax
071-224-0551

MARGARITA ISLAND

U.S.:
Venezuelan Permanent
Mission to the United
Nations
7 E. 51st St.
New York, NY 10022
(212) 826-1660, fax (212)
644-7471

MONTSERRAT

U.S.:
Montserrat Information
Bureau
c/o Pace Advertising
485 Fifth Ave.

New York, NY 10017
(212) 818-0100, fax (212)
818-0200

CANADA:
Montserrat Information
Bureau
c/o TravMark
33 Niagara St.
Toronto, Ont., Canada M5V
1C2
(416) 362-3900, fax (416)
362-9841

U.K.:
Montserrat Information
Bureau
c/o RBPR
3 Epirus Rd.
London SW6 7UJ, England
071-730-7144

PUERTO RICO

U.S. MAINLAND:
Puerto Rico Tourism
Company
575 Fifth Ave.
New York, NY 10017
(212) 599-6262, toll free (800)
866-5829,
fax (212) 818-1866

CANADA:
Puerto Rico Tourism
Company
11 Yorkville Ave.
Toronto, Ont., Canada M4W
1L3
(416) 969-9025

U.K.:
Commonwealth of Puerto
  Rico Tourism Company
67–69 Whitfield St.
London W1P 5RL, England
071-436-4060

SABA

U.S.:
Saba Tourist Office
c/o Medhurst & Associates,
  Inc.
271 Main St.
Northport, NY 11768
(516) 261-7474, toll free (800)
  344-4606,
fax (516) 261-9606

CANADA:
Saba Tourist Office
New Concepts in Canada
410 Queens West, Suite 303
Toronto, Ont., Canada M5V
  2Z3
(416) 362-7707, fax (416)
  368-7818

ST. KITTS & NEVIS

U.S.:
St. Kitts & Nevis Tourist
  Board
414 E. 75th St.
New York, NY 10021
(212) 535-1234, fax (212)
  734-6511

CANADA:
St. Kitts & Nevis Tourist
  Office
11 Yorkville Ave.

Suite 508
Toronto, Ont., M4W 1L3
(416) 921-7717, fax
  (416) 921-7997

U.K.:
St. Kitts & Nevis Tourist
  Board
10 Kensington Ct.
London W8 5DL, England
071-376-0881, fax
  071-937-3661

ST. LUCIA

U.S.:
St. Lucia Tourist Board
820 Second Ave.
New York, NY 10017
(212) 867-2950, fax (212)
  370-7867

CANADA:
St. Lucia Tourist Board
151 Bloor St. West, Suite 425
Toronto, Ont., Canada M5S
  1S4
(416) 961-5608, fax (416)
  961-4317

U.K.:
St. Lucia Tourist Board
10 Kensington Ct.
London W8 5DL, England
071-937-1969, fax
  071-937-3611

ST. VINCENT & THE GRENADINES

U.S.:
St. Vincent & The
  Grenadines Tourist Office

801 Second Ave., 21st floor
New York, NY 10017
(212) 687-4981, fax (212)
  949-5946

CANADA:
St. Vincent & The
  Grenadines Tourist Office
100 University Ave., Suite
  504
Toronto, Ont., Canada M5J
  1V6
(416) 971-9666, fax (416)
  971-9667

U.K.:
St. Vincent and the
  Grenadines Tourist Office
10 Kensington Ct.
London W8 5DL, England
071-937-6570, fax
  071-937-3611

TRINIDAD & TOBAGO

U.S.:
Trinidad & Tobago Tourism
  Development Authority
25 W. 43 St., Suite 1508
New York, NY 10036
(212) 719-0540, toll free (800)
  232-0082,
fax (212) 719-0988

U.K.:
Trinidad & Tobago Tourism
  Development Authority

8a Hammersmith Broadway
London W6 7AL, England
081-741-4466, fax
  081-741-1013

**UNITED STATES VIRGIN
ISLANDS**

U.S.:
U.S.V.I. Division of Tourism
1270 Avenue of the
  Americas, Suite 2108
New York, NY 10020
(212) 332-2222, fax (212)
  332-2223

CANADA:
U.S.V.I. Division of Tourism
33 Niagara St.
Toronto, Ont., Canada M5V
  1C2
(416) 362-8784, toll free (800)
  465-8784,
fax (416) 362-9841

U.K.:
U.S.V.I. Division of Tourism
2 Cinnamon Row
Plantation Wharf
York Place
London SW11 3TW,
  England
071-978-5262, fax
  071-924-3171

INDEX

activities/island matchup, 10–11
airfare tips, 8–9
airports:
  Aerodrome la Tourmente (St.
    Barts), 357
  Bequia, 78, 80
  Blackburne (Montserrat), 297
  British Virgin Islands, 106
  Canefield (Dominica), 148
  Canouan, 200
  Culebra, 134
  Flamingo (Bonaire), 95
  Golden Rock (St. Kitts), 388
  Grantley Adams (Barbados), 66
  Hewanorra (St. Lucia), 407
  Jamaica, 229–30
  Juancho Yrausquin (Saba), 345
  Juliana (St. Maarten), 23, 347,
    429–30, 432
  Lamentin (Martinique), 272
  La Raizet (Guadeloupe), 207
  Las Americas (Dominican
    Republic), 155, 161
  La Unión (Dominican Republic),
    161
  Luis Muñoz Marin (Puerto Rico),
    314
  Newcastle (Nevis), 388
  Piarco (Trinidad), 441, 451, 453
  Point Salines (Grenada), 186
  Queen Beatrix (Aruba), 57
  Simón Bolívar (Caracas), 262
  V. C. Bird (Antigua), 37, 39
  Vigie Field (St. Lucia), 407
Anegada, 106–7, 120
Anguilla, 20–35
  beaches, 24–27
  description, 21–22
  diving, 35
  getting around, 23–24
  getting there, 23
  government tax, 27
  history, 22
  key facts, 22–23
  map, 20
  Prickly Pear Reef, 35
  snorkeling, 26
  tourist information, 463
  where to eat, 33–35
  where to stay, 27–33
Antigua, 36–53
  beaches, 45–46
  description, 37–38
  English Harbour, 48–50
  getting around, 40
  getting there, 39
  going out, 53
  history, 38

Antigua (cont'd)
  key facts, 39
  map, 36
  nightlife, 53
  Sailing Week, 40–44
  South Coast, 48
  Southeast and East Coasts, 50–51
  tourist information, 463
  West Coast, 45–47
  where to eat, 51–53
  where to stay, 45–51
art, artists:
  Caliste, 123, 126–27, 189
  Francis, 127
  on Grenada, 189
  on Jamaica, 236–37
  Manley, 236
  on Martinique, 290
  on Puerto Rico, 340
Aruba, 54–61
  Boca Grandi, 61
  Cellar, 61
  description, 55–56
  getting around, 57
  getting there, 57
  history, 56
  key facts, 56–57
  map, 54
  tourist information, 463–64
  where to eat, 60
  where to stay, 58–60
  windsurfing, 61

Barbados, 62–75
  Atlantis II, 64
  Axis at Ship's Inn, 75
  Bajan Great Houses tours, 64, 75
  Baxter Road, 75
  beaches, 63
  biking, 75
  Club Mistral, 66–68
  Crane Beach, 75
  cricket, 64
  Crop Over, 64
  description, 63
  getting around, 66
  getting there, 66
  Harrison's Cave, 64
  hiking, 64

history, 65
  Jolly Roger, 75
  "Kadooment Day," 64
  key facts, 65–66
  map, 62
  Mt. Gay distillery tour, 75
  nightlife, 64–65, 75
  Sandy Beach Watersports, 68
  Sandy Lane, drink at, 75
  sunset cruises, 75
  tourist information, 464
  where to eat, 73–74
  where to stay, 68–73
  windsurfing, 66–68
baseball, Dominican Republic, 182
Baxandall, Lee, 13
beaches, 10
  Anegada, 120
  Anguilla, 24–27
  Antigua, 45–46
  Barbados, 63
  British Virgin Islands, 120
  Canouan, 199–200
  Culebra, 134–35
  Dominican Republic, 175, 182
  Grenada, 192
  Guadeloupe, 205, 222
  Jamaica, 231–32, 255
  Margarita Island, 263–64, 267
  Marie-Galante, 222
  Martinique, 274, 288–89
  Mayreau, 200
  Mustique, 305, 307
  nude, see nude beaches
  Puerto Rico, 334, 338, 341
  St. Barts, 355, 358–59, 368
  St. John, 372, 381
  St. Kitts and Nevis, 385, 403
  St. Martin, 429, 437
  ten best, 12–13
  Tobago, 454, 455–56
  Trinidad, 450
Bequia, 76–91
  airport, 78, 80
  bookshop, 87
  De Reef, 88
  description, 77–78
  diving, 82–83
  drinks, 88
  Easter Regatta, 88

Frangipani, 88
getting around, 81
getting there, 80–81
Harpoon Saloon, 88
hikes, 81–82
history, 79
Hope Bay, 82
Industry Bay, 88
key facts, 80
Mac's Pizzeria, 87–88
map, 76
Moon Hole, 82
Port Elizabeth, 81
St. Vincent diversions, 88–89
where to eat, 86–87
where to stay, 83–86
Big Drum, Carriacou, 127
biking:
Barbados, 75
Martinique, 289
Montserrat, 294–96
birdwatching:
Dominica, 146
St. Lucia, 411, 415
boats, boating, 10
Antigua Sailing Week, 40–44
bareboats, 109–10, 426
British Virgin Islands, 103, 105, 106–19
brokers, 109–10
Carriacou, 123, 125, 128
catamarans, 148, 207–8, 222, 272, 358
charters, 105, 107–10, 113–14
crewed, 107–8
crewing on, 113–14, 118–19
Dinghy Crawl (St. Lucia), 408–10, 426
Easter Regatta (Bequia), 88
Grenada, 188, 192
packing list for, 118–19
Puerto Rico, 338
Regatta (Carriacou), 128
Regatta (St. Barths), 368
St. Barths Cup, 368
wooden schooners, 124, 188
yacht charters (Martinique), 289
Bonaire, 92–102
description, 93
diving, 93, 96–98, 99–101

flamingos, 93, 102
getting around, 95
getting there, 95
history, 94
Jibe City, 101
key facts, 94–95
map, 92
Marine Park, 98
Photo Bonaire, 100
reef profile, 97–98
slave huts, 102
tourist information, 464
Washington/Slagbaai National Park, 101
where to eat, 101
where to stay, 99–101
windsurfing, 100, 101
British Virgin Islands (BVI), 103–20
Anegada, 106–7, 120
Apple Bay, 119
bareboats, 109–10
Baths, 114–15
beaches, 117, 120
charter boats, 105, 110
Colquhoun Reef, 112
Cooper Island, 115
crewed boats, 107–8
description, 103, 105
diving, 115
Drake's Anchorage, 120
floating bar, 116
Full Moon Party, 120
getting around, 106–7
getting there, 106
Ginger Island, 115
hiking, 113
history, 105
Jost Van Dyke, 105, 116–17, 120
key facts, 105–6
map, 104
Mosquito Island, 113, 119–20
Necker Island, 103
Norman Island, 116, 120
North Sound, 112–13
Peter Island, 115–16, 120
Pusser's Rum Shop, 111–12
Rhone, 115
sailing, 103, 105, 106–19
St. Thomas, 110–11
Salt Island, 115

British Virgin Islands (BVI) *(cont'd)*
  snorkeling, 112–13, 115, 116
  Tortola, 103, 105, 106–7, 110–12,
    117–18, 119, 120
  tourist information, 464
  Virgin Gorda, 106–7, 112–13, 114,
    119, 120
  where to eat, 111
  where to stay, 119–20

Caliste, Canute, 126–27, 189
calypso, 443–44
camping:
  St. John, 374–76
  St. Lucia, 417
Canouan, 199–200, 201
Caribbean:
  climates, 5–6
  maps, x, xi; *see also* maps
  superlatives, 11–13, 16–17
Caribbean Heat, 332
Caribbean National Forest,
  El Yunque (Puerto Rico),
    340–41
Carnival:
  Barbados, 64
  Carriacou, 127
  Trinidad, 441–48
Carriacou, 121–30
  Big Drum, 127
  boatbuilding, 123, 125
  Caliste, Canute, 126–27
  Carnival, 127
  description, 121
  getting around, 124
  getting there, 124
  history, 123
  key facts, 123
  map, 122
  nightlife, 130
  Regatta, 128
  Sandy Cay, 126
  snorkeling, 125, 126
  walking, 124–26
  where to eat, 129–30
  where to stay, 128–29
casinos:
  Puerto Rico, 330
  St. Martin, 430

cerebral activity, 10; *see also* art,
  artists
climate categories, 5–6
codes, 3–4
Columbus, Christopher, 180
cricket, Barbados, 64
Culebra, 131–37, 343
  beaches, 134–35
  description, 131, 133
  Flamenco, 135
  getting around, 134
  getting there, 134
  history, 133
  key facts, 133–34
  map, 132
  snorkeling, 135
  Soni, 134–35
  where to eat, 137
  where to stay, 135–37

Dinghy Crawl, St. Lucia, 408–10,
  426
distillery tours, 75, 191
diving, 10
  Anguilla, 35
  Bequia, 82–83
  Bonaire, 93, 96–98, 99–101
  British Virgin Islands, 115
  Guadeloupe, 205, 214, 222, 223
  Îles des Saintes, 213
  Montserrat, 296–97
  night, 96–97
  resort courses, 97, 223
  Saba, 346, 347–50
  St. Barts, 368
  St. John, 381–82
  St. Kitts and Nevis, 403
  St. Lucia, 426
  Skin Diver, 97
  tips, 96
divorces, Dominican Republic, 182
Dominica, 138–54
  Boeri Valley, 146
  Boiling Lake, 142–45
  Forestry Department, 147
  getting around, 148
  getting there, 148
  guides, 143
  hiking, 140, 142–47

history, 140–41
key facts, 141
Mac's gym, 154
map, 138
Morne Diablotin, 146
National Forest Reserve, 146–47
National Park, 145–46
nature, 141–47
parrots, 146–47
rain forest, 139–40, 141–42
sulphur springs, 147
Titou Gorge, 143, 145
tourist information, 465
Trafalgar Falls, 142
Valley of Desolation, 143–44
where to eat, 153–54
where to stay, 149–53
Wotten Waven, 147
Dominican Republic, 155–82
Altos de Chavón, 175
Barahona, 182
bars and discos, 169–70
baseball, 182
beaches, 175, 182
Boca Chica, 172–73
Cabarete, 178–79
Casa de Campo, 173–75
Colonial Zone, 180
currency changing, 179
description, 155, 157–59
divorces, 182
driving tips, 162–63, 171–72, 177
El Faro a Colón, 180, 182
getting around, 157, 161–63
getting there, 161
going out, 169–71, 179
golf, 173–75, 182
guides, 159
history, 159–60
Juan Dolio, 172, 173
key facts, 160–61
La Catedral de Santa María La
  Menor, 180
La Otra Banda, 176
La Romana, 173–75, 182
leftover food, 180
Magnetic Pole, 182
map, 156
merengue, 163–64, 169–70, 179,
  182

nightlife, 169–71, 179
Our Lady of Altagracia, 175–76
paradas, 177
Puerto Plata, 178
Punta Cana, 175–77
Regional Archeology Museum,
  175
Samaná, 182
Santo Domingo, 164–71, 180–82
Sosúa, 178, 182
tourist information, 465
where to dine, 168–69
where to stay, 164–67, 172–79
windsurfing, 178–79
duty-free ports (St. Martin), 430, 433

Easter Regatta (Bequia), 88
electric beaches, 6–7

flying, tips for, 8–9
focus on:
  Anguilla, beaches, 24–27
  Antigua Sailing Week, 40–44
  Aruba, pampering yourself, 58
  Barbados, windsurfing, 66–68
  Bequia, exploration, 81–83
  Bonaire, diving, 96–98
  British Virgin Islands, sailing and
    charters, 107–19
  Carriacou, walking, 124–26
  Culebra, beaches, 134–35
  Dominica, nature, 141–47
  Dominican Republic, merengue,
    163–64
  Grenada, photo safari, 187–92
  Guadeloupe, Îles des Saintes, 208,
    210–13
  Jamaica, 230–37
  Margarita Island pleasures, 263–64
  Martinique, parlez-vous Français?,
    273–74
  Montserrat, biking, diving, and
    reading, 294–97
  Mustique, exploration, 306–7
  Puerto Rico, San Juan, 315–18
  Saba, diving, 347–50
  St. Barts, fabulousness, 358–59
  St. John, camping, 374–76

focus on (cont'd)
  St. Kitts and Nevis, plantations,
    389
  St. Lucia, Dinghy Crawl/walking
    and hiking, 408–17
  Tobago, exploration, 453–56
  Trinidad, Carnival, 441–48
food, 10
Francis, Frankie, 127
French-speaking communities:
  Guadeloupe, 205, 222
  Martinique, 269, 273–74
  St. Martin, 430
French West Indies, tourist
  information, 465
friendliness barometer, 5–6

ganja, 226, 231, 255, 416–17
gay beaches, St. Martin, 437
gay nightlife, 11
  Dominican Republic, 170–71
  Guadeloupe, 221
  Puerto Rico, 332–34
golf, 10
  Jamaica, 245–48
  Nevis, 395, 403
  Puerto Rico, 336
  "Teeth of the Dog" (Dominican
    Republic), 174, 175, 182
  Tobago, 455, 458, 460
Grenada, 183–202
  basketweaving, 192
  beaches, 192
  boatbuilding, 192
  Carnival, 127
  Concord Falls, 189–90
  Davidall Estate, 190
  description, 183
  fishing village, 192
  Fontainebleu Falls, 190
  Foodland, 198
  getting around, 187
  getting there, 186
  going out, 197
  Gouyave, 190
  Grand Anse beach, 192, 194
  Grand Etang National Park, 192
  Grenville, 192
  guides, 187–88, 189, 198
  Henry's Safari Tours, 187, 198

  hiking, 187, 195
  history, 183, 185
  Honeymoon Falls, 187
  key facts, 186
  Leapers' Hill, 190–91
  map, 184
  Morne Fendue, 191, 192, 196, 198
  National Museum, 189
  nature trails, 195
  Pearl's Airport, 191–92
  photo safaris, 187–92
  Prospect, 190
  rain forest, 192
  Rive Antoine, 191
  rum shops, 190
  St. George's, 188–89
  Sauteurs, 190–91
  tourist information, 128, 465
  where to dine, 195–97
  where to stay, 192–95
  Yellow Poui Art Gallery, 189
Grenadines, 198–202
  description, 199–200
  map, 198
  nude beaches, 14–15
  tourist information, 468
  where to stay/dine, 200–202
  see also specific islands
Guadeloupe, 203–23
  Bas-du-Fort, 221
  Basse-Terre, 203, 205, 214,
    217–18, 221, 222
  beaches, 205, 222
  description, 203, 205
  diving, 205, 214, 222, 223
  Espace Sante de Ravine Chaude,
    222
  getting around, 208
  getting there, 207–8
  Gosier, 205, 213, 216–17, 220–21
  Grande-Terre, 205, 213–17, 219
  guides, 222
  hiking, 218, 222
  history, 206
  Îles de la Petit-Terre, 222
  Îles des Saintes, 208–13
  key facts, 206–7
  map, 204
  Marie-Galante, 222
  nightlife, 205, 221
  Parc Naturel, 205, 222

Pigeon Island, 223
Pointe-a-Pitre, 205, 221
Ste-Anne, 213, 215–16, 219–20
St-François, 205, 213–15, 219
snorkeling, 205, 222
tourist information, 465
where to eat, 218–21
where to stay, 213–18, 222
windsurfing, 205, 213, 222
gyms:
Dominica, 154
Jamaica, 244
Puerto Rico, 342
St. Barts, 368
St. John, 382
St. Martin, 437

hedonism, 10
hiking, walking:
Barbados, 64
Bequia, 81–82
British Virgin Islands, 113
Carriacou, 124–26
Dominica, 140, 142–47
Grenada, 187, 195
Guadeloupe, 218, 222
Jamaica, 256–57, 258
Martinique, 289
Montserrat, 295, 296
Puerto Rico, 341
Saba, 350
St. John, 375, 381
St. Lucia, 410–17, 426
St. Vincent, 88–89
hip locations, 11
Hispaniola, 158, 159
hissing, 17
Historic Sights, 427
Hi-Winds Pro-Am Windsurfing
   Competition (Aruba), 61
horseback riding, Nevis, 397–98,
   403
hot springs:
Montserrat, 296
Puerto Rico, 342
hurricanes:
David, 139, 147
Gilbert, 229
Hugo, 131, 293, 298, 387

Îles des Saintes, 208–13
beaches, 210, 213
diving, 213
Fort Napoléon, 210
getting there, 210–11
map, 209
Terre-de-Haut, 208, 210
where to eat, 213
where to stay, 211–12
island/activities matchup, 10–11
Isle of Spice, 183

Jamaica, 224–58
adventure travel, 258
art, 236–37
beaches, 231–32, 239, 255
Blue Lagoon, 255
Blue Mountain Inn, 258
Bob Marley Museum, 235
Boston Bay, 255
description, 225–27
Frenchman's Bay, 255
getting around, 230
getting there, 229–30
golf, 245–48
guides, 258
Hedonism II, 230–31, 241–42
hiking, 256–57, 258
history, 227–29
Kaiser's, 244
key facts, 229
Kingston, 225, 227, 232–34,
   236–37, 255–58
map, 224
Miss Brown's, 231, 244
Montego Bay, 225, 245–49
MXIII, 244
National Gallery, 236
Negril, 225, 226, 230–32, 538–44
nightlife, 249
North Shore, 225
Ochos Rios, 225
partying, 230–31
Pork Pit, 249
Port Antonio, 225, 227, 250–55
Port Royal, 258
reggae, 232–35, 244
Reggae Sunsplash, 237
resorts, 226
Sense Adventures, 258

Jamaica (cont'd)
  Swept Away Sports Complex, 244
  tourist information, 466
  Trident Villas and Hotel, 250–51,
    255
  University of the West Indies, 237
  where to eat, 242–43, 249, 254,
    257–58
  where to stay, 237–42, 245–48,
    250–54, 255–58
  Y.S. Waterfall, 244
jump-up, 443

Lacour, Brook, 359–60
lesbian bars and clubs, Puerto Rico,
    333–34
LIAT, airfare tips, 8–9
lodging rates, code, 3–4
luxury, 11, 16–17

magic mushrooms, 118, 226, 231
Manley, Edna, 236
maps:
  Anguilla, 20
  Antigua, 36
  Aruba, 54
  Barbados, 62
  Bequia, 76
  Bonaire, 92
  British Virgin Islands, 104
  Caribbean, x, xi
  Carriacou, 122
  Culebra, 132
  Dominica, 138
  Dominican Republic, 156, 181
  Grenada, 184
  Grenadines, 198
  Guadeloupe, 204
  Jamaica, 224
  les Saintes, 209
  Margarita Island, 260
  Martinique, 270
  Montserrat, 292
  Mustique, 304
  Nevis, 386
  Puerto Rico, 310
  Saba, 344
  St. Barts, 354

St. John, 370
St. Kitts, 384
St. Lucia, 404
St. Maarten/St. Martin, 428
Tobago, 452
Trinidad, 442
Margarita Island, 259–68
  beaches, 263–64, 267
  description, 259, 261
  driving tip, 263
  fishing villages, 267
  getting around, 263
  getting there, 262
  history, 261
  Juan Griego, 267
  key facts, 261–62
  Los Roques, 267–68
  Macañao Peninsula, 267
  map, 260
  Mira! The Venezuela Traveler, 267
  Mosquito Coast, 264, 266, 267
  nightlife, 264, 266–67
  Pampatar, 267
  tourist information, 466
  where to eat, 266
  where to stay, 265–66
  windsurfing, 267
Maria Islands, 412
Marie-Galante, 222
marijuana, 226, 231, 255, 416–17
Marley, Bob, 228, 232–35
Martinique, 269–90
  Anse-Mitan, 274, 276–78, 284–85
  art galleries, 290
  beaches, 274, 288–89
  Bibliothèque Schoelcher, 290
  biking, 289
  description, 269
  Diamant, 278–79, 285–86, 288–89
  food trucks, 286
  Fort-de-France, 273–74, 275–76,
    282–84
  French community, 269, 273–74
  getting around, 273
  getting there, 272
  history, 271
  key facts, 271–72
  Le Marin, 279–80
  map, 270
  Musée Vulcanologique, 289

nightlife, 286–87
Parc Naturel Régional, 289
Pointe du Bout, 274–75, 276–78,
  284–85
rain forest coastal walk, 289
Sainte-Luce, 279
St. Pierre, 289
Ste-Anne, 274, 280, 286
tourist information, 465
villa rentals, 282
where to eat, 282–86
where to stay, 274–82
yacht charters, 289
Mayreau, 199, 200, 201–2
meal codes, 4
merengue, 163–64, 169–70, 179, 182
Mira! The Venezuela Traveler, 267
Montserrat, 291–302
  biking, 294–96
  Blackburne Airport ride, 295
  Carr's Bay, 295
  description, 291, 293
  diving, 296–97
  Galways Soufrière, 296
  getting around, 297
  getting there, 297
  HI-FIs, 301–2
  hiking, 295, 296
  history, 293
  hot springs, 296
  key facts, 294
  map, 292
  nightlife, 301–2
  Plymouth, 295, 302
  serenity, 291
  tourist information, 466
  villa rentals, 300–301
  where to eat, 301
  where to stay, 298–301
music:
  calypso, 443–44
  HI-FIs, 301–2
  mento, 234
  merengue, 163–64, 169–70, 179,
    182
  Museum of Puerto Rican Music,
    340, 343
  Radio St. Barths, 369
  reggae, 232–35, 244
  rock steady, 234

for sailing, 118
ska, 234
steel bands, 444
zouk, 287
Mustique, 303–8
  beaches, 305, 307
  description, 303, 305
  explorations, 306–7
  getting there, 306
  key facts, 305–6
  maps, 304
  water sports, 307, 308
  where to dine, 308
  where to stay, 307–8

nature, 10
  Dominica, 141–47
  Grenada, 195
Nevis, 383–403
  golf, 395, 403
  horseback riding, 397–98, 403
  map, 386
  where to eat, 402
  where to stay, 394–401
  see also St. Kitts and Nevis
night diving, 96–97
nightlife, 10
  gay, *see* gay nightlife
  see also "going out"; "nightlife"
    under specific locations
nude beaches, 11, 13–15
  Anguilla, 26
  Bequia, 82
  British Virgin Islands, 117
  Guadeloupe, 205, 222
  Île des Saintes, 210, 213
  Jamaica, 239
  Margarita Island, 267
  Petit St. Vincent, 199
  St. Barts, 359, 368
  St. Martin, 437
nude cruises, Tintamarre Island, 435
nude resorts:
  Bonaire, 100
  St. Martin, 434–35

packing lists, 7–8, 118–19
Palm Island, 199, 200

pan, 444
Papiamento, 55–56, 93
Petit Martinique, 125, 199
Petit St. Vincent, 199, 200–201
photography:
    Grenada, 187–92
    permission for, 188, 406
pirates, 227–28
plantations:
    Carriacou, 123
    Grenada, 191, 192, 196, 198
    Montserrat, 296
    St. Kitts and Nevis, 383, 389–91,
        394–400, 401
    St. Lucia, 422
    Tobago, 457
pretan accelerators, 7
privacy, 10
Puerto Rico, 309–43
    art, 340
    Baños de Coamo, 342
    beaches, 334, 338, 341
    Boquerón, 338–39, 342
    casinos, 330
    Condado, 316, 318, 319–23
    Cordillera Central, 342
    description, 309, 311–12
    Dorado, 334–37
    driving tips, 315
    El Yunque, 340–41
    getting around, 314–15
    getting there, 314
    Gilligan's Island, 339
    going out, 330–34
    golf, 336
    Guánica, 339–40, 342
    gyms, 342
    hiking, 341
    history, 312–13
    Hostería del Mar, 342
    Isla Verde, 318, 323–24
    key facts, 313–14
    Luquillo, 341
    map, 310
    Metropolitan Bus Authority, 315
    Museo de la música
        puertorriqueña, 340, 343
    Ocean Park, 318, 324–26
    Old San Juan, 318, 326–27
    paradores, 318, 337–39

Parque de Bombas, 340
Phosphorescent Bay, 339
Ponce, 340
públicos, 315
¿Que Pasa?, 343
    rain forest, 340–41
    Reserva Forestal Guánica, 339
    Rincón, 337–38, 342
    Río Camuy Cave Park, 342
    San Juan, 315–27
    scenic drives, 341–42
    serenity, 339–40
    snorkeling, 339
    surfing, 342
    tourist information, 466–67
    Vieques, 343
    where to dine, 327–30
    where to stay, 318–27, 334–40
    Windows on the Caribbean, 343
    windsurfing, 342

¿Que Pasa?, 343

Race Week (Antigua), 40–44
rain forests:
    Dominica, 139–40, 141–42
    Grenada, 192
    Martinique, 289
    Puerto Rico, 340–41
    St. Lucia, 413
recipe, Rum and Reggae Punch, 18
reggae, 232–35, 244
Reggae Sunsplash, 237
resort courses, diving, 97, 223
resorts, 10, 16–17; see also "where to
    stay" under specific locations
restaurant price code, 3
Rum and Reggae Punch, recipe, 18

Saba, 344–52
    description, 345–46
    diving, 346, 347–50
    getting around, 347
    getting there, 347
    hiking, 350
    history, 346
    key facts, 346–47

map, 344
Marine Park, 348
Mount Scenery, 350
nightlife, 350
serenity, 346, 350
staying there, 351–52
Third Encounter, 349–50
tourist information, 467
sailing, *see* boats, boating
St. Barths Cup/Regatta, 368
St. Barts (St. Barthélemy), 353–69
  beaches, 355, 358–59, 368
  Christmas, 355
  description, 353, 355
  diving, 368
  getting around, 357–58
  getting there, 357
  Gustavia, 359
  gym, 368
  history, 355–56
  house or bungalow rentals, 359
  key facts, 356–57
  Le Petit Club, 369
  Le Select, 369
  map, 354
  Match!, 368
  Radio St. Barths, 369
  St. Jean, 358
  tourist information, 465
  where to eat, 366–68
  where to stay, 359–66
  windsurfing, 359, 368
St. John, 112, 370–82
  beaches, 372, 381
  best T-shirts, 380, 382
  camping, 374–76
  description, 371–73
  diving, 381–82
  Ellington's, 382
  getting around, 374
  getting there, 374
  hiking, 375, 381
  history, 373
  key facts, 373–74
  map, 370
  Marina Market/Nature's Nook, 382
  nightlife, 381
  Paradise Fitness Club, 382
  snorkeling, 372, 375, 382

tourist information, 468
Virgin Islands National Park, 371–73
where to eat, 380–81
where to stay, 376–80
St. Kitts and Nevis, 383–403
  beaches, 385, 403
  Brimstone Hill, 403
  description, 383, 385
  diving, 403
  getting around, 388
  getting there, 388
  history, 385
  key facts, 387–88
  maps, 384, 386
  plantations, 383, 389–91, 394–400, 401
  serenity, 383, 389
  tourist information, 467
  where to eat, 401–2
  where to stay, 389–401
  see also Nevis
St. Lucia, 404–27
  birdwatching, 411, 415
  camping, 417
  Choisel scenic drive, 426–27
  description, 405–6
  Dinghy Crawl, 408–10
  diving, 426
  drive-in volcano, 413, 427
  driving tips, 408
  Forestry Department, 412–13, 416–17
  getting around, 408
  getting there, 407
  guides, 416
  hiking, 410–17, 426
  Historic Sights, 427
  history, 406
  key facts, 407
  map, 404
  Maria Islands, 412
  Mt. Gimmie, 416
  Mt. LaCombe, 411–12
  Petit Piton, 416
  Pigeon Island, 411
  Pitons, 405, 413, 426
  plantation, 422
  Rain Forest Walk, 413–15
  spa, 418–19, 426

St. Lucia (cont'd)
swimming, 415–16
tourist information, 427, 467–68
where to eat, 422–26
where to stay, 417–22
St. Maarten, St. Martin:
airport, 23, 347, 429–30, 432
beaches, 429, 437
casinos, 430
description, 429–30
duty-free ports, 430, 433
Future Fitness Center, 437
getting around, 432–33
getting there, 432
going out, 437
history, 430–31
key facts, 431–32
lo-lo's, 437
map, 428
tourist information, 465
where to eat, 435–37
where to stay, 433–35
St. Vincent:
accommodations, 89–91
day trip, 88–89
Soufrière volcano, 88–89
tourist information, 468
where to eat, 91
scuba, see diving
serenity, 10
Montserrat, 291
Puerto Rico, 339–40
Saba, 346, 350
St. Kitts and Nevis, 383, 389
Tobago, 453
Sisserou, 146–47
snorkeling:
Anguilla, 26
British Virgin Islands, 112–13,
115, 116
Carriacou, 125, 126
Culebra, 135
Guadeloupe, 205, 222
Mustique, 307
Puerto Rico, 339
St. John, 372, 375, 382
Tobago, 455, 458
Tobago Cays, 199
spas:
Guadeloupe, 222
St. Lucia, 418–19, 426

steel bands, 444
sulphur springs, Dominica, 147
sun, 11
surfing:
Puerto Rico, 342
Tobago, 455
Suzuki Fun Board Championships
(Barbados), 67
swimming (freshwater), St. Lucia,
415–16

tanning centers, 6–7
tennis, 15–16
Ti Gourmet, 219
Tintamarre Island, 435
Tobago, 451–60
Arcadia Records, 460
Batteaux Bay lookout, 454
beaches, 454, 455–56
Charlotteville, 454
exploration, 453–56
getting there, 451, 453
golf, 455, 458, 460
Granby Point, 454
Jemma's, 460
key facts, 451
King's Bay waterfall, 454
map, 452
Pigeon Point, 455
Richmond House, 454
serenity, 453
snorkeling, 455, 458
Speyside, 454
surfing, 455
where to eat, 459–60
where to stay, 456–58
see also Trinidad and Tobago
Tobago Cays, 199
tourist boards, 463–68
touristo scales, 4
Anguilla, 21
Antigua, 37
Aruba, 55
Barbados, 63
Bequia, 77
Bonaire, 93
British Virgin Islands, 103
Carriacou, 121
Culebra, 131
Dominica, 139

Dominican Republic, 155
Grenada, 183
Guadeloupe, 203
Jamaica, 225
Margarita Island, 259
Martinique, 269
Montserrat, 291
Mustique, 303
Puerto Rico, 309
Saba, 345
St. Barts, 353
St. John, 371
St. Kitts and Nevis, 383
St. Lucia, 405
St. Maarten/St. Martin, 429
Trinidad and Tobago, 439
Transderm, 118
Trinidad and Tobago, 439–60
  beaches, 450
  calypso, 443–44
  Carnival, 441–48
  description, 439
  getting around, 441
  getting there, 441
  history, 439–40
  jump-up, 443
  key facts, 440–41
  maps, 442, 452
  street food, 449–50
  tourist information, 468
  where to stay, 448–49
  see also Tobago
T-shirts, St. John, 380, 382

Union Island, 199
United States Virgin Islands:
  St. John, see St. John

tourist information, 468
Virgin Islands National Park, 371–73

Venezuela:
  airport, 262
  Caracas, 268
  Los Roques, 267–68
  Margarita Island, 259, 261–63
villa rentals, see "where to stay" under specific locations
Virgin Islands, see British Virgin Islands; St. John; United States Virgin Islands
Volcanological Museum (Martinique), 289

walking, see hiking, walking
water sports, 10–11; see also specific sports
windsurfing, 11
  Aruba, 61
  Barbados, 66–68
  Bonaire, 100, 101
  Dominican Republic, 178–79
  Guadeloupe, 205, 213, 222
  Margarita Island, 267
  Puerto Rico, 342
  St. Barts, 359, 368
World Guide to Nude Beaches (Baxandall), 13

yachting, see boats, boating

zouk, 287

ABOUT THE AUTHOR

JONATHAN RUNGE, a native of Massachusetts and an ex–
New Yorker, is the author of *Hot on Hawaii: The Definitive
Guide to the Aloha State;* the original *Rum and Reggae: What's
Hot and What's Not in the Caribbean;* and *Ski Party!: The
Skier's Guide to the Good Life.* He first visited the Caribbean
in 1977 on spring break and has been hooked ever since.
After graduating from Tufts, he spent six years working for
ad agencies and is now a full-time travel writer. Besides
being an avid skier, he is also a USCG-licensed captain and
PADI-certified diver.

If you have any comments, suggestions, or information for
the next edition, please write to:

> JONATHAN RUNGE
> *Rum and Reggae*
> Villard Books
> 201 E. 50 St.
> New York, NY 10022